THE COMPLETE HISTORY OF THE HOME RUN

THE COMPLETE HISTORY OF THE HOME RUN

Mark Ribowsky

CITADEL PRESS
Kensington Publishing Corp.
www.kensingtonbooks.com

CITADEL PRESS BOOKS are published by

Kensington Publishing Corp.
850 Third Avenue
New York, NY 10022

All Kensington titles, imprints, and distributed lines are available at special quantity discounts for bulk purchases for sales promotions, premiums, fund-raising, educational, or institutional use. Special book excerpts or customized printings can also be created to fit specific needs. For details, write or phone the office of the Kensington special sales manager. Kensington Publishing Corp., 850 Third Avenue, New York, NY 10022, attn: Special Sales Department, phone 1-800-221-2647.

First printing: March 2003

10 9 8 7 6 5 4 3 2 1

Printed in the United States of America

Library of Congress Control Number: 2002113403

ISBN 0-8065-2433-2

For my son and hero Joltin' Jake Ribowsky,
the home run king of 2015.

Contents

Acknowledgments ix
Introduction x

Part 1
BEFORE THE BABE

1 Lemon Peels and Bottle Bats 3
2 Going Deep Goes Big League 13
3 Baseball as We Know It 26
4 The Arrival 44

Part 2
THE RUTHIAN ERA

5 "A Gift from the Gods" 61
6 Fad Without End 83
7 The Called Shot and Other Fables 101

Part 3
AFTER THE BABE

8 Blood Brothers 115
9 Feast, Famine, Feast 130

10 Baby Boomers 160

11 The Shape of Things to Come 180

Part 4

AND THE WALLS CAME TUMBLING DOWN

12 Deconstructing Babe 205

13 Hammering into History 230

14 Straws That Stirred the Drink 250

15 Foul Balls 274

16 Records Meant to be Broken 298

Appendix: The Top 100 Home Run Hitters of All Time 333

Index 337

About the Author 351

Acknowledgments

Since this book swung for home runs, not infield singles, it could not have been written without the aid of some heavy hitters in the research game. That lineup includes Ben Kopnick of allexperts.com, Bob Waterman of the Elias Sports Bureau, and the Babe Ruth of all home run minutiae, SABR's cleanup hitter, David Vincent. If after reading these pages you have a strong need to see a listing of every single home run ever hit in the big leagues, in order, tell Dave so he can punch up the data base. He may have even memorized it by now.

A figurative pat on the rump goes as well to the helpful folks on the second floor of the New York Public Library, where archival accounts of some of the earliest home runs live in the collections they preserve with such care, and at retrosheet.com—which for a baseball trivia nut with a specialty in vintage history and stranger-than-fiction happenings is the best place to spend an idle afternoon, mouse in hand. And a special shout out to Kirk M. Kandle for the inside skinny on his great-grandfather Matt Kandle's remarkable 16 mm. homemade film of Babe Ruth's "Called Shot" and the press coverage of it, though the best answer to whether Ruth actually called that most famous homer is and will forever be a definite maybe.

Thanks to Bruce Bender and Diane O'Connell at Kensington for understanding the need for this book and for being gentle with the manuscript, and to Sandi Goldstein for good cheer along the way. Finally, my deep appreciation to the home run gods I've gotten to know so well over the past year for providing such wonderfully rich material that it just had to be put in a book.

Introduction

When it comes to the home run, the gods have always been crazy. Sometimes, they're downright preposterous. How preposterous? Try a 328,700-to-1 shot. Those were the odds when a 24-year-old Dominican-born St. Louis Cardinals third baseman of little import named Fernando Tatis was chosen from above to create history in a game at Dodger Stadium on April 23, 1999. On that day, this young man came to bat in the third inning. The bases were loaded. The pitcher was Chan Ho Park. A good pitcher. And Fernando Tatis hit a 2-0 fastball about 450 feet over the left field wall. A nice shot that put the Cards up 4-2. But the beatification of Fernando Tatis was just beginning. The Cardinals batted around, putting 3 more runs on the board, and up came Tatis again. And this is where that math comes in. In the recorded history of major league baseball, from 1876 to 1998, there had been roughly 328,700 games played in the two big leagues, regular and postseason, and no player had ever hit 2 home runs with the bases juiced in the same inning. Only nine men had hit 2 in the same game, and only twice had it been done in the same inning by two different teams. Finally, no Cardinal hitter had ever hit 2 homers in one inning (only twenty players had accomplished it in the National League), and only two had ever hit grand slams in the same game.

Fernando Tatis, though batting that day in the cleanup hole behind Mark McGwire—who hit 70 home runs the year before—seemed to qualify as one of the worst candidates to modify all those equations. In 755 at-bats, he had hit 19 home runs. And then Park, apparently left in the game as a punishment, delivered a fat 3-2 fastball, and Tatis sent it on its way 375 feet into the center field seats. In baseball, where nothing is ever really new, this was really new. And Tatis could be forgiven for talking the talk of a man who had just walked the walk in Nirvana.

"Any ballplayer is looking to be famous," he said afterward. "You want your name to get bigger and bigger. I think my name is going to be famous."

Call Tatis almost famous. He hit 34 homers that season, a new standard for Cardinal third basemen. Then, hampered by injuries in 2000, he got frustrated and began trying to hit a home run every time up. He became a sucker for a curveball and struck out nearly one out of every three at-bats. In 2001 he was traded to Montreal, played in forty-one games and hit 2 home runs. At 27, he was finished, his grand slam record all but forgotten. Almost famous Fernando Tatis was a victim of the capricious and arbitrary fortunes of the home run, touched by the home run gods for just a trice before they moved on.

And just when it looked like this raffish act filled their quirk quota for the foreseeable future, the scamps stopped down for another prank only last season. On May 2, 2002, the Seattle Mariners' Bret Boone and Mike Cameron—both mired in hitting slumps—connected for 2 home runs *each* in the first inning against the Chicago White Sox at Comiskey Park. This was an even weirder quirk than Fernando Tatis's since it took three years longer for it to happen for the first time in creation. But wait. On that night, Cameron couldn't stop hitting homers. He hit 3 more of them his next three times up, becoming the fifth major leaguer to hit 4 in consecutive at-bats and the thirteenth to hit a quad in a game. All told, it may have been the goopiest mélange of home run milestones ever witnessed.

Enough godly flummery, you say? Not so fast. On May 23, during an otherwise nondescript Thursday afternoon game at Milwaukee's Miller Park, another slumping slugger, the Dodgers' Shawn Green—one of the modern era's dime-a-dozen homer hustlers who is one of five players in history to hit over forty long balls in both leagues—pumped 4 homers against the Brewers, the first time there has ever been two 4-homer games in the same season. And it took all of twenty-one days to get it done. But hold on one more minute. Green also went 6-for-6 and had *19* total bases, breaking by one a forty-eight-year-old record, and tied the record of 6 runs scored. The ball on that day, said Green rather unnecessarily, "kept getting bigger and bigger." And bigger still. Green, who had 3 homers in 168 at-bats before his quadruple, hit another the next game, tying the big league record of 5 homers in two games—and then two more in the one after that, setting a new record with 7 homers in three games. Only then, after dogs had begun living with cats, did Green stop this behavior.

What is it about Shawn Green that makes the home run gods so nutty? I don't know, but only a month later the world's best Jewish ballplayer hit 4 homers *again*, over two games against the Chicago White Sox. Meanwhile, Mike Cameron was in home run hell, having hit only 1 more in his next *45* games.

Sometimes, as you are well aware now, those gods just don't play fair. If they did, we wouldn't be here recalling that Hoyt Wilhelm, one of the greatest relief pitchers in history, hit a home run on his first major-league at-bat, then not another one for the rest of his career—23 seasons. Or that Dave Johnson hit 43 home runs in 1973 and had not one other season with more than 18. Or that Brady Anderson hit 50 in 1996 and had not one other season with more than 24. Or that Babe Ruth hit 714 overall and Henry Aaron 755. Oops. Sorry. Sometimes the gods get it right, after all.

The recent home run surge has certainly confounded and distorted all logic, not to mention statistical probability. And baseball is hardly complaining, though some fans and sportswriters are. They make the case that baseball itself has managed to make the home run into the ho-hum, that when a record 70–home run season can be supplanted by a 73–home run season just three years later—and when the once-haughty level of 50 is attainable to, well, seemingly just about anyone—baseball's grande dame has become more devalued than WorldCom stock. And, of course, they're right, though I make a subtle distinction; it's not just that the homer has been marked down—*baseball* has, in ways that have made it unnecessary to have to earn a trot around the bases. Truncated ballparks, juiced-up balls, whip-handled and sometimes corked bats, and all-or-nothing hitting creed has cheapened home runs and taken all the shame out of the strikeout. Then there is the game's now-most-oft-stated ill, its craven capitulation to players beefing up on steroids with implied immunity. For all these reasons, more weight has been given in these pages to eras in which home runs *were* earned by hardy men given few advantages.

Nonetheless, I'd be disingenuous if I didn't add that all the cynicism about cheap homers has a way of melting whenever a long-ball hitter comes to bat in a crucial situation. I still love the dinger, and so do you or else you wouldn't be reading this. Nor would you have been watching Barry Bonds on the final day of the 2001 season. During Bonds' run on Mark McGwire's single-season record of 70, set way back in 1998, there was cynicism, and ennui, aplenty, much of it created by Bonds being such a schmuck. But when Bonds broke 70, the nation turned its lonely eyes on him. Bonds hit the last of his remarkable season, No. 73, before a sellout crowd and hordes of media at Pacific Bell Stadium.

Not that big home run events have always riveted the world. Contemporary wisdom has it that all great home run hitters deserve a free ride of adulation. In the real baseball world, that just ain't so. I know this because, with the home run, history is always a handy reference guide. On the now-historic afternoon of October 1, 1961, on which Roger Maris first beat Ruth's record of 60 by 1, Yankee Stadium was populated by only 23,154 fans on a cool and clear Sunday afternoon. On the Friday night before, when he hit No. 60, there were 19,401. Eleven days before, with Maris at No. 59 and playing game number 154—at which time it was decreed by the baseball commissioner that Maris would have to tie or pass Ruth, who had played a 154-game schedule in 1927, to be recognized as the new king—there were a paltry 21,032 spectators on hand in Baltimore's Memorial Stadium. Now that's ennui. Don't forget, either, that when Babe Ruth hit his 60th, the event did not merit a mention on the front page of *The New York Times*

Much of what is known about the home run is actually the product of years of revisionism, something that is as intrinsic to baseball as Red Man tobacco. Without it, Billy Crystal would have been forced to stick to the truth in his movie about Maris's 1961 run and couldn't have put in those riveting bullshit scenes of Maris being booed at Yankee Stadium after hitting some of his home runs. My mission in these pages is to strip away revisionism and tell you what really happened in the home run evolution. And what has happened has been endless permutations of a simple act. Which is why, as you will see in the following pages, nothing is new anymore about the home run—at least until tomorrow's game.

Think of this book as a user's manual for home run watchers, and in spots for home run hitters. It tells who hit the best of them, the most of them, the most important of them, and the most unlikely of them (the latter segment being dedicated to Fernando Tatis). To get cute about it, what is written here is a biography of the life and times of the home run, an act that, at its point of origin, happens too fast to see but the sound of which—a full-bodied crack (more like a click, actually)—identifies as the most palpably heroic moment in sports, and one that remains anchored in time and mind like no other. Given its visceral hold on the eye of the baseball beholder, the home run has been embellished by figures of speech both modern (dinger, jack, big fly, going yard, touching 'em all) and antiquated (tater, clout, four-bagger, knocking the apple out of the park, knocking the cover off the ball, kissing that baby good-bye, dialing 8), and it is possible that no other act in the human experience—except for one—has spawned so much metaphorical code.

But a home run by any other name is still a home run. And the home run has had a grip on us for about eighty years now, writing a rich, lusty saga of heroes both expected and shockingly unexpected, spanning every generation from the time that it made a drinking, carousing, philandering, gambling slob named Ruth into a living pagan god to the current pop-culture confirmation that "Chicks dig the long ball."

The home run, once a baseball rarity and pariah, has become its savior, its white knight, its vehicle of redemption by which the game hopes to survive its obscene, megaton salaries, contractions and labor fratricide. For that, they can hardly be blamed. Cheap or not, the home run is a lot of things, all of it good. Nothing stands as a better definition of rebirth—or raising the dead—than a 3-2, 2-out, ninth-inning deficit that is turned into a 4-3 victory on the strength of a single swing of a Louisville Slugger. That is what makes the home run so blessed: its simple moral lessons and its promise of instant purification of the soul. While it is complex on the scientific and physiological plane, all we know is that when everything at the molecular level goes right, a wooden bat meets a white horsehide sphere and sends it screaming through the sky and over a fence. It happens nearly every day of the summer and early autumn, and it had better, because Lord knows we need the home run more than we know.

We also need its accompanying fables, it seems. The history of the homer is "Homer-ic" indeed, furnishing an *Odyssey* with an overall plot featuring George Herman Ruth being pursued by lesser gods named Maris, Aaron, McGwire, Sosa, and Bonds. It is Ruth, of course, who owns arguably the most fabled home run of all—the "Called Shot" of 1932. But the home run is within every man's reach, and the ideal allegory of baseball meritocracy is the second most famous dinger—Bobby Thomson's "Shot Heard 'Round the World" of 1951, which of course prefaced the lightning-in-a-bottle heroics of Bill Mazeroski's World Series–ending shot of 1960 and Joe Carter's in 1993. As cruel as the home run gods can be, and Fernando Tatis aside, those wise deities have seen to it that the most profoundly important home runs—the ones that win championships—overshadow the great gobs of homers hit by the more naturally gifted of hitters. (This might help to explain why the most prolific long ball trinity of these times—McGwire, Sosa, and Bonds—had put up a combined one home run in postseason play until Bonds' 7-homer barrage of October 2002. The theory is not infallible, mind you, given that

Part 1

BEFORE THE BABE

1

Lemon Peels and Bottle Bats

Alexander's Ragtime Band

In 1846, Walt Whitman wrote in his journal, "I see great things in baseball. It's our game, the American game. It will take people out of doors, fill them with oxygen, give them a larger stoicism. Tend to relieve us from being a nervous, dyspeptic set. Repair these losses, and be a blessing to us." As prescient as Whitman was, he didn't know the half of it, because he envisioned all of this wonderfulness before practically anyone ever heard of the home run—which, as it happened, entered the lexicon just a year before. Up until then, crude precursors of the modern game of baseball—basically mutations of cricket—had been around for one hundred years before the act of hitting a home run was codified as a round-trip around the bases of a ballfield by—appropriately—a banker.

If Alexander Joy Cartwright were around today, he would hear himself called "the Founding Father of Baseball" by everyone except Major League Baseball, which cast its vote on the issue a century ago with the fiction about Abner Doubleday discovering the sport in Cooperstown. Despite the tale being thoroughly discredited, it is baseball's story, and we're stuck with it, since it's a little late for the game to relocate the Hall of Fame where baseball was really founded: Fourth Avenue and 27th Street in lower Manhattan, or where Fijux's Hotel stood at 42 Murray Street. The former is where Cartwright tinkered with ball-and-bat games and came up with some radical ideas, such as chucking the old square cricket field for a diamond-shaped infield, an outfield, foul lines, and a little thing called "home base" (it wasn't a plate yet, but a square stone). The people who hit the ball and ran around the bases were called "strikers," "knockers," or "peckers."

Born in the spring of 1820 in New York City, Cartwright was a well-to-do bank clerk in 1845 when he proposed that he and his playmates form a team to play the new game. They went over to the Fijux's to hoist a few lagers and when they came out they were known as the Knickerbocker Base Ball Club, so named because Cartwright was a volunteer fireman working out of the Knickerbocker Engine Co. The object, hard as it is to believe, was not to make money. Cartwright and his cohorts were well-heeled blokes—brokers, hatters, insurance men, tellers, even a U.S. marshal—and saw the team as a society of gentlemen playing for the pleasure of playing. Society, indeed. Cartwright was in no mood to play with the "lower orders," and his rules of behavior were strict. One player was fined 6 cents for swearing in the very first game. The Knickerbockers were no party, no disco, no fooling around.

What they were, though, was the structural model for all sports franchises to come. Cartwright was the boss man, but delegated authority to a board of directors made up of his teammates. On August 23, 1845, they ratified their charter and Cartwright's Rules of Baseball—the most important being that the bases were to be "forty-two paces" from first to third base and home to second, which worked out to ninety feet between each, and that any ball not caught on a fly or on the first bounce was a hit. It still was a whacked-out game—21 "aces" (runs) to win, no gloves or other equipment. But, by God, it was baseball, even if Cartwright said nothing specific in his rules about the home run.

The term *home run*, adopted from cricket, simply meant what it said. But at least for now, for a ton of reasons, it almost never happened.

The Knickerbockers spent a year playing the only organized team it could find—themselves. Even by the summer of 1846, when they played the now world-famous "first game ever played" on July 19, their opponents, the New York Club, were actually other Knickerbockers who had split from the "A" team when Cartwright took to playing not in Manhattan but in a lovely green glen across the Hudson River, Elysian Fields, where this first game was played and where the A team lost their knickers, 23 "aces" to 1 in a four-inning affair. A very crude box-score of the match (umpired by Cartwright) tells us nothing except who played and who scored how many runs, leaving official home run history to wait for its beginning.

It would still be years before the game and its future centerpiece would dominate box scores. Before that could happen, however, a herald was needed to be the baseball muse. Enter Henry Chadwick.

"The Baseball Edison"

So you thought all sportswriters were useless? Think again. Henry Chadwick was at least as important as anyone else in the saga of the game and the home run. Indeed, it was Chadwick who unfurled and applied the phrase "national pastime" to baseball and made it a part of the nation's vocabulary. He also invented the prose, the manuals, and the single niftiest vehicle of all to popularize the game—the boxscore—that spread its gospel for half a century.

Born in Exeter, England, in 1824, Chadwick was a kind of sporting royalist. The son of a London newspaper editor, Chadwick came to America at age 13 and in his time worked for nearly every New York newspaper and national sports magazine. As such, he had the clout to give wide attention to baseball, which he stumbled across in 1847 upon seeing a Knickerbocker game. Chadwick was so smitten that he joined the team and then began writing nice things about them.

But Chadwick had bigger ideas for the game, and in time his power led baseball people to cater to his whim. In return, they could expect emotive game stories in Chadwick's blend of American idiom and the King's English, which touted each game as played by manly, moral, swashbuckling warriors. An example is this bite from the June 26, 1869, *New York Clipper* when Chadwick wrote up a Cincinnati Red Stockings game against the Mutuals of New York: "Wright sent a long ball to right centre field, and was on his way to second base when Dick Hunt, after a long run, caught it while the whole field cheered their approbation."

Grammar aside, this passage is actually significant for two reasons. One was Chadwick's use of the term *long ball*, which would of course evolve into the most overused slang for home run. The other is that the batter in the description was possibly Harry Wright, a fellow Brit who had also played for the Knickerbockers and like Chadwick had a greater passion for cricket, yet became the greatest manager of the nineteenth century.

Chadwick's writings may seem painfully quaint now, but back then they pumped life into the game. Chadwick could write about a game that "There never will again be such a struggle for a game that means so much for its winner"—and then write the very same thing the next day. To be sure, Chadwick made so many commitments to cover so many games that he probably wrote those all-purpose sentences on the buggy ride over to the park to save time. In any case, by 1857 Chadwick's power was supreme. That year, Chadwick had done such a masterful job spreading the gospel of the game that all those white-collar baseballers had a league of their own, the amateur National Association of Base Ball Players. Though ostensibly Alexander Cartwright's baby, it was Chadwick who rode herd on the league's rules committee. He did away with the 21 aces rule in favor of a nine-inning, most-runs-wins format. He moved the pitcher up from fifty to forty-five feet from home plate. He allowed pitchers, who were still prohibited from throwing overhand, to snap their wrists on their serves to make the ball curve—an animal cursed by every home run hitter who ever lived (except when they hang).

Chadwick also had something to say about the home run, about which he was very protective. Seeing how a tater could light up a game and a crowd, Chadwick was concerned that a proliferation of the long ball would cheapen the rarely executed lightning bolt of energy he saw as its main attraction. And so he sought to clarify just what kind of hit should carry the name "home run." Chadwick was aghast at the shoddy play of bare-handed fielders (gloves wouldn't come into the game for another decade) who mishandled relays while the batter came all the way around to tally what generous official scorers called a home run. Under Chadwick's policy, "A home run is made, in the literal sense, when the batsman—after hitting a fair ball—runs around the bases without stopping and touches the home base before being put out. But a 'clean home run' is only made when the batsman hits a ball far enough out of the reach of the out-fielders to enable him to run around to home base before the ball can be returned in quick enough to put him out. None other shall be scored on the record as home runs."

When Chadwick barked, the baseball world sat up and obeyed, though in this case his obiter dictum caused some confusion. Did a "clean home run" apply only to balls that left the yard or also inside-the-park ones that skipped cleanly into the alleys out of the outfielders' reach, which was the nature of most home runs of the era? Chadwick didn't clarify it further, and sportswriters began to use the term essentially for any particularly attractive home run, or ones that were crucial to deciding a game. Which of course was exactly what Chadwick didn't want. And Chadwick himself partly answered the riddle in his story of the first game for which a boxscore has been found, played on July 23, 1858, between all-star teams from Manhattan and Brooklyn at the Fashion Race Course on Long Island, New York.

According to Chadwick's story, "[John Henry] Holder was the only one who made a clean home run strike, and a beauty it was, clean over the middle field, which brought him to the home base amidst the most unbounded applause."

The Chadwick PR machine marched on. In 1860, he moonlighted as editor of *Beadle's Dime Base Ball Player*, a regular baseball guide containing rosters, rules, statistics, and Chadwick columns, and later of others of the kind such as *DeWitt's Base Ball Guide*, *Our Boys' Base Ball Guide*, and *Ball Players' Chronicle*. He would write a number of instructional books on baseball as well as contribute articles to the later baseball "bible" *The Sporting News*, and *Sporting Life* and *Outing*. In 1861, Chadwick—who was once dubbed "The Baseball Edison" by the *Cincinnati Enquirer*—began keeping a running account of games on a score sheet. Ever wonder why a strikeout is called a "K"? Here's why: Chadwick took the last letter from "struck" (it being the parlance of the day that to be retired on strikes was to be "struck"). Besides, he'd already tabbed "S" for a sacrifice. Some of the game's most enduring *patois* came about in 1874 when Chadwick, on a baseball tour in England, got the British press to understand the American game by using terms like *assist*, *passed ball*, *grounder*, *pop-up*, and *line ball* (later *line drive*).

As for "HR" on the scorecard, that was not really in the ballpark yet—and I mean literally, since the spacious dimensions of the ballparks (many of which didn't have outfield fences) made "going for the downs" produce no more than a fly ball that made the crowd go "ooooh" but were in reality easy pickin's for good outfielders, bare-handed and all. Even then, the proverbial "long out" was common language. The only way to swing a bat, said conventional wisdom, was to choke up, take a level cut, and try to send a line drive or "daisy cutter"—a sizzling ground ball, not a big bomb—through the infield holes and move up the runners.

Still, human nature being what it is, and the home run being what it is, not all players toed the line. I mean this only semi-literally, since the seminal custom of batters standing on a three-foot line next to home base and not being permitted to move their feet was being devolved with each passing year. And while they liked even then to reach out with their bats and hit all manner of pitches (think of Yogi Berra in knickers, stockings, and a straw cap), hitting was hardly a science. Few men thought it necessary to stride into the pitch and generate what is now known as critical hip and leg power. Some did hold the bat way down at the handle and twist themselves into knots with a furious, all-arms swing. And as much as Chadwick cautioned against doing this, his own vibrant literature about "clean home runs" would have the opposite effect. But it wouldn't turn into a ripple effect until the balls and bats of the day became big-league.

Baked Apples and Mushrooms

In the beginning, baseballs were basically cricket balls with a new name. The earliest ones were small and hard, around 3 ounces and 8 to 9 inches in circumference and had a lead or even cement core, an inner layer of twine, and a chamois or sheepskin cover. Alexander Cartwright correctly saw the need for a larger, heavier ball and commissioned a saddler to manufacture a prototype ball that was 6¼ ounces and 9 to 10 inches in circumference (these would be made the official ball dimensions in 1872). The new core was a crucible of rubber shavings, and the cover horsehide leather—"such as was used for whip lashes," he said. Cartwright had an immediate patent on the ball and hired a shoemaker to mass-produce them. This was possibly America's first sporting goods operation, and off the assembly line came some unique models, either in red, brown, even black (white was the rarest). The most popular ball was the "lemon peel" model, so named for its four-section design, each separated by hand-stitching that could be peeled off. Others were the "half-moon" and "belt" models. The dimensions made these balls about the same size as today's ball, but the added weight made them very home run–unfriendly, and they got unfriendlier because one ball was about all that any team generally had or thought necessary—the home team was supposed to bring it—and it would usually stay in play the entire game. By the end, it looked like a baked apple, though to the winners it looked beautiful because they got to keep it as a trophy of victory.

Bats were also hostile to the homer. The first ones were long and skinny slivers of red oak, hickory, mahogany, poplar, ash, and walnut. Clearly, bats were a popular item from the get-go, perfectly geared to the caveman instincts of hardy men who chopped a lot of wood since childhood. Cartwright also sought to make bats, ordering that they "had to be turned under my personal supervision." But since many a player could whittle a pretty fine piece of wood on the back porch after dinner, homemade bats cropped up in the game well into the next century. While these were of every conceivable shape, most remained long, up to 50 inches, making today's big-league bats look like the souvenir mini ones handed out to stadium crowds at Bat Day promotions. Most also remained thin, usually a mere $2^{1}/_{2}$ inches at the widest part. But in the spirit of seeing what one could get away with, bats appeared that had wider middle sections in the shape of an oar or paddle; still others were contoured like a bottle or lightbulb.

These were all stabs in the dark, and most of the experimental models had negative returns. But then much of what was happening all over baseball was like finding one's way in a darkened room. People simply had no idea what the science of hitting or pitching a ball was. The best guess was that a bat constructed to be long and light would get around quickest and with the most drive. Then too, men were generally of smaller stock, on the order of such all-time great players as George Wright at 5′9″ and 150 or John Montgomery Ward at 5′9″ and 160.

The style of hitting also influenced the bats. Most players would have reeled at the thought of holding a bat way down at the end by the knob, which of course led to the self-defeating practice of lofting easy fly-ball outs. Most everyone choked up for better bat control. A bat was even introduced with *two* handles, 6 inches apart, with the top handle guiding the hands to the choking-up position. If a guy wanted more "power," he would sooner sink a few 10-penny nails into the barrel than go down to the knob, which more than a few actually did. For most, the regular thin knob was inferior for a good grip; those players who were uncomfortable choking up brought into the game bats with large rounded extensions of the knob, called "mushroom" or "ball-knob" bats. So critical was the grip that one player, "Long" Levi Meyerle, took rule-bending to the max by attaching a leather strap on the handle of his bat, tightly slipping his bottom hand through it when he hit. Don't laugh. Not only did he get away with it, but in 1871 Meyerle hit a league-leading 4 home runs and batted .492—the highest single-season average in the history of baseball.

Jim Creighton's Ill-Fated Home Run Swing

The state of baseball changed drastically—and for its purists, horrifyingly as the result of the Civil War. Not only did the game sink roots in the South and Midwest as it was played by Union soldiers who relied on it to take their attention from the pain and carnage around them, but it was also now being played by the "lower orders," which Alexander Cartwright had tried to prevent. Somewhere in that fold of time, bourgeois baseball became associated with playing for pay, as a profession rather than a diversion. The idea of turning the game into a business must have sounded good to the people in baseball, Cartwright and Chadwick excluded, because in the years immediately after the war they were looking around for the best players they could find, at a price.

The professional era had actually begun even before the war when several players were paid under the table. The first may have been Brooklyn Excelsiors' pitcher Jim Creighton, in 1860. Creighton was worth $20 to $40 a month (the going rate in illegal palm-greasing) because he could bend the rules so nicely—by snapping his wrist to make the ball go faster. Creighton, though, would never make it to the first recognized big league when it came into being in 1876. Why? Blame it on the home run.

Like every pitcher who has ever lived, Creighton fancied himself a good hitter (granted, back then there was much less of a hitting gap; as in the Little League, nineteenth-century pitchers often were also a team's best hitter). Unlike most pitchers, he proved he was right, which turned out to be rather unfortunate. In an 1862 game, Creighton swung at a pitch so mightily that when he connected, the ball flew over the fence. But before it got there the shearing force of the backswing doubled him over in pain. Creighton got to his feet and struggled around the bases, but was lifted for "having sustained an internal injury occasioned by strain," as it was reported. If only. The truth was, Creighton had ruptured his bladder. Four days later, he died because of it. Creighton's epitaph was probably spoken by managers and coaches in the wake of the tragedy:

"Didn't we warn you guys about trying to hit them balls out of the park?"

The Orator's Red Stockings

Baseball officially became a play-for-pay game with the formation of the National Association (NA) of Professional Base Ball Players, whose constitution was ratified over a few—okay, a lot of—tankards of ale on St. Patrick's Day 1871 at Collier's Café in lower Manhattan. It just seemed the thing to do after the Cincinnati Red Stockings said the "hell with it" and openly paid Harry Wright to bring his brother George and other great players to the team for around $200 a month each to make the team a winner—and did, in spades, as they racked up sixty-odd straight victories without a loss in '69.

Alexander Cartwright, seeing the day coming when ballplayers would be corrupted by filthy lucre, had folded the Knickerbockers and set out on horseback intending to teach baseball to everyone he could (presumably, he had gone a little daft by now). He subsequently set sail on a boat back from California but wound up beached in Hawaii, where he lived the rest of his life teaching the natives the game and founding the islands' fire department.

The new league's best all-around player was James Henry O'Rourke. Born in Bridgeport, Connecticut, he was nicknamed "Orator" for his tendency to pontificate all day long about most everything—a skill that would later earn him a law degree from Yale. O'Rourke was recruited to join the Boston Red Stockings (forerunner of the Red Sox) in 1873 by the manager, the peripatetic Harry Wright, who took still more money to jump from Cincinnati, bringing with him his brother George and other players. But O'Rourke posed a problem: he was an Irishman, part of the great Irish wave in baseball, and while Boston would become the emerald city of Irish Catholicism in America, back then the city was Puritan. Fearing the reaction to an Irishman at South End Grounds, Wright suggested that O'Rourke change his name to "Roarke."

"Not in a million years," O'Rourke told him. "I'd sooner die than give up my father's name."

The five-foot 8-inch third baseman flourished without a hitch, and today he can be seen as the ancestral prototype for Willie Mays and Barry Bonds. In 1875, O'Rourke led the NA with 6 homers and 17 stolen bases, another baseball gambit that had gained momentum. He also hit over or near .300 as a rule. And he was just starting to make history.

So were the Red Stockings. They were baseball's first dynasty (at a price—the payroll was a whopping $19,000), winning four straight NA pennants behind the bats of O'Rourke, George Wright, Ross Barnes, Deacon White, and George Hall, and the suffocating pitching of Al Spalding, who was the perfect example of the surrealistically iron-armed pitching of the day. In the record books, Spalding is credited with pitching in seventy-one games in 1874 (when the only other pitcher on the team was Harry Wright), going 52-16 in, gulp, 616 innings. The only problem is that the team's record that year was 52-18. (Was he so good in one game that they gave him two wins for it?) The next year, the record was 55-5 also in seventy-one games. He also hit over .300 every year.

And what about home runs? The numbers may not be as excessive, but they are intriguing. In those four title years, the Bostons were the league's most prolific long-ball team, peaking at 18 in '74. To put this in perspective, O'Rourke's 6 homers came in 358 at-bats, which works out to 1 every 60 at-bats, or around 10 home runs in a typical 600 at-bat season today—the output of a weak-hitting shortstop. In the NA's four seasons, which featured around ten teams each season, 217 dingers were recorded (most of the inside-the-park variety, and all in various stages of cleanliness), of which the Red Stockings had 55, dwarfing everyone else. So while baseball was still seen through a one-base-at-a-time looking glass, and the home run was anything but its centerpiece, the Red Stockings did demonstrate the potential and the influence of the long ball.

And as usually happens in baseball when one team wins a lot, other teams would begin trying to do the very same things.

2

Going Deep Goes Big League

Ross Barnes and the Carriages

With so much greed and so little central authority, the National Association (NA) degenerated into a morass of gambling, thrown games, players jumping from team to team, and weak teams collapsing in a heap, leaving the NA to live in history as a brick shy of a "big league." William Hulbert seemed to know this. An officer of the Chicago White Stockings (forefathers of the Cubs), Hulbert had a Darwinist vision of cutthroat businessmen like him protecting the interests of the game by turning the players into indentured servants. In Hulbert's dream, the Chicago club would be the cynosure of the new order. And so while Hulbert railed against low-rent abuses like teams raiding each other for players, his first cannon shot was to raid the Boston Red Stockings and sign Al Spalding as his new player-manager, along with Cal McVey, Deacon White, and Ross Barnes. Then from Philadelphia he looted Adrian "Cap" Anson—the best hitter and worst human being (next to Spalding) who ever lived in baseball.

Hulbert reassured them that they could break their contracts because "you boys are bigger than the Association," but he really meant himself. And when he lined up the owners of the Midwest teams to back his coup d'état of the NA, he strolled in to the league's annual meeting on February 2, 1876, and promptly informed everyone that he was forming his own league, the National Association of Professional Base Ball Clubs, composed of the wealthiest eight teams. The rest weren't invited. Those that came aboard, for $100 annual dues, ratified a constitution that invested ownership as the profit takers. The league jointly vowed to "rescue the game from its slough of corruption and disgrace." How? By creating a baseball monopoly that has remained in force ever since. The difference then was that teams were given rights to keep the players in servitude. Within two years, they would institute the demonic "reserve clause," soldering the players to their clubs with no recourse for most of the next century.

Hulbert did make the trains run on time. There would be a fixed schedule, uniform ticket prices of 50 cents, a lid on salaries, and a ban on gambling, liquor sales at ballparks, and Sunday games (I didn't say everything worked). There would be very rough times ahead for the National League. It would be challenged by player revolts that fueled new leagues threatening its domain. Just like today, the loophole in salary collectivism was that the richest teams reeled in the best talent, inviting the same ridicule among fans and in the press about mercenary players. There would be "contraction" before expansion. But the National League has now been around longer than IBM, U.S. Steel, and the telephone. And in 1876, the flush of a new sun dawning over baseball unleashed the power and majesty of the home run.

Well, actually not. The '76 season brought pretty much the same quality of play—and players—from the NA. Even the first National League (NL) game, on April 22, was warmed-over Association: the Boston Red Stockings won 6-5 over the Philadelphia Athletics at the latter's Jefferson Street Grounds, which like many downtown parks was shoehorned into existing city blocks, making for some crazy dimensions—center field 500 feet away but 250 feet at the right and left field foul lines (a near-exact model for the later Polo Grounds). Appropriately, Orator Jim O'Rourke collected the league's first hit, a first-inning single—and Levi Meyerle, bat strap and all, got the first double and triple. But the first homer waited until May 2 when Chicago played at Cincinnati's Avenue Grounds and Ross Barnes nailed one for posterity in the fifth inning off William "Cherokee" Fisher.

The nature of the blow is a bit of a mystery. According to Lee Allen's 1961 book *The National League Story*, Barnes "smashed it deep into the outfield grass," suggesting it was an inside-the-park homer. But hold on. *The Home Run Encyclopedia* cites "a report of the game" in which Barnes "made the finest hit of the game straight down the left field to the carriages for a clean home run," which seems to say it was into the crowd on the fly—or would if the writer meant to say "into" instead of that nagging "to," which might mean it rolled to the carriages. Maybe we're just not supposed to know.

Likewise, the second dinger of that game, off the bat of Cincinnati's Charley Jones, is just as murky, though it is safe to say this was the more impressive blow, coming off the unhittable Al Spalding, who went 47-13 with nine shutouts as the White Stockings ran away with the first NL title (hitting .337 as a team, a record still). Spalding, though, had other things on his mind—like parlaying his influence into enduring wealth and power. Spalding and his brother had opened a sporting goods store in Chicago and were given an exclusive concession to supply the NL's official ball—a new model called the "figure 8" had been introduced in the 1860s, so named for the two "8"-shaped pieces of horsehide stitched together to cover it, as is the modern ball (though back then it was as "dead" as the older balls). A.G. Spalding & Brother's corner on the NL ball market would last until 1976. Not that Al Spalding was satisfied; his company also sold bats and gloves, and in 1876 he wore one of his fielder's mitts onto the field as a way to pump up sales. Soon, and until the early 1900s, Spalding would be outfitting big league players from head to toe, and providing even those mushroom and ball-handle model bats at discount prices.

Spalding stuck around as a player in 1877, pitching in just four games. By then, he had also begun to publish the *Official Spalding Guide*, the league's annual yearbook, for which he would hire Henry Chadwick as editor. While one can only imagine the stink today if an active figure within the game was also a league's equipment supplier and keeper of records (it would be almost as bad as a club owner serving as baseball commissioner), no one begrudged Spalding, who of course was Willie Hulbert's protégé. After that season, his zeal for playing ball on the wane, Spalding retired at age 27 and was given an executive position with the White Stockings. In 1882, when Hulbert died, Albert Goodwill Spalding—a man who would dig up dirt on his players to fine them and keep their salaries low—became president of the most powerful team in the National League. And Cap Anson, a man who would infamously keep African American players out of the majors, sparking eight decades of segregation, became the team's player-manager for nineteen years.

Anson, who hit .343 that maiden '76 season (he hit over .300 in twenty-one seasons) was the textbook hitter of his time: all singles and doubles. The home run hitters? Even by NA standards, they fell through the floor. There were only 40 of them in 520 games, and it hardly seems worth mentioning that the leader was Philadelphia's George Hall with 4.

A left-handed hitter with a classic southpaw uppercut, Hall portended that lefty power hitters would have an advantage being able to stand in without bailing out against the slants of right-handed pitchers. But before the home run gods sent down just such a man to be their messenger on Earth, they had some games to play of their own with the woebegotten early home run kings.

The Home Run Curse

That Ross Barnes hit the first of 216,943 big-league home runs seems to have been predestined for its irony, since historically he has gotten more attention for it than his major achievement that season: being the NL's first batting champ with a .429 average (it's still .404 if walks aren't counted as at-bats, as they were then). Barnes, who also hit over .400 three times in the NA, led the circuit in runs, hits, doubles, total bases, and walks, and was its best second baseman. Standing 145 pounds dripping wet, Barnes, like poor Jim Creighton, was no power hitter—he hit only 6 in a nine-year career—yet like Creighton, one little homer seemed to require some form of karmic payback.

For Barnes it was a rule change. Barnes' hitting prowess was based on his knack for being able to squib bunts that would kick across the line into foul ground and let him beat the throw to first. In 1877, the league ruled that if a grounder did that before passing first or third base, it was a foul ball. As a result, Barnes hit a puny .272 that year, whereupon William Hulbert cut his salary from $2,500 to $1,500. Barnes took the matter to court, lost, sat out a year, and by 1882 was gone from the game.

Barnes wasn't the only player for whom the home run was a curse. There was also George Hall, the upstanding citizen who hit those league-high 5 homers (and hit .366) in 1876. The next year Hall played for the Louisville Grays. He hit .323, but he failed to hit a single home run in the spacious Louisville Base Ball Park. But wait. It gets scarier. After the season, Hall and three teammates were found to have taken money from a gambler to throw a game (maybe the diamond stickpins and rings gave them away). They claimed they did it because the club's owner refused to pay them their salaries (pathetically, they were only paid $10 by the gambler). William Hulbert wasn't sympathetic. "Damn you, you sold a game. You are dishonest, and this National League will not stand for it," he said, handing down baseball's first lifetime ban for gambling, predating Pete Rose by 112 years. (Footnote: the Grays disbanded before another game was played, and their stadium burned to the ground.)

Then there was Charley Jones, author of the second NL homer. In 1879, he left Cincinnati to play for Boston (now called the Red Caps) and hit 9 homers to top the league. Next season, he got into a dispute with club president Arthur Soden over $378 in back pay and was fined $100 and suspended. When the disgusted Jones went home to Cincinnati, Soden fired him and then blackballed him from the league. Jones appealed to the Common Pleas Court in Cleveland and was upheld, but—as would happen time and again in future years—the game seemed immune to the courts. Soden refused to reinstate Jones, who sat idle for two years before the short-lived American Association (AA) let him play for the Cincinnati Red Stockings (which also had to look for another league to play in when Hulbert expelled them in 1880 for refusing to sign off on banning booze and Sunday games). Jones led the AA with 10 homers in 1883, with 80 RBIs (runs batted in) in ninety games, but unlike the Reds—the name they began to play under when they and other AA clubs were taken in by the NL in 1890—Charley Jones never was allowed back into the only big league that mattered.

Jones wasn't the only home run king to feel the sting of league excommunication. The rawest deal of all went to Lip Pike, unfortunate indeed since he would have made a hell of a standard bearer. The Lip certainly had star power. Born Lipman Emanuel Pike, he began in organized ball a week after his bar mitzvah, then was among the best of the under-the-table pros when he played for the Philadelphia A's (where he was said, probably fancifully, to have hit homers in five consecutive at-bats). Pike led or co-led the NA in homers three times, with a high of 6 with the Baltimore Lord Baltimores in '72. Almost all were inside-the-park jobs, with the 5-foot-8, 145-pound Pike tearing around the bases like a racehorse—a species he proved he could outrun when to win a $100 bet he ran a 100-yard dash against a famous trotter of the day named Clarence. Pike, given a 25-yard lead, won the race in under 10 seconds.

In 1877 Pike won his fourth home run crown, hitting 4 for the Cincinnati club. Then in 1881 came the bum rap. Playing for the Worcester Ruby Legs (I'm not making this up), the team's cellar-dwelling season led the owner to accuse Pike of "not playing his best" and blackballed him for a year. When he was reinstated, Pike said "shove it" and retired (he later made a token comeback with the New York Mets of the American Association).

Somehow, Orator O'Rourke survived intact. He won another (shared) home run title in 1880 when he hit 6 for Boston. By then, the Irishman that Harry Wright had worried wouldn't be embraced in Beantown had become wildly popular. That season, O'Rourke and his brother and Red Stockings teammate John refused to obey the NL's crude order that players pay for their own uniforms, putting them on the edge of a suspension. The crisis was averted when the O'Rourke Fan Club paid the $40 tab. The Orator became player-manager of the Buffalo Bisons, garnering the batting title in 1884 with a .350 average. Three years later he joined five other future Hall of Famers on the pennant-winning 1888 and 1898 New York Giants—which also set a record for most lawyers on one team—2—with O'Rourke and John Montgomery Ward, a former great pitcher and shortstop who was by now simply a great shortstop when he wasn't trying to get players to unionize and stand up to owners. Little wonder that the arguments by O'Rourke and Ward led nearly the entire Giant team to follow them into the maverick Players League in 1890. In all, during his career, only two players had more hits and only six had more RBIs than the Orator, who in 1904 returned to the Giants to catch one game, at 52, the oldest to ever play in a big-league contest.

It's Raining Home Runs

Even though no one will ever confuse Cap Anson's Chicago White Stockings—the National League's first dynasty—with home run–heavy teams like the 1961 New York Yankees, the 1997 Seattle Mariners, or the 2000 Houston Astros, for one season the ancestors of the Cubs set team home run records that turned the game's assumptions upside-down. It happened in 1884, which is significant because the 1880s were when the home run kicked off its diapers and grew to manhood. Of course, it also happened because of a technicality that could only have been possible in the 1880s, but any technicalities that moved along the home run can take a bow in my book.

What is especially bizarre about this is that the White Stockings were the absolute antithesis of a home run–hitting team in the 1870s when they won the first National League flag before hitting a three-year drought and then coming back with three pennants in a row from 1880–1882 and two more in 1885–1886. At the start Anson's teams embodied the '70s ethos of bionic pitching, airtight defense, and one-base-at-a-time hitting. They had two 20-game winners in 1880, a baseball first, and their pitching would remain the team's forte. The offense was sculpted in the image of Anson, who hit 2 home runs in '76, then not another for the next three seasons. In his long career Anson hit over .400 twice, .335

lifetime, yet never hit 40 doubles, and only three times hit 10 or more triples. The name Cap Anson and the term "slugging percentage" (his was an anemic .455) are as compatible as Bill Gates and leather pants. And his teams of the '70s were sculpted in his image. In '77 they were the only NL team without a home run. (Not that the rest of the league did much more. It took until '79 before any of its teams had as many as 10 homers.)

And then came the 1880s, when everything changed. An augury that something was about to break on the home run front came on July 10, 1880. On that day, the strutting White Stockings, working on a 67-17 season (a .798 percentage, a record still), visited the Cleveland Blues after winning twenty-one straight games (a nineteenth-century record). Their ace pitcher Fred Goldsmith was working on a scoreless game with 2 outs and a man on in the bottom of the ninth inning. Up came rookie second baseman Fred Dunlap. Goldsmith dealt and Dunlap promptly took it out of Kennard Street Park. For this Shot Heard 'Round Cleveland, Dunlap won the nickname of "Sure Shot." And although he would hit only 28 homers in a ten-year NL career, Dunlap no doubt tried forever to revisit home run heaven—and did, sort of, when he won the Union Association's one and only homer crown, with 13 for the St. Louis Browns in 1890.

Dunlap's walkoff home run (to use a term that didn't come around for another century) opened the door to heretofore delayed baseball firsts:

- *September 10, 1881:* Troy's Roger Connor hits the first NL grand slam off Worcester's Lee Richmond.
- *1882:* The 100 mark is passed in league home runs hit; *every* NL club hits double-figures in homers.
- *July 6, 1884:* Pat Callahan of the Indianapolis Hoosiers (AA) hits a home run at age 17, the youngest man to hit one until 1945 when Brooklyn's Tommy Brown beat him by five days. (Fun factoid: Cap Anson was the oldest—45 years, 175 days—until the Philadelphia A's Jack Quinn, at 45 years, 357 days, hit one in 1930.)
- *June 17, 1886:* Detroit's Jim Sweeney (a great pitcher who threw so fast he was once dubbed the "Speed King") surrenders 7 home runs in one game, an all-time record.
- *July 17, 1888:* Boston's Billy Klusman is the first NLer to hit two inside-the-park homers in one game, both off Detroit's Ed Beatin.

Overall, the decade rained 2,220 dingers in the NL, an average of 222 a year compared with the league's four-year total of 145 and average of 36 back in the '70s. Add to that 1,429 in the American Association during the '80s, and 125 in the one-year Union Association (1884). But before I go overboard about this surge, some cracks have to be filled in. There was indeed a substantial rise in long balls—but it would have been more remarkable had there *not* been, given that teams began to play more games—rising to 112 in 1884 and then to 139 in '90. But a bigger factor was the rinky-dink ballparks that were springing up faster than mushroom bats to keep up with all those big-league clubs. At its crescent in 1884 the game had room for three major leagues and thirty-four teams in business, four more than the total in the big leagues today. There were six in Philadelphia, five in Ohio, and four in New York State (Brooklyn Gladiators, anyone?). To meet the needs for immediate accommodations, teams threw together ballparks in whatever tract of open space they could find. As with the earlier parks, this meant some Mickey Mouse outfield dimensions. And if space was particularly tight, some Donald Duck home run totals.

Which leads us to the White Stockings fantasy season of home runs, and exhibit A in the stadium follies: Lake Front Park.

Mistake on the Lake

The Chicago White Stockings were the only team ever to lose a ballpark because of a mad cow. When the club joined the National Association in 1871, its home was the Union Base Ball Grounds, which stood a few hundred yards from Lake Michigan next to the Illinois Central Railroad tracks. The Stockings were in a tight pennant race with Boston and Philadelphia when the Great Chicago Fire detonated by Mrs. O'Leary's famous cow raged through the city and razed the park. The team lost its uniforms and equipment but somehow survived the season as a road unit, losing the flag on the last day. But without a home, they had to drop out of the NA until 1874 when they found lodging at the 23rd Street Grounds, which was so inadequate that they moved *up* in 1878 by going to a hovel with a rock and glass-strewn infield called Lake Front Park, until a state-of-the-art facility could be built on the site of old Union Grounds.

That happened in May 1883 when Lake Front Park II opened, complete with a pagoda for the First Cavalry Band to play on over the main entrance. By then, gentrification on the lakefront had required a severely lopsided layout. At a mere 196 feet away, the right field foul pole seemed to be growing out of first base. And that was the *deep* field—the pole in left was 185 feet! That might have been okay except that center was all of 300 feet and the "power" alleys 280 feet in left and 252 in right. Al

Spalding did put up a 6-foot-high fence in right and a 37-foot wood-and-canvas wall in left, but even Spalding agreed to a ground rule that a ball hit over the short left field fence would be called a double.

That season the team had 143 homers and 277 doubles (68 more than anyone else). But all those two-baggers, a record for years, couldn't stop the Stockings from falling from a title to second place. And so Spalding lifted the double rule. As it happened, Spalding also put in a row of private boxes in front of the left field fence (the man was a visionary!), which cut the distance out there to 180 feet. I know what you're thinking. Bombs away! Indeed, all home run records (such as they were) came crashing down in 1884. The team yanked a jaw-dropping 142 of them, a mere 103 more than the next closest team, and 131 were hit at home. In a year when the doubles dropped by 115 and the homers rose by 129, Ned Williamson, a 5-foot-11, 210-pound third baseman whose drives over the scarlet-lettered wall in '83 cost him many homers, went from 5 to an unheard-of 27 dingers. And he wasn't alone. Fred Pfeffer hit 25. Abner Dalrymple hit 22. Even Cap Anson had 21. The year before, this fearsome foursome had hit a total of 4.

In the madness, the weird became the expected. On May 30, Williamson became the first player to hit 3 homers in one game. It took only until August 6 for Anson to become the second. Just playing the Stockings was infectious. When Dalrymple hit a leadoff first-inning homer in a May 29 game against Detroit, the Wolverines' George Wood answered by hitting a leadoff shot in the bottom of the inning, another baseball first.

All those White Stockings homers were beautiful, except for one thing: their own pitchers had to pitch in Lake Front Park, too. And when they did, they gave up 83 of the little buggers (76 at home). When the dust cleared, the club had not reclaimed the pennant but had fallen two pegs further down, tying for fourth place.

Spalding had seen enough. In fact, he never wanted to see Lake Front Park again. The next season he moved the club into West Side Park where the left field and right field foul poles seemed respectably distant. Actually they were a nigh 216 feet away, but center field and the power alleys were canyons. And, just like that, the home run soufflé collapsed. The White Stockings again led the NL in homers—but with a manageable 54. Williamson fell to 43, Pfeffer to 5, Anson to 7, Dalrymple to 11, most in the league.

After a year in never-never land, the National League's home run pulse was back to its resting rate. Now, the forsaken homer turned its lonely eyes to other big leagues.

The Hot Stovey League

The challenges to the NL's self-ordained primacy came about because of William Hulbert's and Al Spalding's spiteful arrogance about the teams that played east of the Ohio state line. Although the Boston Red Stockings were a stable team, the New York, Brooklyn, Detroit, and Philadelphia entries were the league's poor stepchildren, their tenuous, shadowy owners kept hungry by Hulbert and Spalding, unable to afford good players, and always a day away from going under. This left an opening for leagues to till that territory, and the American Association got there first in 1882 with six teams skewed to the east (but anchored by its showcase team, the Cincinnati Red Stockings). Not that the stability of the AA was anything to brag about, but one can imagine the distress in Spalding's office through the '80s as AA teams outdrew the NL's, and as the AA's long-ball hitters flourished while the NL's stagnated.

In 1880s the AA introduced baseball to its first great home run king: Harry Duffield Stovey. A native Philadelphian who played seven seasons with the league's team in the city, the Athletics, Stovey was the archetypical slugging first baseman. At 6 feet and 180 pounds, the right-hand-hitting Stovey mashed balls deep and far, and could muscle a pop fly over a shallow wall—a trait that certainly came in handy since he played half his games at Jefferson Street Grounds, where more than a few Stovey shots wound up in the swimming pool behind the wall.

No one, though, ever accused Stovey of hitting cheap homers. Before jumping to the AA, he had led the NL when he hit 6 for Worcester in 1880, no small change at the tureen-like Agricultural County Fair Grounds. In the AA Stovey won or shared the homer title four more times. The first was in 1883 when he clocked 14, a new record (such as it was) in a signal year when three hitters hurdled the "magical" double-digit barrier—Charley Jones hit 10 for Cincinnati, and Buck Ewing did the same for the NL's New York Gothams. Stovey topped out at 19 homers in 1889. But this is only part of the story. Stovey rang up numbers that in future years would be called Triple Crown level, that is, ones that could lead a league in homers, batting average and RBIs in a season. He hit over .400 twice, led the AA in runs four times, in doubles once, in triples three times (with as many as 25), in steals three times (as many as 156), in RBIs once, and in fielding percentage once. And for good measure, when he returned to the NL with Boston in 1891 he shared another home run crown, with 16. He was the first player to reach triple-digits in career homers, ending up with 122.

The problem for Stovey and other versatile hitters of the nineteenth century was that such stats were not the holy grail of baseball in their time. While the leagues did keep running batting average tallies during the season in the 1880s, albeit with dubious accuracy, loads of home runs were likely missed unless someone from the team's office was there to see it. And RBIs weren't kept at all; not until the early 1900s did it become an official league stat. From what numbers-crazed baseball historians have dug up, Harry Stovey never did finish No. 1 in the Big Three in any one season. The closest he came was when he led the AA in homers (19) and RBIs (119) in 1889 but finished ninth in hitting (.309).

So, if not him, who was the first Triple Crown winner, in the retroactive sense? The answer, to baseball's great dismay, turned out to be Paul Hines. If only he knew it. When he died in 1935, it was still believed that the first Crown had been won by Boston's Hugh Duffy in 1894, the most productive season any player has ever had, as Duffy hit .440—highest in major league history—along with 8 homers and 145 RBIs. To the baseball panjandrums Duffy was the preferable choice for several reasons. One, he was a Hall of Famer. And two, he wasn't Paul Hines. Not that Hines wasn't a superb hitter. His .302 career average says he is. So does the 1878 season he had with the Providence Grays when he hit .358 with 4 homers and 50 RBIs. The problem was that, at the time and for years thereafter, it was baseball boilerplate that Hines had finished second in hitting to Abner Dalrymple, then with the Milwaukee Grays. Only after Hines was gone was it proven that he beat out Dalrymple and thus had earned the Triple Crown.

But Hines was a man with a bad reputation, a strange thing to say about a man who got to the majors even though he was partially deaf. (It was to accommodate Hines that umpires began using hand signals to indicate balls, strikes, and outs.) Hines might have been deaf, but he wasn't mute. He constantly argued with those accommodating umpires. He also injured opponents with hard slides. William Hulbert once wrote an open letter upbraiding Hines for "a lack of hustle" and a "poor attitude." After his baseball career, Hines seemed to rehabilitate his reputation when President William McKinley—an old friend—named him postmaster for the Department of Agriculture. Then in 1922 Hines was arrested for being a pickpocket.

Actually, this Triple Crown thing is a little complicated. If you believe—as major league baseball does not—that AA records should count, then there is a third nineteenth-century winner: James Edward "Tip" O'Neill, who was the greatest Canadian-born hitter in history if you don't count Stubby Clapp, or Larry Walker. Tip O'Neill, whose identity was stolen by a future Speaker of the House, had the Big Three in 1887, though a note of clarification is in order. That year, the AA counted bases on balls as both a walk and a hit, thus O'Neill's staggering .492 average (to go along with his league-leading 14 homers and 123 RBIs) is the highest ever by that standard, which of course would be unfair. (Trivia fun: if Barry Bonds' 198 walks in 2002 were counted as at-bats and hits, his batting average would have been .577.) Not by coincidence, other AA hitters from that season hold down places 2, 3, 5, 13, 18, and 19 among highest all-time averages, using the absurd standard. Using the real-world standard, O'Neill's average is actually .435—still the second-best in history behind Duffy's .440.

There were other Triple Crown–type guys of the 1880s and '90s. One who deserves a mention is Dan Brouthers, a huge man and a six-time batting champ and two-time home run champ. Brouthers had 106 homers, 1,296 RBIs, and a .342 average in a nineteen-year career, and in one 1889 game he had 3 homers, a double, and a single while playing for Boston. Another is Roger Connor, who held the career home run record—138—for four decades until Babe Ruth came along. In 1898 he led the NL in homers with 14 and RBIs with 130, and in 1885 he led it in averages (.371). Five times he led the league in triples. Connor also hit the longest home runs of his era. After one particularly awesome shot he hit while with the New York Giants in 1883, they passed the hat in the grandstand and bought Connor a $50 gold watch. It was as good an omen of the future as any.

The Tortured Louisville Slugger

In that same 1887 season, Pete Browning hit .402 (by the official standard) with 118 RBIs and 4 home runs with the AA's Louisville Colonels. And if you don't think a man who hit 4 home runs as late as 1887 belongs in the home run pantheon, Browning himself may have anticipated such disdain or otherwise he wouldn't have laid the blame on his home field—Eclipse Park, which had "big league" dimensions, 320 feet and 360 feet at the foul lines, 405 feet in the left-center-field alley, and 495 feet to dead center. After one of many drives he hit died in the outfield, Browning invoked a variation of a common slugger's lament.

"That would count [as] a home run in St. Louis," he said.

Browning's stats, though, are irrelevant to the invaluable contribution he made to the game in general and to the home run in particular.

Having been born and raised in Louisville, and having played there for nine years in the AA and NL, Browning was given the moniker of "The Louisville Slugger" in a thirteen-year career that produced a .359 average and 49 homers. Most players valued their bats, but Browning was so picky that he went through dozens of them. In 1884 he began to pay a Louisville woodworker named John Hillerich, the son of a German immigrant, to make bats for him according to his specifications. While many players used woodworkers to turn bats for them, the obsessive Browning collected more than two hundred of them, each of which he called by name, usually biblical names. Soon other hitters were coming to Hillerich and the demand for what was first informally, then by copyright called "Louisville Sluggers" burgeoned into Hillerich & Bradsby Co., makers of fine baseball bats. By the turn of the century Louisville Sluggers had cracked the market that the Spalding company had cornered. Other bat-makers got into the act as well, such as the "Leader" bat made by W.B. Jarvis Co. of Detroit favored for a while by Ty Cobb. But by the mid-1920s nearly every star of the game used and endorsed the Slugger, in return for which they got their names carved into the barrel, and a few dollars in royalties.

Pete Browning never knew the profound effect his bat obsession would have on baseball. Although bats became a huge business in itself, and their evolution a critical component in that of the home run by harnessing the power within a long piece of wood (after some more design modifications, as we will soon see), in his later years Browning probably couldn't have distinguished a bat from a fir tree. After his career ended in 1894, he was so "batty" that he was confined to a Louisville insane asylum. Let out in 1905, he died in a city hospital later that year at age 44. Every form of art, science and philosophy must have its essential tortured genius. The sacred discipline of hitting a baseball had Pete Browning.

3

Baseball as We Know It

The Folly of Fungo-Ing

For all the colorful and loopy characters who intrepidly carried forth the home run during baseball's evolution, up until the 1890s the game that was played was only a facsimile of the game we know today. The contributions of George Hall, Charley Jones, and Harry Stovey are important, but how fair is it to compare them with Babe Ruth or Mark McGwire when they hit underhand-throwing pitchers standing 50 feet away and delivering it where they called for the pitch, with up to 9 balls for a walk and 4 strikes for an out? This was baseball seen through the acid haze of Timothy Leary. And we're not even talking about pink uniforms with horizontal stripes and all those handlebar mustaches.

And yet gradually, haltingly, they somehow got it right. Step by step, the brick and mortar of the modern game was falling into place by the early 1890s. Mercifully, they ended the chaos of balls and strikes in 1888 when they made it 3 strikes and stopped tinkering. A year later they did the same with 4 balls. In 1887 they made a rough "strike zone"—somewhere between the shins and neck was a strike. Of course, baseball hasn't stopped tinkering with that. Another important alteration was that a sacrifice fly, like a walk, was not to be counted as an at-bat. And now, as well, all catchers had masks and chest protectors (shin guards came a few years later), and nearly every fielder had one of those mitts that once made people laugh.

By far the most critical change came in 1893 when the distance between pitcher and hitter became 60 feet 6 inches. Aptly, for this bumbling baseball crowd, this fatefully perfect range wasn't the result of anyone's genius but rather by accident—a surveyor's error that nobody realized. The back line of the old pitcher's box was replaced by a 12- by 4-inch rubber slab atop a raised "mound" which pitchers pushed off of. No more 4-step or 1-step jog before they threw. A final tinkering in 1895 enlarged the rubber to 24 inches by 6 inches. Finally, in 1900, the 12-inch diamond-shaped home plate was made into a pentagon 17 inches across the front. This gave the pitcher angles to aim for, and the umpire a clear look at balls and strikes.

Predictably, the immediate practical effect of moving the pitcher back was to fatten up batting averages. In no decade has there ever been as many .400 hitters—it was accomplished ten times by seven different players, including of course Hugh Duffy's .440 for Boston. Both Cleveland's Jesse "Crab" Burkett and Philadelphia's "Big Ed" Delahanty did it in successive seasons, in 1894 and '95. But the new distance also forced pitchers to get better, or sneakier, by developing a variety of motions and speeds that now featured breaking balls and change-ups. This was portended when hurlers first got away with bending the rules, encouraged when they were freed to throw overhand in 1884, and mandated when batters were no longer allowed to call their pitch.

Accordingly, pitchers' lexicons suddenly percolated with arcane terms that make today's splitters and two- and four-seam fastballs seem prosaic. These included incurve, outcurve, reversing curve, drop, inshoot, downshoot jump ball and rising ball. What's more, the spitball was legal and beanballs commonplace. One head-hunting pitcher of the day, the New York Giants' Jouett Meekin, counseled that when facing a good hitter, the first two pitches should arrive "within an inch of his head or body," which would set him up for an outside curve. "Driving the batsman away from the plate is an essential part of baseball," he said. So don't be blaming Roger Clemens.

More pitchers were being taken into clubs, as well, up to four or five per staff, and though the aces were still expected to go the route—one would practically have to shoot Hoss Radbourne, John Clarkson, Tim Keefe, Amos Rusie, and a new sensation named Cy Young to get them to come out of a game—relief pitching was a viable option for managers now. Free substitution was the rule, so usually a pitcher who came out simply switched positions with a player who could pitch, generally the right fielder.

One can reasonably assume that the baseball brass had come to appreciate the drama and spectacle of a ball flying over a wall. But they also rigorously wanted to strike a balance between offense and pitching. For example, the same year the 60-foot 6-inch rule came in, the flat-headed bats were thrown out. Bats could still be of any weight, but still no wider than 2¾-inches in diameter and, now, 42 inches in length. However, this even-handed approach did not mollify the more vocal, and powerful baseball traditionalists, who to their horror watched the home run grow in prestige and romance. Its pluck was evident in 1891. That year, when the jaunty abbreviation "homer" entered the vernacular in a *Chicago Tribune* game story, Brooklyn's Tom Daly got the first pinch-hit in history—and it was a "homer." Then the 60-foot 6-inch rule was enacted, giving potential long ball hitters now taking a full stride to meet the ball a longer look at the pitch. Now, some sportswriters were less impressed with the one-base-at-a-time game and new tools for executing it like the hit-and-run and sacrifice bunt. One, Sam Crane, of the *New York Commercial Advertiser,* turned it into a hormonal issue. Strafing the bunt as a "baby play," he asked, "Who wants to see big Roger Connor—who can hit a ball a mile—make a puny, little feminine bunt?" The walls of Jericho seemed to be cracking.

Up stepped one of the most rock-ribbed of the game's guardians to keep them standing. The redoubtable Henry Chadwick, now in his late 60s, counterattacked in *Spalding's Official Base Ball Guide* in an 1895 piece entitled "The Batting of 1894." In the article, which was as much a rebuke of writers like Sam Crane, Chadwick derisively called long-balling fungo hitting, the pregame ritual of throwing a ball in the air and hitting practice flies to outfielders. He wrote:

> A good deal of bosh has been written—mostly by the admirers of "fungo" hitting—about sacrifice hitting being something that should not be in the game, just as these fungo-hitting-advocates try to write down *bunt* hitting—the most difficult place hit known to the game. This class of writers think that the very acme of batting skill is the home run hit, a hit which any muscular novice in batting on amateur fields can accomplish without difficulty, and where more home runs are made in a single season than in two seasons by the best managed professional teams.
>
> The effort to make home runs leads to more chances for catches by outfielder in one game than there are home runs made in fifty. The exhaustion which follows a home run hit, with its sprinting run of 120 yards at full speed, is entirely lost sight of by the class of patrons of the game who favor home runs. One season, a few years ago, the tail-end team of the League excelled all its rivals in scoring home runs,

> while the pennant-winning team took the honors and the prize solely on account of its excellence in team-work at the bat. . . . (T)he object of the batsman (is) to send the runner home the best way he can, either by a base hit or a sacrifice hit. In striving to do this, the very worst plan is to try solely for a home run hit, as it only succeeds once in thirty or forty times, and not that against skillful, strategic pitching. Time and again were batsmen, last season, left on third base after opening the innings with a three-bagger, owing to the stupid work of the succeeding batsmen in trying to "line 'em out for a homer," instead of doing real team-work at the bat.

In other writings, Chadwick admitted that fans dug "the splurgy long hit which yields a home run," but that it was the "intelligent minority" who understood effective hitting. Swinging for the fences, he said, was "veritable stupidity."

Much of Chadwick's polemic is relevant even today (though it is least relevant, and most amusing—especially to Barry Bonds—for its ancient notion that home run hitters might actually exhaust themselves running out drives). Yet, in truth, he protested too much. This was typical for Chadwick, who blistered players like Orator O'Rourke and Monte Ward for forming the "Brotherhood" union that stood against the reserve clause and led to mass jumping to the Players League in 1890 (which fell apart after one season). The constitution of the Brotherhood, Chadwick wrote, was a "revolutionary pronunciamento" and its methods "terrorism." Still, on this one, he was just plain wrong. To be certain, hitting did spike after the 60-foot 6-inch rule; one manifestation was that the previously unthinkable feat of hitting four home runs in one game was accomplished *twice*, within *two* years! The first time it was ever done was on May 30, 1894, by Boston's Bobby Lowe, then matched on July 13, 1896, by Philadelphia's Ed Delahanty. Still, look at the progression of overall hitting numbers:

Year	Runs per Game	Home Runs	Batting Average	ERA	Strikeouts
1892	5.10	417	.245	3.28	5,955
1893	6.57	460	.280	4.66	3,335
1894	7.36	627	.309	5.32	3,304
1895	6.58	484	.296	4.78	3,602
1896	6.03	404	.290	4.36	3,522
1897	5.88	367	.292	4.30	3,727
1898	4.96	299	.271	3.60	4,247

By the time Chadwick's harangue ran, the spike had ended and the numbers were melting back to 1892 levels—indeed, by '96 *fewer* homers were being recorded, and by '97 fewer runs, while there still was a much higher batting average, which should have delighted Chadwick (except that he also was riled up by singles hitters fattening up their averages without regard to building runs; there was just no pleasing the man).

In fact, the league's top teams, the Baltimore Orioles and the Boston Beaneaters, who combined for eight straight pennants in the '90s, played the "team-work at the bat" game so well that they left behind rubrics of endearing value. Boston's was the first use of hand signals, developed by manager Tommy McCarthy and relayed from base runner to hitter when the time was right for the hit-and-run—a play McCarthy pioneered. In time, of course, the chain of command of such signals would be from manager to coach to players. The Orioles, a dirty bunch more suited to brass knuckles than clever strategy, nonetheless had one—the "Baltimore Chop," which was perfected by "Wee" Willie Keeler who swung down on the pitch, chopped it off the plate or turf high into the air, then beat the throw to first. Wee Willie's credo was to "hit 'em where they ain't," which didn't mean behind the fence but in the gaps, such as they did in a series against Boston in 1897, ringing up 22 doubles in three games.

Not to be outdone, Monte Ward, now managing the Brooklyn Bridegrooms, brought in bats made of soft willow, which made bunting easier. Ward was tricky; he used identical-looking hardwood bats to throw opponents off the scent. Ward, and all managers, were not averse to a good long ball once in a while, but the general sentiment, as elucidated by Henry Chadwick, was that "any soft-brained heavyweight"—as another sportswriter said—could give it a good ride, but in the end it was brains that won games.

The nastiness of the debate surely deadened enthusiasm for the home run, but it has never been proven that the game responded to the long-ball backlash by unilaterally deadening the ball such as by using a mushier core—though individual teams, it is clear, did so on their own in wonderfully creative ways. With the home team now responsible for supplying a dozen balls per game, Connie Mack, who managed the Pittsburgh Pirates in the 1890s, would stick a half-dozen balls meant for the next day in an ice box overnight to deaden them. He'd mark them and try to run those in when the other team batted.

The pitchers didn't really need help, anyway. Which is why, with an actual dead ball or not, what is called the "Dead Ball Era" had cast its shadow over the majors. Fortunately, another big league would change the landscape again, in ways no one could have figured in 1900.

Buck, as in Babe

The home run, which had been caught in the undertow all throughout the nineteenth century only to keep its head popping up every once in a while to remind baseball it was still around, resurfaced again in 1899 in a way that was so out of context that it probably seemed at the time to be a mirage. But, as history relates, it was really a scouting mission for a future intercession by the home run gods, who with perfect timing chose the final year of one era to be the jump-off point of a new era with endless possibilities to do some fine-tuning.

That year, a 27-year-old Washington Nationals outfielder named John Frank "Buck" Freeman, in his first full big-league season, cranked out 25 home runs—and they weren't a Ned Williamson, dinky ballpark 25, either. The Nats' home grounds, Boundary Field, had deep foul poles and power alleys and rewarded few hitters. Indeed, many homers were lost there when drives struck oak trees that hung over the outfield walls and caromed back into play. What's more, the team as a whole hit only 47 dingers in 155 games, and no one else had more than 6. Freeman himself, in eleven seasons, only hit 82, with 13 his second-highest total in a season.

Freeman was obviously a home run anomaly, a former-day Brady Anderson unloading a truckload of long balls for no apparent reason and then falling off precipitously. But don't overlook how much of an oracle he was. He threw and batted left-handed, he began his career as a pitcher, and he played with the Boston Red Sox of the new American League. And Freeman left a neat little home run legacy, too. When he led the league in 1903 by bagging 13 homers, he became the first of only three players in history to have paced both the NL and the AL in the department (the others: "Wahoo" Sam Crawford, who led the Cincinnati Reds with 16 in 1901 and the Detroit Tigers with 7 in 1908; and Mark McGwire). Freeman also led the AL in RBIs in 1902–1903 and hit .294 overall. When Freeman retired in 1907, Babe Ruth was 12 years old and being kept off the streets and saloons of Baltimore at the St. Mary's Industrial School and Reformatory. Within seven years, the Babe would begin his big-league incarnation. As a left-handed pitcher who could also put a ball into orbit. With the Red Sox. When the gods were ready to do business.

Power Games

Because the American League gave the home run its star power, the long ball owes its fame if not its life to the dogged survival of the league over the long haul, and by extension, to the work of Byron Bancroft Johnson.

"Ban" Johnson, a former Cincinnati newspaperman, was the force behind the only successful challenge to the National League. In the 1890s Johnson had become president of the Western League, a minor league until Johnson had a vision in 1899 when he changed the circuit's name to the American League and enlisted some powerful allies to help him muscle in on the NL's domain by going head to head with it in Cleveland, Chicago, Boston, Detroit, St. Louis, and Philadelphia. For the center of gravity, Chicago, he gave majority ownership to Charlie Comiskey, the former great first baseman who had allied with Johnson when he owned a Western League team in St. Paul.

Bancroft positioned the new league as a "clean" alternative to the bullying, boozing NL, but he was hardly above playing dirty to get started, by taking advantage of the NL's internal troubles and seducing some its biggest—and most ambitious—stars. Many NL players came aboard the ship in 1900 when the elder league contracted from twelve to eight teams, sending players looking for work. Many others came over because Johnson recruited Connie Mack and John McGraw, who were given minority ownership of the Philadelphia Athletics and reconstituted Baltimore Orioles, respectively (both would also manage, and McGraw would play as well). But even more important was Clark "The Old Fox" Griffith, the wily pitcher who had been a fixture on Cap Anson's White Stockings since 1893. In 1901, Griffith, acting as head of the Players' Protective Association (a seminal players' union), demanded that the NL end the reserve rule. When he was told to take a hike, Griffith wired Johnson, who waived the rule, "Go ahead, you can sign all the players you want." Griffith himself jumped to Comiskey's White Sox as pitcher-manager.

Of the 182 players in the AL its first year, fully 111 were ex-NL players, including Buck Freeman, Big Ed Delahanty, Rube Waddell, Jesse Burkett, and Cy Young. The NL, under new president Harry Pulliam (and Al Spalding, who watched in horror as the White Sox took fans from the Cubs) fought back. When three members of the Philadelphia Phillies, including the wondrous Napoleon Lajoie, jumped to Connie Mack's Philadelphia Athletics in 1901, the Phillies filed for relief in the Pennsylvania Supreme Court. While the case dragged on, Lajoie gave the A's a season that still stands as one of the all-time greatest, winning the AL's first Triple Crown by hitting .426 with 14 homers, 125 RBIs, 232 hits, 76 extra-base hits, a .463 on-base percentage, and .643 slugging percentage. Finally, in April of 1902, the court ruled that the jumpers could not play for anyone but the Phillies. But because the court's jurisdiction was only Pennsylvania, Ban Johnson cannily ran an end-around and transferred the players to the AL's Cleveland Bronchos, where Lajoie again led the league with a .378 average and, in the first of thirteen seasons there, helped establish the team that later became the Indians.

For the NL, though, the most depressing number was the 1.7 million fans drawn by the upstart league, which, while 200,000 behind the NL, was a shot across the bow that would only intensify. Stocked with outstanding players, the White Sox took the league's first pennant. But the real test for the AL was 1902, when it had to survive its own upheaval, caused by John McGraw's power play. The 5-foot 7-inch McGraw showed why he was called "The Little Napoleon" in a war of nerve and dare with Ban Johnson. McGraw's Baltimore team was so awful that plans were made to move it to the lucrative New York market and challenge the Giants. But McGraw—whose incorrigible bullying and bleating run-ins with umpires led Johnson to fine and suspend him in 1901—reckoned that Ban would never trust him with a New York team, and he pulled off a mind-numbing conspiracy with the Giants' owner, Andrew Freedman. Early in the 1902 season, McGraw was ejected from a game that led to a forfeiture and another suspension. In a huff, he divested his Oriole stock and moaned that "ballplayers are not a lot of cattle to have the whip cracked over them." The next morning, he was named manager of the Giants, with a contract (dated days before) for $11,000 over four years. McGraw wasn't through. He somehow arranged for Freedman to assume covert control of the Orioles, whereupon he released four players—including future Hall of Famers Joe "Ironman" McGinnity and Roger Bresnahan, who came right to the Giants—before Johnson could take back control of the club.

Within a year, Freedman sold the Giants to John T. Brush for a large profit. Johnson, meanwhile, did move the Orioles to New York to play as the Highlanders in 1903. When the newly-renamed team began play, its manager was none other than "The Old Fox," Clark Griffith, who had gotten Johnson to give him the job by vowing to bring over six NL players. By then, the AL was here to stay, having outdrawn the NL in 1902 by 2.2 million to 1.7 million.

Some of them even saw a home run every now and then.

Pitchers' Paradise, Hitters' Hell

Not that anybody really noticed, but the AL's first homer was hit on April 25, 1901, when Cleveland's Erve Beck went yard on Chicago pitcher John Skopec. That season, the AL eked out a 228-227 edge in four-baggers in the first dual-league season, in twenty-four fewer games and 829 fewer at-bats than the NL, and handily won the league home run derby the next two seasons as well, recording a 258-98 blowout in 1902. If it strikes you that this was a conscious effort by a league that recognized the value of a good long ball, it just ain't so. The truth is, the home run, and all hitting, was ceded to the AL, a gift if ever there was one.

In 1901, the senior circuit made a radical rule change. It began calling foul balls as strikes. Up until then, foul balls weren't balls or strikes or anything but do-over pitches, meaning that hitters could chill out knowing they would not fall behind in the count except when they swung and missed. Now, all that changed. Not only were those fouls now strikes but a two-strike foul tip caught by the catcher on the fly was now a strikeout. This brought about another structural change: catchers moved up right behind the hitter to snare the foul tips. With the ensuing increase in two-strike counts, hitters became discombobulated. For the first time they learned that being behind changes everything. They now had to swing defensively rather than slash away. Result: in 1901, the NL average fell from .267 to .259; by 1908 it was .239. Meanwhile, strikeouts rose from 2,697 in 1900 to 4,241 in 1901. Home runs sagged from 350 in 1899 to 98 in 1901 and would remain in the mid-100s, until 1910 when they reached 200.

The fledgling AL, trying to build a fan base, did not wish to crimp any offensive weapon, and the league's hitting numbers were markedly better: a .277 league average in 1901, .275 in 1902, scoring runs at a clip of 5.35 and 4.89 runs per game while the NL was mired at 4.63 and 3.98. And home runs, as noted, were really moving. In 1902, the AL's leader, Philadelphia A's outfielder Ralph Orlando "Socks" Seybold, socked 16 over the wall, a record for seventeen years.

But the party in the AL had to end, and did in January 1903. After two years of trench warfare between the leagues, détente was reached. What ripped it was a new round of league-jumping players that season, the most important being Wahoo Sam Crawford, who signed a new contract with Cincinnati, then days later signed one with the Detroit Tigers. Crawford, the home run king of 1901, had hit .333 with an NL-high 23 triples in 1902, and his defection threatened to consume the leagues in self-destructive warfare if not settled in good faith. Both circuits took the occasion to go beyond these cases and establish a working agreement that would preempt future disputes and territorial encroachments. And so the National Commission was born, consisting of respected Cincinnati owner Garry Herrmann, who was chairman, Ban Johnson, and Harry Pulliam. This essentially put the two leagues on equal footing (Hermann's integrity was demonstrated by his crucial vote to allow Crawford to go to Detroit, where Wahoo would soon team up with Ty Cobb). For the NL it was good business because Ban Johnson's league was the more popular one, and the alliance offered the promise of a postseason World Series, which when played between intra-city rivals would bring astronomical profits.

The enduring effect of the détente was the sanctifying of the five shared big markets and the territorial exclusivity of the remaining three teams from each league. As a result, the same eight teams in the two leagues would remain intact for more than fifty years. The restrictive and salary-choking reserve clause, which was now adopted by the AL as well, would last until 1975. More immediately, when play began in 1903, baseball's uniformity included a 154-game schedule that would be played without pause for the next fifty-eight years (except for the World War I years 1918 and 1919), as well as the AL's acceptance of the foul-strike rule—meaning that both leagues now could suffer hitting indignities in solidarity. That year, the AL's overall batting average fell to .255 and home runs to 184. By 1907, homers had bottomed out to 107, an all-time AL low. Indeed, it did not take long for the NL to catch up again, winning the homer race 175-156 in 1904. The senior circuit would win in fifteen of the next sixteen seasons, though not until 1911 did the general home run malaise end, and not by accident. Read on.

It surely didn't help matters that the dominant teams of the early 1900s were McGraw's Giants and Mack's Athletics, who each won five pennants between 1902 and 1913—overseen by two old-line devotees of "scientific" ball. Nor did it help that another old lion, Charlie Comiskey, was putting out winning teams without much hitting of any kind—the most egregious example being the White Sox "Hitless Wonders" of 1906, who won an actual championship hitting .236, a record low for any pennant winner, while hitting 20 homers. Conditions were such that Harry Davis, the Athletics' great third baseman and captain, could actually lead the AL in homers for four straight seasons—and become the first of only four players in history to turn that trick—by hammering 10, 8, 12, and 8. It was that bad.

Moreover, the old Homer Hex seemed to be lingering on, as some unlucky sods found out. Ed Delahanty, for one. In his sixteen-year, Hall-of-Fame career, "Big Ed" hit .346 playing mainly for the Phillies. His Kodak home run moment came on July 13, 1904, when against Chicago he hit 4 inside-the-park home runs, 3 of them in consecutive at-bats, which hadn't been done before and hasn't since. In 1902 he jumped to Washington in the AL, then a year later signed with the Giants, but the National Commission sent him back. Big Ed decided to go anyway. On July 2, 1905, he hopped a train for the Big Apple, but en route he got drunk and disorderly and was put off the train. He tried to walk across a railroad bridge over the Niagara River and fell to his death.

Still, one wonders if the homer would have had its day much earlier had either, or both, Honus Wagner and Nap Lajoie not played the bulk of their home games where they did. Wagner, the incomparable shortstop, was the very prototype of the long-ball hitter. At 5 feet 11 inches and 200 pounds, Wagner was a bow-legged, square-jawed hard pumice of a man who came out of the western Pennsylvania coal mines to play for the Pittsburgh Pirates in 1900. With his huge hands all but making cornmeal out of the bat, he had a vicious swing that exploded out of a bent-kneed crouch. Many years later, Ed Barrow, the longtime Yankee front-office boss who had a major influence on Babe Ruth's genesis, opined that "If Wagner had batted against a lively ball, he would have hit fifty homers every year."

That could be, but Wagner's big problem was Exposition Park, a lovely twin-spired Taj Mahal where he had to contend with foul lines that stretched to 400 feet and a 450-foot corridor to center. Though he did hit 101 career homers in a glorious twenty-one-year career (including a grand slam at age 42, the oldest player to do that), Wagner adjusted his swing to pierce the outfield gaps, cracking drives that ran to the wall and sent the deceptively fast "Flying Dutchman" streaking around the bases. Wagner had 3,418 hits—a record until 1962, won the batting title six times, hit .327 lifetime, had 643 doubles, and a NL-record 252 triples. And he stole 722 bases. Oh, if only one could add those 500 homers Barrow talked about. Such is the stuff of dreams. Still, fueled by Wagner's endless gappers, the Bucs swept to the pennant three straight years, 1901–1903, and another in 1909.

As for the great Lajoie, the Napster never equaled his home run output in Philadelphia, and maybe I'm overstating his power potential since he hit BBs rather than cannon shots. Ring Lardner, the great sportswriter of the 1910s and 1920s, once noted that Nap "wasn't a fly-ball hitter.

When he got a hold of one, it usually hit the fence on the first bounce, traveling about five feet three inches above the ground most of the way and removing the ears of all infielders who didn't throw themselves flat on their stomachs." Still, when Lajoie was with the Phillies, his home field was the Wee-Kirk of baseball, Baker Bowl. Lajoie was a sinewy 6-foot-1, 195-pound man, and he could drive a ball a long way to the opposite field. At Baker Bowl, that field was right field and it was all of 272 feet to the alley out there, and only 300 feet to center. When Nap went to Cleveland, home was League Park, where the 400-foot alleys were nearly as deep as the center field fence. In one spot just left of center, the fence was—get ready—505 feet away!

So, as things stood, with coddled pitchers loading up the ball, with fielders' gloves getting bigger and better, with the rules skewed against hitting, with prevailing attitudes about how to play the game set in concrete, and with many ballparks' almost audible giggling at long-ball hitters, Babe Ruth was still far, far away.

Certainly, pitchers weren't complaining. With little to fear in most hitters, the hurlers partied on. The numbers posted by the best of the game's pitchers during the early 1900s never fail to amaze. Start with the Giants' Ironman McGinnity, the last of the great underhand pitchers. He worked both ends of a doubleheader five times over the 1903 and 1904 seasons and won 9 of the 10 games. In 1903 he had 47 starts, 44 complete games, 434 innings, a 31-20 record, and a 2.84 ERA (earned run average). In 1904 the numbers were 44, 38, 408, 35-8, 1.61. But McGinnity was just one of many "Ironmen" to take the hill. His famous moundmate, Christy Mathewson, who took the screwball to dizzying heights, started 42 games in 1904, completing 37, in 366 innings, with a 30-13 record.

Believe it or not, both of John McGraw's aces were outdone that year by the ace of the other New York team, the one McGraw knew he'd never manage: the Highlanders, for whom "Happy Jack" Chesbro, a gnarly spitballer, went 41-12 with 48 complete games in 51 starts and 454 innings—all but the innings records. Although I'm betting Jack was not Happy on the last day of the season when a wet one got away from him for a wild pitch in the bottom of the ninth to lose the pennant.

Want more? How about Connie Mack's dynamic duo in Philadelphia—Rube Waddell and Eddie Plank. The eccentric southpaw Waddell—baseball's answer to R. P. McMurphy—went 25-19 with 39 complete games in 46 starts, 349 strikeouts (a record that stood until Sandy Koufax broke it in 1965), and worked 383 innings in 1904. All Plank did was to go 26-17 with 7 shutouts, 43 complete games in 44 starts and 357 innings.

Then there was the Boston Pilgrims (Red Sox) tandem, Cy Young and Bill Dinneen. Young, whose given name of Denton True Young had long given way to the truncated form of "Cyclone" for the effect of his pitches, had a perfect game in 1904, one of his three no-hitters in his career, and against Waddell, to boot. Young actually totaled a record twenty-four straight hitless innings that year, at age 37.

Young really had two Hall-of-Fame careers, coming to Boston after starring in the NL for eight seasons with the Cleveland Spiders. His first year as a Red Sox, he went 33-10 with 38 complete games and a 1.62 ERA over 371 innings. He would win more than 30 games twice more in Boston, to bring his career total to 5, and would start no less than 30 games or pitch no less than 287 innings for the next eight years. Pitching in his shadow, Dinneen produced nothing but complete games—37 straight of them—in 1904, working 335 innings. Finally, St. Louis Cardinals' Jack Taylor threw 187 consecutive complete games (yikes) and one season worked 352 innings. And still waiting in the wings was Walter "Big Train" Johnson, who wouldn't arrive until 1907.

Just reading these numbers today can make one exhausted, but apparently compiling them was candy because most of baseball's cumulative pitching standards were set in the Dead Ball Daze—most notably Young's 511 unreal victories. The next two in line—Johnson's 416 and Mathewson's 372—were nothing to sneeze at, either. Young also set the standard for complete games (750) and innings (7,356), and Johnson for shutouts (110). And there is this fact: no one from the era is even close to the top in all-time walks. Which immediately explains a fact of life of those times: hitters didn't give much truck to walking and swung at pretty much everything, one reason why pitchers' jobs were so easy.

They were that good, statistically, because people didn't hit home runs, and as a result never had to worry about the consequences of laying a ball in. In their thought-provoking book *The Diamond Appraised*, Craig R. Wright and ex-major-league pitcher Tom House (who in 1974 caught Hank Aaron's 715th home run in the Atlanta Braves' bullpen) make a convincing case that the home run's absence was the X-factor in the inner game of baseball, and thus nearly singularly responsible for those ridiculously inflated innings. They write:

> To understand the differences between work levels of pitchers in [that] era and those of today, we have to keep in mind the different

> strategies of the period. Without the constant threat of the home run hanging over their heads, the pitchers faced fewer crucial batters to whom they would need to pitch carefully and use setup pitches. In the modern era, even the average player is capable of hitting a home run, and so he's in scoring position whenever he goes to the plate. And if a modern player reaches first base, he is more of an immediate threat to score because of the higher incidence of extra-base hits with the live ball. The old-time pitchers didn't have to worry as much about runners scoring until they were in scoring position.

They go on:

> Given the absence of the long ball, the pitcher's need to pace himself for complete games, and the long haul of the season, the practice of "coasting" became prevalent in this era. Besides Cy Young's noted habit of pitching just well enough to win, Grover Alexander openly admitted he did not bear down until a runner reached base, and Christy Mathewson was notorious for letting up with a lead . . . [T]he pitchers of this era threw significantly fewer pitches per batter than in modern times. . . . From 1903 to 1919 [pitchers] had the potential for throwing far more innings and far more complete games, while needing less time off between starts.

Inevitably, however, even the ironmen rusted. Their innings slackened and their arms and shoulders paid the toll for those high times. Ed Walsh, who followed up his incredible 464-inning carnage of 1908 with 393 in 1912 at age 31, was a shell of a pitcher from then on. No one would ever get near 400 again, as baseball began demanding less of starting pitchers and realizing the values of moving fresh arms into games, especially when the hitters finally started waking up. By 1909, the change was evident: historians have determined there were 110 saves in the two leagues (this was long before saves became an official statistic), up from 32 in 1901. That year, only three hurlers rang up more than 300 innings in the NL, two in the AL.

In the end, those monster inning totals were fool's gold. By throwing fewer pitches per batter, Wright and House conclude, Ed Walsh averaged about 95 pitches per start in 1908—about five hundred fewer than Mickey Lolich in 1971. When Walter Johnson threw his career-high 373 innings in 1910, he threw probably 4,060 pitches, or the equivalent of 265 modern innings.

"Seen in this light" they write, "we know the pitchers of this era were not supermen."

This would be proven when baseball saw the light about the home run and the real supermen came out to play.

Shortball in the Fall

As baseball's climactic event, the World Series has done more than anything else to magnify home runs into aristocratic currency. Nothing about a World Series dinger is common, even if some players who hit them are. Such was the case with Jimmy Sebring. On October 1, 1903, the 21-year-old Pittsburgh Pirate outfielder (career: 363 games, .261 average, 6 homers) came to bat at Boston's Huntington Avenue Grounds in the first inning of the first game of the first World Series and—against Cy Young, no less—hit the first Series homer, keying the Pirates' eventual 7-3 victory. This is such a feel-good moment for this book that I really hate to report that, according to the *Boston Globe*, on Sebring's "drive into the alley, the Boston outfielders [took] their time in fielding it, permitting a home run." In other words, inside-the-park. Damn.

Sebring did have 4 RBIs that historic game, so give him his due. However, it was actually the slugging of a man with the perfectly heroic American name of Patrick Henry "Patsy" Dougherty who turned the Series around in Game 2—yes, home runs could do that, even then. The hard-nosed outfielder who hit 17 round-trippers in a ten-year career, hit an inside-the-park homer leading off the first inning against Sam Leever. Then, amazingly, he hit 1 in the sixth over the left field wall off Bucky Veil to ice a 3-0 win for Bill Dinneen. This was no easy feat, since Huntington was a continent, 350 feet down the line, 440 in the alley, and nearly *600* feet to center. Boston went on to take the best-of-nine series, 5 games to 3.

As historic as Jimmy and Patsy were, the hex got them, too. In 1905 Sebring had to leave the Pirates when his wife took ill, soon to die, and he himself died at age 28 of Bright's disease on December 22, 1909. As for Patsy, his brawling ways led the Pilgrims to dump him. He landed with the White Sox in 1908 and while he led the AL with forty-seven steals in 1908, he played in fourteen more World Series games and never hit another homer.

Which only proves that, this virtual avalanche of 3 homers aside (none others were hit), the World Series was not markedly different from the regular-season dribble of home runs. In fact, there would not be a single one hit in each of the next three Fall Classics. Back then, the bigger picture was that there even *was* a World Series. Residual bitterness between the two leagues forced the Boston and Pittsburgh owners to make the series on their own, not as a sanctioned event. This was similar to the NL-AA "World Series" of the 1880s that were played as pseudo-barnstorming tours and drew scant interest. This time there was much more at stake financially and in prestige, and attendance of more than 100,000 swelled the players' shares to $1,316 each for the losing Pirates and $1,182 each for the winning Pilgrims (Pittsburgh owner Barney Dreyfus gave his team extra from his own pocket). Total gate receipts cleared $50,000.

But that wasn't enough to make John McGraw lift his grudge against Ban Johnson, and when the Giants took the 1904 NL pennant, he and owner John Brush refused to play the Pilgrims, calling the AL a "minor league." Such hubris, though, only left McGraw open to ridicule for cowardice. Besides, the money was just too good to ignore, so Brush put forward a plan for a permanent best-of-7 World Series that was adopted by the time the Giants repeated as league champs in 1905 and strode into the Series in new black uniforms—a sight that must have scared the hell out of the Pilgrims, who lost in five games, every one of which was a shutout.

While the home run played no vital role in any World Series or pennant race during the century's first decade, a 1907 controversy involving a long fly ball and a fan is worthy of a mention as a preface to future home run madness. It involved Wahoo Sam Crawford, who by now was hitting cleanup right behind Ty Cobb in the Tiger batting order. Crawford, like everyone else, detested the scabrous Cobb, who was in his third season. But the two men worked together beautifully, developing synchronized double-steals that often delivered the Georgia Peach from third base—when Crawford wasn't clearing the bases with a homer or one of his record 312 triples. These two were why the Tigers won three straight AL pennants from 1907 to 1909. Crawford figured into the 1907 race too, though it may have been decided late in September by an umpire named Silk O'Louhglin, who ruled that Crawford was interfered with trying to catch a long drive to left field—not by a fan but by a Philadelphia policeman standing at the edge of an overflow crowd on the left field grass. This kept the Athletics from beating the Tigers and moving into first place. Eight decades later, another long-ball interference controversy involving a certain 12-year-old Yankee fan would prove that nothing aberrant that happens in baseball is ever really new.

Cobb's Way

Speaking of Cobb, I don't want to but I must, because he was baseball's first supernova. Cobb may have been a cretin but he took his self-hating insecurities out on the world with such passion that the *New York Evening World*'s Bozeman Bulger wrote, "He was possessed by the Furies." Cobb won the batting title every year but one from 1909 to 1919, and, with the dotage of the press—it was a *Detroit Free Press* sportswriter, Joe Jackson, for example, who nicknamed him "The Georgia Peach"—and to baseball's great dismay, he supplanted the cultured, hunky Christy Mathewson as the game's top attraction. This happened as masses of people streamed from the countryside to the big cities, and the press reflected the new paradigm. By the time Henry Chadwick died on April 20, 1908, blue-collar natives and immigrant readers wanted some red meat on the sports page. The benefactor: Ty Cobb.

The influential New York and Chicago sportswriters of the 1910s—Hugh Fullerton, Fred Lieb, Ring Lardner, Paul Gallico, Frank Graham, *Reach Guide* editor Francis Richter, pseudo-sportswriter Damon Runyon, and of course Grantland Rice—bled Cobb over the newspaper like an open wound, breathlessly charting his lethal dirt-cloud slides and flying spikes as well as his endless contract holdouts. Anyone who believes the depiction of modern ballplayers as greedy brats should read Frank Richter's take in the *Reach Guide* of Cobb's 1910 batting title quest, which ended in controversy when on the season's last day the St. Louis Browns tried to keep the title (and a Chalmers automobile) away from him by allowing Napoleon Lajoie to lay down seven straight bunt singles. Ban Johnson was so ticked off by the conspiracy he credited Cobb with enough hits to prevail (though Chalmers gave both men a car). Richter, though, laid into Cobb for the losing Tigers' "factional troubles," which "were apparently augmented by rows growing from Cobb's personal ambition and his desire to win an automobile offered as a batting prize."

In actuality, Cobb was captive to the owners' tight-fisted grip on salaries. Making $9,000 after winning the 1909 and 1910 batting titles, he made not a penny more after winning three more. Don't pity him too much; he was also an early investor in Coca-Cola, which turned him into baseball's first millionaire player. But Cobb skillfully manipulated the press to lobby for more money, and that he became the highest salaried player as a result was a lesson to all.

It may surprise one to know that Cobb was a home run king, that in his 1909 Triple Crown season (.377, 115 RBIs), he homered a league-best nine times—every last one of them an inside-the-park job. In fact, of Cobb's 117 career homers, 46 never left the yard, and until 1910 only 2 of his 28 homers did. This was consistent with the ratio of the day. Wahoo Sam Crawford, for example, had 51 inside-the-park homers out of a career take of 97. The home run still mostly happened as an accident, the result of a fielder slipping on the slick grass and letting a line drive roll a mile and a half through the outfield. Cobb hit at least 1 homer in a record twenty-four straight seasons, yet the idea of swinging for a home run was anathema to him. "Don't grip your bat at the very end, leave say an inch or two," he once wrote in a letter to Crawford. "Don't slug at full speed. Learn to meet it firmly, and you will be surprised at the results." This is still a sacred baseball canon, and who would argue with a guy who hit .367 in his career, the best ever.

But Cobb's way ruled only until another way could come around. And in 1909, it did, by way of a Philadelphia machine shop.

4

The Arrival

A Rabbit in the House

One of the great unsung heroes in the argosy of the home run is Ben Shibe, a man whose contribution to the Industrial Age—making horsehide baseballs better than anyone else—rewarded him with corporate wealth, a ballpark named for him, and best of all a section about him in this book. Back in the 1880s, Shibe, a Philadelphia machinist, became partners in a sporting goods company with Al Reach, who after his playing career as a left-handed second baseman had followed Al Spalding into the business of selling bats, balls, and the like (as well as into team ownership; Reach helped to found the Phillies and served as their president until 1903). The A.J. Reach Co. quickly took off mainly because of one thing—the lovely balls that came out of Shibe's machines. One wound yarn more tightly than had been possible before; another perfectly punched out those figure-8 covers for them. Spalding thought so much of the operation that he bought it out in 1889, though A.J. Reach retained its identity with Reach and Shibe as officers. When the AL began play, the Reach became its exclusive ball (and the *Reach Guide* its promotional vehicle) until into the 1940s, long after both men had died.

In 1909, Shibe, always the innovator, made a design change. To the rubber-shavings core of the ball he alloyed hard cork, which made it come off the bat with more pop than the old tomatoes. In 1911 A.J. Reach began marketing the ball, and while the baseball elders believed this was a rather innocuous alteration, Ban Johnson didn't mind if it coaxed some more runs off those iron-armed pitchers. Then, too, Spalding knew he had to start rolling off those cork-balls, necessitating the NL's use of it. And so both leagues adopted the ball, and from day 1 it proved anything but innocuous. All it seemed anyone talked about was the "rabbit ball."

By all rights, this should have been the wellspring of what historians call the "Lively Ball Era," and technically it is. However, the fact is that *no* ball was going to profoundly change the game just yet. To be sure, the bunny balls ran wild for a while. Hitting stats popped like, well, corks in 1911—when Ty Cobb hit .420 and Cleveland's "Shoeless" Joe Jackson .395. (Until recently, Jackson was actually credited with hitting .408 that year.) Here's how the overall numbers stacked up:

AMERICAN LEAGUE

	Runs per Game	Hits	Batting Average	Home Runs	Slugging Average
1910	3.64	9,948	.243	147	.313
1911	4.61	11,239	.273	198	.327

NATIONAL LEAGUE

	Runs per Game	Hits	Batting Average	Home Runs	Slugging Average
1910	4.03	10,384	.256	214	.338
1911	4.42	10,675	.260	316	.356

Interestingly, strikeouts also rose dramatically, meaning that free-swinging was in, and home runs didn't have to hide in shame. Indeed, it was in 1911 that baseball found itself with a player, born in Maryland, possessed of an insanely heavy bat, whose very name became a billboard for the home run. And, no, it ain't who you think!

Home Run Baker

John Franklin Baker was known as Frank Baker when he broke in with Mack's Athletics in 1908. Born in Trappe, Maryland, in 1886, Baker was a 5-foot-11, 173-pound third baseman with great hands, a lot of speed, and the strength of a moose—using a *52-ounce* bat either out of ego or because he just liked to swing a Sequoia tree. In 1909 Baker had a league-high 19 triples (and 4 homers), but made news mainly for being spiked on the arm by Ty Cobb on a slide into third, an act that nearly set off a riot in Philadelphia. In 1910 Baker hit .409 in the A's five-game World Series triumph over the Cubs and won a rave notice from Fred Lieb in *Baseball Magazine.* "Never did a young slugger live up to his reputation more," wrote Lieb. "[He] plays with his heart and soul. Many a time with the Mackmen far behind, a long-distance swat from Baker's war club has put the White Jumbos back in the game."

For those confused, the A's wore an elephant logo on their uniforms. More confusing was that Baker hit 2 home runs all that year, none in the Series. Meaning that he was already a pet of the press when 1911 rolled around. That year, the year of the rabbit, Stuffy McInnis replaced Harry Davis at first base for the A's, completing what the sportswriters called the "$100,000 Infield," with Baker, shortstop Joe Barry, and the incomparable second baseman Eddie Collins. (The four men didn't actually make $100,000; that was their market value to Mack.) Early on, Baker, who threw right and batted left, began sailing shots over the right field wall at Shibe Park—the first in a wave of new ballpark construction that from 1909 to 1915 replaced old, wooden firetraps with six opulent brick and steel "green cathedrals." (The others were Comiskey Park, Forbes Field, Fenway Park, the Polo Grounds, and Ebbets Field.) Right field at Shibe Park was very reachable at 340 feet, helping Baker hit 11 for the year to lead the AL—blessedly, only 1 was inside the park—and also batted .334 with 115 RBIs.

Even so, those dingers were small change next to the NL champ, the Cubs' Frank "Wildfire" Schulte, another lefty-swinging banger who swatted 21, the most the century had seen. Schulte also hit .300 with 121 RBIs, also had more than 20 doubles, triples, homers, and steals, and *that* wouldn't happen again until Willie Mays did it in 1957. And he also had 4 grand slams, which stood as a record until Ernie Banks clocked 5 in 1955.

But it was the glare of that year's World Series spotlight that makes Baker's name still famous. The Series against John McGraw's Giants crackled with excitement to begin with. It was a rematch of 1906 and McGraw again sent his boys out in black uniforms when the Series began on October 14 at the Polo Grounds, hoping to unglue the A's again—and came away with a 2-1 win behind Christy Mathewson. But Baker changed the vibe in Game 2 at Shibe Park two days later. Facing Rube Marquard in the sixth inning with two outs, man on, 1-1, Baker jacked a fastball over the right field wall to win the game 3-1 for Eddie Plank. Afterward, McGraw and Mathewson wanted to rip Marquard's spleen out. Matty, who was writing a column for a New York newspaper during the Series, blistered his teammate in print for ignoring McGraw's explicit orders not to throw a fastball to Baker.

Now, in Game 3 back at the Polo Grounds on October 17, Matty was on the hill, and again he was nearly unhittable. He was up 1-0 and had one out in the ninth. Up came Baker. Matty, working on a skein of 44$^{1}/_{3}$ World Series innings with one tiny run allowed, got Baker in the hole, 0-and-2. Then he, too, tried to sneak one by that 52-ounce bat—and paid, dearly. Baker once more yanked it over the 12-foot right field wall to tie it and circled the bases in surreal silence. McGraw, who almost imploded, retaliated by having Fred Snodgrass spike Baker on a slide into third in the tenth. But the stunned Giants fell apart, committing three errors in the eleventh to lose 3-2.

"Will the great Mathewson tell us exactly what pitch he made to Baker?" Marquard dryly asked later.

By now even the pugnacious McGraw was demoralized, moaning, "We just can't seem to get him out when we need to." Worse, the Giants had to live with the loss through a week of rainouts and expired in six games, over which Baker hit .375. And for his dinger off Mathewson—still one of the most spine-tingling of all World Series moments (and one likely made possible by Mack's team stealing the Giants' pitching signals)—he would see himself in the papers being called "Home Run Baker." Baker wore it well. Over the next three seasons he led or co-led the NL in homers (with 10, 12, and 9) and as an encore he again killed the Giants in the 1913 World Series, cranking yet another dinger off poor Marquard—a Hall of Famer whose career was near spotless when he wasn't being battered by this man—in Game 1. Baker went on to hit .450 in the A's five-game conquest. Then, with his bat at its most blazing, and the team on a roll of five pennants in six years, Mack could no longer afford his own team. Like I said, is anything in baseball today new?

The Rabbit Dies

Baker's fireworks show, as it turns out, wrote *finis* to baseball's new power generation. In 1912, the numbers already began to parachute. Cobb did hit .408 that year, and Cubs' second baseman Heinie Zimmerman came up three RBIs shy of the Triple Crown (for many years it was accepted that he did win it) when he led the NL with a .372 average and 14 homers. Hardest of all to believe, Pittsburgh's Owen Wilson collected no less than *36* triples, not merely a big-league record but 10 more than were ever hit in any season by the runners-up in the twentieth century, Wahoo Sam Crawford, Joe Jackson, and Kiki Cuyler. And yet the AL composite batting average fell to .265 that year, and homers to 156. In the NL the homer total fell to 287. Oddly, the league batting average actually rose, to .272, but this was a temporary aberration; in 1913 it fell 10 points. The numbers would then hang at roughly the same levels through 1919—when AL home runs shriveled all the way to 96, an all-time league low, and plummeted in the NL to 139, the fewest since 1902.

Tellingly, as the hitting returned to homeostasis, strikeouts remained way up, as if the sluggers of 1911 were in denial. Which, of course, played into the crafty fingers of the clever pitchers who had quickly adapted to the new ball—by defiling it as best they could.

Left alone by the rules to do whatever they wanted, pitchers scarred, tarred, and all but feathered the rabbit ball, going on the very logical theory that a player can't hit what he can't see—especially if what he can't see is aimed at his head. At the turn of the century, the spitball and the beanball were meant to rattle hitters, not decapitate them. A great old spitballer like Big Ed Walsh would rarely let a wet one get away. In a game annexed by thugs, thieves, and worse, the pitcher-hitter face-off had been the last shred of honor among men in knickered uniforms. Now, batters ducked, dodged, and cowered as sticky, grimy horsehides careened plateward, pregnant not merely with saliva but tobacco, licorice, and who knows what else, courtesy of pitchers or their infielders who would spit such mucilage into their gloves and rub the ball in it. These serves would dart and dip wildly, with no rhyme or reason, and in shades not of lily or off-white but rather baleful shades of brown, gray, and black. Hitting anytime was no bargain, but in the twilight it was literally a stab in the dark.

Baseball, of course, could have contained this form of substance abuse had its Brahmans not been overly afraid to tip the balance too far to the hitters. As well, owners were still too niggardly to conscript a sufficient supply of balls that could replace too-dirty or dingy ones. Umpires were still under strict orders to keep a ball in as long as possible. Only because fans were now apt to hold on to foul balls hit in the stands did fresh ones come in at all, and they would soon look like they were dipped in axle grease. Within this lax environment, men with only middling talent but the impulses of a larcenist could become creative geniuses—and reliable pitchers. While it was technically illegal to "doctor" a ball by cutting, scraping, or otherwise defacing it, not since the beginning of the game had pitchers been reined in, and now they pushed it to the limit.

The Yankees' Russ Ford, for example, went beyond the usual scuffing of the ball. As a semi-pro, Ford had stuck a piece of emery board in a slit in his glove to grind the ball on, and when he came up in 1910 he went 26-6, then 22-11. Ford, though, wasn't very good at keeping what he was doing a secret, and when other pitchers started throwing the "emery ball," baseball specifically banned it in 1915. Not that it mattered. Because umpires often looked the other way, hurlers gashed and slashed the ball with their belt buckles or rings, or with coins, metal, or glass hidden under the strap of their mitts. Some even managed to stick pins in the stitching, which someone must have called "voodoo ball."

All this more than explains the hitting drought in the 1910s, which seemed to water down everybody's averages except those of Ty Cobb and Tris Speaker and put a damper particularly on the long-baller hitters. There was, however, one glaring exception—Gavvy "Cactus" Cravath, a Phillies outfielder who won six home run crowns (1913–1915, 1917–1919), with a rousing high of 24 in 1915. Cravath was quite a story in his day. Rejected by three AL teams, he came to the Phillies in 1912 and in the Year of the Rabbit popped 11, which was a prelude to his spectacular 1912 season when he led the NL in homers (19), RBIs (128), hits (179), total bases (298), and slugging (.568), and was second in hitting (.341). He was not a wild swinger, either, striking out only 63 times in 525 at-bats. In 1916, Cravath missed leading the league in homers for seven straight years by one. From 1911 to 1920 he slugged 119, more than anyone, beating Home Run Baker by 43 and Wildfire Schulte by 52. Cravath had four doubles in one game and won the RBI title for a second time in 1915. In 1914 he also led all outfielders with 34 assists.

Cravath had a habit of hitting nearly all of his home runs at home. Of the 117 he hit with the Phillies—all but 2 over the wall, bless him—93 came in his home park including all 19 in 1914, 19 of 24 the following year. There's a reason for this math: the same reason that Nap Lajoie lost his power groove after leaving Philadelphia—the notorious bandbox of Baker Bowl, where the Little League fences also helped Fred Ludurus bang out 16 in 1911 and 12 in 1913 (all but 7 at home), and the Phillies as a team to lead the NL from 1913 to 1916. Still, something was going to have to keep hope alive for the home run during these years of guerrilla pitchers, so Baker Bowl gets my thanks.

For most everyone besides Cravath, the home run had returned to being a novelty item, its purveyors an afterthought. One indicator of how low in the jockocracy the sluggers were was the paucity of them in the era's developing pop culture centered around baseball heroes. In the pages of Ralph Henry Barbour's twenty-three baseball novels like *The Double Play* and *Bases Full*, or Ring Lardner's anthology of short stories in the *Saturday Evening Post*, later adapted to a comic strip and the novel *You Know Me, Al*, or Lester Chadwick's "Baseball Joe" books, the protagonists embodied down-home values surviving in an increasingly complex world and were team players not generally given to the selfish pursuit of the home run. The first ballplayer to pen his memoirs was that bane to batsmen, Christy Mathewson, in the 1912 *Pitching in the Pinch*.

When the new medium of motion pictures was born, ballplayers—being the best-known celebrities—were invited to show their acting skills. Ty Cobb appeared in a movie called *Somewhere in Georgia*, crusty John McGraw in one called *Touch of Nature*. The knight-errant of the home run, Frank Baker, did get into a movie of his own, but his signature hit seemed somewhat pallid to draw public attention. The film's title: *Home Run Baker's Double*. Of course, the most famous of baseball refrains for years, Franklin P. Adams' "Tinker to Evers to Chance," chose as its heroic standard-bearers the Cubs' double-play trinity.

Salaries, too, were a barometer, more so when yet another big league, the Federal, tried to crash the AL-NL monopoly in 1914, giving the players leverage to bleed owners for more money. While the average salary about doubled from $3,800 in 1913 to $7,300 in 1915, the Tigers bumped Cobb up from $12,000 to $20,000. The Red Sox gave Speaker an unheard-of two-year contract for $36,000. When Washington owner Clark Griffith refused Walter Johnson's demands, Big Train signed a *three-year* contract with the Federal League's Chicago club, including a $6,000 bonus—forcing Griffith to sweet-talk Johnson into rescinding the deal and re-signing with the Senators for $12,500.

Down the list was Home Run Baker, who enjoyed no such tribute from the flinty Connie Mack. After his 1914 championship team lost $65,000, Mack sold off his biggest assets—his "$100,000 Infield"—refusing to pay those gifted players inflated salaries, and trading them before he could lose them to the Federal League and get zilch. For the great Eddie Collins, Mack got $50,000 from the White Sox. But when Baker pledged not to go to the Federal, Mack believed he could keep him at the same $8,500. Baker, however, sat out the whole 1915 season. Mack peddled him to the Yankees (the Highlanders' new name as of 1913) for $35,000 the following year. The proud A's, left in ruins, turned from champs to the worst team of the era and arguably of all time that season, going 36-117 in 1916.

Actually, only eighty-one players under contract to the AL and NL jumped to the FL, mostly has-beens like Hal Chase, Johnny Tinker, and Russ Ford, who took his emery boards with him and went 20-6 for Buffalo in 1914. The real effect of the Federal was felt at the minor-league level where thriving bush-league teams in Kansas City, Indianapolis, Buffalo, and Baltimore saw their fans stream away to new ballparks built by FL interlopers. Baltimore's minor-league Orioles were hit the hardest, causing reverberations that would soon tear baseball asunder. Still, while the FL was in business, the NL and AL trembled. Appeasing tottering players, the National Commission gave in to some demands of the newest pseudo-union, The Players' Fraternity, such as making the clubs pay for and clean players' uniforms, and giving players with ten years of service the latitude to sign with other teams rather than be sold to minor-league teams. Then, in 1916, after two seasons, the FL died on the vine. For months, the league had a restraint-of-trade lawsuit on the docket of a Chicago judge known for his antitrust inclinations. Hoping for an earth-shaking ruling that would end the established leagues' grip on their players, and foment a free-for-all in the game, the judge instead sat on the case until finally the FL could hold on no longer. The judge, a baseball fan named Kenesaw Mountain Landis, would be repaid by the baseball barons for his help.

That was when the air came out of the players' balloon. The Fraternity, rendered impotent, frittered away and the owners again effectively put the game in a lockbox. Not by coincidence there came scuttlebutt about gambling and possible game fixing. Any such incidents were passed off as idle rumor or dealt with quietly, out of the public eye, but the fetid smell of scandal was unmistakable, and growing.

Unmistakably as well, home runs were in that lockbox, Cactus Cravath notwithstanding. Back in 1912, Christy Mathewson, who like most pitchers could toy with grunting hitters who swung only for the fences, became so worked up watching the Giant hitters try to go yard that he raked them over in *Pitching in the Pinch,* writing that they were seeking to be "free-swingers overnight and . . . trying to knock the ball out of the lot, instead of chopping at it." Five years later he had no such irritation, now that the fascination with the home run had practically vanished, at least among ballplayers. The fans, as ever, had an abiding sense of wonderment about the home run. Indeed, things were so dreary for power-hitting by the end of the decade that a big galoot of a *pitcher* was causing a real buzz up in Boston for pounding 'em out higher and further than anyone else could.

A Babe in the Woods

In 1914 George Herman Ruth came to the big leagues as a 19-year-old man-child about whom no one saw anything saintly, but about whom many saw something marketable. Born on February 6, 1895, he was the son of a Baltimore saloon keeper who grew so tired of trying to keep his kid out of trouble that he and his wife squirreled him away to the Xaverian Brothers at St. Mary's Industrial Home for Boys when he was 7. He stayed there for a dozen years, so long neglected by his parents that it was assumed he was an orphan. Ruth had a prodigious appetite for food and breaking the rules and the only way to keep his mind off of trouble was to give him a school baseball uniform and let him whack away at a ball or throw it with mustard past other kids. He grew into a rather odd creature, with spindly, pigeon-toed legs under a then long-and-lean body and a cherubic, pork-nosed mug. At 6 feet 2 inches and 195 pounds, Ruth had more growing to do; plainly, he would bloom into a very big man, yet at 19 those piano-bench legs carried him around the bases as fast as the wind. Thus he was an unmistakable presence on the ballfield, for a host of reasons, and it did not faze him in the least that while he was left-handed, he could simply slide on a righty's glove—the only kind St. Mary's had—backward on his right hand and play as smooth a game at shortstop or catcher as anyone, but only on the days he wasn't burning his fastball and bending his curve to dispose of hitters.

At 18 Ruth was paid $60 a month to play for the International League's Baltimore Orioles, a thriving team whose owner, Jack Dunn, was an ex-big-league player and had connections. Because Ruth was still underage, Dunn had to take legal custody of him, so he was snidely dubbed "Jack's Babe" by the players and sportswriters. Yet "Babe" Ruth's immense talent and unique black-swan appeal was evident from day 1. Ruth's first home run as a pro, though it didn't count officially, came in an intrasquad practice game at the Fayetteville Fair Grounds in North Carolina on March 7, 1914. This minor event was big news. The shot supposedly went more than 500 feet and earned the headline "Ruth Makes Mighty Clout" in the next day's *Baltimore News Post*. Roger Pippen's game story said the blast "will live in the memory of all who saw it. Th[e] clouter was George Ruth, the southpaw from St. Mary's School. The ball carried so far to right field that he walked around the bases." One can glean from this description that Ruth was a strange hybrid: he had massive entertainment value for his ability to hit the ball out of sight, yet his *real* function was as a pitcher. The first start Ruth made for the O's he blanked Buffalo 6-0—and hit a triple. Such was the conundrum of Babe Ruth, the kind no one had ever had to make sense of before and one that wouldn't fully resolve itself for years.

Besides, once the IL season began and wound into midsummer, Ruth had only 1 home run while winning thirteen of nineteen on the mound. Remarkable find that he was, though, Jack Dunn couldn't keep him. The Orioles were being bled dry by the Federal League's Baltimore Terrapins, sending Dunn on a selling spree. For Ruth he wanted $10,000. First he called Connie Mack, who of course was into his own fire sale of his Athletics players and declined. The Reds were interested but instead chose two lesser Orioles on the cheap. Dunn finally found a taker in Red Sox owner Joe Lannin, who dropped $14,000 on the Ruth kid as part of a $25,000 deal that also included pitcher Ernie Shore and catcher Ben Egan.

Ruth arrived in Boston, and on July 11 he made his first start, beating Cleveland 4-3. (For the record, his first big-league at-bat was a strikeout.) Ruth was shuttled to and from the Red Sox minor-league team in Providence and finished 2-and-1 in four starts with the big club. On his own and away from the Xaverians, he also drank a lot, caroused a lot, and married a 16-year-old waitress. In 1915, at age 20, he drank and caroused more and went 8-8 with a 2.84 ERA and 112 strikeouts, though he was left out of the World Series rotation—except as a pinch-hitter, which bespeaks Ruth's schizoid existence with the team. That season Ruth batted .315 and blasted 4 home runs (with 21 RBIs) in 92 at-bats in the games he pitched, twice as many homers as anyone else on the roster and just 3 behind league leader Braggo Roth—in 292 fewer at-bats. Ruth's slugging percentage of .576 was 85 points higher than any hitter in the league.

What's more, Ruth, with exquisite timing, hit his first big-league dinger in Metropolis, on Thursday, May 6, 1915, against the Yankees at the Polo Grounds before a small crowd of 8,000, but the always sizeable coterie of big-gun New York sportswriters—all of whom went home humming about Ruth after he pitched thirteen innings. Although he lost 5-3, he seemed to be a mutant baseball life form. In the third inning Ruth—in his eighteenth big-league at-bat—hammered the first pitch off right-hander Jack Warhop, an underhand pitcher, that landed in the upper deck in right, hitting seat 26 in section 3. He also singled twice and struck out on a mighty cut in the fourth with runners on first and third.

In the papers the next day the raw-boned youngster with the gooney-bird legs was the story line, complete with the ascension from St. Mary's. Ruth, wrote Damon Runyon in the *New York American,* "is quite a demon pitcher and demon hitter—when he connects." Fred Lieb, in the *New York Press,* described how the "sensational kid" had "rifle[d] the pill far up in the upstairs section of the rightfield stands for a merry-go-round trip." And Wilmot E. Griffin of the *New York Evening Journal,* who wrote under the pseudonym "Right Cross," led with:

> Ruthless Ruth, the stem winder, is some hurler. A pitcher who is so versatile that he can not only shoot all sorts of deliveries from the port turret, but can besides this hit a home run and a couple of incidental singles in one game is some asset, ladies and gentlemen, some asset indeed. When he is not pitching they can use him for an outfielder or pinch hitter. In these days of efficiency he is the ideal player.

This of course was not a new concept; not only had some pitchers hurled every other game for their teams during the 1860s and 1870s, but had also played in the field on nonpitching days. But that was a less trying game, when the schedules ran fifty or sixty games. Still, while it was easy for others to venture Ruth for double-duty, the Babe kept making the case seemingly every time he played. Indeed, Jack Warhop was a useful Ruth prop. A month later, again at the Polo Grounds, Ruth took him deep his first time up—a 2-run blow, some ten feet farther up in section 3—and won the game 7-1. Before the season was out he hit shots in Fenway Park and Sportsman's Park in St. Louis, each farther than had ever been hit there.

However, Red Sox manager Bill "Rough" Carrigan did not utilize Ruth's bat between starts save for pinch-hitting, preferring not to mess with his team's "Golden Outfield" of Tris Speaker, Harry Hooper, and Duffy Lewis, nor with the chemistry that won the pennant. Then, too, giving Ruth more time in the field would cut into his pitching, which just kept getting better. In 1916 he went 23-12 and topped the league both with a 1.75 ERA and nine shutouts. That year, too, he made his first World Series start, in Game 2 against Brooklyn. He gave up an inside-the-park homer in the first inning to Hy Myers, then shut out the Dodgers for thirteen innings to win 2-1, giving the Sox a 2-0 game lead in a Series they would win in five.

The next season he was 24-13 with a 2.02 ERA and a league-high thirty-five complete games. Certainly Ruth was among the elite pitchers in the game. Check some comparisons from 1915 to 1917:

	Won-Lost	ERA	Innings Pitched	Strike-outs	Bases on Balls	Shut-outs	Complete Games
Ruth	65-33	2.07	868	410	311	16	74
Walter Johnson	75-49	1.91	1,080	619	205	18	100
Grover Cleveland Alexander	64-35	1.53	1,153	608	170	36	109
Rube Marquard	61-43	2.71	851	418	176	6	72

Remember, this was still the baby Ruth, in his early 20s. By now, Christy Mathewson was finished. A burned-out Marquard would never again win twenty games. Johnson and Alexander were both reaching age 30, and only once (by Alexander) would either win more than 23—and Big Train lost to Ruth five straight times head-to-head. But Ruth himself was diffident about pitching. From the start, he had joined in taking batting practice every day, a breach of etiquette that didn't sit well with the hitters. After one such foray, Ruth found his bats sawed in half in his locker. Which might explain why only one teammate—team captain Harry Hooper—pushed for him to play on nonpitching days. For four years it didn't happen, and still he sent twenty "reach" balls into the seats. In 1916 he hit 3 homers in three consecutive games. One of those, in St. Louis, came when he was down 3-0 and he blasted a 3-run shot that according to one account went "completely over the bleachers," which made it the first ball to be hit out of Sportsman's Park. In 1917 he put one into the center field seats at Fenway Park, something no one had done. By now, the Ruth conundrum had reached critical mass: still a pitcher by trade, he was expected to hit a tater when he came to bat. One game, when he could only muster a single, one reporter lamented, "Babe Ruth was not able to make any home runs."

All along Ruth made it clear he preferred to give up pitching, but Rough Carrigan put him off, fearing such a precipitous move would crippled his staff. And while Carrigan quit after the team finished second in 1917, his successor, Ed Barrow, was also resistant to the idea—until a frustrated Ruth split and threatened to play for an industrial league team back in Baltimore. To get him back, Barrow compromised: Ruth would pitch every fourth day instead of every third, and he would play first base or in the outfield and hit cleanup on the days in between. In the end Ruth pitched even less than that, making just 20 starts over 166 innings, about half of his figures for the previous season. His lack of focus on these days is seen in his awful ratio of 49 walks to 40 strikeouts. But Ruth, it seemed, could always throw a win and finished 12-7 with a 2.22 ERA.

Though he had no trouble focusing on hitting, because of the heavy workload he was worn out by midsummer and began sitting out games altogether. In all, he played 95 nonpitching games, and while he had white-hot streaks of 3 home runs in 3 games, and 4 in 4, his final take was "only" 11 homers—tying for the league lead with the Phillies' Tully Walker (in 97 fewer at-bats)—and 64 RBIs (fourth best). Then again, this was a season conducted in the pall of World War I and seemed less important by the day as casualties mounted in the "Great War." As attendance fell off amid headlines of mustard-gas attacks and trench carnage, baseball—which was buffeted by the attrition of 120 players being swept off their rosters and into the military—dithered for months about whether to call the season early, and how to prop up teams suffering heavy financial losses. More strife occurred when, after it was agreed the season would end on Labor Day, players on the pennant-winning Red Sox and Cubs—who like everyone else lost a month's pay—were close to calling a wildcat strike before the World Series if it was played on the customary pay scale of 75 percent to the winners and 25 percent to the losers. With that year's attendance slippage, it would leave the losing players with table scraps. At the last minute they agreed to a new 60-40 deal.

When the Series was played, it was owned by Babe Ruth—the pitcher. He won twice in Boston's six-game conquest, 1-0 in the opener and 3-2 in Game 5. Until Ruth gave up a run in the eighth inning of the latter he had hurled an astonishing 29⅔ scoreless frames, going back to 1916. That record would stand for forty-three years before Whitey Ford bettered it. It was also Ruth's farewell to arms. In 1919, when baseball would again truncate its schedule due to the fact that nearly every team was losing too much money to complete a full schedule, the Red Sox would play 138 games. Ruth played in 130 of them, 113 as a nonpitcher, and batted 432 times. He made only 17 starts, going 9-5 in 133 innings with a 2.97 ERA but his 58 walks to 30 strikeouts indicate his head was even less on the mound. Simply, Ruth didn't want to pitch anymore, and the fans didn't want him to. He was now a rhinoceros-sized novelty act for one reason: just how far could he go with these home runs? Ruth's home run count was charted daily on the nation's sports pages. And he didn't even get crazy until August, when he went on a tear, hitting 7 in twelve days including his fourth grand slam of the season (which would be a record for forty years).

On September 8, when Ruth broke the "modern" record of his turn-of-the-century stalking horse Buck Freeman by hitting No. 26, sportswriters dug through old *Spalding Guides* and found Ned Williamson's "mistake on the lake" 27. Twelve days later, Babe clocked 1 off Chicago's Lefty

Williams to tie, then four days later he put No. 28 over the right field roof at the Polo Grounds, whose short right field fence seemed organically suited to him rather than the pitcher's sanctuary that was right field at Fenway Park. His parting shot was hitting No. 29 in Washington on September 22, completing a cycle in which he had hit at least 1 homer in every park in the league over the season, another first.

Drink in Ruth's total numbers that season, hitting and pitching. They're intoxicating: a .322 average to go along with the game's top totals in homers, RBIs (112), runs (103), total bases (284)—all, again, in 130 games. He was also second in walks (101). He out-homered the rest of his team 29 to 5—and he nearly tripled the AL runner-up in homers, the now-downgraded Home Run Baker, who had 10. The NL leader, Cactus Cravath, had 12. Now factor in Ruth's 9 pitching wins and what we have is the single greatest season any athlete has ever had in any sport. Don't even try to argue.

Overlooked about 1919, however, is that homers were up all around baseball, just not on an individual level except for Ruth. In the AL the number jumped from 98 to 241, in the NL from 139 to 207. And while Ruth's exemplar certainly brought the homer out of the closet, the credit should justifiably go to Ben Shibe—or rather to his son and heir, Tom, who had taken over the A.J. Reach Co. from Ben, who was now in his 80s and retired (he died on January 14, 1922). Before the season Tom Shibe had made yet another tiny modification to the ball, with large implications. After the war, Reach was able to import a finer-grade wool from Australia, which could be wrapped even more tightly around the rubber-and-cork core and accordingly had a little more bounce and lift, most electrifyingly it seemed off the bat of Babe Ruth.

Intriguingly, and propitiously for the Babe and for baseball, Ruth's cosmic season didn't do much for the Red Sox, who dropped to fifth place. In retrospect, this was eerily well timed given that the game was lurching into its darkest days and that only Ruth could have brightened them—if he could go where he could move onto a grander national stage. The first augury of trouble came during that 1919 season when two veteran players now with the Giants—Heinie Zimmerman, who nearly won the Triple Crown seven years earlier, and first-base star Hal Chase, along with an itinerant player and former Chase teammate named Lee Magee, were all fired for taking (and offering) bribes to fix games. Then during the World Series between the White Sox and Reds, the tentacles of these scandals engendered rumors that the Series was fixed, though baseball leaders vehemently denied it. That season as well, no less public idols than Ty Cobb and Tris Speaker may have conspired to throw a Tiger-Indian game in the Tigers' favor. (The charge came up seven years later when both men were player-managers in the AL, and they were eased out of the game; while later reinstated as players, neither would be able to manage again.)

Whether baseball knew it or not, it was going to need one hell of a savior. Providentially, it had one already, as would be emphatically clear after one more rule change and the bamboozling of one incredibly dumb owner.

Part 2

THE RUTHIAN ERA

5

"A Gift from the Gods"

A National Curiosity

Among baseball's non-uniformed civilians, the two most pivotal figures in the evolution of the home run were Ben Shibe and Harry Frazee, each for a very different reason. Shibe of course was the great horsehide innovator. Frazee, on the other hand, was the great horsehide rump.

For eight decades Frazee has been cursed in Boston, even by those who don't know his identity other than as the guy who traded Babe Ruth to the Yankees. As bumptious as Frazee was, however, he shaped baseball's own modern identity, not only because of Ruth but because he undermined and helped bring down baseball's old power structure. Frazee, a Broadway show producer, bought the Red Sox in 1917 for $400,000 only to see them pummeled by the wartime attendance decline and finish fifth in 1919. Frazee saw little return for Ruth's $10,000 salary, nor any upside in keeping the team intact. His first move to dismantle it came in July when pitcher Carl Mays, who had won forty-three games the past two seasons, walked out of the park after taking a two-inning beating in Chicago, blaming his teammates' ineptitude, and said he wasn't coming back. Frazee then sold Mays to the Yankees for two pitchers and $40,000—flaunting Ban Johnson's directive not to move Mays until the situation was resolved. When Johnson voided the deal, the thin veil of league unity was torn off in a morass of anti- and pro-Johnson infighting.

Rapidly, the blocks began falling. With all the disarray, the three-man

National Commission now had two ineffectual league presidents: the NL's John Heydler who was always no more than a cipher and Garry Herrmann, a chairman who couldn't get the votes he needed to keep the job. This left the entire game leaderless and stumbling like one of the many drunks in its midst (including Johnson).

But for Frazee and Yankee owner Colonel Jacob Ruppert, the Mays episode produced a fast friendship—which for the vulturous Colonel meant he had found a pigeon. On the day after Christmas, 1919, the two owners broke bread in New York. Frazee was trying to line up backing for his new musical, *No, No, Nanette,* and they agreed on the most famous (or infamous) sports transaction in history: the Yankees would take Babe Ruth off Frazee's hands for $125,000 and a $350,000 loan, with Ruppert taking a mortgage on Fenway Park as collateral. When Ruth assented to a two-year contract worth $41,000—or $500 more per year than the game's top-paid player, Ty Cobb—the deal was announced a week later. Frazee delivered a soliloquy (recalled in *The Baseball Hall of Fame 50th Anniversary Book,* 1988) that would haunt the Red Sox and their rooters from that day on:

> The sale of Babe Ruth will ultimately strengthen the team. It would be impossible to start next season with Ruth and have a smooth-working machine. Ruth had become simply impossible, and the Boston club could no longer put up with his eccentricities. I think the Yankees are taking a gamble. While Ruth is undoubtedly the greatest hitter the game has ever seen, he is likewise one of the most selfish and inconsiderate men ever to put on a baseball uniform.

Few in Boston were mollified. Ed Barrow nearly had to be sedated when he heard. Harry Hooper, a future Hall of Famer who, with most of those on the championship Red Sox teams would also go in a Frazee fire sale, he to the White Sox, later said, "He sold the whole team down the river to keep his dirty nose above water. What a way to run a ball club!" Indeed, the hull of Frazee's team would from 1922 to 1930 finish dead last. Not that Harry would be around to feel the sting. He sold the team in 1923 for $1 million—twice Ruppert's tab for the Yankees in 1915—to a group of Ohio businessmen. Six years later, Frazee died in infamy of kidney failure. The Red Sox, winners of five of the first fifteen World Series, would not play in another for twenty-eight years, and if they ever do win, it will be the first since 1918. Of course, with the "Curse of the Bambino" on their heads, that may be never.

Almost all of the 1920s and much of the 1930s, meanwhile, would belong to Jake Ruppert and his "babe," aided in part by the second precondition of Ruth's reign, and the home run's. That came about on February 9, in the shadows of the intramural baseball warfare and the fallout of the Ruth sale. On that day the joint rules committee, hoping for a cosmetic upgrade to rid the game of all those disgustingly defiled balls, banned foreign substances on and alterations to the ball, specifically but not limited to saliva, resin, talcum powder, paraffin (!) and the already interdicted emery ball. The penalty for violating the rule was a ten-day suspension and fine. However, to ease the transition, two pitchers from each team were permitted to keep throwing the spitter for one more season. This deadline would be extended a year later for seventeen stipulated pitchers who could keep throwing it until the end of 1923. By then, the lot had shrunk to only five spitballers, including Hall of Famers Burleigh Grimes and Red Faber, and the immortally named Urban Shocker.

No longer would those snow-white balls degenerate into mud balls, eclipsed from sight and with no direction home. Hitters still could be, and would be, dusted at any time but at least they could see the next pitch linger. And as if that wasn't momentous enough, there was yet one more little alteration of the ball by Tom Shibe that would potentiate the rule changes. By sinking the stitches deeper into the surface of the ball, it became slicker to the touch, and thus harder for the pitcher to get a good grip on it. This would make for more fastballs sailing without movement and more curveballs failing to break—the proverbial flat fastball and hanging curve.

For a batter like Babe Ruth, this was not unlike presenting him the pitch on a velvet pillow. Yet not everyone in baseball expected Ruth to thrive in New York on a middling team in a town owned by their landlords, John McGraw's Giants, and against pitchers who would be prepared for him. "Perhaps, and very likely, Ruth will not be so successful in 1920," opined John B. Foster in the *Spalding Guide*. "The pitchers will eye him with more than ordinary caution."

Foster would have hedged in writing those famous last words had he considered the impact of Ruth playing half his games at the Polo Grounds instead of Fenway Park. It wasn't only Babe's blasts at the former that foretold what was to come. It was simple math. In five years at Fenway, where the left field "Green Monster" then as now was a very inviting target standing just 324 feet away, right field was only a target at the foul line, 313 feet away, before jutting sharply out to 475 feet in right-center and to an astonishing *550 feet* just right of dead center where the bleachers angled back. (This would become nearly *600 feet* from 1931 to 1934.) Ruth, who rarely sneaked a cheapie right down the line, was out of even his league here. Of the 49 homers he hit with the Red Sox, he hit all of 11 at Fenway—*none* of 11 in 1918 and 9 of 29 in 1919. The Polo Grounds (actually the fifth reconstruction of the stadium) may have been famous for its own center field infinity—nearly or over 500 feet to the elevated clubhouse in dead center through much of its history—but in 1920 it was only 433 feet out there. The right field porch, scene of more cheap homers than in any other "modern" big league park, was then a ridiculous 256 feet down the line and even less, 249 feet to the overhanging second deck. Left field was similarly 277 feet down the line but 270 feet to the upper deck.

In this circus funhouse, a pop fly could be a homer, and a line drive to the same area an out. Of course, Ruth needn't ponder that proposition, having already hit the only ball over the roof of the joint in 1919. However, for the first month of the 1920 season, John Foster seemed on target. Through April, Ruth was homerless. Then on May 1 he kissed No. 1—against the Red Sox—that came to rest on the street after yet another roof-clearing shot at the Polo Grounds. Ruth lost 12 balls in May, 12 more in June. On July 15 he tied his record of 29 with a game-winning homer in the thirteenth inning against St. Louis. He cleared the 30 mark with two shots off Chicago's Dickie Kerr. By August's end he had 37. By mid-September he'd passed 40. On September 24 he smacked Nos. 50 and 51 in a doubleheader against Washington. On September 29 came No. 54 in Philadelphia.

Then Babe Ruth rested.

Actually, Ruth hit his then-preternatural 54 home runs—more than any other *team* in baseball that year—in 130 games, missing more than a few with curious minor ailments and, ahem, indispositions. (The Babe was allowed to trash curfews at will.) Ruth as a young man could hit homers while in a semiconscious state, and he would carry that skill into his later, fatter years. Moreover, he had a legendary habit of hitting not only a lot of homers but a lot of them when they were needed most, which is why the Yankees were in contention for the pennant to the end, coming up just three games behind the flag-winning Indians. Stories of Ruth telling teammates he'd hit one out and then doing just that became fodder in the avalanche of publicity around him. Ruth was reshaping the pediment of hero worship in America—and incidentally making the misbegotten and nearly forgotten home run into nearly a metaphysical life form.

Don't think every other hitter didn't notice Ruth garnering headlines every day, even when he was not doing anything newsworthy. Even the stuffy *New York Times* was swooning over him. In 1920 the newspaper of record gushed, "He has become a national curiosity, and the sightseeing Pilgrims who daily flock into Manhattan are as anxious to cast eyes on him as they are to see the Woolworth Building."

As a tourist attraction, Ruth's year in the big town doubled the Yankee attendance from 619,164 (or 8,482 per game) to 1,289,422 (16,746). It was the first time a team cleared a million, a baseball record that would stand for twenty-six years. As this beat the Giants by 300,000 in the same park (and the NL pennant–winning Dodgers by 400,000), it also pretty much wrote the Yankees' eviction notice from the Polo Grounds, the consequence of which would be seen in 1923. Thanks to Ruth, AL attendance spiked from 3.7 million to over 5 million for the first time (8,240 a game). Riding the wave, the NL also enjoyed a record rise, from 2.9 to 4 million (6,542). All these levels would roughly hold right through to the end of World War II. Would there have been a rise without Ruth? Absolutely. Would there have been the excitement of a new baseball order? Yeah, right.

Indeed, Ruth didn't only arise as a demigod in the sports pages. In 1920, the highbrow magazine *Current Opinion* called him "the most talked of American." By the time *The Literary Digest* in 1922 captioned a photo of Ruth, "Everybody knows him," everybody already knew that. As the *Digest* reported, "Backwoods citizens (and) darkies way out there in the wilderness and swamps who may not know President Warren G. Harding would surely know Babe Ruth." Given that Ruth had become a messiah with enormous populist appeal, the question must be asked, Did Ruth make the home run or did the home run make Ruth? Call that the real Ruth conundrum, and damned if I have the answer. The fact is no one before him had ever taken the homer to "Ruthian" heights, and it certainly is a little scary that the first to come along and do it seemed to have been sprung fully formed as if from Medusa's head. Ruth was a walking impressionist painting of what a home run is: he objectified its awesome power, its individualistic excess, its instant gratification. Ruth owned the game by owning its life force, allowing him to live his own excesses with impunity (exactly what they tried to get him not to do back at St. Mary's).

Yes, I'll say it—the power was with him. And a good thing, both for him and for the game, since neither may have survived intact if he hadn't come along when he did. So, if you have to answer the conundrum, go with Ruth making the home run.

No one ran with the premise more than the Babe himself. When Ruth traveled to new cities during spring exhibition tours, banks and businesses would close and people would line the streets near the local park hoping to see him. Jake Ruppert, never one to miss a chance to exploit him, would demand and get 85 percent of the sold-out gate. Not by surprise, a horde of would-be agents, hucksters, and leeches were lining up to get their hooks into Ruth, with mixed results at the start. During his very first week with the Yankees, he arrived late and wearing makeup after mornings filming a movie called *Heading Home.* Not only was the movie laughed out of theaters, Ruth's checks from the producers bounced.

The Home Run to the Rescue

In the new order spawned by Babe Ruth, the home run snuffed out the old metered style of hitting. And, in the weirdest of turns, the baseball patriarchs cheered it on. Never before had homers been fully embraced, or anticipated. Even when Home Run Baker batted, few seriously expected a home run. Everyone did with Ruth. Before, the reflexive reaction to an upswing in homers within the game had been to scold, cajole, and tinker to bring them back down again. Now Ruth had swung the pendulum in the opposite direction, and with such a benediction from the press that, in a fillip, the old concept of "scientific" batting was suddenly out of touch. Ruth, marveled writer F. C. Lane in 1921, "throws science to the wind and hews out a rough path for himself by the sheer weight of his unequaled talents." How significant was this? It appeared in *Baseball Magazine,* which almost always took its cues from the baseball establishment. Not that this shift in attitude required any great epiphany beyond all that additional ticket revenue in the till.

About the only sour note in the choir was from skeptics in the press (the usual suspects) who understandably were dubious that Ruth could hit so many homers without the help of a friendlier ball than baseball was letting on was in use. These allegations, which began in the whispering stage in 1920, would grow more voluble in the coming years. One of the skeptics, Ring Lardner, formed a good bit of conventional wisdom on the matter when he wrote with literary and grammatic license, "(T)he master minds that controls baseball says to themselves that if it is home runs that the public wants to see, leave us give them home runs, so they fixed up a ball that if you don't miss it entirely it will clear the fence, and the result is that ball players which used to specialize in humpback liners to the pitcher is now amongst our leading sluggers."

Alas, Lardner had no evidence of this conspiracy, the very notion of which so offended baseball that in 1920 it enlisted the U.S. Bureau of Standards to test the ball, which the agency confirmed was no different in elasticity than the old ball. And Tom Shibe, who didn't think the minor changes to the ball had any great effect, dismissed the charge out of hand that same year, telling *The New York Times*, "It has not been changed one iota and no effort has been made to make the ball livelier. . . . With all the freak deliveries dead and the spitter almost dead, batters are able to hit the ball more solidly." In the coming years, when balls began flying out in farragoes, similar denials and studies would be issued, doing nothing to convince contemporary critics and latter-day historians who would blithely accept 1920 as the commencement of what has been designated the Lively Ball Era.

To all of them I say: live ball, hooey. Undeniably, the ball got friendlier, as noted. But it seems the only real beneficiary of it in 1920 was the Bambino. Overall, while homers did go up, if you take out Ruth's 54, the AL's rise from 240 to a then-record 369 isn't all that outrageous. (Remember, the schedule was restored to 154 games.) Homers per game? They moved up from 0.21 to 0.30, less than the previous year's jump. The NL, untouched by Ruth, had a modest increase from 207 to 261, still below 1913 levels. The runner-up to Ruth in the AL, George Sisler of St. Louis, had 19. The NL leader, Philadelphia's Cy Williams, had 15. Even for Ruth the biggest difference wasn't the ball but, again, the Polo Grounds—he hit 29 dingers there. What all this means is that, as Shibe said, the rule changes and the phasing-out of the spitball were even bigger contributing factors than the ball itself, but while all these things made a difference, they only made a profound difference to Ruth. When people finally began to hit home runs as a way of life it was simply because Babe Ruth had made everybody *want* to hit home runs.

Still, it also helped a great deal that 1920 placed the game firmly in the hands of the hitters, all of whom seemingly benefited from the favorable conditions. Throughout the game batting averages went through the roof—from .268 to .284 in the AL and .258 to .270 in the NL—along with runs, which shot up to 4.67 per game in the AL, 3.97 in the NL. As for Ruth, he again proved he was not of the Earth. So feared was he that, showing a great deal of sense, pitchers walked him 148 times, or 51 times more than anyone else, yet he still hit .376 (only good for fourth place in this hit-happy year) with a big-league-best 137 RBIs, 158 runs, 99 extra-base hits. His slugging percentage of *.847*, or over 200 points more than Sisler, and his home run percentage of 1 every 8.5 at-bats were higher than when he hit 60 in 1927. Ruth also stole 14 bases, had 21 outfield assists (though with 19 errors), and pitched 1 game—which of course he won.

But it would be the last season Ruth had all to himself. From now on, he would have a lot of company circling the bases. And the baseball brass, of course, would pretend that nothing was more natural in the world than those sacrosanct home runs. Maybe they actually believed it since Ruth and his homers saved their behinds when a rush of ugly headlines threatened to scatter the game into a thousand pieces. That happened in September of that 1920 season, when all hell broke loose about the 1919 World Series.

For months, the full weight of the baseball establishment came down on anyone who raised the scenario that the White Sox had tanked against the Reds. The most persistent, and for a time the only one who did in the press, was Chicago sportswriter Hugh Fullerton (Ring Lardner and Fred Lieb were among many who knew but kept a stony silence), who was ostracized as a "visionary and erratic writer" by the *Sporting News*. Fullerton, added *Baseball Magazine*, "should keep his mouth shut when in the presence of intelligent people," and ventured that "only fools would say there was 'something screwy' about the Series."

But the lid blew open when eight "Black Sox"—including one of the game's greatest hitters, "Shoeless" Joe Jackson, and one of its greatest pitchers, Eddie Cicotte—were indicted by a Chicago grand jury looking into gamblers and game-fixing, leading owner Charlie Comiskey to showily suspend them pending their trial the following summer. The truth was that Comiskey—whose parsimonious plantation system had led the players to accept the blandishments of game-fixers in the first place—had actually known that the fix was in but kept it under wraps by insisting he was conducting his own in-house whitewash, er, "investigation," during which he, too, derided any suggestion of foul play.

In the interregnum before the trial, when baseball faced potential ruin just when its popularity was at its highest, the game's lords knew they could not stand pat. With its divided owners incapable of running a candy store, they looked outside the game for a CEO. On October 18 they axed the National Commission for good and turned to the judge who was so helpful in stalling the Federal League's lawsuit in 1915. On November 12, Kenesaw Mountain Landis was unanimously elected the first commissioner of any sport, with carte-blanche latitude to make all decisions and take any and all actions to preserve the integrity of the game as he saw fit. Landis, a grim-faced man with unruly white hair and a look of perpetual heartburn, looked and played the dictator. The tainted "eight men out" (who had all originally confessed to taking bribes from gambler Arnold Rothstein to throw the Series) were acquitted in a dubious trial, on August 2, 1921. Still, Landis, "for the good of the game," banned them anyway, sending Shoeless Joe, a career .356 hitter, to the sticks to play on rag-tag teams for the next decade, and Ed Cicotte to a life as a game warden. Both would be ineligible for entry to the future Hall of Fame.

For all the hand wringing about this seeming injustice, with special sympathy for the illiterate Jackson, who may not even have understood that he was taking a bribe, Landis's castor oil was just the right medicine for baseball. While it skirted due process, no active player, or another judge, would have dared question his authority. (Four of the condemned did sue the White Sox, with two accepting a small settlement from Comiskey.) The gambling scourge was ended, never to rise again. And there would be no messy episodes to distract the game from its newfound repast at the gate. In the future, not even Babe Ruth would be bigger than the game when it came to being disciplined.

Baseball had a czar at the helm and a Sultan of Swat on the field. Just in time for the Golden Age of the home run to proceed without pause.

Babe Ruth and the Science of the Home Run

F. C. Lane's observation that Ruth had thrown science to the wind is of course absurd. As unparalleled as Ruth was, the man didn't hit home runs by accident or on will. Ruth was in fact a waddling lesson in longball hitting at the molecular level, otherwise a lot of big galoots would have hit 714 home runs. Ruth's swing, to begin with, while big enough to ventilate the upper deck, was neither wild nor random. It created homers because Ruth was a powerful and disciplined hitter who swung at strikes. If there is one mistake would-be sluggers make over and over, it is trying to hit any semi-decent pitch out of sight, doing nothing except to squander their power by diffusing it. Most hitters of the 1910s and 1920s were indoctrinated to swing only at good pitches, and Ruth's power was remarkably efficient, concentrated within the hitting zone. Springing at a hittable pitch, every joint, tendon, and muscle would fuse in a way that would optimize power. Look at any old picture of Ruth in mid-swing. Forget the Jocko the clown exterior and check the form, the way upper and lower body knitted, the head staying level. Take a pencil and draw a line from the tip of the bat to the shoulders—it will be straight all the way through the arms. Science.

Ruth was known to strike out some, okay a lot, but his career total of 1,330 whiffs is *twenty-sixth* on the all-time list led by Reggie Jackson's 2,597. Jackson, in case you're wondering, batted 1,549 times *less* than Ruth. Not convinced? Here's how Ruth stacks up against baseball's other famous longballers:

	Years	Strikeouts per Year	Home Runs per Year	Batting Average
Sammy Sosa*	14	131	36	.278
Reggie Jackson	21	123	27	.262
Willie Stargell	15	122	30	.282
Harmon Killebrew	16	105	35	.256
Mickey Mantle	16	105	33	.298
Mike Schmidt	18	104	31	.267
Manny Ramirez*	10	101	31	.316
Mark McGwire	16	100	37	.263
Alex Rodriguez*	9	97	33	.309
Ken Griffey Jr.*	14	89	34	.295
Eddie Mathews	17	87	30	.271
Duke Snider	14	87	28	.295
Juan Gonzalez*	14	85	29	.296
Hank Greenberg	10	81	32	.313
Barry Bonds*	17	80	36	.295
RUTH	16	79	43	.342
Frank Robinson	20	76	29	.294
Ralph Kiner	10	75	37	.279
Mike Piazza*	11	73	32	.321
Willie Mays	21	70	30	.302
Willie McCovey	22	70	23	.270
Rafael Palmeiro*	17	68	29	.293
Ernie Banks	19	65	27	.274
Carl Yastrzemski	23	61	21	.285
Hank Aaron	24	56	31	.305
Lou Gehrig	16	49	31	.340
Ted Williams	15	46	34	.344
Mel Ott	22	41	24	.304
Stan Musial	22	32	22	.331
Joe DiMaggio	13	27	27	.325

*Still active, statistics through 2002

Shockingly, Ruth's home run-to-strikeout ratio is inferior only to some of history's greatest contact hitters whose at-bats weren't homer-centric—Williams, Musial, Gehrig, and DiMaggio (as an aside, Joe D's 1 : 1 ratio is one of the game's most remarkable and overlooked achievements) and is only a tad behind the wrist-hitting Aaron, whose record 755 homers were a product of unshakable consistency over the long run, with not more than 47 in any season. And Ruth's .342 average (ninth all-time) is higher than all of them except Williams (who beats him by a whole two points). Ruth, who struck out 90 or more times only twice, had a high of 93, about half that of Barry Bonds' unspeakable record of 189—pursued by such glorious practitioners of the swing and miss as Rob Deer, Pete Incaviglia, and Gorman Thomas. There are singles hitters today who strike out far more often than Ruth did (see Rey Oronez), and Ruth isn't even among the top thirty-five highest ratios of strikeouts-to-at-bats. Neither, incidentally, is any of his contemporaries, which proves how misread Ruth is by modern generations of ersatz sluggers. For many of them, a homer is often literally hit or miss. For Ruth, a miss could easily mean a hard RBI single or double.

What of Ruth's size? (By this I don't mean Babe's favorite appendage, "Little Babe," which he bragged about often—and lamented later on that the worst part of getting fat was that he could no longer see it when he stood up.) By the vintage pictures of the Babe one might think he was a mastadon. In fact, he was 6 feet 2 inches tall and only around 200 pounds for most of his career, a virtual pygmy next to the big boys of today and even a few light-hitting shortstops. While he had a massive upper body, next to Lou Gehrig's chiseled-in-stone physique he was a sack of Velveeta with girly legs. And yet he was beastly strong and could generate colossal power swinging as much as a forty-ounce bat.

However, Ruth's lumber was no mere mallet; it is a major historical signpost in itself, a radical departure from the railroad spikes players had used as bats since the 1850s. Indeed, as much as the Reach balls and the rule changes, it was Ruth's transformation of baseball bats—based on nothing but instinct—that wreaked home run havoc. Anyone looking at Ruth's timber would know it was his—and not only by the notches he carved into the barrel after hitting many of his home runs, like a gunslinger out of the Old West marking his kill. Since Ruth wouldn't have choked up even with a gun held to his head, he had no use for those thick handle bats and, for his purposes, using one of those would have been like trying to get blood from a stone. So he ordered his thirty-six-inch-long bats be made as thin as possible in the handle, only a couple inches in diameter. This shifted the overall weight—generally around thirty-eight ounces during the bulk of his career—to the barrel, which would whip around like a bolo, with more aerodynamic force and concentrated power, and set in motion by a flick of the wrist instead of the forearms.

There had been a pioneer of sorts in bat evolution pre-Ruth: the "bottle bat" popularized by Heinie Groh, who played from 1912 to 1927 in the NL. Groh's bat also had a thin handle, which stretched six inches then sharply flared to a thick barrel. But Groh's bat was traditionally rooted. It was heavy, over forty ounces, and Groh choked up on it mainly to hit curveballs through the infield. The bottle bat wouldn't have supplied much power, because its weight was not distributed smoothly as with a gradually tapered bat. It took Ruth, baseball's idiot savant, to get all this straight, and don't think the folks at Hillerich & Bradsby weren't grateful because orders on new thin-handled, tapered bats began pouring in after 1920.

But just how did Ruth make his homers happen? How does anyone make one happen? For this it is necessary to break down the science and turn to the laws of physics. Simply, if the center of the ball meets the center of the bat—scientists call this the "ideal line alignment"—one is in business. But not all the time. The bat's sweet spot, or "center of percussion," is about a six-inch swath around the label. Dead solid contact here will hardly be felt in the hands because every ounce of kinetic energy from the bat is transferred into the ball (whereas a Sammy Sosa swing and miss will dissipate this energy as heat). Miss the center of the sweet spot by even a few millimeters and the bat will twist and turn in one's hands. A few more millimeters toward the handle and it will reverberate like a tuning fork (not pleasant on a cold day) or saw the bat off in one's hands (not pleasant any day).

But a solid shot can be a line drive single or a long fly out, so other variables come into play—such as the physical properties of the bat and ball and air density (air is 12 percent less dense at 95 degrees than at 30 degrees, and air pressure decreases 3 percent for every 1,000 feet of elevation; at 5,000 feet a moving ball has 15 percent less drag on it than at sea level—a phenomenon that I will return to). There is also the velocity of the bat and the pitch at the point of contact. A bat can go fast either by brute strength (Mantle, Frank Howard, Jimmie Foxx) or perfectly meshing biomechanics (Aaron, Musial, Mel Ott)—or both, as with Ruth. For all the dangers of the hanging curve, a live fastball is by far easier to pound out, because of the "rebound speed," or change in momentum from bat to ball.

Amazingly, on a molecular level, the ball actually *stops* upon collision, for an infinitesimal moment. It must in order for the laws of momentum to work. The pertinent equations are *momentum = mass × velocity* and *force = change in momentum/time to change momentum*. What this means is that the larger mass and force of the bat stops the light ball dead and gives it its momentum. So a 30-ounce bat going 70 mph striking a 5-ounce ball for about two milliseconds will send the ball on a ride at around 100 mph. (The bat gets the ball's momentum and slows down.)

Even more amazing is that Ruth accomplished this turnaround with a 38-ounce bat (or that Home Run Baker could take as many over the wall as he did with his 52-ounce monster). Logic says the bat can't possibly move that fast due to inertia and would take longer to move in the split-second interval a batter has to decide to swing or not. This explains why almost all of those snazzy new slim-handled Louisville Sluggers were lighter (and, it follows, shorter) and would keep getting lighter still—even Ruth went down to a 36-ounce bat by the late 1920s. Over the years players would use ingenious (read illegal) methods to tinker with the dynamics, such as the time-tested practice of drilling out the center of the bat and filling it with cork, or anything else fluffy short of duck down. Rule 1: When in doubt in picking a bat, go with the lightest feasible one. Except if your name is George Herman Ruth, but then you wouldn't be human.

The list of home run variables is endless. For example, the angle of the swing. A good power swing is normally angled slightly upward. But emulating Ruth's natural uppercut, as with emulating his massive swing (which was in fact tidy and economical), has done more harm than good, since the best home run swing may be a level one for some, and for others no swing will work. Home runs are in the genes more than the bat. Some men are born to swing big and efficiently at the same time—Mantle, Sosa, Griffey, Ruth. But swinging way too hard, way too upward, or trying to pull every pitch, will net fewer home runs than very weak outs. Look at the swings of other home run nobility—McGwire's was nearly a one-handed chop at the pitch, Bonds' could be executed in a phone booth, Aaron's didn't seem hard enough to break a pane of glass. All were or are as quick as an eyeblink, and like Ruth's weren't often wasted on bad pitches. Willie Mays hit most of his homers in wind-swept Candlestick Park by taking *inside* curve balls to right field, into the wind draft that carried balls out that way. "Ask me how I did it. I don't know,"

Mays says now. All one needs to know is that the laws of science never take a rest.

There is also the inner game of pitcher versus hitter, figuring out when and whether a pitch will be a home run pitch. For example, there was George Sisler, a .340 career hitter who twice hit over .400 and frequently finished second to Ruth in the home run derby. Sisler wasn't a Hall of Famer for nothing. He was no dummy, having delayed his career with the St. Louis Browns to earn a degree in mechanical engineering at the University of Michigan. Smarty-pants that he was, Sisler said he spent ten years building up the fiction that he could not hit a high inside pitch—to the point of striking out on that pitch just so he could get pitchers to throw it to him in an important at bat. (Where have all the great baseball thinkers gone?) In its goofy way, this confirms what scouts have been saying for a century—right-handed power hitters generally like the ball high, left-handed hitters low, due to the biomechanics of their respective swings—though it's more complicated when great hitters adjust. Science also governs what makes a pitched ball go fast or break, depending on the drag coefficient, magnus coefficient, and spin frequency. But that's a treat for later.

Roaring in the Twenties

It has already been determined that Babe Ruth made the home run, but to even things out a bit, Ruth was made by his era, not the other way around. Only because there was a confluence of conditions that met with nuclear force was there a Ruth Era. Speaking of equations, the Ruth equation was *New York City* + *postwar economic boom* × *the disposable money that grew on trees* (for everyone of course but those on the lower economic rungs) × *the home run* + *arrested adolescence* = *Sultan of Swat*. Suddenly, there were more upwardly mobile Americans and manifold ways to spend money in excess. And Ruth naturally congealed as his generation's paradigm of excess on and off the field.

Even though awe-struck sportswriters only hinted at Ruth's habitual drinking and womanizing, his grotesquely corpulent appetites were a badly kept secret, hardly masked by his publicized hospital visits to sick kids. (Don't get me wrong; the Babe really liked those forays.) As baseball historian Jules Tygiel writes in his book *Past Time: Baseball as History*, Ruth "elicited divine comparisons, evoking images of Bacchus and Dionysus, the gods of wine and sensual pleasure. . . . Ruth's prodigious sexual appetites [and] profligate lifestyle . . . were well known. . . . This excess of humanity, however, endeared him to people even more."

Indeed Ruth's decadence and insatiability mirrored the times. These were the Roaring Twenties, when Ruth sat atop an Olympian summit with Jack Dempsey, Bobby Jones, Big Bill Tilden, and Red Grange, and one can just imagine the pagan temptations as recreational sex and bathtub gin bubbled up like never before. Manly men were exempted from moral compacts as long as they spoke of God, family, and country—and performed on the field. Ruth practically wrote the script. "The greatest thing about this country," he effused with practiced humility in his memoirs, "is the wonderful fact that it doesn't matter which side of the tracks you were born on, or whether you're homeless or homely or friendless. The chance is still there. I know."

As the "Twenties" went on, the chroniclers of Ruth's feats propped him into broader context, in ways normally reserved for historians searching retroactively for context. For example, Westbrook Pegler wrote that Ruth was "an unequaled exhibition . . . of a pace with the madness for crazy pleasure, unheard of speed, and aimless bigness convulsing the nation." Thus, one can see how Ruth was a product of the press that followed his every move—and very soon, the *media*, with the birth of radio in the early 1920s, allowing the nation to be able to experience Ruth's at-bats in real time in the World Series.

It would be difficult to overlook that baseball and sportswriting had dual comings of age. In the early 1920s the baseball press was living through a "Golden Age" of its own, when the young turks of the 1910s had become entrenched and had pooled their influence through the Baseball Writers Association. Many were as famous now as the men they wrote about—Grantland Rice's lead for the 1924 Notre Dame–Army game ("Outlined against a blue-grey October sky, the Four Horsemen rode again. . . .") may just be the most famous piece of twentieth-century American literature. While these men kept a safe distance from the cold and humorless Ty Cobb, they salivated on and fawned over Ruth, trampling over each other, currying his favor.

The luckiest of the lot, to whom Ruth entrusted the full-time job of marketing him like so much Burma Shave, was a former newspaper cartoonist, Christy Walsh, who in 1921 began playing Svengali to Ruth's Trilby. Walsh booked the Babe's endless endorsements and appearances everywhere, from bowling alleys to wrestling matches to men's smokers. He ghost-wrote countless newspaper and magazine articles, and half a dozen books bearing Ruth's byline (if he couldn't do it he would hire suitable lackeys to handle the chore, such as a certain sportswriter named Ford Frick). He handled matters large and small, from getting Ruth fifteen bucks per home run from one newspaper for a few "exclusive" words (made up by Walsh) to booking him onto the vaudeville circuit at $3,000 a week for twenty weeks during one off-season to negotiating all of Ruth's Yankee contracts, taking a cut of everything Ruth made. So blame Walsh for serving in the role of sports' first agent, and a mega one when his work for Ruth led many other players to hire him as well. Thus, you can understand what Walsh meant when he once called Ruth "a gift from the gods."

For the press in general Ruth was a self-fulfilling prophecy, and as a result the press would find it impossible to cut him back down to size when Ruth's act wore thin. When *Baseball Magazine* said of Ruth that people "will always idolize the man that can do something that no other man on Earth can do," the irony was that when their own infatuation with Ruth would cool in a few years, these words would become his epitaph.

A House for Ruth

In the red-letter year of 1921, another superlative season by Ruth led the Yankees to ninety-eight wins and their first-ever pennant, by four and a half games over the Indians. By now, conditions were even more favorable for Ruth. For one thing, pitchers were kept on yet a tighter leash, as the result of a Carl Mays submarine pitch that caved in the skull of Indians' shortstop Ray Chapman in August 1920, causing Chapman's death a day later. That made him the only on-field fatality in big-league history if you don't count Jim Creighton's previously noted ill-fated home run swing. The accident so traumatized the lords of the game that, because the ball that killed Chapman was a gray color that Chapman's eyes couldn't distinguish, the next season the rules went beyond *intentional* discoloring of the ball. Teams were now instructed to have a plentiful supply of balls, and umpires were told to chuck the one in play if it got even slightly soiled and replace it with a glossy white one that was harder for pitchers to grip for a hard fastball or biting curve (and thus actually *more* dangerous).

How different were those times? Back then pitchers complained about *too many* new balls put in play; today, they will replace one with a speck on it, or if doesn't *feel* right. The only concession the pitchers got was that umpires would rub down a new ball to get the gloss off, and, in

1925, to dry their fingers on a resin bag placed on the mound. But whatever gloss was left on the ball was knocked off by Ruth and, now, his apostles. That 1921 season was really the birth of the home run as an egalitarian tool—the AL zoomed from 369 to 477 (134 by the Yankees alone), the NL from 261 to 460. And while no one came within even half of Ruth's astounding 59, three others in the American and two in the National cleared the 20-homer level—both the Browns' Ken Williams and the Yankees' Bob Meusel had 24, the A's Tilly Walker 23; the Giants' George Kelly had 23 and the Cardinals' incomparable 25-year-old second baseman Rogers Hornsby had 21.

As for Ruth, at 26 he too was still on the climb. Playing in all but two games, by mid-July he had more career homers than anyone, passing Gavvy Cravath's post-1900 mark of 119 and Roger Connor's 136 overall. On September 15 he broke his own season record with No. 55. On the last day he blasted No. 59, a 3-run shot against the Red Sox. Ruth hit .376, third behind Harry Heilmann and Ty Cobb, and led the majors in runs (158), RBIs (137), slugging (.846), walks (144), and total bases (378), and a home run percentage of 1 every 9.1 at-bats. And this time, the pennant was the reward, as Ruppert had surrounded Ruth with a solid cast—again, courtesy of Harry Frazee's willingness to pawn important people for cash. First came Ed Barrow, who became general manager and quickly got Frazee to deal pitcher Waite Hoyt and catcher Wally Schang.

Ruth, who clinched the flag when he hit 2 homers in a critical late-season win over the Indians, felt right at home in his first Yankee World Series, because he was home, in the first of back-to-back Series against the Giants. Unfortunately, so was John McGraw, who would have sooner chugged arsenic than lose to his Polo Grounds tenants, though in the first of the only two times a Series was played in one ballpark, Ruth stood in the way. He hit his first Series dinger against Phil Douglas in the ninth inning of a Game 4 loss and his *bunt single* sparked a Game 5 win that put the Yankees up three games to two in the best-of-nine Series. Hitting .313, a swollen elbow and bad knee took Ruth out for the remaining games, and the Giants won the last three to save McGraw's pride. (Because of dwindling attendance, Landis made this the last best-of-nine Series.)

The following year Barrow looted five more Red Sox, including shortstop Everett Scott and third baseman Jumping Joe Dugan, who made Home Run Baker expendable. That helped bring another pennant—despite a sour Ruth ruining his own season. Though Babe had inked a stratospheric five-year, $52,000-a-year contract, he lost a sizable chunk of it before playing a single game, having run afoul of Kenesaw Mountain Landis when he and Bob Meusel joined a barnstorming team—the kind that earned ballplayers several thousand dollars—right after the World Series. This violated a baseball injunction against World Series participants playing on such units during or so close to the Series. It was, Landis said, "a question of who is the biggest man in baseball, the Commissioner or the player who makes the most home runs." Landis had the answer, withholding Ruth and Meusel's Series share of $3,500 and suspending them until May 20, 1922, when they were reinstated and paid their shares.

An out-of-sorts Ruth subsequently was suspended five times for verbal abuse of umpires, prompting Ban Johnson to send a scathing letter to Ruth calling his behavior "shameful" and questioning whether "a man of your influence and breeding" belonged in the game. Ruth should, he said, "allow some intelligence to creep into a mind that has plainly been warped." Limited to 110 games, Ruth hit .315 with 35 homers (third behind Kenny Williams's 39 and Tilly Walker's 37) and 99 RBIs. He even had a pregame fistfight with teammate Wally Pipp in July—then went out and hit two homers against St. Louis. While the Yankees managed to win the flag by one game over the Browns, McGraw's Giants starched them in four straight games in the World Series, holding Ruth homerless and to two hits in seventeen at-bats with a simple plan: the Giant pitchers would throw him curveballs in the dirt and hope he swung at them. He did, too often.

Beating the Yankees wasn't enough for McGraw. Mortified that the Yankees were outdrawing him, McGraw, or "Muggsy," had evicted them from the Polo Grounds in 1920 effective in 1923, giving Ruppert two years to build his own stadium. The Colonel annexed a lumberyard in the South Bronx, on 161st Street, right across the Harlem River from the Polo Grounds, and constructed an appropriately excessive (and at $2.5 million, expensive) basilica to stand as baseball's unchallenged mecca. Yankee Stadium was an architectural wonder, a peach-shaped, shale-blue, three-tiered basin with exterior cathedral windows and seating for 65–70,000 people—most of whom Ruppert knew would be there to see his right fielder, who was envisioned from the start as the St. Jude of this abbey.

Already it was being called "the House that Ruth Built," but it was also the house Ruth contoured, as the right field pole was 294 feet and the fence out there stood only 3 feet 7 inches high. Right-center flared to 344 feet where the bleachers began and then to the wide acreage of the famously dubbed "Death Valley": 429 feet to deep right-center, 490 feet to center, 460 feet to left-center, 415 feet to the left field bullpen before shortening to 280 feet at the pole. Lying in wait for the Babe, the lower right field grandstand and the steep, massive upper deck above it were called "Ruthville," though the notion of Ruth reaching the elevated subway tracks behind the bleachers was not preposterous.

Construction began on May 5, 1922, and still wasn't completely finished on April 18, 1923, when the Yankees met the Red Sox—who had as much to do with the stadium's majestic rising as anyone—in the inaugural game. On that day 74,217 people, a good 5,000 who paid to stand, squeezed into every inch of space and the Babe, who always seemed to excel when the glare was on him, personally stamped the game with a 3-run homer to Ruthville off Howard Ehmke, sealing a 4-1 win. Six days later President Warren G. Harding came to the park and Ruth hit one out against the Senators. By August the travails of 1922 were gone. Ruth had hit over .400 with 31 homers, and on September 21 he won the AL's MVP award by unanimous vote of an eight-man committee of sportswriters, the second since the AL revived the concept of the defunct Chalmers Award, applied to a most valuable player, which George Sisler had won the year before. (The NL would begin its award in 1924.)

Ruth's season was another jaw dropper. While everyone now was aping his home run swing, Ruth, having learned from his disastrous World Series, became a more patient, controlled hitter. As his homers slipped to 41 (still a league high but no better than the Phillies' Cy Williams), his average soared to .393, behind only Harry Heilmann's phenomenal .403. He led the majors with 130 RBIs, 151 runs, 399 total bases, and a whopping 170 walks, an all-time record until Barry Bonds' magical mystery 2001 (when he batted 46 times more than Ruth had and walked 7 times more).

And when the Yankees faced the Giants in October for the third straight year, this time Ruth imposed his will on McGraw.

October Thunder

The 1923 World Series proved a truism about home runs and the Fall Classic. In these games, when the best meets the best in a short round, many stars fall short of expectations. Consider some Series averages—Cobb .262, Wagner .275, Hornsby .245, DiMaggio .271, Williams .200, Mays .278, Mantle .257. Even Ruth's .326 Series average was 18 points below his career average, and is not among the top twenty Series averages. Many great pitchers haven't fared better—Mathewson 5-5, Marquard 2-5, Johnson 3-3, Feller 0-2. Sandy Koufax, with an *0.98* ERA, was 4-3. What's more, even hitting safely in all seven Series games, or even pitching three victories, might not leave as lasting an image as a well-timed home run to break up just one game. This calculus was nectar for Ruth, who left his mark 15 times in 41 games—1 every 8.6 at-bats.

In that 1923 Series, Aaron Ward hit .413, Bob Meusel had 8 RBIs and Herb Pennock (another steal from Boston) went 2-and-0 for the Yankees. Frankie Frisch hit .400 for the Giants. But no one would remember anything else but five dingers—3 by Ruth and 2 by Charles Dillon Stengel. To the redoubtable Casey, then a good-hitting outfielder better known for hijinx, such as the time he let a bird fly out from under his cap, goes the honor of hitting the first Yankee Stadium World Series home run, and what a home run! Few four-baggers have ever had the brio of Stengel's "mad dash" on October 10, 1923, when he tore around the sacks in the top of the ninth of Game 1—with a loose shoe coming off—to tally the winning run in a 5-4 game. Ruth one-upped him in Game 2, slamming homers in consecutive innings in a 4-2 win. Unlike the year before, the Giants didn't try to get him to fish after bad balls, growing out of McGraw's hubris about Ruth, which he displayed before the game by chest thumping, "Why shouldn't we pitch to Ruth? We pitch to better hitters in the National League."

Noting this in his game story, Heywood Broun wrote in the *New York World*, "Ere the sun had set on McGraw's rash and pompous words that the Babe had flashed across the sky fiery portents . . . sufficient to strike terror and conviction into the hearts of all infidels."

Then at the Polo Grounds, Stengel, who hit .417 in the Series, one-upped *himself*, ending a scoreless affair with a homer in the seventh, the only run of the game—and waltzed around the bases blowing kisses to the Yankee bench, prompting Ruppert to complain to Landis.

"I didn't mind it," the commissioner told him. "Casey's a lot of fun."

But the Yankees took the next two games and in his first at-bat in Game 6 Babe broke more new ground with his third Series shot. But the Series' dramatic crest was reached in the eighth when with the Giants up 4-1 Art Nehf walked home 2 Yankee runs. Now leading 4-3 Nehf had to face Ruth with the bases jammed. After getting two strikes he threw one wide of the plate that an overeager Ruth chased and missed—capping a moment of high drama heard across a rapt nation on the radio, told in the melodramatic tones of announcer Graham McNamee. In recalling his on-air quatrain, McNamee later wrote of Ruth's at-bat: "Only one little crack—just a solid connection between ash and leather and the series would be over," and that Ruth "squared his shoulder and set himself menacingly enough," only to suffer an "ignominious moment, his face almost green where before it had been white."

Fortunately for the green-faced Babe, Meusel singled in 2 runs to win the Series, a single few waxed about. Indeed, in a Series that drew 310,000 people and earned a million-dollar gate, Ruth again was the exemplar of "bigness." And, now, so would the World Series be.

For Ruth, though, another Series would have to wait for two years. In 1924 he rang up another spectacular season (.378, 46 homers, 121 RBIs) but the Cinderella Senators held off the Yankees to win the pennant—prefacing the aging Walter Johnson's famous Game 7 relief victory against the Giants. Then in 1925 Ruth pushed his vices too far. On April 5 he collapsed in a train station, and when the news spread one newspaper reported that he was dead. He might have been if he hadn't been taken off the train (they had to remove a bay window to get him out), rushed to a hospital, and operated on—for what the protective press wrote up as a big bellyache brought on by a routine Ruth carnage at the dinner table. Only years later was it revealed that Ruth was nearly blown open by a massive case of gonorrhea and syphilis. Bedridden until late May, an unchastened Babe kept to his usual late hours and brothels and in late August he disappeared for two days in St. Louis—during which time a detective hired by the Yankees reported he slept with six women in one night.

Finally showing up at the park, Ruth winked to Miller Huggins, "Sorry I'm late, Hug."

The diminutive manager didn't wink back. Instead he suspended and fined Ruth $5,000. Livid, Babe gave a "Hug-or-me" ultimatum to Ruppert, who supported the manager, forcing a humiliated Ruth to apologize.

Given his insane pagan lusts—which also included heavy gambling on the ponies that could cost him as much as $75,000 on a single race—the most remarkable thing about Ruth was that he lived as long and as comfortably as he did. It was a dicey proposition that Ruth could even bounce back from that horror show season when he hit .290 with 25 homers (second to Meusel's 33) and 66 RBIs in 98 games, still a ton for most players—and do it without materially changing his lifestyle. Indeed, as Ruth's belly was expanding some in the press ceased believing his excesses were so endearing. That year, a disillusioned F. C. Lane broke ranks by decrying Ruth as "crude, uncultured, ill-educated," and prone to "wild license . . . utter disregard of regulations . . . and coarse escapades."

Dubious as well was whether the Yankees could recover from a seventh-place season. That they did can be traced to the saving grace of 1925, which took hold on June 2 when first baseman Wally Pipp had a headache and was replaced by a sinewy 21-year-old local kid, Lou Gehrig. He had been signed for $400 after starring on the Columbia University team, had a cup of coffee with the Yankees in 1923, and played three years in the bushes. Early in 1925, sportswriter Frank Graham watched him take batting practice and as retold in *The Ultimate Baseball Book* (1988), wrote this soliloquy:

> The boy picked up a bat—one of Ruth's, by some curious chance—and advanced to the plate. He was obviously nervous, missed the first two pitches, then bounced one weakly over second base. Then he hit one that soared into the right field bleachers, high up, where only Ruth had ever hit a ball. . . . He hit another in there another—still another. His nervousness had slipped from him now. "That's enough," Huggins cried. He turned to the players. "His name's Gehrig," he said, and walked slowly behind the hulking figure of the youngster toward the dugout. The players looked after them in silence.

Gehrig, of course, could be found at first base for the next fifteen seasons—although revisionists often ignore that he was not an instant star, and was even pinch-hit for three times in June, didn't start on July 5, and came into the game later on. Still, it became evident that Gehrig almost never looked bad on a pitch, and while he hit white-blur line drives more than towering fly balls, he could easily reach Ruthville, or any grandstand of any distance. On September 10, Meusel, Ruth, and Gehrig hit back-to-back home runs, and the three of them combined for 68 homers. With Gehrig (who hit .295 and had 20 homers and 68 RBIs) in tow, the Yankees now had the pieces for a home run "row" no one had ever seen before.

But there were other grade-A sluggers around the baseball map as well. And with Ruth temporarily deconstructed as the Sultan of Swat, into the home run glare came his disciples, led by a cantankerous cuss of a second baseman who was in every way a ball-buster.

6

Fad Without End

Swinging from the Hip

As electrifying and rewarding as the home run cloudburst of the 1920s was, a fair number of people around the game fretted about the game being cheapened, dumbed down into a kind of carnival attraction. As it was, the baseball panjandrums constantly had to contend with the ongoing charge about the ball being juiced up, though Babe Ruth made it all very simple to understand.

"The ball is all right," he said in the *Reach Guide* in 1925. "It's the same ball as 10 years ago. Only reason for the increased hitting, especially home runs, is that seven of every 10 batters used to choke up on their bats—now nine out of 10 are swinging from the hip."

Whatever the reason, the trend caught many of the game's longtime barons off guard, none more than Connie Mack, whose unbroken string of lowly finishes in Philadelphia did not alter his worldview of the game. Mack—who was pleased when Harry Davis and Home Run Baker habitually led the league back when 15 was a ton of homers—was unmoved by Ruth and his flock racking them up by the bushel, including the A's own Tilly Walker who tied Ruth with 11 in 1918 and zoomed to 37 five years later. In 1923, Mack called that kind of long-ball hitting "a fad" and did his part to end it by moving the fences back at Shibe Park and announcing he would from now on stress speed and defense.

As a result, Walker sank to 2 homers that year and thereafter could only find work in the minors. The A's? They won four more games and soared from seventh to sixth place. But Mack would move his team up, way up—when he found room in the mid- and late 1920s for Jimmie Foxx and Al Simmons, big boys whose long-ball ways made Mack move the fences back *in*.

Mack wasn't the only convert in the sclerotic old guard—even *Ty Cobb*, the scourge of power-hitting, hit 5 homers in two games in 1925 (none inside the park), becoming the first player to do that in the twentieth century. During the mid-1920s, fences were also moved in at five National League parks, to accommodate both homers and more seating capacity for fans who wanted to see homers. Another, Wrigley Field, built by the Federal League's Chicago team and then annexed by the Cubs, was already a hitter's haven. One holdout was Pirates' owner Barney Dreyfus, who refused to truncate the spacious dimensions at Forbes Field and pushed in vain for a return to the withered custom of calling a ball hit into too-shallow stands a double.

That John McGraw capitulated to the new order was the white flag of surrender. Once, back when he was leading the Orioles' Baltimore chop, bunt-and-run attack, Muggsy would give hell to free-swingers. But seeing Ruth steal the Polo Grounds from the Giants, he needed fire to fight with. McGraw encouraged first baseman George "High Pockets" Kelly and Emil "Irish" Meusel, Bob's brother, to go deep. Kelly even hit a homer in six straight games in 1924 (a league record) and 3 in one game. The Giants, who had 347 steals in 1911, had a mere 82 in 1924—when they led the NL in homers, as they did in 1925. A year later, a little guy with a big swing—Mel Ott—would arrive from Louisiana. But McGraw failed when he offered the Cardinals $300,000, more than the value of many *teams*, for the NL's answer to Babe Ruth—Rogers Hornsby.

Rajah's Ruckus

As the decade was developing, several hitters vied for recognition as baseball's second-best home run hero. Two of them, the Browns' Kenny Williams and the Phillies' Cy Williams, shared a surname and a reliable long-ball swing. At a time when the 40-homer plateau was still a cosmic milestone for everyone but Ruth, Cy Williams smacked 41 in 1923, tying Ruth and leading the NL by 19—though again it must be qualified as a "Baker Bowl 41" (26 came at the infamous bandbox where that season the Phillies and Cardinals combined to hit a record 10 homers in one game).

Cy Williams was a left-handed, dead-pull-hitter, jerking shots down the line, and had led the league with 12 in 1916 with the Cubs before being traded to the Phillies. He won his second home run crown with 15 in 1920 before unloading in 1923—when he also hit 15 in one month, a record for twenty-six years. An accurate history would give him the honor of hitting against the first "Williams Shift," the defensive alignment, with the shortstop on the second base side, that was named for a certain lanky Red Sox pull-hitter with the same last name a decade later. Cy Williams won his fourth homer crown with 30 in 1927, tying with the Cubs' rising slugger Hack Wilson.

Ken Williams came agonizingly close to 40 in 1922, leading the AL with 39, part of a wicked season when he hit .332 and also led with 155 RBIs—and stole 37 bases to boot, the first time any player went 30-30-30-.300. Williams, who threw right and batted left, pounded 3 homers in one game and 2 in one inning, as well as 1 in six straight games. But this too was a factor of friendly fences—Sportsman's Park being one of those parks where they shrunk the outfield, shaving 10 feet down each line, to just 315 feet in right. Of those 39 bombs, Williams sent 32 out at home, and over an eleven-year career 142 of his 196 homers came in a white uniform.

As it happened, another Sportsman's Park resident was making noise, so loud that it drowned out all of the other would-be home run caliphs. Rogers Hornsby, the Cardinals' second base *enfant terrible*, was also succored by the fences, but he needed little help. In fact, he hit home runs mainly because he was simply the best all-around hitter in the game then. In retrospect, he was quite likely the best all-around right-handed hitter in baseball history. Unlike the others, he didn't swing at a 45-degree angle. His swing was as level as Ty Cobb's, and much deadlier because at a compact 5 feet 11 inches and 200 pounds, with huge butcher-sized hands, Hornsby could make any spot on the bat a sweet spot with his strength and fluid mechanics.

Hornsby, born in Winters, Texas, in 1896, was signed as a skinny kid by St. Louis for $400 in 1915. He might have washed out after a year had the Cards succeeded in selling him to Little Rock of the Southern Association, but the $500 price was too steep. Under manager Branch Rickey, the young Hornsby developed his highly unorthodox batting stance, with his back foot dug into the extreme left corner of the box. Seemingly vulnerable to outside pitches, Hornsby took a large diagonal stride to reach them, yet had such quick reflexes that he could set himself and lash his heavy thirty-five-ounce bat to hit inside serves as well. In 1920 he bounced from .318 to .370, leading the league in hits, RBIs, slugging and total bases. That year, the last for the team at roomy Robison Field, he had 9 homers. At Sportsman's Park the next year, he was suddenly Triple Crown material. He led baseball with a .397 average and the league with 235 hits and 126 RBIs as well as doubles, triples, runs, slugging, and total bases—and was second with 21 homers, after High Pocket Kelly's 25.

Then came 1922 and a season that rivals any by Ruth. Having signed a three-year $18,000-a-year contract, he played in every game for the second straight year and, amassing a thirty-three-game hitting streak (a record at the time), he passed Gavvy Cravath's league standard of 25 homers on July 20 in dramatic fashion—a 2-out, 2-run, bottom-of-the-ninth shot that beat the Braves 7-6. Two weeks later he passed Ned Williamson's pre-1900 27. With a no-doubt Triple Crown in his pocket, he banged out an amazing 250 hits—still an NL record. On the season's final day, flirting with .400, he went 3-for-5 to finish at .401 (the first NL .400 of the century—though it seemed almost paltry next to George Sisler's .420 in the AL that year). Remarkably, Hornsby also had 42 homers, 152 RBIs, 141 runs, 450 total bases, .722 slugging.

Hornsby's alliterative nickname—"Rajah"—was aptly given since even the Triple Crown seemed inadequate for a man who would win a second Crown and *again* hit over .400 doing it. That happened in 1925 when he batted .403 with 39 homers, 139 RBIs, and slugged .756—an NL record that withstood even McGwire and Sosa until it was destroyed by Bonds in 2001. For Rajah, who won the first of his two MVP awards (and actually should have won three or four), that .403 average could have even been considered a *slump*, since the year before he merely hit *.424*, only the highest average of the twentieth century. Obviously, I'm not talking about a mere commoner here. Hornsby's career .359 average is second only to Cobb. Yet like Ruth, Gehrig, and later Ted Williams, Hornsby's high average was never inconsistent with the home run.

If Hornsby's lifetime take of 301 dingers seems a little light, it's only because he packed his epic years into the 1920s before burning out, his erosion hastened by his incurable habit of getting into distracting hassles with nearly everybody. To put it mildly, Hornsby went against the grain. Like Pete Browning batting sans hat to aid his vision, Hornsby assuaged *his* batting eye by refusing to watch movies or read the paper. A heavy gambler, Hornsby would have the Racing Form read to him. As dedicated and courtly as he was on the field, he was a blunt, foul-mouthed man with a disposition as knotty as his bat off it. The *Sporting News'* Bob Broeg once wrote that Hornsby was "majestically aloof and taciturn, independent and a loner. In fact, to be as honest as Hornsby, he was a petty, prejudiced person, though a frank, outspoken man who hated hypocrisy almost as much as he did baseball general managers."

The latter became clear almost as soon as Hornsby—who may have been less suited by temperament to be a manager than anyone in history—became the Cardinals' player-manager, as well as being given 15 percent of the team's stock, in 1925, replacing Rickey after twenty-eight games. His managerial style was once described by Hall of Famer Billy Herman, who played under him later with the Cubs. Hornsby, he said, "ran the clubhouse like a gestapo camp. You couldn't smoke, drink a soft drink, eat a sandwich or read a paper." Rajah could go a month without saying hello to his players, but would burn their ears if they screwed up. Still he drove the Cards to their first pennant in 1926 and led them into the World Series against the revived Yankees—and a very much alive Babe Ruth.

Ruth, apparently through the wonders of penicillin, had stayed healthy and found his stroke again in 1926, missing the Triple Crown himself by just 6 batting points, hitting .372 while leading baseball with 47 homers, 145 RBIs, and 365 total bases. At the same time Gehrig hit .313 with 16 homers and 112 RBIs. As a team the Yankees clocked 121 four-baggers, with Gehrig, Meusel, and rookie second baseman Tony Lazzeri combining for 46, as well as 307 RBIs. Lazzeri may be the most underrated Yankee of all time (if there is such a thing). Called "Push 'em Up" because of his knack for moving runners up, Lazzeri was much more than a supporting actor. An immensely popular man, he was arguably baseball's first Italian American idol. Working each off-season in his father's butcher shop, Lazzeri developed blacksmith-thick arms and in 1925 he had hit 60 home runs—and driven in *222* runs in 200 games playing in the Pacific Coast League. While his 18 rookie homers were creditable, as a right-handed hitter he had to contend with the wide acreage of Yankee Stadium's Death Valley, as would another Italian Yankee icon soon to follow, Joseph Paul DiMaggio.

Still, Hornsby's team was hardly anemic, having hit 90 homers that season. When the Series began it was the Cardinals who showed the early power when Billy Southworth hit a 3-run game-winning shot off Urban Shocker in Game 2, giving them a two-games-to-one lead. That was when Ruth arose at cramped Sportsman's Park, cranking the first pitch he saw for a homer, before slamming one completely out of the place in the third. For Ruth hitting a ball out of Sportsman's was not new, but this shot may have been the longest ever hit there, possibly going 550 feet before ending its journey. Then he came up in the sixth and took a 3-2 pitch over the center field wall—a record third Series homer, icing a 10-5 Yankee win.

In Game 5, the teams were tied 2-2 in the tenth when Hornsby ordered Ruth intentionally walked, loading the bases for Lazzeri, who hit a sacrifice fly for the gamer. The Cards now had the daunting task of having to sweep the last two games at Yankee Stadium. It also set the stage for 39-year-old Grover Cleveland Alexander to write a baseball roulade. Alex, whose alcoholism was an open secret among baseball people, first hurled a complete game 10-2 victory to win his second Series game. With the Series down to a climactic seventh game, the Cards weathered Ruth's fourth Series homer, and took a 3-2 lead into the seventh when the Yankees loaded the bases with 2 outs. Now Hornsby—appropriately—gambled. He put a call out to the Cardinals' bullpen for Alexander, who may or may not have been conscious at the time, sleeping off a late night celebrating his Game 6 triumph. Helped to his feet, "Old Pete" took an agonizingly slow walk from the pen to face Tony Lazzeri, who on a 1-1 pitch hit a screamer into the right field seats that hooked foul by a few feet. Alexander focused his eyes as best he could and on the next pitch broke off a roundhouse curve that Lazzeri cut on and missed, pricking the Yankee balloon. Alex would breeze through the eighth and the ninth.

With 2 outs, Ruth came up, but only long enough for Alex to walk him, recording the Babe's fourteenth Series walk, an all-time record until Barry Bonds' 2002 Series walkathon. Now came one of baseball's truly goofy moments, one that makes you wonder just who was really drunk that day, Alexander or Ruth. With Bob Meusel up, Ruth, taking it upon himself to get into scoring position, tried to steal second. Bad idea. Catcher Bob O'Farrell pegged him out by a country mile to end the Series right there, the only one to end *during* an at-bat.

Hornsby, though, had little time to savor the Series win. His autocracy took a lot out of his players, not to mention Hornsby, who that year fell to .317 and 11 homers. When he wrangled with owner Sam Breadon over a new contract, Breadon had the excuse to be rid of him. Hornsby was traded to the Giants in a deal that brought Frankie Frisch to St. Louis, but before Rajah would sign with the Giants he refused to cash out his Cardinal stock at Breadon's price. NL president John Heydler disposed of the unsightly matter by having each league team kick in $2,000 each, and the Giants $17,500, to bring Hornsby's windfall up to a staggering $112,000.

And for all that *mishegas* Hornsby lasted all of one year with the equally prickly John McGraw before being traded to the Braves, and then to the Cubs, with whom as player-manager he won his second MVP in 1929 (.380, 39, 149). This could have been his fourth MVP if repeat winners had been allowed (that didn't come about until the 1930s).

Even when he got rickety, Hornsby could still hit, and hit long. In 1931 he had homers in three consecutive at-bats, and became the first to hit a game-winning pinch-hit grand slam in extra innings. But his declining years were a sad game of shuffleboard. In 1932 the Cubs fired him as manager in midseason before going on to win the pennant. When the team voted on its World Series shares, the players stiffed Hornsby. Later, he returned to the Cards for an inconsequential season and left to manage the Browns, to be fired by owner Bill Veeck after another rocky run. On the day he was canned, the Browns players gave Veeck a trophy in appreciation.

But give the man his due. Hornsby did a lot for the home run during its golden age. He hit 12 grand slams. He was the first and only second baseman to lead the league in homers until 1990. And most significantly of all, he proved that Barry Bonds was far from the first asshole to hit a lot of balls out of the park.

60

Now quietly genuflect and speak in hushed tones as I address the 1927 Yankees—history's best team considering the premise that men who lived in 1927 can be compared physically with bigger, faster, better-coordinated men who live today. And maybe so, since the former crowd was a much more exclusive club. When eight teams played each other all season, chances are there were fewer lardbutts on the field than there are today when thirty-one teams (more or less according to how many Bud Selig can get away with liquidating) play each other. I know. I know. It was a picnic playing only day games back then, and getting around on trains instead of draining cross-country flights. Hitters also must have had it really easy not to have to face purebred relief pitchers.

But a bigger difference between then and now is that pitching in general is a sieve today, and applies to all but a couple of big-time closers out of the pen. Even with the home run bombardment of the 1920s, the American League ERA in 1927 was 4.14; in 2001 it was 4.47. Yeah, let's hear it for that great relief pitching. Pete Rose, who broke Ty Cobb's all-time hit record, once said that if Cobb had to hit against today's relief specialists, he would have hit .250. Actually, given the paucity of middle-relief especially today, he might have hit .500.

The fact is, no sane person would make the case that the 1993 world champion Toronto Blue Jays were a better power team than the '27 Yankees because they had the edge in home runs, 159 to 158. Indeed, the Yankees' then-record was broken by the 1930 Cubs, who hit 171. History has done everything it could to ignore them. The '27 Yankees are deified as Murderer's Row. Of course, being in New York helped just a little.

As did the fact that this was Ruth's 60-homer year. Because the margin of a single home run—the difference between Ruth's seasons of 1921 and 1927—wound up lifting the latter year from being simply superlative—as was '21—to being simply elysian.

The irony of the story is that the Babe may not have even been the best player on the '27 team. Even hitting 60 homers Ruth was beaten out for the MVP by his own teammate, Lou Gehrig, and while this is partly explained by the fact that the voting then was done in early September, even when all was said and done Gehrig was the logical choice. He hit 47 homers of his own that season as part of a frightening onslaught in which he beat Ruth in batting average (.373 to .356), RBIs (175 to 164), and total bases (447 to 417) and elevated himself nearly to Ruth's level of media fawning, though Gehrig rarely courted the attention that Ruth clearly needed. In fact, his prudish sensibilities were always offended by Ruth's crude narcissism. The notion of Gehrig going on a vaudeville tour in 1927 for $8,000, as Ruth did, or selling his name for such things as Babe Ruth Gum, Babe Ruth Home Run Shorts, and Babe Ruth Smoking Tobacco was less probable than Ruth having a quiet evening at home with his wife.

Still, as popular as Gehrig would become, he did almost nothing to advance the home run, even with as many as he hit. Ruth had made the homer a vehicle for narcissism, and only those with an air of self-absorption would from here on out stand as home run gods. Even those who wouldn't get to that level would betray how much of a celebrity the home run had become. It's why a .220 hitter that happens to manage a lucky homer will come out of the dugout for a curtain call.

The '27 Yankees, to be sure, made the home run into celebrity chic, as about everyone in the batting order could hit one out, including Meusel, Lazzeri, center fielder Earle Combs, and second baseman Mark Koenig. Miler Huggins was a vital component as well, as that season he decided to bat Gehrig in the cleanup spot and put Ruth in the three-hole. Babe still led the league in walks with 144 (thus creating Gehrig's RBI bonanza) but the poison of facing the Iron Horse cost teams dearly. This explains why the Yankees won 110 games (no one would win more until the 1954 Indians), won the pennant by 18½ games, and blew away the Pirates in a four-game World Series sweep highlighted by a Ruth homer in each of the last two games.

More has been written about Ruth's 60-homer season—when he outhomered each of the seven other AL teams by himself—than about the fall of Rome. But the feat cannot be fully appreciated without knowing that as late as mid-August Gehrig had him beat, 37 to 36. Ruth, who never really knew why Gehrig disliked him so much, knew he owed a lot to the muscular man batting behind him, and that without their natural rivalry (a friendly one on Babe's part, but not on Gehrig's), he may have settled into a 45- to 50-homer groove. With it, he turned the last six weeks of 1927 into a shooting gallery. He hit 6 in as many games the first week of September, then No. 50 on the eleventh. No. 57 was a grand slam off Lefty Grove—his second slam in three days—then came a pair on Sepember 29. He was sitting on 59 on the penultimate day of the season, September 30 at a barely populated Yankee Stadium. After getting a couple of hits against Senators' southpaw Tom Zachary (against whom he had already hit 3 out during the season), Ruth came to bat in the bottom of the eighth in a 2-2 game, 2 outs and Koenig on third.

As Zachary later recalled, he wasn't in the mood to challenge Ruth and threw him "the kind of ball no other hitter would even have tried for. It was a curve ball, high, straight at him. You might call it a bean ball. I wanted to get the Babe away from the plate. Instead of stepping back, he waded into the ball. He lunged for it before it ever got to the plate and pulled it around into the stands. He never hit a worse ball in his life."

The New York press corps hadn't become fixated on 60 as a mythical chef d'oeuvre until the last week. Now with the deed done, the writers went shamelessly overboard on the theme (if not the managing editors of their papers, none of which put the Ruth story on the front page), dishing up a hyperbolic spectacle of adulation that seemed improbable given the meager crowd.

> Well, the Babe went and did it! Ten thousand fans shouted themselves hoarse when a terrific clout from George Ruth's bat sailed into the right field bleachers for the big fellow's sixtieth home run. . . .
>
> The demonstration which followed was the greatest seen in New York in years. Everybody was on his feet, cheering and yelling. It sounded like one of those Al Smith demonstrations at the last Democratic convention, but this was all spontaneous. (Fred Lieb, *New York Post*)

> As the mighty Babe galloped around the base paths, the stands became one tumultuous ovation. Nothing like it has been seen since the

> Stadium was built. . . . No star of the great White Way was ever acclaimed so fervently. Even the veteran newspapermen, whose calloused souls have been accustomed to such demonstrations, stopped their typewriters, rose to their feet, and applauded.
>
> The players chorused their approval. They jumped to their feet as the ball descended among the bleacherites, and they stamped their feet and slapped each other on the back. (Charles Segar, New York *Daily Mirror*)

> A child of destiny is George Herman. He moves in his orbit like a planet.
>
> Succumb to the power and the romance of this man. Drop your cynicism and feel the athletic marvel that this big, uncouth fellow has accomplished. . . .
>
> I get a tremendous kick out of that egg. I like to have illusions about him. I like to believe that everything about him is on the level. I don't trust many things in sports, but Ruth I do, and I still get that silly feeling in my throat when he conks one. I'm tickled silly over his breaking the record. (Paul Gallico, New York *Daily News*)

And if there had been a backlash against Ruth among the literati, John Kieran of the *Times* made it abundantly clear all was forgiven:

> Supposedly "over the hill," slipping down the steps of Time, stumbling toward the discard, six years past his peak, Babe Ruth stepped out and hung up a new record at which all the sport world may stand and wonder. What Big Bill Tilden couldn't do on the tennis court, Babe Ruth has done on the diamond. What Dempsey couldn't do with his fists, Ruth has done with his bat. He came back.
>
> Put it in the book in letters of gold. It will be a long time before any one betters that home-run mark, and a still longer time before any aging athlete makes such a gallant and glorious charge over the comeback trail.

From prose, Kieran leaped to poetry, some of which went:

> You may rave, I say, till the break of day, but the truth remains the truth:
> From "One Ole Cat" to the last, "At Bat" was there ever a guy like Ruth?
> He has manned his guns and hit home runs from here to the Golden Gate;
> With vim and verve he has walloped the curve from Texas to Duluth,
> Which is no small task, and I beg to ask: Was there ever a guy like Ruth?

The Babe himself was a bit giddy—and overly gracious to the man who was becoming more and more alienated from him. "Will I ever break this again?" he said. "I don't know, and I don't care, but if I don't I know who will. Wait till that bozo over there"—meaning Gehrig—"gets waded into them again and they may forget that a guy named Ruth ever lived."

Then in a more unguarded moment, he smiled hard and said, "Sixty. Let's see some son of a bitch beat that."

Ruth was the first SOB to try. In the season's last game, he went without a homer. And from then on even he would become secondary to the power and mythology of that number.

Ruth was hardly getting irrelevant. Making $70,000 in 1927, he would top out at $80,000 in the 1930s—and was worth every penny of it. Over each of the next five seasons he would notch at least 41 homers—including 54 in 1929—137 RBIs and a .323 average. His last great year, 1931, in fact, may have been his finest writ. At age 36 he hit 46 homers with 163 RBIs and a .373 average (though he again lost the MVP, this time to Lefty Grove). Still, as Benny Bengough, the Yankee catcher in 1927, later mused, "We felt Babe Ruth might hit 65 the next year. He hit 60 and I imagine the next year Babe figured, well, I'll probably hit 65 or 70. He figured, if I played tomorrow, I might hit another."

But Babe was wrong, and gradually his hold on the game slipped—although he did have one more other-worldly moment stored up, to come in 1932. As for the Yankees, they too lost their groove, leaving as their final testament to their Roaring Twenties dynasty a sixth pennant in eight years in 1928 and victory in the World Series—settling a score with the Cardinals by sweeping them aside in four laughers. In that Series Ruth hit .625 and had 3 homers in Game 4, while Gehrig hit .545 with 4 homers to equal Babe's record. Gehrig's first shot, a three-run blow in the first inning of Game 2, made Grover Cleveland Alexander pay for '26, and he hit two off Jess Haines in Game 3 after being walked five straight times. In all the Yankees hit 9 dingers that Series, a record at the time.

Then in 1929, the year of the stock market crash, when the country would turn upside down and the era of raw excess reached its end, came a reversal of fortune in baseball as well. Now it was Connie Mack's turn to live large, by riding the long ball.

Beast and Bucketfoot

In finding his lost legacy, Mack's epiphany about the home run was delivered by its once-famous namesake player, Home Run Baker. In 1924 Baker was managing the Easton, Pennsylvania, club in the Eastern Shore League when he tipped off his old boss about the Easton catcher, James Emory Foxx, then a blocky 17-year-old with bestial power. Mack invited the kid, called "Jimmie," to the Athletics' camp, signed him, and over the next three years played him sparingly behind All-Star catcher Mickey Cochrane. In 1927 Mack switched him to first base to get him into games, and Foxx hit over.300 for two seasons, tacking on 13 homers in 1928—including the longest blow likely ever hit at Shibe Park that went completely over the left field stands. The following season he was being called "The Beast" and, inevitably, "the right-handed Babe Ruth." That year Foxx, who bore a striking facial resemblance to Ruth, cracked 33 homers (the Babe and Gehrig were 1-2 in the league with 46 and 35) and had 117 RBIs and a .354 average.

There were other long-ball turks around—most notably Foxx's teammate, left fielder Al Simmons, who hit 34, led the loop with 157 RBIs and was second with a .365 average. Still, Foxx was the first to stir up a Ruth-like sense of anticipation when he came to bat. He was apt to hit one as high and deep as the Babe. He also looked the part. At 5 feet 11 inches and 190 pounds he was so muscular and his neck so thick that people would swear he was much bigger, say, the size of a bank vault. How tough a bird was Foxx? Before playing ball, he tried to enlist in the army but failed—primarily because he happened to be 10 years old at the time! He talked the part, too.

"Let me get a good grip on the bat, as if I wanted to leave my fingerprints in the wood," he once explained his hitting approach. "Let me swing with a quick snap which comes with a powerful wrist, and if I've gotten the back of the ball it sure will travel."

Everything about these A's would have curdled Mack's prim sensibilities a decade before. Foxx, for example, liked to intensify his beastly image by cutting out the sleeves of his uniform shirt, giving more freedom to a pair of biceps that seemed pumped with freon. Simmons (real name Aloysius Szymanki) had a batting stance that invited reprobation—left foot striding away from the pitch toward third base, the proverbial "step in the bucket," which is supposed to sap any authority from a swing. Yet "Bucketfoot" Simmons, as he was called in grudging admiration, somehow maintained his hip balance even while bailing out, and also had very long arms and used a very long bat—more than forty inches—which he controlled through the teeth of the hitting zone.

Simmons, who had a sallow complexion and looked pale and sickly, was quite a sight when he let his fiery temper control him, which was often. At those times, when his disposition was as foul as his mouth, he could be relied on to trash dugouts and locker rooms. Rather than order him to cool it, though, Mack timidly groveled to Simmons, even making sure to ask him whether he approved of each day's lineup card. After Mack brought in as charity cases the hoary Ty Cobb and Tris Speaker in 1928, Simmons played in center field between them and had to run down so many balls they couldn't reach that he complained undiplomatically, "If this keeps us, I'll be an old man myself." At season's end, both old-timers were cut loose and were gone from the game.

That Mack paid $50,000 to obtain Simmons from Milwaukee of the American Association was out of character, too. But Mack was determined to win again, and so the man who had sold off his championship teams and balked at paying Jack Dunn $40,000 for Babe Ruth now went as far as to pay Dunn $100,000 in 1927 for pitcher Lefty Grove. In 1929, Mack was faced with Simmons' demand for a three-year contract with $100,00. The two wrangled all during spring training until just moments before opening day when Mack gave in. Simmons then went out and hit a home run on the first pitch he saw. But then Simmons' flair for the dramatic was akin to Babe Ruth's. In the first game of one doubleheader he injured his knee. Told the only way he could play is if he could walk around the bases, he was sent up to pinch-hit in the nightcap and did just that, by hitting a game-winning 3-run homer. At least that's how the story goes.

With Foxx and Simmons, the A's had not only a right-handed Ruth but a right-handed Ruth-Gehrig tandem. The pair made the comparison plausible when they drove the team to the 1929 pennant by seven games over the Yankees and played the Cubs in the World Series. Foxx set the tone in the opener with a seventh-inning blast that broke open a scoreless game, then mashed a 3-run shot in the Game 2 win. Simmons, who also homered in Game 2, left his mark in Game 4. With the A's trailing 8-0, he led off the seventh with a homer, whereupon the team batted around—the key was when Hack Wilson misplayed a Mule Haas fly ball into a 3-run inside-the-park homer—and Simmons came up again with the score now 8-7. Simmons singled to tie it, and the A's tacked on two more in an historic 10-run inning to win 10-8. They ended the Series the next day.

In 1930 Beast and Bucketfoot had 37 and 36 homers, respectively, to Ruth's 49 and Gehrig's 41. The order of the RBI finish was Gehrig (174), Simmons (165), Foxx (156), Ruth (153). Simmons led in average with .381, nipping Gehrig by 2 points. However, the Yankees dropped to third place and Mack again went to the Series, against the Cardinals' "Gas House Gang." Again Foxx came up big. With the Series tied two games apiece the Beast came up in the top of the ninth at Sportsman's Park, the game scoreless, a man on. Facing the old spitballer Burleigh Grimes, he put 1 deep into the bleachers for the margin of the 2-0 win. The next day Simmons popped his second homer of the Series to sew up a 7-1 series-clinching victory.

However, as awesome a combo as they were, the big home run story of 1930 was written in the NL, by a human bowling ball with the perfect nickname for a free-swinger who swung his forty-ounce bat the way he went through life—with not one ounce of discipline.

Hack Attack

For two years the Depression didn't dent baseball's gate appeal. Attendance spilled over 10 million for the first time in 1930 and the $2 million profit turned by the big leagues tripled that of 1929. The arrival of a new decade, in fact, marked the absolute apex of the game's home run-intoxicated Golden Age. In the NL particularly the pitchers must have been shell shocked, as the league batting average spiked at .303 (the first and only time post-1900 a league batted over .300). That year, which still makes historians quiver, no less than *eleven* Cardinals hit over .300, as did nine Giants, eight Phillies, and seven Pirates. New York's Bill Terry, who led the league with a .401 average, had 254 hits, Philadelphia's Chuck Klein 250, and Brooklyn's Babe Herman 241—three of the top 10 one-year totals of all time. (The AL was no slouch, either, hitting .288.) Carried by this ebb tide came 892 home runs, 138 more than the '29 record, which included five men hitting 32 or more four-baggers led by Klein's then-league-record 43 and Giant Mel Ott's 42. In 1930, five NLers had 35 or more. But it was the guy who had tied with Rogers Hornsby for third place the year before with 39, Cubs outfielder Lewis Robert "Hack" Wilson, who made even Ruth, Gehrig, Foxx, and Simmons look like small change.

Wilson, who was surely the strangest put-together ballplayer ever (even counting Yogi Berra and Smokey Burgess here), looked like two different halves stuck together. He stood just five feet 6 inches and 195 pounds, and if Ruth had gooney bird legs Hack's were like coasters under a big sofa. The definition of the word *compact,* Wilson's chest and arms were immense. He wore a size-18 collar and a size-6 shoe. Like Foxx, he could break a person in half as a pubescent. Born in Ellwood City, Pennsylvania, in 1900, he worked in the steel mills for $4 a week on a finishing gang, swinging a sledge hammer. He made the big leagues with the

Giants in 1923 but washed out under John McGraw, then rescued from the minors by the Cubs in 1926 for $5,000.

Wielding a long truncheon of a bat, over forty inches and forty ounces, Wilson may have looked like a troll but he didn't milk his small strike zone; instead he swiped vicious "hacks" at high fastballs over his head (though like Ruth he was far more controlled than today's sluggers, never striking out 100 times in any season). At the same time he hit over .300 six straight seasons, and five times over both 30 homers and 100 RBIs. He led or shared the league homer crown in 1926 (21), 1927 (30), and 1928 (31). Then in 1930 he let his wad go in one stupendous gush that gets my vote as baseball's most outrageous power-hitting season (yes, even after all the Ruth-crooning—and yes, Barry, even better than yours).

Hack, who got that nickname because he looked like a pile, or hack, of bricks, found out what Ernie Banks and Sammy Sosa would years later—hitting at cramped Wrigley Field is a lot of fun when the Lake Michigan wind is blowing toward the outfield. Not that the Cubs were smart enough to take advantage of it. When Joe McCarthy broke in as a manager with the team in 1926, they had powderpuff hitters. Marse Joe brought in such heavy hitters as Kiki Cuyler and Hornsby to complement Wilson and in the pennant-winning season of 1929 the club hit 140 homers. With the 171-homer orgy of 1930, that two-year total of 311 beat the 1927–1928 Yankees (to whom the sports world is still genuflecting) by 20 homers.

For Wilson, who had hit .471 in the '29 Series but was crucified for his shoddy fielding, the homers just kept on coming. He hit 3 on July 26 and by mid-August he had 44 big ones, breaking Klein's very short-lived league record. On September 5 he had 50. Five days later he had a new RBI record in his pocket with 176, breaking Gehrig's mark. On the twenty-seventh he hit his last 2 dingers against Cincinnati—55 and 56—only 4 shy of Ruth's standard and better than the Babe would do getting near it—and the only time Ruth was ever beaten out by a NL home run hitter when playing a full season. More amazingly, his RBI total ran out at, gulp, *190*. Not only is this number seemingly inviolate—no one has gotten closer to it than Gehrig's 184 in 1931. Hack embellished it sixty-nine years later, or twenty-one years after his death, when in 1999 baseball heeded newfound data and credited Wilson with one more RBI from that season, bringing it to 191.

This opens up the thorny issue of baseball's selective application of postdated stats. The truth is that if baseball had any courage, by all rights

Babe Ruth would be credited with *715* homers. Indeed, because of other statistical digs, in 1999 Ruth had 6 additional walks added, bringing his then-record—since broken by Rickey Henderson—to 2,062. But that sepulchral 714 is a different matter, apparently off-limits to revision. The game's record keepers sigh in relief that—so far—no one has uncovered Ruth having hit any balls into the stands on a bounce, which until 1931 would have been home runs, not the familiar ground-rule doubles. The closest call, ferreted out by retrosheet.com's Bob McConnell, came on June 16, 1923, during a game against the Browns. As the *New York Times'* game story read, "A near home run by Babe Ruth featured the fifth [inning]. The ball dropped at the base of the left field stand—away off the Babe's usual channel—and almost bounced into the stands. But Ken Williams rescued it in time and held his home-run rival to second base."

A potential bug did arise, however, two decades before when baseball empowered a special committee to verify all stats for the impending first edition of the *Baseball Encyclopedia* in 1969. Uh-oh. The panel determined that Ruth had *lost* a home run during the eleven years prior to 1931 when the author of a game-winning homer in the bottom of the ninth only got credit for as many bases as was needed to push home the winning run to score; even if he ran all the way home, if the bases had been loaded in a tie game, all he'd get was a single. To restore the homer would have meant the hallowed Ruth number would be 715. It also meant baseball said "never mind." So that 715th homer is still orbiting in the ionosphere.

Wilson made the most of his empyrean year. After the season he signed for a salary of $35,000 and as the Baseball Writers Association's selection as the league's MVP pocketed another $1,000 from the Cubs. But, like Ruth he was doomed to live in the shadow of his own masterwork, for a couple of reasons. First was the introduction for the 1931 season of yet another new and improved ball, this one with a cushioned cork center that the Spalding and Reach people intended to extend the life of their horsehides by keeping them from becoming lopsided, as they were from getting whacked so hard. Again, lazy revisionists have blathered the canard that baseball intentionally "deadened" the ball that year when hitting got out of control. They've made this induction because hitting collapsed in 1931.

However, it seems highly specious that the baseball establishment would have wanted to obviate hitting and with it the home run just as the Depression was forcing people to choose between their leisure diversions. More likely is that the collapse was an unfortunate by-product of the new ball, which in any case failed to prevent the ball-bending. And yet it is intriguing that the game's lords did nothing to ditch the ball, since it remained on the field until the early 1940s. It's plausible that baseball had become somewhat jaded to the homer, and always expected it to come to the rescue anyway.

Wilson had a greater handicap still. The NL went a step further, raising the seams of its ball and thus allowing pitchers to once again get a tight grip, especially on the bat-deflating curveball. In fact, as Bill Starr points out in *Clearing the Bases*, 1931 was "the year the National League acquired its reputation as a curveball league," the result of which was that balls that had flown over moved-in fences became pop flies or strikes. Along with a 26-point drop in batting average to .277, homers plunged by *400* to 493, the first time in a decade the senior league had fewer than the junior league, where the drop was held to 10 points (to .278) and 97 homers (to 576). Wilson took the biggest dive—from 56 to *13*, from 191 RBIs to 60, from .356 to .261.

Other men like Hack, who parlayed shallow home-field dimensions into inflated homer totals, also suffered. The Braves' Wally Berger fell from 38 to 19, Klein from 40 to 31, Gabby Hartnett from 37 to 8, Babe Herman from 35 to 18. And while dingers would rise again, the NL would go through the decade firmly behind the AL.

Fortunately for the NL, the Gas House Gang was a perfect fit for the new/old order, as nickel-and-dime hitters such as Frankie Frisch, Pepper Martin, and Sparky Adams took a team with 60 homers to the championship in '32, beating the mighty A's of Foxx and Simmons in a seven-game World Series in which the Cardinals hit exactly 2 homers (only one less than the A's 3, all by Foxx and Simmons). But, again, with paranormal World Series capriciousness, the crucial hit in the 4-2 Game 7 victory was a 2-run shot by light-hitting George Watkins.

Just as damaging to Hack Wilson as anything about the ball, though, was that he could deal with pitched high balls far better than glass-enclosed highballs. Unlike many of the game's heavy-drinking stars—Ruth, Alexander, Foxx, Cochrane—Wilson was a mean drunk. Since he was drunk most of the time, he was mean a lot, often precipitating a number of on- and off-field incidents, including going into the stands after heckling fans and into the Reds' dugout after pitcher Ray Kolp, earning an ejection. Later, as both teams waited at Chicago's Union Station for their trains, he got into a fight with another Reds' pitcher, Pete Donohue, and knocked him cold.

During his horrific 1931 season, an inebriated Wilson was benched by Hornsby before an early September game in Cincinnati. That night, on the train back to Chicago, Hack and his Cubs drinking buddy, Pat Malone, argued with two sportswriters, both of whom Wilson decked. He also went looking for Hornsby, but when that human callous of a man came out of his berth in his boxer shorts and his fists up, Hack sobered up quick, though he was suspended for the rest of the season and then dumped to the Dodgers for chump change, $45,000, and a bush-league pitcher.

Amazingly, Wilson hit .297 and 23 homers for the Dodgers—including one as a pinch-hitter after being roused from a deep slumber in the clubhouse, surrounded by beer cans—but by 1934 he was in the bushes. He would live only fourteen more years before dying of alcoholism at age 48, penniless and forgotten, much like Pete Browning. It took another thirty-three years for him to get into the Hall of Fame.

Hack Wilson's plight was a parable of the Depression, which caught up to baseball in 1931, lending overall context to the new "dead ball" era as a time of drought and ruined lives. As attendance fell by 3 million, and profits to just $217,000 in 1931, home runs suddenly seemed less like materialistic accessories and more like little uplifting homilies. And in the depths of the big chill of 1932 came one home run in particular that would come to be baseball's Holy Grail.

Even if it didn't happen quite like they say it did.

7

The Called Shot and Other Fables

Raging Beasts

Besides the ball issue, the home run shrinkage had much to do with the fact that players in the '30s simply weren't as good as those in the '20s. Consider that sixty-eight players were elected to the Hall of Fame who played between 1920 and 1939—and forty-four of them were playing in 1930 alone. (Though to keep this in context, the entire twenty-year period produced more Hall of Famers than any other two-decade slice of history.) Actually, hitting didn't really die; it basically returned to the levels of the mid-1920s, which wasn't exactly cream cheese. The paroxysm of 1930 may have been gone but during the '30s the AL regularly kept its batting average near or above .280. Compare that with the AL's .267 average, and the NL's .261 in 2001, in what is considered a "hitter's era."

And the home run? While they weren't as copious, it was in this decade that not one but two sluggers came closer than Hack Wilson did to Ruth's 60, only proving again that once the homer got into baseball's blood no mere softened core was going to transfuse it out. Even after the great fall of 1931, Chuck Klein and Mel Ott *increased* their homers in 1932, Klein from 31 to 38, Ott from 29 to 38. And Klein and Jimmie Foxx each won a Triple Crown, Klein in '32, Foxx in '33—and the Beast missed by 3 batting points of doing it in '32.

Foxx also made the first of those serious runs at Ruth during 1932. In fact, he got to 50 faster than Ruth had in 1927—getting there on September 3 when he smacked Nos. 50 and 51 against Boston. In a late September series against the Yankees, he clocked 3 to tie Wilson's 56, and on September 24 against Washington he hit his second grand slam in three days. A day later in the season finale came No. 58, to go with a .364 average and 169 RBIs. The problem for the A's was that while they slammed a then-record 173 homers (just how big was that chill anyway?), and while Simmons came in third with 35 (behind Ruth's 41) and tied for second with Lou Gehrig with 151 RBIs, the pitching was awful and the resurgent Yankees mauled them by 13 games to win the pennant.

This catastrophic season by the team that had won 107 games the year before slapped Connie Mack out of his home run fantasia and into Depression-era reality. With profits vaporizing around baseball, in 1932 the owners colluded to cut salaries by $1 million and Mack was more than willing to do his part. In a 1914 déjà vu, Mack was prepared to go back to losing if he could do it with black ink. After the season, he sold Simmons and two other veterans to the White Sox for $100,000.

Foxx, whose 1933 Triple Crown and MVP season (48 homers, 163 RBIs, .356) included home runs in four consecutive at-bats over two games and a record 9-RBI game, would go too. Mack was not happy when Foxx had the nerve to ask for a raise, Triple Crown or not, and gave in kicking and screaming to a bargain-basement salary of $18,000. Foxx hit 44 homers in 1934 and a league-high 36 in 1935, but the team sank to dead last, giving Mack an out to sell Foxx and pitcher John Marcum to the Red Sox, who were now owned by 32-year-old millionaire Tom Yawkey, for $150,000, plus pitcher Gordon Rhodes, and catcher George Savino. (Yawkey also lifted Eddie Collins from Mack's coaching staff to become the Red Sox' general manager.) This was every bit the heist that the Babe Ruth trade was in 1920, only now in Boston's favor. Indeed, the "Curse of the Beast" did no less than bring the Sox back to the ranks of the living, albeit the frustrated living—and commit the A's to the walking dead for the next fifteen years.

Ruth, too, felt the Depression sting. He was earning $80,000 in 1931, when he hit .373 (second to Simmons), tied Gehrig with 46 homers, and was second to him in RBIs (181 to 163). Ed Barrow, though, cut him back to $75,000, and he had to bitch and moan to get that much. This was now the Ruth most familiar to later generations—the fat Elvis, and yet at 37 he was still a monster. While 1931 was the last of a dozen times he led or co-led the league in homers, in '32 he pounded 41, drove in 137 runs and hit .341.

By now it was no sin being worse than Gehrig in his prime. As it was,

Babe was lucky to tie Gehrig for the homer crown in '31, since Lou lost one in April when a runner mistakenly thought a Gehrig shot was caught and left the field. Gehrig, rounding third, passed him—making it a triple. The Gehrig rampage was in full throttle. He hit 3 grand slams in four days that season among 6 dingers in as many games. In 1934, when he won *his* Triple Crown (.363, 49, 165), he would homer in four straight at-bats and hit his 17th career grand slam, bypassing Ruth en route to his still-all-time record of 23. He'd lead the league in homers again, with 49 in 1936, and score a career-high in runs, 167, at age 33. And, of course, he hadn't missed a game since 1925. Indomitable, that was the Iron Horse.

And yet, as eminent as Gehrig was, even when Ruth eroded, he could not do what the Babe had done in the early 1920s—take the Yankees to a pennant on the gale-like force of his being. It's why Gehrig will always live in Ruth's shadow. Of course, Ruth also hit a lot more homers in all, which might matter even more. But even when Lou was on a par in the home run production business, the force was with Babe.

As proof, consider the 1932 World Series.

"It's in the Papers, Isn't It?"

Time to genuflect again. For now we have come upon baseball's greatest, most irreducible myth—Babe Ruth's "Called Shot," a folk ballad so grand that even though several generations of cynics have pin-pricked it to death, no one has clinically exposed it as a fraud. The clichéd response to the fable is that its veracity is irrelevant anyway, that baseball needs this magic flute as a buffer against reality, such as $5 beer at ballparks and rotating free agents. Well, I don't know about you but I'm too old to be Peter Pan, and I don't need a home run from 1932 to convince me that the game can be joyously preternatural—hell, I think the two Yankee game-winning homers on consecutive days in the 2001 World Series make Ruth's famous blow seem like a no-pressure lark.

Still, don't come to me to puncture the myth. I'm just as powerless against its mythic brick and mortar. But I can give you my opinion and it's that Babe, God bless him, didn't call anything that October 1st except maybe room service and a few whorehouses after the game. But he was being Babe, which meant he was having just a little too much of a good time and put himself out on a limb that would be morphed into a high wire by, well, the force of his being.

Actually, the World Series was a confection for Ruth after a trying season, when he missed games with leg and other injuries (not VD-related, I don't think). He was feeling weak when the Series began against the Cubs, but the bad blood between the two teams juiced him up. For one thing, Joe McCarthy, who'd become Yankee manager in 1931, was facing the team that fired him. Ruth, who had put in for the manager's job only to be rebuffed by Ed Barrow, resented McCarthy but was mollified when Marse Joe continued the usual double standard of behavior for him. For another, the Cubs had acquired Mark Koenig in midseason, yet weren't going to pay him a full Series share. From the start Ruth ragged the Cubs for it. In return, wrote Robert Creamer in his book *Babe*, the Cubs "call(ed) him fat and old and washed up, and they dragged out the old 'nigger' cry. Guy Bush, a dark-haired, swarthy Mississippian, was [the game one pitcher] and the Yankees yelled back, 'Who are you calling a nigger? Look at your pitcher!'"

This Algonquin round table debate broke out into bench-jockey warfare, but it did nothing for the Cubs, who were ravaged 12-6 and 5-2 in New York. When the Series moved to Chicago, Ruth and his second wife, Claire, were spat on by a crowd outside the hotel. At Wrigley Field, as he waited to hit in the first inning, he was bombarded by oranges, apples, and other things, and showily pointed to the right field bleachers, then came up and hit the first pitch from Charlie Root for a 3-run homer.

Gehrig hit his second homer of the Series in the third, but in the fifth it was a 4-4 game when with 1 out Ruth waddled plateward to lusty booing by 30,000 people. Several Cubs came up the dugout steps to heckle him as Root's first pitch came in for a called strike. Now Ruth, hearing some inner voice, lifted a finger (no, not that one) on his right hand, acknowledging the strike. After 2 balls, Root watched another called strike and Ruth did the same thing, with two fingers, but in the myth he "pointed" them to center field while iterating to catcher Gabby Hartnett, "It takes only one to hit it." Ruth and Root exchanged words—Gehrig, in the on-deck circle, later said Ruth's were, "I'm going to knock the next pitch down your goddamned throat."

A 16-mm film exists of the fateful at-bat, shot by a Cubs fan named Matt Kandle sitting on the third base side behind home plate, but the grainy images of Ruth jabbing his hand seem to prove that Ruth did not point to center field but rather to the Cubs dugout. After kicking a lemon thrown at him toward the Cubs' dugout, Ruth then slammed Root's next pitch, a change-up low and a bit away, out—*way* out, over the center field bleachers just to the right of the scoreboard and through a large tree across the street, arguably the longest ball ever hit at Wrigley. Ruth all but danced around the bases, dodging thrown garbage. When he got to third, he slapped his knees and yelled to the Cub bench, "Squeeze the Eagle Club," a reference to Koenig's nickname. We only wish that this excursion—Ruth's 15th and last World Series blast, had been preserved by even one camera. Curiously, the only photos of the occasion show Ruth crossing the plate, head down, greeted by Gehrig, without flourish.

It is possible that while Ruth certainly enjoyed the moment, he never believed he would be spinning yarns about it years from then. Right after Ruth, Gehrig hit another shot out on the first pitch, sending the Yankees to a 7-5 win. And Ruth's first reaction in the victorious locker room was to warble, "Did Mr. Ruth chase those guys back into the dugout? Mr. Ruth sure did!"

Not, say, "Did Mr. Ruth call his shot? Mr. Ruth sure did!"

That angle emerged the next day, after a game story by Joe Williams in the *New York World-Telegram*, headlined RUTH CALLS SHOT AS HE PUTS HOMER NO. 2 IN SIDE POCKET. Of the big blow, Williams wrote:

> In the fifth, with the Cubs riding him unmercifully from the bench, Ruth pointed to center and punched a screaming liner to a spot where no ball has ever been hit before.

The "paper of record," the *Times*, was more oblique—although John Drebinger's game story did make page one, the headline was a prosaic YANKEES BEAT CUBS 7-5 FOR THIRD STRAIGHT IN WORLD SERIES BEFORE 51,000. The text, noting the lemon incident, read:

> It seems decidedly unhealthy for any one to taunt the great man Ruth too much and very soon the crowd was to learn its lesson. . . . In no mistaken emotions, the Babe notified the crowd that the nature of his retaliation would be a wallop right out of the confines of the park.
>
> Root pitched two balls and two strikes while Ruth signaled with his fingers after each pitch to let the spectators know exactly how the situation stood. Then the mightiest blow of all fell. It was a tremendous smash that tore down the centre of the field in an enormous arc . . . easily one of his most gorgeous [home runs]. The crowd, suddenly unmindful of everything save that it had just witnessed an epic feat, hailed the Babe with a salvo of applause.

In the ensuing days, other writers chimed in on this theme—with Paul Gallico laying it on thick: Ruth, he wrote in the *Daily News*, "pointed like a duellist to the spot where he expected to send his rapier home." Even so, nobody made that much of the Called Shot that winter, and rather than trail Ruth around the following season it seemed like a sidebar. The *Reach Guide*, in its review of the 1932 season, gave it one sentence, noting Ruth's "tremendous drive after indicating in pantomime to his hostile admirers what he proposed to do, and did."

What of those newsreel films of the moment? Actually, there are none; those that have been presented as such in documentaries are recreations, the kind which were often made *ex post* to stand in as real history. A radio broadcast? You may have heard a call of the Called Shot that was featured on a CD a few years ago that accompanied an anthology of great sports moments, *And the Crowd Goes Wild*. This is a purported NBC Radio broadcast of that game, and on it announcer Tom Manning nearly comes unstrung as he describes the storied at-bat this way, after the second called strike:

> Boy, the Cubs are giving it to Babe now! . . . And he steps about two feet away from home plate. Now he steps towards the Cubs' dugout! We thought for a moment that he was going over and toss his bat at them or something. No, he's smiling at them. He takes off his hat, he holds up his two fingers with his right hand. Now he drops his bat and he's indicating that the count is ball two and strike two. He gets back into the batter's box. The umpire again warns the Cubs. Charlie Root gets his signal.
>
> And Babe Ruth steps out of the batter's box again! He's holding up his two and two. Oh, oh, and now Babe Ruth is pointing out to center field. And he's yelling at the Cubs that the next pitch over is going into center field! Someone just tossed a lemon down there. Babe Ruth has picked up the lemon and now he tosses it over to the Cubs' bench. He didn't throw anything, he sort of kicked it over there. After he turns, he points again to center field! And here's the pitch. It's going! Babe Ruth connects and here it goes! And it's a home run! It's gone! Whoopee! Listen to that crowd!

The only problem with this wonderful tableau of the times is that Manning's pitch sequence—ball, strike, strike, ball—is wrong. Which means Manning was extremely dyslexic or that it was an audio recreation that was influenced by the fact that ever since that day at Wrigley, even the people who had been on the field later became seriously confused about what the pitch count had been—including no less than the Babe himself, who in his 1947 autobiography said he hit an 0-and-2 pitch. This was the way it went down in the movie made of his life in 1948, the year he died. The movie, *The Babe Ruth Story*, with William Bendix in the lead role, may now be the *grand bouffe* of bad movies but then it was a major event that deified the Ruth legend, including the Called Shot, portrayed the way it might be today on *Saturday Night Live*, with a grim Bendix, clay nose attached to his face, gesticulating with comically absurd exaggeration.

Before this, on the rare occasions when Ruth had spoken of the homer, he had been coy, once confiding that "I didn't exactly point to any spot, I just sorta waved at the whole fence," and admitting, "It was damned foolishness." Ford Frick later recalled that only days after the game he asked Ruth if he had really pointed at all. "It's in the papers, isn't it?" was all Ruth would say, and all he needed to. And a Brooklyn Dodger trainer, Ed Froelich, said that Ruth had once told him that those who believed the tale are "full of crap up to their eyeballs. I may be dumb but I'm not that dumb. I'm going to point to the centerfield bleachers with a barracuda like Root out there? On the next pitch they'd be picking it out of my ear with a pair of tweezers." That was an assessment that Charlie Root vehemently agreed with, saying that if Ruth would have done any pointing, Root would have "knocked him on his ass" on the next pitch instead of giving him a hittable ball. But, of course, it wasn't an 0-2 pitch; it was a 2-2 pitch, limiting Root's options.

Unaware of the confusion he was causing, all a dying Ruth evidently wanted to do was ensure the Called Shot would outlive him, in all its mythical glory. And of course it has.

Conversely, Lou Gehrig's own Series shining (.549, 3 homers, 8 RBIs to Ruth's .333, 2, 6) has been dimmed by time. And Gehrig, who by then had stopped talking to Ruth because of an unflattering remark Babe made about Lou's mother, may have unwittingly coined the best epitaph of the whole manic episode.

"What do you think of the nerve of that big monkey calling his shot and getting away with it?" he said.

More than seventy years later, the big monkey still is.

Master Melvin's Mash

With the exception of Hack Wilson's barrage of 1930, the NL home run theme from the late 1920s through the mid-1930s was mainly the tug-of-war between the Phillies' Chuck Klein and the Giants' Mel Ott. The battle was joined in 1929 when each man had 42 homers coming into a doubleheader pitting their teams on the season's final day. After Klein popped one off Carl Hubbell in the opener to take the lead, the Phillie pitchers went wimpy and intentionally walked Ott *five* times in the nightcap rather than giving him a fair shot—the last time with *the bases loaded,* one of only three times that has happened in history. Over the next four years Klein won the home run crown three times and the two tied in 1932, each hitting 38.

Such was the homer anorexia in the league, however, that when Klein won the Triple Crown in '33 (trivia time: with Jimmie Foxx winning it in the AL, this was the only time one season had two Triple Crowns), he had his lowest homer count in five years—28 (with a .368 average and 120 RBIs). The feat was so humdrum that Klein was deemed replaceable and traded to the Cubs after the season for three players including Mark Koenig. Displaced from the homer factory of the Baker Bowl, Klein still hit over 20 homers three more times, and after being traded back to the Phillies in 1936 he had a 4-homer game against the Pirates—at Forbes Field, no less. Yet Klein was never quite the pistol he had been and faded into a pinch-hitting spare wheel.

Ott, meanwhile, settled in for the long haul, clearing .300 and 30 homers six times, leading or co-leading in dingers five times. No year, though, was quite the rush for "Master Melvin" as was 1933, when his final swing of the season delivered the ultimate victory.

Ott, of course, had the nuttiest batting style ever. Al Simmons and other hitters may have stepped in the bucket, but the left-handed-swinging Ott stepped into it by lifting his right leg the way a dog would coming upon a hydrant. Many players today do a quick leg lift and kick during their swing to drive harder into the pitch, but Ott did it in slow motion, lifting and *holding* his leg up in midair until the very last moment, his hands dropping down below his belt level, before lashing a forty-inch bat that seemed bigger than the diminutive Ott was at 5 feet 9 inches and 170 pounds.

The immensely popular, mild-mannered Ott didn't only go through this ritual for more drive; the pause was designed to keep his back foot affixed to the ground to prevent too soon of a power-sapping weight shift and utilizing his great lower body strength. While freeze-frame photos have shown many power hitters, such as Ruth, Mantle, and Williams, pounding a ball with their back foot barely touching or even off the ground, Ott made sure not to do that even as a 16-year-old in the Louisiana semipro leagues. Scouts didn't know what to make of him, but a tryout at the Polo Grounds in 1925 convinced John McGraw to sign him and order his coaches not to tinker with the kid's swing. He resisted sending Ott to the minors even for a day, saying "No minor league manager is going to have a chance to ruin him."

And so in 1926, at age 17, Ott became the youngest big leaguer until a 15-year-old Joe Nuxhall came around in 1944, though for two seasons Ott was a student on McGraw's bench. Ott did, however, get in his first homer on July 27, 1927—and is still the youngest ever to hit one, at 18. But wait, it gets better. That first one was an inside-the-park homer—the *only* one of the 511 homers he hit in his twenty-two-year career.

But then, playing in the Polo Grounds, with the right field wall 257 feet away and an overhanging second deck even closer, who needed to run hard to get four bases? Not Ruth and not Ott, who in his career hit 323 homers at home and 188 on the road—at 135 the widest gap between home and road dingers in history. Following are some comparisons of other sluggers who played when a home-park home run advantage was real:

	Home	Away
Chuck Klein	190	110
Babe Ruth	347	367
Lou Gehrig	251	242
Jimmie Foxx	299	235
Hank Greenberg	205	126
Rogers Hornsby	163	138
Ralph Kiner	210	159
Mickey Mantle	266	270
Reggie Jackson	280	283
Willie Mays	335	325
Hank Aaron	385	370
Frank Robinson	321	265
Tucker Ashford	3	3

Give Ott credit. He trained himself to adapt to his park, learning to pull balls right down the line without crimping his overall hitting. Anything outside he would punch the other way. And while pitchers constantly buzzed and beaned him to get him off the plate and disrupt that subtle timing, Ott never backed away. Which explains why he held the NL record for home runs until Willie Mays broke it in 1967, and for walks (1,708) until Joe Morgan broke it in 1982. In 1933, Ott was walked in seven consecutive at-bats over two games. (And I'm not even talking about his superb glove and arm in right field.)

Actually, 1933 was something of a downer for Ott. That year, when McGraw took ill and was replaced by Bill Terry, Ott slumped to 23 homers, 103 RBIs, and a .283 average, the lowest he would hit until 1943. But Terry, as player-manager, hit .322 and drove the team to the pennant and into the World Series against the Senators, who were sparked by their own rookie player-manager, Joe Cronin. The Senators, who would never win another pennant again, beat out the Yankees because of strong hitting (a team .287 average), but with just 60 homers were no fence-busters, while the Giants, who hit an NL-high 82, presented one-swing peril. They also had Carl Hubbell, who hurled two complete game wins, one in eleven innings, and gave up no earned runs in twenty innings.

Ott came out smoking, staking Hubbell to a 2-0 lead in Game 1 with a 2-run homer and also had 3 singles and 3 RBIs in the 4-2 victory. After Hubbell's Game 4 win, the Giants led 3 games to 1. Looking to close the deal in Griffith Stadium on October 7, they let a 3-0 lead get away when Fritz Schulte (no, not Wildfire Schulte) ripped a 3-run shot in the sixth to tie it. The game went to the tenth still tied and the first two Giants made out. This brought up Ott against reliever Jack Russell, who'd been unhittable since coming in, in the seventh. Russell busted 2 strikes on Ott, then decided to go for the kill instead of wasting 1 (what Babe Ruth *thought* Charlie Root did with him).

Bad idea. Ott spanked a low line drive. Schulte, in center, tracked it to the wall, stuck up his glove, and the ball ticked off it and over the fence. At first, the closest umpire, Cy Pfirman, apparently thinking it bounced in, signaled ground-rule double, sending Terry up the dugout steps in hysterics. The other umps, knowing Terry was right, huddled with Pfirman and the call was changed to a homer—a blow as suddenly stunning as Home Run Baker's ninth-inning bolt in 1911 *against* the Giants. In the bottom of the inning Dolf Luque, with the tying and winning runs on base, struck out Joe Kuhel on three pitches to win it for Muggsy McGraw, who would die happy four months later at age 60.

Ott, who hit .389 in the five games, played in two more Series, 1936 and 1937, and had a homer in each—which unfortunately did very little against a new Yankee thresher that began to churn when Joe DiMaggio arrived. Even more unfortunate for Ott was that he chose to manage the Giants in the 1940s with teams that were so bad it earned him a most unwelcome, and undeserving, epitaph from the man who replaced him in 1948, Leo Durocher. Of Master Mel, Durocher famously averred, "Nice guys finish last." This from a guy who had missed managing Jackie Robinson's rookie year because he was stupid enough to play footsy with gamblers and was suspended as Dodger manager. Who is going to listen to him?

Farewell, Babe

Babe Ruth's denouement was the 1933 season when the creaky Bambino, at age 38, mustered his last semblance of a Ruthian year with 34 homers, 103 RBIs, a .301 average, and his last big-time home run—which put the *Good Housekeeping* seal of approval on a new and very bright idea that no one expected to last. This of course was the All-Star Game, an event that had been planned as a one-shot promotion during the Chicago World's Fair that summer, with the game's elite players chosen by the fans in newspaper balloting. When the two leagues' squads took the field at Comiskey Park on July 6, the place was sold out and scalpers were getting *$40* a ticket outside. Most observers thought the game would be stamped as the last appearance on a ball field by John McGraw, who came out of his sick bed to manage the NL team against Connie Mack's AL.

But the game gained cosmic gravitas as the players were introduced with no team fealty but for the names on their shirts. This was the ultimate vehicle of baseball's individualism, a showoff's paradise—and, like the World Series, an easy mark for the ultimate in instant and everlasting gratification, the home run, performed for all baseball fans at once.

For Ruth, it was a familiar cue. Introduced to a tumultuous roar, he came up for his second at-bat in the third inning with the AL up 1-0, Charlie Gehringer on first, Cardinals' southpaw Wild Bill Hallahan the pigeon. Hallahan had walked five by the time he got to Ruth but didn't want to look craven, so he put one in the strike zone that Ruth jacked into the right field stands. That was the only thing anyone would ever remember about the AL's 4-2 win and as such the main dynamic force that necessitated turning the All-Star Game into an annual benediction.

One can only hope Ruth enjoyed that radiant trip around the sacks, because for all purposes it was his farewell tour. His skills and aura dimming fast, in 1934 he had his last whacks in an All-Star Game, at the Polo Grounds, where he first captured baseball. But he would end up a footnote to someone else's glory, Carl Hubbell, whose mercurial screwball whiffed five consecutive Hall of Famers–to–be: Ruth—on three straight called strikes—Gehrig, Foxx, Simmons, and Cronin, though the AL took the contest. Ruth still hit 22 homers and .288 as a decrepit sack of lard that year, and his last Yankee dinger came on September 30 against Washington. Though he had hoped to stay in the Bronx, the Yankees were dying to ease him out, and put out signals to that effect by cutting his salary in half to $17,000 and pointedly naming Gehrig captain that season, when he won his first and only home run crown, with 49.

Told he should make his own deal somewhere else, Ruth got an offer to play part-time and draw fans full-time back in Boston, with the NL bottom-feeding Braves. On February 26, 1935, with none of the fanfare of his arrival, the Yankees gave him his release. Babe turned back the clock on opening day 1935. Playing before a huge crowd in Boston, he cracked a 430-foot homer off Carl Hubbell. But by June 2, hitting .188 in 28 games worth 72 at-bats, he quit. Still, Babe Ruth didn't leave without a last big bang. Ruth hit 4 homers that sad season, but 3 came in one game, on May 25 against the Pirates at Forbes Field—suddenly a favorite venue for aging sluggers to prove a point.

On that day he hit a 2-run homer in the first inning, another 2-run homer in the third, and an RBI single in the fifth. He came to bat in the seventh against his old verbal sparring partner, Guy Bush, who had already given up 2 dingers that day and just may have been grooving a few for the Babe that game, because Ruth now smashed his third of the game and last ever—number 714 (or if one wants to get technical, 715). And this was no commoner among homers. The ball screamed over the 86-foot-high roof of the right field grandstand, something that had not been done before—and was done only sixteen times in the park's history—and landed on a rooftop across the street. The Pirates' head usher would later step off the distance from home plate to the rooftop and made it out to be a highly unscientific 600 feet, which no doubt was stretching things a wee bit. But when Bush spoke about the homer in his golden years, saying "I never saw a ball hit so hard," he meant it. And when I say Ruth forever made baseball an offshoot of the home run rather than the other way around, I mean it.

Not that it takes much debate to back up that point, but there is a certain irritability about Ruth among modern baseball annalists. Bill James, in his *Historical Baseball Abstract*, vents, "If you think [Ruth] was responsible for the change in baseball that took place about 1920, you're dead wrong. [He] came along at one of the gates of history when the old ways had been destroyed. . . . Ruth's role was in leading the way to and defining the rules of the new order." This is what is called 20-20 blindsight. (To be fair, Babe had these kind of Philistines in his day, too, otherwise he would have won more than one MVP.) Ruth defined the rules, all right—by smacking more home runs by himself a few seasons than any other team, and that happened as late as 1927, years after James' gate of the new order was wide open. That other people started hitting home runs, some almost as many as Ruth did, came about only because Ruth changed baseball at the cellular level.

So rest easy, big guy. You're the man.

Part 3

AFTER THE BABE

8

Blood Brothers

New Day, Old Habits

Baseball in the mid-1930s could no longer be called "prehistoric" or even "overly vintage." But for the glaring and ghastly exception of its racial intransigence, the vestiges of the old order were fading fast with the retirement of Ruth and the deaths of baseball's Bickersons, John McGraw and Ban Johnson. Connie Mack was now consigned to the second division for the rest of his time in the game. The All-Star Game was entrenched. Night baseball became a reality in Cincinnati on May 24, 1935, for a Reds-Phillies game and within six years light towers graced ten ballparks used by eleven teams, and by 1948 all except Wrigley Field. Bats were slim handled and tapered and gloves were large and cushy, if still not fully evolved. And, of course, the home run was king, on a permanent throne.

With Ruth now history, his immediate legatees broke out of his shadow. A month after Ruth hung 'em up, Jimmie Foxx broke up the All-Star Game with a homer and 3 RBIs. A year later, after Mack had sold him to the Red Sox, the Beast, still not 30 years old, cut "The Monster"—Fenway Park's looming left field wall—down to size with 41 homers, 143 RBIs, and a .338 average. Over the next four years he had at least 35 homers and 105 RBIs. In 1938 Foxx tore out a season reminiscent of his Triple Crown rampage of '32. He hit 50 taters to reach the half-century mark for the second time, which only Ruth had done, and hit 2 in a game *nine* times (breaking the record set by Ruth and Hack Wilson) while leading the AL with 175 RBIs and a .349 average.

Foxx properly won the MVP that season, but he *didn't* lead the league in homers, coming in second to Detroit's own beast, Hank Greenberg, who smacked *58*, the highest single-season total anyone would ring up until 1961. And if you think 50 and 58 homers in the AL sounds a little odd during what was supposed to be a Depression in and out of baseball, so did folks back then. Like the NL in 1930, in 1938 the AL was another of those wacko anomalies that was, on the surface, unexplainable. And in baseball, when something is unexplainable, the first suspect to be fingered is the baseball itself.

In fact, even before this, in the mid-1930s, there had been much mewling about the ball again getting too lively. Although home runs were still way down from the 1930 levels, and the two leagues were in remarkable symmetry (the NL hit 663 homers and the AL 662 in 1935), *St. Louis Post* columnist John E. Wray sounded a lot like Henry Chadwick had in the 1890s when in 1934 he upbraided fans for "worship[ing] at the shrine of the Big Wallop. [For them] the climax of a game is not a steal of home but a knock over the wall. Whether the lively ball or the batter's prowess accomplishes this doesn't concern them. But the old 'die hard' boys who like to see a run earned will never be reconciled to seeing a tally gained by intelligence and planning offset by a rubber cored wallop over the roofs."

New York sportswriter Garry Shumacher echoed the refrain, caviling that "the new dynamite laden pellet has taken the science and skill from the game." By 1938, when two 50-homer hitters made these opinions plausible, the assumption in the game was that something had to be up with the ball. But the assumption flew in the face of the truth: that the home run binges of the late 1930s were produced by some of the strongest and smartest home run hitters of all time. They had to be, since in reality the ball had actually regressed in its liveliness. For all the refinements by Reach and Spalding, by the late '30s the ball was as lumpy and dead-spot-ridden as in the late 1910s. In 1940, in fact, Mel Ott went 4-for-4 in a game against the Dodgers and *complained*, saying the balls were like "overripe grapefruits."

Ott's home runs dropped from 27 to 19 that year, and had dropped from 36 the previous year, 1939, when Foxx dropped to 35 (leading the league at that) and Greenberg from 58 to 33. Pretty damning evidence about the ball, isn't it? So then why did Johnny Mize's NL-high home run totals go from 28 in 1939 to 43 in 1940? And why did Greenberg go back up to an AL-leading 43 in 1940? It's true that 1940 did see a mushier ball, when the country was readying a war machine and put restrictions on rubber and leather goods that would last until 1945. But while Mize dropped to 16 home runs in 1941, the Dodgers' Dolph Camilli went from 23 in 1940 to 34 in 1941. I could go on, but you get the idea now how inane the whole lively ball versus dead ball issue is, and what a fraud the Lively Ball Era was. In *Clearing the Bases*, Bill Starr pored over the minutes from baseball's annual executive meetings during the 1920s and 1930s and concluded, "There [was] never a decree by the owners to enliven the ball." Claims of juiced-up balls, he wrote, "are indicative that 'Orwellian newspeak' functions in baseball, too."

The only thing I know for sure is that, with a ball anything but lively, some of the greatest pure home run hitters baseball has ever known made those grapefruits disappear in bunches. Take Foxx. Lefty Gomez, the Hall-of-Fame Yankee pitcher, said that when Neil Armstrong walked on the moon and reported seeing an unidentifiable white object, "I knew what it was. That was a home run ball hit off me in 1937 by Jimmie Foxx." By 1942, at age 34, the Beast had hit 509 home runs—only 7 less than Ruth had at the same age—and if he had averaged what Ruth had over the next six years, 33 homers, he would have ended up with 707 homers. Not that 534 home runs is pimento loaf (or for that matter 1,922 RBIs, sixth-best all-time), but Foxx's burnout is a pity. For that, don't blame the ball but the bottle.

Like Hack Wilson, Foxx's drinking ate into his greatness. Ted Williams once recalled that when he joined the Red Sox in 1939, he would see Foxx in uniform before a game with a flask of Scotch in his hip pocket. He held his booze well enough to win his fourth home run crown that year (and hit .360), then hit 1 more dinger, 36, in 1940, including 1 that rocketed over the left field roof at Comiskey Park—a 550-footer regarded as the longest ever hit there. (He also hit 1 into the center field bleachers at Comiskey, 1 of only 4 men to do that.) A week later, he hit grand slams in consecutive games. As with Roger Hornsby, if Foxx could stand, he could hit. But even that became a task, and on June 1, 1942, he was put on waivers and claimed by the Cubs, hitting 3 homers in 70 games.

Foxx was not too proud to eat his pride to stay in the game, putting in a five-game minor league hitch and even managing a women's pro-league team (providing juicy material for the Tom Hanks character based on him in the movie *A League of Their Own*). He then came back for a big-league curtain call in 1945 with the Phillies, when he hit 7 homers on his clear-eyed days, had 38 RBIs and hit .268 (and also *pitched* in nine games, two as a starter, going 1-0 with a 1.57 ERA). The Beast's parting shot was a pinch-hit grand slam (the second in his career) against St. Louis on May 18.

But he was already an echo. Baseball, the ever-regenerative life form that it is, by then had seamlessly replaced Foxx and most everyone else who toddled in the Ruth era with new blood, which began flowing hard in the mid-1930s when a Jewish kid from the Bronx came to Detroit and an Italian kid from the Bay Area came to the Bronx.

Hank G and Joe D

How was it that the Yankees let Hank Greenberg get away from them, leaving the first New York–born Jewish ballplayer to wear pinstripes to be not one of the greatest hitters of all time but rather the immortal Ron Blomberg some thirty-five years later? The answer is that Greenberg was too smart to dream that impossible dream. Born Henry Benjamin Greenberg in the Bronx to Romanian immigrants, Greenberg grew into a huge and gangly man at 6 feet 4 inches and 215 pounds. While attending New York University he tried out for John McGraw, who loved how he hit the ball a mile but felt he was too clumsy. Undaunted, Greenberg, who could only play first base, looked at other teams—but not the one in his own backyard, where first base was kind of occupied. In 1930 he signed with the Tigers for $9,000 and by '33 he was their starting first baseman, hitting .301 with 12 homers including a ninth-inning shot that ended the Senators' thirteen-game winning streak that year.

Greenberg was the linchpin of the Tigers' salad years as a baseball power, when they won pennants in 1934, 1935, 1940, and again in 1945, and titles in '35 and '45. But it is doubtful any team has ever had three better players in its lineup than the Tigers' core of Greenberg, second baseman Charlie Gehringer, and catcher Mickey Cochrane, who arrived in 1934 as the last piece of dry goods in Connie Mack's fire sales, for $100,000. A second-division team since Ty Cobb left in 1926, the Tigers went from a .269 team average and 57 homers to a *.300-hitting*, 74-homer, 101-victory juggernaut in 1934, landing in the World Series against another Cardinals' Gas House Gang bunch. Greenberg, who hit .339 with 26 homers and 139 RBIs that season, homered in a Game 1 loss, had three hits and three RBIs in a Game 4 win that evened the Series, and hit .321 with 7 RBIs overall. But the rub was that the Tigers could only break even in homers against the light-hitting Cards—each team hitting just two—and went down in the famously anarchic seventh game, 11-0 (when Tiger fans pelted the pugnacious Cardinals with garbage, leading Kenesaw Mountain Landis to order Joe Medwick off the field in the ninth for his own protection).

The Tigers came back in 1935 behind Greenberg's phenomenal MVP year, tying Foxx for the home run crown with 36, leading the league with 170 RBIs (*51* more than runner-up Lou Gehrig), and hitting .328. The Tigers hit 106 homers and .290 and also had the league's best pitching. And they didn't even need Greenberg to finish off the Cubs in the World Series. His 2-run first-inning blast in Game 2 broke open the 8-2 win that evened the Series, but he later tried to score from first on a single, hurt his wrist, and didn't play again as the Tigers won a stranger-than-fiction scenario: the Cubs out-homered them 5 to 1 and still lost in six games.

Greenberg signed a $20,000 contract for 1936 but re-injured his wrist on April 29 and missed the rest of the season, giving rise to scuttlebutt that he would never make it back. But Greenberg had overcome his awkwardness as a youth with a fanatical work ethic and obsession for the subtleties of hitting, and when he came back in 1937 he didn't miss a beat. Nor did he ever miss keeping his faith, each September sitting out games that fell on the Jewish holidays, pennant race or not, at first to the bewilderment of his more provincial teammates. One of them, pitcher Eldon Auker, once said, "I came from Kansas and I never knew what a Jew was."

Looking at old films of Greenberg it is a wonder the man was an athlete, much less a great one. He appears barely mobile with nearly no flexibility in his joints and he ran with the teeny steps of a man trying not to spill a drink. But I just got through singing hosannas to Babe Ruth, who proved that big, cloddy white guys with unbelievably well-meshed swings could make it big back then. Greenberg crowded the plate, not giving an inch, and was quick enough to get around on the inside pitches. When he did, it was look out below. Joe Falls once wrote in the *Detroit News* that Greenberg's home runs left no doubt. They "were never line drives or high flies; they were towering shots, skyscrapers, majestic blasts." When he returned after his injury, he sent 40 balls over the wall, second in the AL to a fellow I'll be getting to in a moment, though what really turned him on was driving runs home. Like a mantra, Greenberg used to order teammates, "Just get the runner over to third," leading Gehringer to rib him, "You'd trip a runner coming around third just so you could knock him in yourself."

The order of the AL home run and RBI leaders in 1937 is a good barometer of the sea change in the game. In both departments, Gehrig came in third behind Greenberg and the aforementioned league leader who had 46—a guy named Joseph Paul DiMaggio, whose instant messiah-like gravitas was unveiled when he came to the Yankees in 1936 after tearing up the Pacific Coast League's San Francisco Seals. Because DiMaggio had also torn up a knee in 1934, most big-league scouts lost interest in him, leaving Yankee scout Bill Essick free to sign him for $35,000. But DiMaggio's exploits, including a sixty-one-game hitting streak, forced the Yankees to accede to the Seals' demand to let him play one more year, 1935, with them.

The plank-lean, fluidly graceful DiMaggio came to New York in 1936, greeted by enormous fanfare. "Here is the replacement for Babe Ruth," wrote Dan Daniel in the *World Telegram*. Not fazed in the least by the attention, DiMaggio had 3 hits in his debut and thereafter set AL rookie records for runs and triples and hit .323 with 29 homers and 125 RBIs, and he played the caverns of the Yankee Stadium outfield nearly flawlessly. "DiMaggio didn't glide; he proceeded. He segued. He always seemed to be waiting, not pursuing," Roy Blount Jr. once wrote. Joe McCarthy recalled that DiMaggio could have stolen 50 or 60 bases a year if he let him. "He wasn't the fastest man alive, he just knew how to run the bases better than anybody," said Marse Joe. DiMaggio's most skilled weapon was an absolutely flawless hook slide on which his front foot would graze the base or the plate as his body pulled in the opposite direction—a move not one player today knows how to execute.

In fact, all of DiMaggio's baseball instincts seemed to be innate, not invented. As with Greenberg, his swing had not an ounce of squandered movement and thus met every pitch with full force, but unlike Greenberg his biomechanical perfection was not the product of empirical design, merely second nature. "There's no skill involved," he once insisted. "I'd just go up there and swing at the ball." Jimmy Cannon may have hit it as squarely as Joe D did when he wrote, "DiMaggio has never had a superior. [His] is the most unselfish skill possessed by any man who ever played the game for a living. It is an accidental gift, I think."

DiMaggio must have been blessed, since no one could have stood in the batter's box the way he did and still hit a buck and a half. But like Ruth's radically different kind of swing, there was science to how DiMaggio made that famous spread-eagle batting stance work. First, he was a stronger man than people thought; at 6 feet 2 inches he was a tightly packed 215 pounds, as heavy as Greenberg. Anchored by his wrists, forearms, and long fingers, a thirty-eight-oz. bat would feel light in his hands. With his feet spread a yard apart, DiMaggio could hang back as long as humanly possible before springing into a pitch with a small, nearly imperceptible stride. His backswing was so torrential that the bat would whip around his back and twist his upper body into a knot.

Even though as a right-handed hitter he had to contend with the stupefying dimensions of Yankee Stadium's Death Valley, DiMaggio didn't shorten up his stance to punch pitches to right field. Several generations have speculated about how many homers he lost playing in the park—a reasonable question since he hit 148 homers at home and 213 on the road in his career. Still, in advancing the theory that he was shortchanged, some historians would do well to ponder a few points. To be sure, when he was young DiMaggio was snakebitten at home. As a rookie, he hit 8 at home, 21 on the road. But as he began to fill out more, and gauge big-league pitching, the stronger and more experienced DiMaggio began to hit opposite-field homers. The home-away demarcation from 1937 to 1941 looked like this: 19-27, 15-17, 12-18, 16-15, 16-14. When he got older and his power began to dissipate the gap widened again: in 1950, his last year, it was 9-23.

Then, too, DiMaggio was as much helped as hurt by playing where he did. Remember, his power was more in line drives, not fly balls, and the power alleys at the Stadium were a line-drive-hitter's paradise. Joe D's power year, 1937, came at a time when pitchers still believed that his spread stance left him vulnerable to inside stuff and he sent a goodly number of not-inside-enough serves over the Stadium's short left field wall by the foul pole. That year, he hit 15 homers in July, then a big-league record. As well, he was hitting third in front of a still-frightful Lou Gehrig. For all these reasons he finished with 46, the most in baseball that year and still a Yankee record for right-handed hitters, while also carving a .346 average, third in the league, and running up 167 RBIs, second.

That may have been the last time DiMaggio saw those inside pitches as a rule. Most pitchers began staying away from that inside corner, though ironically the closest thing to a weakness he had was inside pitches, and sinkers, which few pitchers threw then. One who did, Cleveland's Mel Harder, was the toughest arm he faced. But all those homers in '37 gave rise to the "book" on Joe D. As Bob Feller recalled, when he was a young pitcher "I used to pitch him outside and he kept wearing me out. Finally I got enough nerve to pitch him inside and started to have success." DiMaggio, who was almost never fooled on a pitch, rarely had to guess-hit. He knew he'd be pitched outside, and geared that mile-long swing so that his arms would be fully extended when he slammed balls into the alleys.

DiMaggio's microscopic strikeout totals are simply beyond belief, especially for a guy who could hit it out. The chart in chapter 5 shows how few times he struck out, but that is just part of the story. For a slugger, a 1 : 2 ratio for strikeouts to home runs is boffo. DiMaggio's was less than *1 : 1*—361 to 369, which works out on average to 29 homers and *27* strikeouts a year. Compare this with, say, George Sisler, he of the .340 lifetime average and the reputation as maybe the best contact hitter ever. His per-year strikeout average is 22, not much better than Joe D's—and his home run average is 6.6 a year. The lowest strikeout average in history belongs to Lloyd Waner, around 11 a year—but Waner also has the lowest home run average, 0.4 a year. Pete Rose? He struck out 48 times a year. Ty Cobb, a.k.a. Mr. Anti-Homer? Struck out 15 times a year—with a homer average of around 5 a year. Really, the only bona fide home run hitter whose ratio is comparable with DiMaggio's was the last of the 1930s young bloods, who in 1939 arrived at Fenway Park for a two-decade run of unequalled brilliance.

Before I get to you-know-who, though, let's pay homage to the half-decade DiMaggio had to himself, for it was a breathtaking ride. The only downer was that Joe D's upward ride coincided with Lou Gehrig's decline and fall. In 1939, at age 36, the Iron Horse was coming off his first sub-.300 season since his rookie year and first sub-30-homer season in eleven years (though 1 of his 29 was his 23rd grand slam, a record no one has ever come near). Rickety and weak, Gehrig never could get untracked in '39. Hitting .143 on May 2, he told Joe McCarthy he was finally going to sit down after those 2,130 consecutive games. This was followed by the subsequent news on June 21 that he was retiring because of amyotrophic lateral sclerosis, an incurable illness few knew of. Then and thereafter, it came to be called "Lou Gehrig's disease."

Gehrig's indelibly heart-wrenching July 4 valedictory address in the well of a packed, deathly silent Yankee Stadium was baseball's saddest day, its vibe of pain and loss echoed by John Kieran's printed elegy the next day: "Idol of cheering millions. / Records are yours by the sheaves, / Iron of frame they hailed you / And decked you with laurel leaves." Unlike Babe Ruth, who in his terminal state nine years later managed to drag his ravaged body to the plate at the house he had built in two ceremonial requiems, the last just days before he died on August 20, 1948, Gehrig repaired to the solitude that always comforted him and on June 2, 1941, he died, the signet of the young athlete taken before his time.

Despite Gehrig's tragic exodus from the lineup, the '39 Yankees, at 106-45, may have been the finest Yankee team of all, albeit one sans the picaresque, manic charm of Murderer's Row. This too was a factor of DiMaggio. Painfully insular, at times neurotically withdrawn, his sullen, surly vibe washed over the Yankees, who were petrified of drawing one of DiMaggio's cold, baleful stares for any against-the-grain behavior. The story is told that DiMaggio and teammates Tony Lazzeri and Frank Crosetti were sitting in the lobby of the Hotel Chase in St. Louis one day. While the latter two were voluble, animated Italians, they would not say a word until Joe spoke first. And so for ninety minutes they all sat there, silent. Then DiMaggio cleared his throat.

"What did you say?" Crosetti eagerly asked.

"He didn't say nothing. Shut up," Lazzeri sternly rebuked him, and the threesome sat mute for another half an hour.

Because of that DiMaggio vibe, the Yankees, then and for around forty years after, were all but shorn of most basic human emotions as they went about their game with all the joy and abandon of a cement mixer. The days of Ruth's phallic jokes and boozy Falstaffian reveries were not a part of the new Yankee dynasty. The legion of those who swoon at the mere mention of DiMaggio's name say that, emotion or not, to see DiMaggio was to see God himself in knickers, and fans will humor them about that. But what this crowd overlooks is that even in New York, DiMaggio was not entirely popular among the fans and the media. At times, he was ragged as a man who roused little excitement—yeah, yeah, I know, he was so good at everything he did, he just *looked* unexciting. Red Smith addressed the issue when he wrote, "He'll never threaten Babe Ruth's home-run record, nor will he ever grip the imagination of crowds as Ruth did. If he were not such a matchless craftsman, he might be a more spectacular player . . . and so more highly regarded [but] you must rank him off the sum total of his component parts, and on this basis there has not been during Joe's big-league existence a rival close to him."

As well, DiMaggio often caught the brunt of anti-Italian prejudice in the culture at large. His nickname—"Big Dago"—was innocuous put-down patois in the Yankee clubhouse but it was heard in a far different vein after he committed a Depression-era taboo, holding out for a raise from $15,000 to $35,000 in 1938. DiMaggio missed the first weeks of the season before Ed Barrow gave in at $25,000, and the press savaged him, egged on by Barrow, who would bring the writers into his office and show them piles of mail from fans, which he said ran heavily against DiMaggio.

In May 1939, *Life* magazine ragged him. The mass-circulation magazine's slug of a publisher, Henry Luce, the Babe Ruth of American bigots, gave the go-ahead for a charming piece by Noel F. Busch that cobbled every ugly Italian stereotype. Among other slurs, Busch wrote that DiMaggio was rebellious, had "squirrel teeth," and that his "rise in baseball is a testament to the value of general shiftlessness." Under a photograph of DiMaggio and Joe Louis was the caption, "Like Heavyweight Champion Louis, DiMaggio is lazy, shy and inarticulate."

Busch did note a few admirable qualities, such as that DiMaggio "speaks English without an accent and is well adopted to most U.S. mores," and that "instead of olive oil he keeps his hair slick with water. He never reeks of garlic and prefers chicken chow mein to spaghetti."

The fact is, not until DiMaggio's last few years as a player, after more holdouts and injuries many deemed to be questionable, was he a universal icon of class and dignity. Still, in the '30s his imprimatur was already deeply embossed in baseball, as the Yankees devoured four straight championships from 1936 to 1939. During that span, they had a 16-3 edge in World Series games, a 23 to 7 edge in World Series home runs. In decimating the Reds in a four-game sweep in '39, they hit 7 homers to the Reds' none, 3 by Charlie Keller. In the '37 Series against the Giants, Lazzeri blasted a grand slam, just the second in Series play. In 1936, the Yankees hit 182 home runs for the season, more than the Ruth Yankees ever had and then a record—including one doubleheader in which they hit 8 homers in the first game and 5 more in the nightcap, a record for a twinbill. And their pitching, headed by Red Ruffing and Lefty Gomez, led the AL in ERA all four years, three of them as the only staff to give up under 4 runs a game.

As their kingfisher, DiMaggio basked reluctantly in a supernatural kind of fame, tasted previously only by King Babe. Decades before Paul Simon asked, "Where have you gone, Joe DiMaggio," the man was a pop culture standard, in the song "Joltin' Joe DiMaggio," a chart-topping hit of the 1940s, and in literature by Hemingway ("'I would like to take the great DiMaggio fishing,' the old man said. 'They say his father was a fisherman. Maybe he was as poor as we are as a kid and understands . . .'"). The Yankee Clipper "segued" to the MVP award in '39, only now he was no longer without peer.

Teddy Ballgame

Here's a little-known fact: Ted Williams, yin to Joe DiMaggio's yang, might actually have played with DiMaggio in the Yankees' outfield had not fate determined that this would have been just too damn unfair. This was surely behind the Yankees missing the boat on Williams the way everyone else did on DiMaggio. It happened when Williams was a skinny teenage *pitcher* in his hometown San Diego. When pro teams came calling on him, his mother demanded a $1,000 bonus from the Yankees, who passed, and the kid stayed at home, signing in 1936 with the Padres of the Pacific Coast League, the league that made DiMaggio famous, for $150 a week.

Williams the pitcher gave up a home run to the first man he faced and was switched to the outfield. He didn't hit .300 in the league, but when Red Sox general manager Eddie Collins made a scouting trip out west, he signed the Padres' second baseman Bobby Doerr and Williams, paying $25,000 for Williams' contract.

At 6 feet 4 inches and a stringy 150 pounds, Williams was all arms, legs, and bushy eyebrows. And mouth. Even then, he had a tendency to talk big, crack wise, and piss people off. Williams called himself "The Kid" in solipsistic admiration of his precocious abilities. People still called him that when he was 40. But his most striking quality was the pure innocent rush he had swinging a bat—the kind that DiMaggio would rather have imploded than display publicly. A bat in The Kid's hands was like a rattle in a real kid's. While playing the field was drudgery for him, no one ever came to the plate with the flounce of a Ted Williams.

And you would, too, if you could hit like that. DiMaggio was a great natural hitter, but even he looked like he was doing manual labor next to Williams' blithe ease. When he stepped in, there was no wide stance, no crazy leg lift. He stood with slightly hunched shoulders, and with a tiny twitch of the hips his long tensile wrists and forearms unfurled a long-armed swing that was as level as a table. Williams never seemed to be fooled by a pitch and while he could discourse all day about the science of hitting, nothing was more vital in his catalog than his eyes. Don't ever think Williams was just talking big when he said he could see the seams of the ball spinning so clearly that he knew exactly what the pitch was. If he said he could see a worm wiggle under a rock, I'd believe him. The evidence is his .344 lifetime average and 521 home runs—a brew of hitting idioms only Babe Ruth has matched. Chalk it up to hand-eye coordination not generally given to Homo sapiens. The next time you see a .250 hitter taking a wild, shoelace-popping swing trying to hit one out, think of Williams in the box, the tiny twitch of the hips as the ball came in, his thewy wrists and forearms sending the bat around in a tight arc, the ball pouring off the wood like buttermilk.

As with DiMaggio and Yankee Stadium, Fenway Park posed a problem for Williams. In his overview, pulling a ball was the manhood of hitting. It was proposed that he tailor his swing to dent the Green Monster in left. Williams said forget it. In fact, his resistance to temper his stubborn ways earned him a ticket to the minors before the 1938 season began. Williams went, but changed nothing and hit .368 with 43 homers with Minneapolis in the American Association. When he came back in '39, they left him alone. His first game, on April 20, he doubled off the Yankees' Red Ruffing. Three days later he blasted his first homer off the A's Bud Thomas and went 4-for-5. Williams never dropped below .300 that year, finishing at .327, with 31 homers—only 4 behind his teammate Jimmie Foxx, the league leader, and 2 behind Hank Greenberg. The most outrageous thing he did was driving in 145 runs, the most in baseball—a first for a rookie, by miles. And yet as immaculate a rookie season as this was—and no other has come close to it except Albert Pujols' in 2001—everyone seemed to know it was just a teaser. It was.

Not that Williams would ever be good enough for large segments of Red Sox fans and the press that covered the team. His contretemps with critics of his at-best mediocre fielding and the fans who shouted abuse at him kept Williams from ever rising to DiMaggio's level of reverence; in turn, he built walls around him higher than the Green Monster. Befriending no one on the team, his consorts were usually faceless, disposable people like cab drivers and clubhouse attendants. This was the Williams paradox, that a man so great and so idolized, and with such ingenuous tastes—all he wanted, he would say, "is that when I walk down the street folks will say, 'There goes the greatest hitter who ever lived,'" a wish he was granted—could also be so unlovable. The poet John Updike, whose longtime Red Sox obsessions run cheek by jowl with those of the self-tortured souls in his short stories, tried to put his finger on the pathology of being—and watching—Ted Williams in a 1960 *New Yorker* confessional, writing:

> The dowagers of local journalism attempted to give elementary deportment lessons to this child who spake as a god, and to their horror were themselves rebuked. Thus began the long exchange of backbiting, bat-flipping, booing and spitting that has distinguished Williams' public relations. . . . The left-field stands at Fenway Park for 20 years have held a large number of customers who have bought their way in primarily for the privilege of showering abuse on Williams. Greatness necessarily attracts debunkers, but in Williams' case the hostility has been systematic and unappeasable. His basic offense against the fans

> has been to wish that they weren't there. Seeking a perfectionist's vacuum, he has quixotically desired to sever the game from the ground of paid spectatorship and publicity that supports it. Hence his refusal to tip his cap to the crowd or turn the other cheek to newsmen. It has been a costly theory—it has probably cost him, among other evidences of good will, two Most Valuable Player awards . . . but he has held to it from his rookie year on. . . .
>
> The affair between Boston and Ted Williams has been no mere summer romance; it has been a marriage, composed of spats, mutual disappointments and, toward the end, a mellowing hoard of shared memories. It falls into three stages, which may be termed Youth, Maturity, and Age; or Thesis, Antithesis, and Synthesis; or Jason, Achilles, and Nestor.

Through all his incarnations—as The Kid, The Thumper, The Splendid Splinter, or Teddy Ballgame—Williams never changed. Fenway or no, he was an intractable, ego-driven hitter. This explains why he liked the home run more than DiMaggio, and the numbers show it. Williams' 521 were 160 more than DiMaggio hit—yes, in 881 more at-bats. But before anyone thinks that means Joe D would have made up the difference had he played as long, here's the math: Williams hit 1 homer every 15 at-bats; DiMaggio 1 every 19. So at that rate, DiMaggio would have had 37 more, or 398, in the same number of at-bats. Still, let's not put them on dead-even playing fields. Williams' Fenway was not Babe Ruth's Fenway. Even before he got there, the center field fence was brought in 80 feet, to 388, in 1934. Then in 1940, expressly to aid Williams, the bullpens were moved from center to in front of the right–center field bleachers and fenced in 23 feet closer to the plate, from 405 to 382. The right field pole was moved in from 332 to 304. Death Valley this wasn't.

Consequently, the home and road home run breakdown cracks the mirror-image fiction of the DiMaggio-versus-Williams debate. Williams did hit fewer at home but it's hardly decisive—248 home, 273 road. Nine times he hit more at home. Only once, in 1957, was the gap significant: 26 road, 12 home. Clearly, Williams went for the fences more than DiMaggio, and his power was superior. Logically, he should have struck out far more and had a lower average. But check the stats. Williams' worst strikeout year was 51 to DiMaggio's 36, and his 706 career K's work out to 37 a year, all of ten more than Joe D. His homer-to-strikeout ratio of $1 : 1\frac{1}{2}$ (521 to 709) is not quite DiMaggio's 1 : 1 but still remarkable. And the kicker is that Williams rolled up a .344 lifetime average—19 points higher than DiMaggio's.

Ah, but the argument isn't over, because Joe averaged 100 RBIs to Teddy's 97. (Both men would have had many more homers and RBIs but for the interruption of their careers by World War II.) And Williams could only once carry his team past the Yankees and to a pennant. So what am I trying to say here? That Williams may well have been the peerless one and still he loses the argument because DiMaggio had the team, and the timing. One season, as to be related in a bit, would prove that point for all time.

Big Jawn

Contrary to what you may be thinking, there was a National League during this time, and there were some home runs hit there, some big ones. The biggest was hit by Gabby Hartnett in 1938. Hartnett, by then the Cubs' player-manager, led a late-season run by the team that chopped a 7-game Pirate lead on September 1 to a 1½-game lead when the two teams opened a series on September 26 at Wrigley Field. The Cubs won the first game behind a retread Dizzy Dean. Then, as clouds shrouded the ballpark, they were tied 5-5 with 2 outs in the bottom of the ninth when Hartnett came up. Pitcher Marc Brown broke 2 curveballs by him for called strikes, then tried another curve. Gabby swung and hit it . . . somewhere, though in the dense fog no one really knew where until the ball thudded into the left field bleachers. The shot, poetically dubbed "The Homer in the Gloamin'" by the Chicago sportswriters, put the Cubs in first place, and they went on to win the pennant.

By gloamin' or by clear daylight, though, home runs were hard to come by in the senior circuit. In 1940, when the AL had 883 homers to the NL's 688, no less than six AL teams compiled over 100 dingers, while the NL had but one team, the Cardinals, who had 119—and that was due mainly to one man, left-handed-hitting first baseman John Mize, who led the league with 43 homers, 137 RBIs, and a .636 slugging average, and was fifth with a .314 batting average. (Typically, the boneheaded baseball writers gave the MVP award to the Reds' first baseman Frank McCormick, who hit .309 with 19 homers and 127 RBIs.)

Mize was a wonderful slugger who broke the mold of the slash-and-burn Gas House Gang. Not that this was such a good thing in the Twinkie-fied National League, in which the 6-foot-2, 215 pound Mize—nicknamed "The Big Cat" or "Big Jawn," as he called himself in his Georgia twang—stood out like a giant mutant spud. After five minor-league seasons he broke in with 19 homers, 93 RBIs, and a .329 average in 1936, and he would increase his 4-baggers each of the next five seasons (while hitting no lower than .314 or driving no fewer than 100 runs), leading the loop in 1939 (with 28) and 1940. Yet all this seemed almost counterproductive as the Cards, who had won it all in 1934, would win nothing until 1942—after Mize was traded to the Giants. That year, without him, St. Louis put up only 60 home runs and hit a meager .268. With Mize, who hit 26 homers behind teammate Mel Ott's league-high 30, the Giants were the only league team with 100 homers. They finished third. Henry Chadwick would have said, "I told you so."

Of course, Mize was hardly to blame for the Cards' drought, having come along after Dizzy Dean's fastball went south and the Gas House Gang got old. But clearly, he was in the wrong league—and on the wrong team. Mize came to the Cards through the famous Branch Rickey minor-league pipeline that supplied the raw goods for eight pennant-winning and five championship teams from 1920 to 1945, including Pepper Martin, Joe Medwick, Dean, Country Slaughter, and Stan Musial. But Mize, like Musial, was only technically a Gas Houser, being far too courtly and solicitous to fit in—not to mention too lead footed to join in any base-running games.

Even so, how lame must those late 1930s' Cardinal teams have been not to benefit from a hitter like Mize? In 1938 he blasted 3 homers in a game twice, did it 2 more times in 1940, and 6 times overall in his career, a big league record. Mize had 30 3-homer games, 7 pinch-hit homers, at least 1 homer in all 15 ballparks he played in, and 359 homers in all. And he did all of these things while hitting .312—and striking out a mere 524 times, creating a Williams-like 1 : 1½ homer-to-strikeout ratio. (He too would be robbed of a ton more homers by the war.)

And yet for the first seven years of his career, his long balls and his mastadon guise marked him as an endangered species in his league. As John Lardner wrote in *Newsweek*:

> Big John Mize is a "whale" in every sense of the definition. He can pull the ball, but he also has power in all directions. He owns sharp eyes and enough "plate intelligence" to be a consistent hitter. The pitchers in his league fear no man as much, and that is the ultimate tribute.
>
> There are other potential "whales" in the National League. . . . But just for now, for this department's doubloons, the only full and ripened specimen of Physeter macrocephalus outside the American League is J. Robert Mize.

In time, J. Robert would get competition of his own in the league that couldn't hit deep. But the world would have to change first.

9

Feast, Famine, Feast

Black Babes

Entering the new decade of the 1940s, baseball's fresh blood had transfused the game's Depression-induced inertia with a growing confidence that reflected the nation's own recovery. In 1938, NL attendance jumped to more than 4½ million and 7,000 per game for the first time in seven years; in 1940, AL attendance hit a then-record 5½ million and 8,700 per game. Still, with the dark omens of war now looming larger by the day, there were sticking points retarding both game and country, reminders that neither was home free just yet.

Indeed, baseball was trying hard to avoid its own war, one it had made inevitable ever since the 1880s when Cap Anson ran African American ballplayers off big-league diamonds. While segregation had become melded to the game's status quo for six decades, the major-league bureaucracy had to know the status quo could not hold much longer. The unwritten but unwavering injunction against non-white baseball was never more indefensible as on the eve of war, when black men were being conscripted to serve and die in combat. Not that this caused any great crisis of conscience among the game's pharisees, who continued dishing up the same feeble canards that integrated ball would devalue their teams. In fact, the freezing effect of war would actually provide useful if ironic cover to keep the stall going—and even after it was over only one big-league capo, Branch Rickey, would go about razing the color line, albeit delicately and pragmatically.

Thus, until the late 1940s, black players would go about their business the only way they could, and had, by playing with distinction in parallel "big leagues," which for all their struggles to stay afloat were successful commercial enterprises—and a coat rack for the entire civil rights crusade. They established cult status for a legion of Negro League players whose exclusion ate at the white game's credibility. "Blackball" adopted the structure and rituals of the big leagues, such as by playing a World Series and an All-Star Game (called the East-West Game, played annually at Comiskey Park, often before sellout crowds). They rented big-league stadiums from owners whose resistance to black players did not preclude making money off of them. And over time the best of these players came to challenge the superiority of the white game. White big leaguers hardly needed to be convinced these men could play with them. For years, barnstorming big leaguers had engaged black stars in the off season, and had the tar beaten out of them by Negro Leaguers who took these meaningless games as rites of manhood.

Position by position, blackball could offer up their best to make their case—such whip-armed pitchers as Satchel Paige, Smokey Joe Williams, Bullet Rogan, and Hilton Smith; slick and blinding baserunners like Cool Papa Bell; flashy glove men like Pop Lloyd, Judy Johnson, and Willie Wells; drop-anchor catchers such as Biz Mackey and Roy Campanella. They even had an Al Spalding clone in legendary pitcher-turned-executive Andrew "Rube Foster," who founded the Negro National League (NNL) in 1920, owned its marquee franchise, the Chicago American Giants (forging ballpark-sharing agreements with the White Sox), and served as the league's commissioner until a mental breakdown confined him to an asylum, chasing imaginary fly balls.

And, of course, there were sluggers.

The home run, after all, was not copyrighted by white men—a point duly and frenetically noted in the black weeklies that thoroughly covered the "other" big leagues. When African Americans began sending balls over fences, many of them took turns being dubbed "The Black Babe Ruth" in these papers, a sobriquet rooted both in envy and conviction. The first to wear it, Norman "Turkey" Stearnes, was like the Babe, a rotund outfielder and left-handed hitter who from 1924 to 1926 led the NNL with 17, 10, and 10 dingers while playing for the Detroit Stars. I must point out, however, that citing Negro League statistics is a very "iffy" proposition. For one thing, league schedules were usually unbalanced and many games fell into a black hole, with not a box score in sight. For another, black clubs had to play against many levels of competition to make any money, and so games against the local shopkeepers could be counted in a player's yearly record. Stearnes, for example, was reported to have hit 50 homers in 1924 against all comers—sounds good but couldn't matter less. Of Satchel Paige's reputed 2,000-something wins, 300-something shutouts, and 55-something no-hitters, no better fiction has ever been written. (Far more trenchant is that Paige's $35,000 salary in the early 1940s was higher than all but a few white big leaguers.)

Still, if the white game had its legends of the summer, so would the black game. When another big St. Louis Stars slugger, first baseman Mule Suttles, who hit the first East-West Game home run in 1933, cracked 1 in the bottom of the ninth to win the 1935 East-West Game, the *Pittsburgh Courier* smothered him in vespers:

> "For the West, Mule Suttles at bat!"
>
> That's the resonant voice of the [public address] announcer. . . .
>
> "T-H-E M-U-L-E!"
>
> Reverberating through the reaches of this historic ballpark and bounding and rebounding through the packed stands comes the chant of some 25,000 frenzied spectators.
>
> They're yelling for blood! They're yelling for their idol, the bronzed Babe Ruth of colored baseball to come through. . . .
>
> Suttles threw his mighty body into motion. His foot moved forward. His huge shoulder muscles bunched. Came a swish through the air, a crack of the rifle, and like a projectile hurled from a cannon the ball started its meteoric flight. [It] CLEARED the distant fence in far away right center, landing 475 feet from home plate. It was a herculian swat, one of the greatest in baseball. . . .
>
> And then pandemonium broke loose. . . . [T]he third-base line was filled with playmates anxious to draw him to their breasts. Over the stands came a surging mass of humanity.

The *Chicago Call* chose to run this piece of understatement: "Not since the celebration following the news that the armistice had been signed [ending World War 1] has Chicago seen its citizenry so stark mad for a few minutes. Score cards were torn up and hurled into the air. Men tossed away their summer straw hats and women screamed."

In truth, this sort of hyperbole was itself cribbed from the white sporting press' unctuous treatment of baseball heroes, and most overtly to venerate Babe Ruth's home runs on the spot. And it worked just as well for the black press in spreading the gospel that *uber*men came in all colors. The proof was that in time the white media began to take notice of the black game. *The New York Times*, in fact, reported that dramatic East-West Game, though with much less steam in two lines of agate type.

Other bronzed Babes came through, like the Homestead Grays' cleanup hitter, Walter "Buck" Leonard, a tremendous all-around first baseman who hit 3 homers in East-West Games. But by 1940, all had been dimmed by blackball's most potent metaphor of power and pain, catcher Josh Gibson, who between stints with the Grays teamed with Paige on blackball's answer to the '27 Yankees, the '32 Pittsburgh Crawfords—forming possibly baseball's greatest battery ever. A 6-foot 2-inch, 220-pound block of granite with a forty-ounce bat, the Georgia-born Gibson set off Ruthian echoes by hitting balls long and longer, though unlike the Babe most of his homers didn't shoot up in a wind draft but rather began as line drives that just kept going, often not climbing fifty feet above the ground. The longtime Kansas City Monarch first baseman John "Buck" O'Neil, who played against Ruth on the barnstorming trail, recalled that the only other time he ever heard the unique "click" made by Ruth's bat meeting a ball was when Gibson tied into one.

Again bearing in mind the caveat about Negro League statistics, Gibson is credited with hitting 963 home runs over a seventeen-year career, against all competition. Of these, he had 75 in 1930, 69 in 1934, and 84 in 1936. Also consider that a team might play over 200 games each year. He hit over .400 six times between 1929 and 1939. In 1938 and 1939, Gibson's slugging percentage was computed, possibly in Disneyland, as 1.389 and 1.190. Against white big leaguers he hit .412 and had two homers in one game against Dizzy Dean. In the Gibson catalog of mythical long balls is a shot in Monessen, Pennsylvania, that was paced off at 568 feet, and one at the Polo Grounds that the night watchman found in the last row of the upper deck. Another, the story goes, left the park, landed in a truck and wasn't discovered until the next day—baseball's only 500-*mile* home run.

And then there was the one he hit clear out of Yankee Stadium. Or didn't. Or did. Or didn't. This tale, blackball equivalent of Ruth's Called Shot, is also a tale told with varying degrees of conviction over the years. What's more, according to lore, Gibson may have done it *three* times. Or more. Or less. Or not at all.

The reason for the confusion, other than unreliable record keeping, is that Gibson hit a number of dingers at Yankee Stadium, and any Gibson homer there was said by *someone* to have left the building. The first one came in 1931 when he was just 19 and Homestead was playing the New York Lincoln Giants in the league championship series. In the first game, played at Forbes Field, Gibson smoked one an estimated 475 feet. When the teams shifted to New York, he ripped a ball into the third deck in left field that apparently fell to the back of the bullpen below, about 500 feet away, leaving the impression among those who were there that he had hit it on some kind of weird curve over the roof and into the pen.

Gibson was supposed to have hit another cannonball in 1934 with the Crawfords. At least he did according to a retrospective account in the *Sporting News* in 1972 (when he was elected to the Hall of Fame) by Ric Roberts, who had covered the Negro Leagues for the *Courier*. Roberts wrote that the blow came against the New York Black Yankees and was "a rifle-shot that rattled off the escarpments in front of the 161st Street Elevated Railway [which] probably would have traveled 700 feet had it been two feet higher. It was a 650-foot explosion!"

It also likely never happened. For one thing, the only recorded Crawford games at Yankee Stadium that year were against the Philadelphia Stars. For another, the elevated subway runs beyond the *right field* bleachers, and not even Josh Gibson could have hit a 680-footer the other way. Roberts may have been thinking of June 3, 1937, when Gibson did hit 1 out against the Black Yankees that by one report hit "just two feet below the rim" of the left field roof—a mere 580-footer. Conclusion? No one has ever hit a fair ball out of Yankee Stadium. And I mean *nobody*.

Actually, Gibson's homers weren't the only ones to rattle this stadium in Negro League play. In 1930, in the first game league teams played there, Rap Dixon of the Baltimore Black Sox hit 3 out and Lincoln's Chino Smith 2. But, as with Ruth on the white side, Gibson's were on a higher level. This may be why Walter Johnson once said that Gibson would be worth $200,000 to a major-league team, adding with a tsk, "Too bad this Gibson is a colored fellow."

Too bad, indeed. For the big leagues and for Gibson, whose self-image wasn't the greatest to begin with. Though he was portrayed as a carefree giant who would quip things like "I don't break bats, I wear them out," Gibson never was able to reconcile the traumatic death in 1930 of his teenage wife during childbirth; and he crept ever inward—eventually taking refuge in the bottle, the reefer, and ultimately the needle. Under the radar screen he lived hard and, seemingly by choice, not long. Having grown obese by the mid-1940s, he could still whack 'em long—pounding a 500-foot homer in 1946—and he was the epicenter of six straight Grays pennants in the 1940s. But he was a dying man. Diagnosed with a brain tumor, Gibson refused treatment and died on January 20, 1947, at age 35.

That year, of course, would see Jackie Robinson break the color line, and because Gibson had been denied entry so long, his premature demise cut more deeply than Lou Gehrig's for an entire race of Americans who reckoned that white baseball had sacrificed him to intolerance. The *Courier*'s Wendell Smith carved this onto parchment.

> They're laying Josh Gibson in the cold, cold ground this week. He was the "King of Sock" and he ruled with majestic splendor . . . the personification of destruction and devastation, and though he lies motionless in death, the baseball skies still vibrate and resound from his thunderous wallops. . . .
>
> Had his color been of another hue, Josh Gibson would have been a major leaguer, swinging at the slants of such greats as Dizzy Dean, Bob Feller [and] Carl Hubbell. . . . But he had the unfortunate experience of being born a Negro and he paid a penalty for that carelessness his baseball life. . . . Perhaps if Josh Gibson hadn't been a victim of the vicious color line in the majors . . . he might be living today. For he was a big leaguer, and he knew it. He was a thoroughbred and he should have been with them. But they slammed the door in his face, his kindly black face, and left him standing on the outer fringes of the glistening world to which he belonged.
>
> This treatment, more than anything else, sent the "king" to his grave. It made him morose and synical [*sic*], downhearted and resentful. It sent him to the "land of drink" and into the pitfall of human errors. Finally, his health went and he slipped into eternal darkness.
>
> I know the real reason Josh Gibson died. I don't need a doctor's report to confirmation, either.
>
> He was "murdered" by Big League Baseball!

This gross revisionism—not only white sportswriters do it—ignores that Gibson was just one of hundreds of men in the Negro Leagues stuck in a stalled elevator, and that none of the others chose the slow suicide he did. The fact is that few of these men left behind by history lived in a morass of self-pity—least of all Gibson, whose emotional scarring had little to do with the game. By the 1940s, he was too far gone for the big leagues to even matter. Near the end, as white scouts fanned out across the black landscape seeking suitable candidates for promotion, Gibson was arrested after wandering naked and dazed through an airport in Puerto Rico.

But neither did baseball care enough to make Gibson and men like him feel like complete human beings. So let's just say the great American game threw a few handfuls of dirt on that kindly black face.

It would be nice to be able to show a definitive list of the black game's all-time leading home run hitters in league games. Instead, following is a list of the leading home run hitters according to Negro League statistics laundered by modern-day historians. So for what it's worth, here are the names and numbers from the Macmillan *Baseball Encyclopedia*, not to be taken as close to the last word:

Turkey Stearnes* (primar. Detroit Stars, Chicago American Giants, Kansas City Monarchs), 1923–40, 185
Mule Suttles (primar. Birmingham Black Barons, St. Louis Stars, Chicago American Giants, Newark Eagles, New York Black Yankees), 1923–44, 183
Oscar Charleston* (primar. Indianapolis ABCs, Harrisburg Giants, Philadelphia Stars, Pittsburgh Crawfords), 1915–41, 151
Josh Gibson* (Homestead Grays, Pittsburgh Crawfords), 1930–46, 141
Willie Wells* (primar. St. Louis Stars, Chicago American Giants, Newark Eagles), 1924–48, 123
John Beckwith (primar. Chicago American Giants, Baltimore Black Sox, Homestead Grays), 1920–35, 104
David Malarcher (primar. Chicago American Giants), 1920–34, 81
Frog Redus (primar. St. Louis Stars, Chicago American Giants), 1924–40, 80
Jimmy Lyons (Chicago American Giants), 1914–21, 76
Dewey Creasey (primar. St. Louis Stars, Philadelphia Stars), 1924–38, 73
Buck Leonard* (Homestead Grays), 1934–48, 71

Blaze of Glory

Although baseball didn't know the full impact of impending war, everyone in the game was living on borrowed time at the turn of the decade. In retrospect, the 1940 and 1941 seasons seem to have been scripted to give the country two years to savor a full-bodied taste of baseball in bloom before famine would hit again. As usual, the real action was in the American League, where the home run was still the main dish.

In 1940, Hank Greenberg made mincemeat of Joe DiMaggio and Ted Williams in the homer derby, 41 to 31 and 31 and Greenberg's Tiger teammate Rudy York had 33 of his own. In fact, the theme of the season was that Greenberg had willingly switched to the outfield so that the fielding-challenged York could play first base, upon which both men drove the team to the pennant with a molten-hot last month. From September 4 to 26, Greenberg hit .410, on 34 hits in 82 at-bats, with 15 homers and 38 RBIs, earning the MVP with league highs in homers, RBIs (150), and doubles (50), and a .340 average, fifth behind DiMaggio's .352.

*Hall of Famer

And it was a hell of a story. It just wasn't the *real* story, which had more to do with stealing—not bases but signs.

It seems that in late August, pitcher Tommy Bridges came to the park with a high-powered rifle with a telescopic lens, to use for hunting after the season. As Greenberg recalled to author Bill Starr, "Some of us looked through the lens and were astonished how close the most distant objects appeared. Someone suggested that we equip one of our bullpen pitchers with high-powered binoculars to zero in on the catcher's signs. Then, by a hand signal, the catcher's sign could be relayed directly to the batter."

I'm not talking rocket science here, but the best sign-stealing is always the simplest kind. Which is why the Tigers suddenly began atomizing the ball—eventually leading the league with a .286 average and coming in third with 134 home runs—and passed the Yankees and Indians into first place. When they heard that Joe McCarthy had become suspicious of the bullpen guy with the binoculars, they moved the snoop to the outfield bleachers, usually a pitcher on his off-day who dressed undercover in civvies. Sometimes, the hitters would have to peer through a sea of white shirts to get the sign, but it worked. The Tigers won the flag by one game over Cleveland. Then they got to the World Series against Cincinnati and all players had to be present and accounted for, ending the binocular snooping. Greenberg still hit .357, and his 3-run tater in Game 5 put the Tigers up three games to two. However, it was a dinger by a *pitcher*, Bucky Walters, that helped win Game 6, 4-0, letting the Reds stay alive. They then won Game 7.

Of course, Greenberg hardly needed help to go long—no spy was in the center field bleachers at Yankee Stadium on September 19, 1937, when he became the first man to put a homer into those distant seats—but he accepted the little push in 1940 without moral qualms. "I never had a more enjoyable month," he admitted. And because this was Hank Greenberg, the guy who dutifully observed the high holy days, one can safely assume that the hitter hasn't been born yet who wouldn't gladly take a pilfered sign. The hidden history of baseball, in fact, includes larcenous lengths to which teams have gone to intercept catchers' digital communications. (If you don't think deciphering a pitcher is important, ask the Yankees' Andy Pettitte, whose telltale windup variations the Arizona Diamondbacks read like a book in two World Series victories in 2001.)

Greenberg pointed out that many teams used binocular espionage, from behind cracks in outfield fences and through holes in scoreboards. Checking the little windows in Fenway Park's Green Monster scoreboard has been an age-old ritual among visiting managers for eight decades. A slightly more sophisticated espionage technique, now known, may have led to the most famous home run of all. But you'll have to wait until 1951 for that story.

For the Tigers, the snooping had a brief life. In 1941, they fell to 75-79 and into fifth place. But then not even the Hubble telescope would have helped that year, when with the stench of war in the air and the Selective Service Act passed, Greenberg's number came up and he was gone with the draft nineteen games into the season. Days later, Dodger outfielder Joe Gallagher got his draft notice. Now there was a minor panic in the game as men of privilege realized they would be given no special dispensation, nor did they believe they could avoid serving without cries of favoritism. As it happened, no other big leaguers were drafted in 1941, but with Europe burning and nerves on edge in and out of baseball, it seemed clear the Summer of '41 would be the last blaze of glory and innocence before everything changed. And a blaze it was, thanks to Yin and Yang.

The '41 season, of course, is the fodder for baseball's most heated argument of all time: who was better, Joe DiMaggio or Ted Williams? History tells us that Joe D—with his epochal 56-game hitting streak, 30 homers, .357 average, league-leading 125 RBIs, and Yankee pennant—beat out The Thumper—with his equally epochal .406 average (baseball's last .400 season), major league–high 37 homers and .735 slugging average, and 120 RBIs—for the MVP award, by a curiously large margin of 291votes to 254. The vote—or the stiffing of Ted Williams, according to his courtiers—now as then sent Red Sox fans into apoplexy, but you already know how loathed Williams was by the sportswriters. You also know how wildly unreliable an indicator the MVP was back then. So why don't I try to give the debate a new twist, by refracting it through the light of the home run. Because, as always, it had a large role to play.

Doesn't the edge go to Williams since he beat DiMaggio in homers that year by 7? Well, partly. But it was also the dinger that made Joe D's hitting streak even more magnificent, by giving it guts and muscle, as opposed to, say, the single and double parade of Pete Rose's 44-game hit streak in 1978 or, to a lesser degree, Paul Molitor's 39-game streak of 1987. DiMaggio's 15 homers and 55 RBIs during the run gives higher meaning to the .408 he hit in those 56 games. He had 1 more homer than he had doubles, and if you think he may have gotten single-hungry as the streak wore on, chew on this: over the two-month adventure, from May 15 to July 17, he hit 8 homers by June 15 and 7 thereafter. No less than *seven* times a homer saved the streak as his only hit in a game—including back-to-back in July, in Games 45 and 46, the first a 3-run blow, the second a 2-run shot. DiMaggio went 91-for-223 in all, hitting a homer once every 15 at-bats and slugging *.717*. In a June 8 doubleheader he slammed 3 homers and had 7 RBIs.

Here are all the home runs during the streak:

Date	Against	Streak Game	Hits–At-Bats	Home Runs	RBI	Pitcher
May 16	Chicago	2	2-4	1	1	Thornton Lee
May 27	Washington	12	1-4	1	3	Red Anderson
June 3	Detroit	20	1-4	1	1	Dizzy Trout
June 8	St. Louis (Game 1)	23	2-4	2	4	Elden Auker
June 8	St. Louis (Game 2)	24	1-4	1	3	George Caster
June 12	Chicago	26	2-4	1	1	Thornton Lee
June 15	Cleveland	28	1-3	1	1	Jim Bagby
June 19	Chicago	32	3-3	1	2	Eddie Smith
June 22	Detroit	35	1-5	1	2	Hal Newhouser
June 25	St. Louis	37	1-4	1	3	Denny Galehouse
June 27	Philadelphia	39	2-3	1	2	Chubby Dean
July 2	Boston	45	1-5	1	3	Dick Newsome
July 5	Boston	46	1-4	1	2	Phil Narchildon
July 11	St. Louis	50	4-5	1	2	Bob Harris

As for Williams, he wrote quite a home run tale himself in '41 during his march to .406—a march that saw him hit .436 in May and .402 in August. Not generally known is that Williams would have actually hit *.412* by today's standards because he hit 6 fly balls that before 1940 and after 1945 would have been scored as sacrifice flies and not official at-bats. In fact, Williams was for many years hurt by another rule—the one requiring that a man must have 400 official at-bats per season to qualify for a league batting title. Because Williams walked so much—he led the league for eight years, with as many as 162 twice, and is fifth all-time with 2,019—it threatened to disqualify him during seasons when injuries took him out of the lineup for any appreciable time. Finally, in 1957, expressly because of Williams, the rule was modified to read 400 *plate appearances*.

During the '41 season, Williams also hit what is arguably the greatest All-Star Game home run when he came to bat with 2 outs in the bottom of the ninth, the AL down 5-4, runners on second and third. Facing Cub pitcher Claude Passeau, he turned on a fastball and hit a rocket that clanged off the facing of the right field roof at Detroit's Briggs Stadium—still the only walk-off homer in All-Star competition. Williams' clapping, light-footed trip around the bases in the old newsreels buffs up baseball's enameled virtues like no other remnant of history. (Thank God they learned to film these things since the Called Shot.) It has also wiped from memory what could have been that game's signature: 2 homers by Pirate shortstop Arky Vaughn, the first time that was done. It figured. Vaughn, a Hall-of-Fame singles and doubles hitter, had only 96 dingers in 14 big-league seasons.

Williams's most astonishing stat that year was his *.551* on-base percentage—by far a record until Barry Bonds wasted it in 2002. His problem was that 37 homers and 120 RBIs weren't fat enough numbers to be ammunition against DiMaggio (he did miss some early games with injuries). Moreover, he showed a remarkable flaw against left-handed pitchers. Williams could hit lefties, of course; he just couldn't hit them long, because he couldn't get around on them quickly enough to pull the ball. In 1941, he hit 35 of his long balls against righties, just 2 against southpaws. And this was no one-year anomaly. In his career, Williams would not hit more than 8 homers in any year against the lefties. One year the gap was 31-1, another 25-1, another 38-5. Overall, the gap was—gulp—457 to 64. For those weak in math, *88 percent* of his homers were against right handers.

By contrast, DiMaggio, from the other side of the plate, hit 241 homers against righties, 120 against lefties. Jimmie Foxx, the classic right-handed-hitting pull-hitter, went 438 and 96, or 82 percent hit against righties. You say I'm being too hard on Williams because there are tons more right-handed pitchers than left-handed ones? Nice try, but check out the splits of history's great left-handed sluggers:

Babe Ruth: 495-219 (80 percent of total hit against righties)
Lou Gehrig: 350-143 (70 percent)
Mel Ott: 400-111 (79 percent)
Johny Mize: 274-85 (80 percent)
Reggie Jackson: 384-179 (70 percent)
Barry Bonds: 427-186 (70 percent)

So chalk us up as an assenting voice for DiMaggio's MVP in '41. Williams' consolation prize was the 1942 season when he won the Triple Crown, hitting .356 with 36 homers and 137 RBIs. But his second straight second-place finish in the MVP voting, to another Yankee (second baseman Joe Gordon, who hit .322 with 18 homers and 103 RBIs), was a far more indefensible snub than in '41—only five years before, Ducky Joe Medwick had won the MVP in the NL with a Triple Crown season much like Williams'—.374, 31 homers, 154 RBIs. And if the reason was that Williams again hadn't won a pennant (the Red Sox came in second, by nine games, though they won ninety-three games that year), it didn't seem to matter for Medwick, whose Cardinals had finished in fourth place.

But this was a different game now, one that had a cheapening effect on Williams' crown. By the time the season began, the country was at war, Americans were fighting and dying in the North Africa desert, and baseball rosters were in their first stages of depletion. Missing were Greenberg—who had been discharged two days before Pearl Harbor, then re-enlisted in the Air Force—Feller, and DiMaggio. The next year, 1943, nearly every marquee name was wearing fatigues, including Williams, who enlisted in the Naval Air Corps, Mize, Mickey Cochrane, Charlie Gehringer, Stan Musial and Billy Herman. The epilogue of baseball normalcy was—fittingly—a home run, and as fate would have it, a home run by another Everyman, George "Whitey" Kurowski, who made the Cardinals that year after five seasons in the bushes. Despite a childhood accident that required a four-inch removal of bone from his right arm, Kurowski played a superb third base for nine big-league seasons and hitting a career .286. But his shining was the 1942 World Series.

That October, the Yankees were after their sixth championship in seven years and ninth straight Series conquest.Then, as now, people bemoaned the Yankees' greatness and habit of catching all the breaks, but even they would be victimized by the World Series law of random hero selection. Then again, the post-Mize Cardinals were no rummies. They won 106 games and 41 of their last 48 that year to streak to the pennant. In their reversion to the Gas House Gang style, they hit only 60 homers, third lowest in the NL, to the Yankees' AL-high 109. The young Musial hit .315 with 10 homers, Country Slaughter .318 with 13, and they were the only ones on the team in double figures. In the blood-starved NL, timely singles hitting and tight pitching were the way to success—the MVP in '42 was the Cards' 22-game winner Mort Cooper.

Arms the Cards had, and after a 7-4 loss in Game 1 of the Series, they shut down the Yankee lumberjacks, tearing off the next three games without benefit of a single home run. Then, in Game 5 at Yankee Stadium, Phil Rizzuto and Slaughter matched early solo homers. The score was tied 2-2 as the Cards came up in the top of the ninth. Cooper led off with a single against Red Ruffing, was bunted to second, and up came Kurowski, who had hit .254 with 9 homers during the season and was a meager 3-for-14 in the Series. Ruffing threw a fastball, a little high, a little inside, but not enough. Kurowski took a quick cut and hit a liner down the left field line that bent and bent but stayed fair by a few feet as it landed in the short grandstand for a cheap yet glorious dinger that put the Cards up 4-2. A half-inning later, that was the final score of the Series clincher.

The shot put Kurowski into home run heaven with Baker, Ruth, Gehrig, Foxx, Ott and . . . Harry Hooper, whose ninth-inning blast won the 1915 World Series for the Red Sox, and Elmer Smith, who hit the first Series grand slam for Cleveland in 1920.

As previously stated, the home run gods are nuts. The World Series? Forget about it.

War and Leftovers

Imagine waking up and seeing your home team replaced by twenty-five factory seconds. This was baseball during the duration, when most of the players in the premier sporting enterprise in the world were deemed by their draft boards to be in worse physical shape than the average man of their age on the street, too old or too young to be trusted with a carbine, or too domesticated as the sole provider of a large family. Among those finding a home on big-league rosters were a 15-year-old pitcher (Joe Nuxhall), a one-armed pitcher (Pete Gray), and codgers coming out of retirement for a belated paycheck (Babe Herman, Arky Vaughn, Pepper Martin).

One need only intone three words to imbue the flavor of baseball during the war: St. Louis Browns. In 1944, the Brownies rose up from their invariably moribund existence to end the Yankees' dynasty by winning their first and only pennant in fifty-three years of competition (to be generous), and did it with a gaudy team batting average of .252.

The curdled cream of the "big league" crop were a few fading stars like Mel Ott, who at age 34 in 1943 fell to 18 homers, 47 RBIs, and a .234 average—then, in '44, rose to 26, 82, and .288, followed by .308 in '45. Paul Waner, who turned 40 in 1943, boosted his average from .258 to .311, and his brother Lloyd came out of retirement to play in '44, hitting .321 as a pinch hitter. Jimmie Foxx, of course, came back in 1945 as a pitcher, and probably could have played any position he wanted, for the asking.

Younger talented men found that their batting eyes were now like a Cyclops'. The still-green Stan Musial, only 22 in 1943 and in his second season, feasted on cut-rate pitching, hitting a NL-high .357 and winning the MVP award. In '44 he hit .347—every reason why the Cardinals took the pennant both years, a title the latter year, and nothing in '45 when Musial was called into the service. Rudy York, whose number wasn't called, led baseball with 34 homers and 118 RBIs in 1943. York is actually one of the great underrated homer heroes; in 1937, as a Tiger rookie, he broke Babe Ruth's record for home runs in a month, hitting 18 in August—bettered since only by Sammy Sosa who hit 20 in June of 1998.

But the biggest beneficiary may have been Cubs' outfielder Bill Nicholson, whose nearsightedness kept him out of the service but not the big leagues. Nicholson would swing in the general vicinity of pitches with an enormous hack, and the sound made by his whipping bat when he missed—*swish*—became his nickname. In 1943 and 1944, though, Swish Nicholson led the NL in homers (29, 33) and RBIs (128, 122), and he lost the '44 MVP by one vote to Marty Marion. That year, Swish, the scourge of wartime ball, hit 4 straight homers over two games against the Giants. On his next at-bat, he was walked intentionally with the *bases loaded*, on orders from Mel Ott, who of course had once been walked in the same manner.

Overall, hitting was as awful as pitching during the four years of war. Batting averages in both leagues hovered around .250 to .260 each year, and homers remained under 500 in the homer-proud AL; the NL, by simply staying in the upper 500 range, was now the home run league. (Remember, too, the ball used those years was certifiably deader because of inferior materials for non-war industries.) But for Bill Dickey's climactic 2-run home run in Game 5 of the 1943 World Series against the Cardinals, which avenged Whitey Kurowski's blow the year before, no homer of note distinguished any Series during the war. Not by coincidence, it seems, the most outrageous wartime home run feat was turned in by a *pitcher*, the Braves' Jim Tobin. On May 13, 1942, Tobin pounded *3* homers in one game agains the Cubs—the first and still only time in history a pitcher has done that. And get this: the day before, Tobin hit a pinch-hit dinger, meaning that he had 4 homers in 5 at-bats!

So it was almost unfair when Hank Greenberg was one of the first players to return home midway through the 1945 season—and promptly banged a homer in his first game. He had rung up 12 by the season's final day, September 30, when the Tigers sat a game up on the Senators. Now, in the ninth inning against the Browns at Sportsman's Park, they were down 3-2. With first place in deep peril, Greenberg came up with the bases loaded and smacked a Nelson Potter screwball over the left field roof for a grand slam, a 6-3 lead, and the pennant. Greenberg, who lost none of his brutish power after three years on the shelf, found himself in the culture shock of the World Series of the mid-1940s, facing the Cubs, a team that in 1945 rivaled the Gas House Gang as the modern era's scrawniest home run–generating teams, with 57 homers, or one more than the worst power team in the NL.

And so of course the Cubs took Game 1, 9-0, behind a homer by Phil Cavarretta and three hits by Swish Nicholson. But Greenberg restored order in Game 2, slamming a 3-run shot to pace a 4-1 Tiger win. Detroit then ran out to a three-games-to-two edge when the Cubs took a 7-3 lead into the eighth inning of Game 6 at Wrigley Field and began thinking of Game 7. Only the Tigers broke back with 4 runs to tie it, as Greenberg capped the rally with another homer. Eventually, the Cubs went on to win in 12, but the roller-coaster ride left them out of gas for Game 7, which Detroit won 9-3 for the championship. In a Series with precious little hitting, Greenberg's 2 homers were the only ones Detroit had (the Cubs never had another one after Cavarretta's) and the Tigers hit .223 as a team. But Greenberg hit .407 with 7 RBIs and 7 runs. It was a little sign, bare months after V-E and V-J Days, that the big guns were coming off the battlefield and back to baseball.

The real significance of wartime baseball was that the game held up. After initial fears that the Germans or Japanese would bomb ballparks, attendance kept steady, dipping in both leagues to 3½ million in 1943 but rising in 1944 to the upper 3 million range in the NL and upper 4 million in the AL. In 1945, fans began streaming back, over 6 million strong in the AL and more than 5 million in the NL. In 1946, when the game reclaimed its nobility, came the explosion. But before I go there the point cannot be stressed enough that the war acutely altered baseball's all-time home run totals.

How much? Well, let me try to come up with an answer by playing with the numbers of those who lost the most. While the following model is not foolproof because it can't factor in variations such as injuries, here are the projected home run totals of the longball kings of the era, based on the average number of homers each hit over the previous three seasons before departing for boot camp:

	Career Home Runs	Years Missed	Average Homers (3 prev. yrs.)	Projected Career
Williams	521	3	32	587
Greenberg	331	4½	44	529
DiMaggio	361	3	27	442
Mize	359	3	28	443

Keep in mind that Williams missed nearly all of two more seasons during the Korean War, costing him maybe another 45 homers. So what these figures mean is that Williams would have had something like 632 home runs over an undisturbed career, and today he would be sitting at No. 4 all-time instead of No. 13. But Williams' fate was far better than poor Greenberg's, who may have lost *200* homers, which would have moved him up from No. 73 to No. 12. No wonder his bat was so angry when he came back.

The Peacetime Bomb

Because baseball was one of the most trenchant symbols of American cultural continuity during the war, and had suffered its own sacrifices and degradations, the game had a prominent place in the warm glow of victory. As one of the major things America was fighting for, baseball's quasi-patriotic properties received a laying on of hands in the nation's return to normalcy. In 1946, with all teams again intact, attendance swelled by more than 30 percent in the NL, to nearly 9 million, and by nearly double in the AL, to 9.6 million—and that was a mere warmup for 1947 when postwar domestication made the game an adopted member of the family, spawning a gate of 10.3 million in the NL and 11.1 million in the AL, records that would endure for thirteen and nineteen years, respectively.

So too did the home run go through the roof shingles. Ted Williams gave the cue, hitting the first pitch he saw in spring training in 1946 over the wall, and the dingers just kept flying—at least in the AL, which with the repatriation of Williams, DiMaggio, and Greenberg brushed aside the senior league's fleeting long-ball advantage, clanging 132 more homers than in 1945, up to 653, with the Yankees alone beefing up from 93 to a league-high 136. Indeed, how loopy is it that NL home run production *fell*, even with the return of Mize, Slaughter, et. al, from 577 to 562?

But if it seemed as if this was the same old National League, little clues told a different tale. Mize, first of all, was limited by injuries to 101 games and 377 at-bats. And while his 22 homers were still enough to be second-best in the league, the top dog with 23 (the lowest league high since 1921) was a new face that crashed the party with a portentous noise. This was Ralph Kiner, a hulking Hank Greenberg clone who had been signed by the Pirates in 1940 as a Santa Rita, New Mexico, high school boy for an $8,000 bonus. Brought up in early 1943, Kiner instead enlisted as a Navy bomber pilot and went off to war for three years. In '46, his belated rookie season, the 6-foot 1-inch, 195-pound Kiner showed that he was at best semicoordinated, snail-slow, and a liability in the outfield. But his swing was as smooth as butter, hair-trigger quick and fused by his huge hands and upper torso. With it, he became the first rookie to lead a league in homers and he was still green, doing it on pure power—he hit just .247 and struck out 109 times, most in the league.

The immediate home run glut in the AL fit into a dynamic not unlike the confluence of excesses in the Roaring Twenties, when decadence met Babe Ruth in happy union. Only now, good times were well behaved and the product not of laissez-faire capitalism and bathtub gin but a war machine that jolted the economy into high gear, creating jobs and suburban split levels as far as the eye could see. In high gear it would stay, solidifying middle-class creature comforts like two cars in the garage, fast food, and—you knew this was coming—the home run, which outlived its Perseus—Babe Ruth—as the savior of the game. By now, its mythological properties had become infused into society, and coming out of a wartime psychology, was a perfect totem for strength, power, and victory. It was, in every sense, America's peacetime bomb.

And, as such, the focal point of baseball more than ever before. Consider the statistical oddities of the half-decade following the war, when batting averages remained much the same but the long ball blew sky high—the NL turned on the home run spigot in 1947—until the early 1950s. Not by surprise, walks grew concurrently, by well over 200 in each league in 1946—then by 300 more in the NL and *700* more in the AL in '48, *1,000* more in '49 to over 5,600—unheard of numbers then.

Clearly, pitchers were becoming terrified of laying one in over the plate, and hitters more patient waiting for the meatball they could take long. In fact, after strikeouts rose for a few years, they leveled off even as homers soared. For pitchers too jittery to challenge home run hitters, the operative word was "wimp."

Baseball's Favorite Mistake, and Other Postwar Four-Baggers

In 1946 Ted Williams hit .342 with 38 long balls, 123 RBIs, and a league-high .667 slugging average. He also owned the All-Star Game, played at Fenway Park, going 4-for-4—with 2 homers, tying Arky Vaughn's record, and a new record of 5 RBIs—in the AL's 12-0 blowout victory. Rather than for any of the minutiae, however, Williams' masterpiece performance lives on for one swing, the one that produced the second homer and the kitschiest moment in the game's history.

Though the contest was long-decided, Williams came to bat in the eighth inning against Pirate pitcher Truett Banks "Rip" Sewell, a man whose very presence in the All-Star Game was a tour de force of lower-case wartime baseball. Sewell, who had lost part of his right foot in a hunting accident, was classified 4-F by his draft board but 1-A by the big leagues, and in fact was a decent pitcher, wining twenty-one games in 1943 and 1944. (He also went 13-3 in 1946.) But Sewell would forever be branded as a kind of harlequin because, to ease the stress on his foot, he would occasionally throw an absurdly mutant form of change-up that he lobbed twenty-five feet into the air before coming down—the "eephus pitch," he called it, a perfect non sequitur for a nonsensical pitch, the success of which was purely incidental: hitters were so over-anxious to hit the slow-moving target that they usually tied up in knots trying. Not once had anyone ever hit it solidly enough for a homer.

Enter the Thumper. When Williams came up, he easily engaged in the vaudeville-type shtick presaged by the inevitable drama. The eephus pitch would meet its greatest challenge, right now, in Fenway Park. And so as Williams assumed his stance, he grandly shook his head "no," in a pantomime, as if to say, "Please don't throw me that thing." Sewell, of course, nodded "yes, oh yes." So here came the eephus, in all its goofy glory . . . up, up, up, then down, down, down. Williams waited, waited, waited. And when it reached the plate, even the great Williams looked silly, hacking with a mighty fury and fouling it back. Next Sewell got coy. He threw a fastball outside. Then he threw a fastball for a called strike. Then Sewell stopped being a well-rounded pitcher and again did what he was there at that moment in time to do. The ball went up, up, up, and down, down, down. Then, a *crack*. And a rocket that came to rest in the right-center-field bullpen.

As Sewell recalled in the *Sporting News*, Williams "took a couple of steps up on it—which was the right way to attack that pitch, incidentally—and he hit it right out of there. And I mean he *hit* it. . . . I walked around the bases with Ted, talking to him. 'Yeah,' I told him, 'the only reason you hit it is because I told you it was coming.' He was laughing all the way around. He was the only man ever to hit a home run off the blooper."

A deep thought for the day: If only Williams could have been that happy more than a handful of times in his career. Now back to the real world.

Actually, not to ruin the moment, but Williams was technically out when he hit that legendary home run. Those steps he took to meet the ball took him out of the batter's box—in the old photographs his front foot is a good yard in front of the box and his *back* foot is so far up it's ahead of the plate. But it would have taken the Massachusetts National Guard to enforce that call in Boston that day. So let's call this famous dinger baseball's favorite mistake.

The eephus pitch wasn't the only ploy foiled by Williams in '46. In June, when the Red Sox played Cleveland, Lou Boudreau, the Indians' young shortstop and player-manager, began stationing himself just to the right of second base, and had his second baseman stand back twenty feet on the outfield grass between Boudreau and first base—the heralded "Williams Shift," which originated thirty years earlier to fend with Kenny Williams. The alignment was designed to screw with Williams' id more than his bat. Boudreau, playing a little reverse psychology, wanted him to give in to the temptation to till all that fertile open ground, but Williams didn't bite. Instead he resolved to rip the ball through the tiny cracks in the shift—although he did pick a wonderful time to change his mind, as we'll see in a minute.

This time, at least, Williams could not be kept from the MVP, though the biggest reason was that Joe DiMaggio was slow to regain his form and hit only .290 and 25 homers during a chaotic Yankee season that featured three managers and a third-place finish. In the upheaval, the Red Sox did Harry Frazee's ghost proud and actually won the pennant by an immense 12 games over Detroit, winning 104 games—not that Williams would care to recall the World Series against the Cardinals, when he went 5-for-25 without an extra base hit. (He wasn't the only high-octane flop: Stan Musial hit just .222.) That the Sox came close to winning the Series was due in part to Rudy York, who was traded to Boston that year and had 119 RBIs. York had half of the team's 4 Series homers, including a solo in Game 1 and a 3-run shot in Game 3. This being the Red Sox, though, a

3-to-2 lead in games only meant that they would have to lose the last two, the finale on Country Slaughter's famous mad dash from first base to score on a single when Johnny "Needlenose" Pesky inexplicably held the ball on the relay from the outfield.

Hank Greenberg, too, had mixed blessings in '46. Before the season, the hunky Greenberg not only married Coral Gimbel, heiress to the department store fortune, but pocketed his own fortune when he signed for $60,000. Thus stoked, he went yard 44 times and had 127 RBIs, both AL highs. Though his average slipped to .277 and he began having back problems, he put the Tigers on notice that he wanted "real" money—DiMaggio and Williams money. Let's say the team's management didn't react well. Without bothering to tell Greenberg, they shopped the 36-year-old slugger around and in January 1947 pawned him for peanuts—$35,000—to the Pirates, who envisioned Greenberg and Kiner interlocking in the kind of power nexus that would have been anathema at Forbes Field in past years.

Greenberg wasn't amused. Mortally offended by the trade—and more so by hearing about it first on the radio—he huffed about retiring. The Pirates talked him out of it, with a $100,000 salary (the NL's first) and by coincidentally deciding to construct a new bullpen enclave in front of the distant horizon of the left field wall that cut home run distances from 365 feet to 335 feet in left and from 406 feet to 355 feet in the left-center alley. This new gaping repository for medium-deep fly balls immediately was hung with the name of "Greenberg Gardens."

This architectural bow to the home run left Washington's Griffith Stadium as the lone holdout against shrinkage among the game's venerable ballparks—unbelievably, in 1945 the Senators hit only *one* homer all year at home, and that was an inside-the-park job by Joe Kuhel. Everywhere, though, the inside-the-park home run (or IPH)—once the sina qua non of the "clean" home run days—was becoming semi-extinct, deflating from 126 in 1914 to 106 in 1921 to 70 in 1926 to 37 in 1931 to 19 in 1946, the level at which it has stayed ever since, with exceptions (ranging from a low of 9 in 1981 to a high of 43 in 1995). Since 1939, when the number of times a player had hit 2 IPHs in a game hit 10, it has only happened twice, by Hank Thompson in 1950 and Richie Allen in 1972.

That the IPH fell out of favor was not a matter of players' choice or speed, but rather of cramped-up ballparks and the final death of the notion of manufacturing runs instead of getting them on one swing. That's not to complain, nor yearn for a return to the days of the 360-foot dash, but I do get a little misty that an act once routinely called "the most exciting play in baseball" generally can only happen today if the outfielders are Dennis Franz, James Gandolfini, and Drew Carey.

Leave it to Ted Williams, though, to write a fabulous footnote to the IPH. It happened on September 15, 1946, when the Red Sox played the Indians, needing a win to clinch the flag. Again Lou Boudreau put on the Shift, and further dared Williams to go the other way by bringing in left fielder Pat Seerey to play shallow as a kind of deep shortstop, leaving left field completely naked. He also instructed his pitcher to pitch outside. Unable to resist all that open acreage, Williams figured the time was right to break form, dunked one over Seerey's head, and just kept running. By the time the center fielder ran over and recovered the ball, Williams had come all the way around the bases. How remarkable was this? Greatly, given that it happened to be Williams' *only* inside-the-park home run in twenty-one years and 7,706 at-bats.

In 1947, Williams slammed 32 of the outside-the-park variety, good enough to lead the AL. But then Williams led in everything that year, romping to his second Triple Crown. On May 13, he skewed not 1 but 2 homers over the Green Monster, the first times he had homered twice to the opposite field at home. He had a 5-for-5 game en route to hitting .343 and he was the AL's only 100-RBI man with 114. Williams also led in walks, slugging, and on-base percentage. The only thing he didn't do was win the pennant again; the Red Sox finished third as the Yankees once more found their way under a new manager, Bucky Harris, and with a toadish-looking catcher, one Yogi Berra. So you know what's coming. Joe DiMaggio, who still had the postwar blahs, hit .315 with 20 homers and 97 RBIs—and got the MVP, his third, by a single point over Williams.

Here is why it pays to be nice to crabby sportswriters. Williams lost because a Boston scribe, Mel Webb, *left him off the ballot*. It was an unconscionable personal slight by a man Williams called "a grouchy old guy, a real grump," but it stood, rendering another Triple Crown into useless hardware. Williams must have thought a lot of other writers were grumps, too, since a mere three of the brethren gave him first-place votes. No, it wasn't easy being Ted Williams.

DiMaggio, on the other hand, had grown into veteran iconhood easily, with nary a word or a need to make his case. While Williams' far more perilous war tenure in the cockpit of fighter planes had earned him few Cub Scout points, DiMaggio's baseball-exhibition tour of Army bases all but wiped away the old Italophobia. Even Henry Luce wouldn't have dared try to print another hatchet job on Joltin' Joe, though there were a few whispers now that he had lost his groove in those three years out of the game. DiMaggio hit only .231, though with 2 of the Yankees' 4 home runs in the melodramatic seven-game World Series victory over the Dodgers. This included the one that decided Game 5, 2-1, at Ebbets Field—canceling the horror of the day before when Bill Bevens lost a no-hitter and the game on one ninth-inning pitch to Cookie Lavagetto, who doubled home 2 runs to give the Dodgers a 3-2 victory. Joe D had to suck up another crusher in Game 6 when he mashed one about as far as anyone could into the teeth of Death Valley. Dodger left fielder Al Gionfriddo chased it as a speck in the sky all the way to the Yankee Stadium bullpen railing, then stuck out his glove and the ball landed in it. DiMaggio's famous show of emotion, kicking the dirt around second base, is a newsreel classic. But while Gionfriddo saved the game, the Yankees won Game 7 on a clutch hit by Tommy Henrich (who also won Game 1 with a walkoff game-winning homer).

The most compelling home run story of 1947, however, was that the NL at long last caught and passed the AL (though Brooklyn could only muster one in the Series, by Dixie Walker). Remarkably, homers in the league zoomed by *58 percent*, to 886, 6 off the big-league record the league set in the aberrational 1930 season. A good part of the story was written in New York, where the Giants exploited the Polo Grounds' niggling fences with alarming ease, peppering the grandstand at Coogan's Bluff with 137 dingers there alone—more than all but one other team had *in total*. The Giants' bounty came out to be 221, more than shattering the old record of 174 by the '38 Yankees and the league record of 171 by the '30 Cubs.

The longest canon belonged to Johhny Mize, who recovered his health and prewar home run groove. The Big Cat was a monster everywhere, blasting a co-league-high 51, with 29 at home and 22 on the road, while notching a league-high 138 RBIs and a .302 average. That was not totally out of line for a power source like Mize, but what to make of Willard Marshall and Walker Cooper—whose previous home run highs were 13 each—yanking 36 and 35, and Bobby Thomson, essentially a rookie, going yard 29 times? Did anyone say rabbit ball? Well, no. Not in 1947. Probably because everybody was enjoying the peacetime bombs flying around too much to kvetch about it. At the new Forbes Field bandbox, in fact, long balls were the only thing that made bearable a Pirate team that gave up a league-worst 4.68 runs a game and finished last at 62-92, and that wouldn't smell a pennant race for the next decade.

The Pirates were right about yoking Greenberg and Kiner, and the union was a boon to the latter. The burly, free-swinging Kiner seemed as subtle as a rhinoceros on roller skates, but he learned from Greenberg the nuances and cerebral tiers of power hitting. While the only cards most players knew from came in a deck of 52, Kiner kept a file on 3-by-5 cards cumulatively charting every pitch he saw, gleaning patterns and probabilities of getting a meatball according to pitcher and count. He sprung for a movie projector and had someone film his at-bats, to study his form and whether pitchers tipped off their pitches. He took batting practice at all hours. And he did all of this because of Greenberg, in whom he found his St. Thomas of Aquinas.

Saint Hank's tutelage of Kiner was far more important than Greenberg's own bat, which produced 25 homers but just a .249 average as his back pain worsened beyond relief, forcing him to quit after the season, whereupon he took his baseball earnings and bought into the Indians' management. He became the team's second-largest stockholder and GM from 1949 to 1958 (later he held the same position with the fledgling Los Angeles Angels).

Greenberg left the game with two legacies, his own and Kiner's ascendance. In the transition, Greenberg Gardens neatly morphed into Kiner's Korner and became the young slugger's ticket to the home run pantheon. Kiner, who had little use for the opposite field, hit 28 dingers at Forbes Field in '47 and 51 in all, tying Mize for the big-league high in the NL's first double-50-homer season. Greenberg's most telling influence? Kiner's strikeouts—which dipped from 109 to 81, and in 63 more at-bats than the previous year; nevermore, in fact, would he reach 100.

Kiner recalled that Greenberg "impressed several principles on me. He showed me the sense of standing closer to the plate. That immediately made it tougher on the pitchers. In effect, I reduced their strike zone. He insisted that I knew my particular hitting zone. And, above all, practice, practice, practice."

Greenberg, who was able to break down the complex science of the home run to simple math, told of Kiner's education to author Bill Starr: "Ralph was an apt pupil. He caught on quick. I gave him some calculations to consider: 'Suppose you play 150 games and average 4 times at bat. That's roughly 600 times at bat, totaling about 2,400 pitches. Suppose 1,000 of those were strikes? Do you think you could hit 35 of those strikes out of the park?' Ralph said, 'Of course.' That thought stayed with him. He looked for strikes. He hit 51 homers that year . . . and [h]is batting average jumped from .247 to .313."

Later, I will show how ridiculous inefficient home run hitters would get when they stopped looking for strikes, much less reserving heavy swings for them. It would become a totally forgotten practice.

The great Mize-Kiner home run race of '47—which was fairly murked by the seismic story of Jackie Robinson's rookie year—must have shocked Mize, who had the year of his life (he also led the league with 138 RBIs and hit .302) and looked like he'd put the kid away by August 1 when he led Kiner 31 to 25. But Kiner, who then broke Johnny Rizzo's Pirate home run record of 25, went on some historic binges. He hit 3 homers in a row on August 16 against the Cardinals (that day, Greenberg also hit 2 and both clubs hit 10, then a record), giving Kiner 7 four-baggers in four games, 6 in three, 5 in two, and 4 in consecutive at-bats.

Then on September 11 he banged out 3 straight homers *again*, against the Giants, thus becoming the first to do it twice in a season (a feat since matched only by Mark McGwire in 1987 and 1995). A day later, when Kiner hit his 8th homer in four games—breaking Tony Lazzeri's 1936 record of 7 in four games—he finally passed Mize, 49-48. On the 18th, he passed him again with No. 50 against St. Louis and topped out at 51 on September 23 against the Cards' Jim Hearn. Mize squared things 51-51 on the 25th against the Braves' Johnny Sain and both men flailed away in vain over the remaining three games trying to break the deadlock.

As the young turk, Kiner got more attention than Mize, though it's debatable whether Kiner's streakiness—his 10 multihomer games that season was a record that still stands, tied only by Sammy Sosa in 1998—was more impressive than the Big Cat's steadiness. When the pair would redo the race in 1948, Kiner again hit in bunches, setting another record on September 12 with *8* long balls in four games. A classic Kiner home run came on May 9 when the umpires allowed the second game of a Sunday doubleheader against the Dodgers to break the 7:00 P.M. curfew, on grounds that the Pirates were stalling with a 5-4 lead. Brooklyn then took a 7-5 lead, but only until Kiner came up in the last of the ninth with two runners on and launched a game-winning homer into the night. But then Kiner had a thing for Sunday homers. He hit at least one dinger on that day for eight consecutive weeks over May and June, and *17* in 38 Sunday games in all.

But Mize kept up, smacking No. 40 on October 3 to tie for the lead, and that's how it ended, 40-all, with Mize beating Kiner in RBIs 125 to 123 and in average .289 to .265. How much did their home fields help? A lot. Kiner hit 31 at Forbes Field, Mize 25 at the Polo Grounds.

The late-blooming power skills of Stan Musial, however, had little to do with Sportsman's Park. Musial that year hit 39 homers and missed by 1 winning the Triple Crown, with his .376 average and 131 RBIs (and other league-highs in hits, doubles, triples, and slugging). He also slammed his first All-Star Game homer in the NL's 5-2 loss. Rather than inflating his homer stash with cheap home-field taters, Stan the Man—who had already won two MVP awards as a line-drive contact hitter—jacked 15 at home and 23 everywhere else. This was a stark metamorphosis for a guy who had hit just 19 homers the year before. But while his numbers in '47 were career highs, this was no rabbit ball–induced fluke. For the next nine seasons Musial crushed at least 21 homers and five times hit 30 or more, 475 all told. Talk about swinging at strikes; Musial never hit lower than .310 in this time and twice hit over .350, the last time in 1957 when at age 36 he won his eighth batting crown.

Brilliantly consistent, Musial was as humble as Williams was—well, not humble—yet his career eerily mirrors the Kid's, although their origins were a continent apart. Stanislaus Frank Musial, son of a Polish immigrant, was so humble that he seemed unprepossessing even at 6 feet 1 inch and 180 pounds. But Musial was constructed like the bituminous coal he lifted as a teenager in the mines of eastern Pennsylvania. Those excursions built his wrists and forearms into steel springs. Like Williams, Musial began as a pitcher before a shoulder injury led him to the bat rack, and at his first spring training with St. Louis he showed so much promise that Branch Rickey tore up his $400 bonus and gave him $700. Musial wouldn't forget; in 1946, when the Mexican League was trying to raid big-league talent, one league honcho came to see El Hombre, dumped $75,000 in big bills on his dining room table and said he could keep it if he signed a four-year, $200,000 contract. Musial, who was making $15,000 in St. Louis, told the señor no dice, that he didn't want his two young sons to hear, "There go the kids of a guy whose word was no good." Later, Musial would do something even more bizarre: request a pay *cut*. I'll leave that for now as a tantalizer.

Musial hit his 475 lifetime homers without sacrificing average—he stands 24th all-time at .331, 3rd with 725 doubles, 5th with 1,951 RBIs—or plate sense. Musial broke a Cobb record with six 5-hit games in '47 and tied Cobb and Wee Willie Keeler with four 5-for-5 games in '48 (a record until nonslugger Pete Rose did it five times in 1986). Strikeouts? Musial couldn't abide them. He never struck out more than 46 times in a season and with his 475 dingers his homer-to-strikeout ratio is a phenomenal 1:1¼. Like Williams, too, Musial could read the label and the break on a spinning ball. And, like Williams, he pretty much sucked in the World Series, adding little to the Cards' three championship rounds in his first five seasons, whereupon he was able to go home without playing October baseball for seventeen straight years. But for all of his years, the image of Musial in his strange hunchbacked, closed, feet-together stance peering at the pitcher around his right shoulder—and absolutely perfect swing—was a marker of baseball royalty.

The early and mid-1940s Cardinal dynasty burned out with second-place finishes in 1947, 1948, and 1949, as the seat of power in the NL came back east, in '47 to Brooklyn and in '48 to Boston, where the Braves relied not on big bats but the big arms of Warren Spahn and Johnny Sain, in vivid contrast to the bombast created in the AL by the Red Sox and the newly revived Indians in their fabulous "down to the wire and then some" pennant race that year. The Tribe, in particular, lived by the sword, ringing up a big-league-high 155 home runs, with two men clearing the 30 mark, Joe Gordon (31) and Ken Keltner (30). In this, the first of successive years when the Red Sox almost nearly won the pennant, the teams finished the season with identical 96-58 records that necessitated a one-game playoff, played in Boston on October 4. And once again, Williams shrunk from sight. Instead, it was Lou Boudreau who pulled out the Red Sox' heart by smacking a first-inning homer off Denny Galehouse and another in the fifth off Ellis Kinder to get the jump, and Ken Keltner iced it with a shot of his own in the Indians' 8-3 win.

The Braves, though, seemed to put a clamp on the Cleveland big boys in the World Series, which quickly turned into a pitching duel. Over the first three games neither team scored more than 4 runs, and two of the contests were shutouts. But the Tribe won two of them, meaning that when their bats woke the Braves were toast. In game 4, Larry Doby—the AL's first African American player—homered in the third to put the Indians up 2-0 while pitcher Steve Gromek weathered a Marv Rickert homer in the seventh to win 2-1. Game 5 was a home run fest; both teams hit 5 dingers, with Boston's Bob Elliott notching a pair and 4 RBIs in the Braves' 11-5 win. But all it took was one homer—by Joe Gordon—early in Game 6 to stake pitcher Gene Bearden to the lead he never relinquished in a 4-3 victory that clinched it for the Tribe.

In 1949, when the Dodgers again took the NL flag, Ted Williams had his last great chance to get a ring, given that the Yankees were learning they couldn't depend on Joe DiMaggio anymore. While Joe D had finally relocated his swing the year before, leading the AL with 39 homers and 155 RBIs, he was slow to recover from an off-season foot surgery and was limited to seventy-six games in '49, in which he hit .346 and 14 homers. DiMaggio's erosion made moot the last of a series of rumors about Williams trading uniforms. Actually, the closest to fruition the rumor ever came was in 1941, apparently in exactly the same way Jake Ruppert and Harry Frazee had cooked up the Babe Ruth deal—during a night of extended elbow bending in a New York watering hole, this time featuring Tom Yawkey and the Yankees' GM and part-owner, Larry MacPhail, a brilliant baseball man and quite possibly its most unstable of all time. MacPhail (who during World War I was involved in an unsuccessful plot to kidnap Kaiser Wilhelm) had made lucrative winners of the Reds, the Dodgers, and the Yankees, but after the 1947 World Series he became drunk in the clubhouse, punched out a sportswriter, and announced he was quitting the game. Had the biggest trade of all time gone down in '49, however, it would have been as big a disaster for the Red Sox as Frazee's deal, because DiMaggio's career was now becoming terminal. So props to Yawkey for averting another Red Sox catastrophe.

It was the only break the Red Sox had in 1949. On the surface, nothing should have stopped them that year. Here's what they did: they led baseball by far with 908 runs, scored a then-record 14 runs in an inning, and had two games with 3 consecutive homers. They had Bobby Doerr and Vern Stephens, each of whom hit more than 220 career home runs. Their team ERA was only marginally higher than the Yankees'. Williams, coming off his fifth batting title, resolved to go more for the money ball, and increased his homers from 25 to 43, his RBIs from 127 to 159. He and Stephens went 1-2 in the AL homer derby all year, pushing the Sox to a league-high 131 dingers. They also hit .283 as a team to the Yankees' .269, and they had four .300 hitters and two 150-RBI men (Williams and Stephens had 159 each).

And yet it took all season for them to catch the Yankees, who found nirvana with another new manager—Casey Stengel, whose previous managing forays with the Dodgers and Braves had yielded exactly one season above .500 and hardly seemed to qualify him a job at the scene of his legendary inside-the-park mad dash in the '23 World Series. But Stengel was smarter than his buffoonery suggested. Juggling talent wisely, he found a winning formula in flip-flopping his lineup according to left- or right-handed pitchers—the platoon system, in which only Phil Rizzuto got over 440 at-bats. Stengel also was given a hell of a replacement part when in August the Giants dealt Johnny Mize for a chump-change $40,000—leaving the NL home run field to Ralph Kiner, who clocked 54 big ones, and, as did Musial, one in All-Star Game. Used mainly as a high-priced pinch hitter, the Big Cat would have one last great resurgence in the 1950s.

The Yankees had one other thing that made life miserable for the Red Sox—DiMaggio, who—hobbled or not—was born to torment Williams. The year before, when the Yankees were out of it and the Sox battled the Indians toe-to-toe all the way, a 4-for-4 game by DiMaggio in the final game sunk them. Now, during a June series at Fenway Park, DiMaggio flew to Boston after being fitted with an orthopedic shoe, which had no spikes, and a reinforced heel to ease the pain in his foot. In the first game, he popped a 2-run homer into the screen above the Green Monster to give the Yankees a 5-4 victory. In the second game he helped erase a 7-1 deficit with a 3-run blast, then hit another to win it, 9-7. He put the third game away with yet another shot—his 4th in 11 at-bats.

Still the Sox kept breathing. On September 25, when Williams hit his 43rd and final homer to help twenty-five-game winner Mel Parnell beat Allie Reynolds 4-1 at Fenway, the Red Sox tied the Yankees for first place (DiMaggio was in the hospital at the time with pneumonia). They then came to Yankee Stadium for the last three games, leading by a game and needing only one more win to clinch. Yeah, right. Of course, they lost all three. Days later, the Yankees were back in the World Series against their perennial butt-boys, the Dodgers, who were in the process of forming a dynasty of their own with a core of young hitters—Gil Hodges, Duke Snider, Carl Furillo—and by getting a jump on the first wave of great black talent. By 1949 Jackie Robinson and Roy Campanella were fixtures in the lineup, and Don Newcombe was their best pitcher, even on a staff with Preacher Roe and Ralph Branca. They would go on cultivating the Negro Leagues into the '50s as all but a few big-league clubs made even cursory moves to sign black players. The Yankees, for one, wouldn't take on their first until 1955, the Red Sox not until 1959.

Indeed, in Game 1 of the 1949 World Series, Don Newcombe matched zeroes with Allie Reynolds inning for inning in a splendid scoreless game that wasn't decided until Tommy Henrich—the gritty right fielder who more than earned his moniker of "Old Reliable" that catch-as-catch-can season—led off the bottom of the ninth and hit a Newcombe pitch screaming into the right field grandstand for a 1-0 Yankee win—a moment that, as preserved in the wry and knowing prose of the newest press box vaunt, the *Herald-Tribune*'s Red Smith, barely disturbed the air of bored, communal tedium that had become the overriding Yankee Stadium vibe:

> Humphrey Bogart and Baby Bacall sat looking on, as silent as the 62,222 other witnesses. They've put on more spectacular battles, and stirred more excitement, in El Morocco.
>
> There was nothing to holler about except the pitching, and World Series fans don't holler much at pitching duels. And then, all of a sudden, it was over.
>
> Spectators sat there, struck speechless before they'd had a chance to yell. They had seen Henrich whack Newcombe's third pitch of the ninth inning into the right-field seats, but it took a moment for the meaning of the hit to sink in. In that moment, Newcombe started for the bench. Some in the stunned crowd thought, for just an instant, that he was taking himself out of the game in disgust.
>
> Then they got the idea; Henrich had taken him out of the game. There was no place to go but home.
>
> Henrich is the guy who hit a home run in the Yankees' first game of the season, when they went into first place; a home run in their last game of the season, when they won the American League pennant; and now the home run that sent them away ahead of the Dodgers, one game to none.
>
> Between those first two [homers], he hit a wall in Chicago and disarranged a string of vertebrae. They said then—this was August 28—that he was through with baseball for the year and maybe forever. His injury was the most serious suffered by any of the patients in ward 4, the huge hospital wing formerly known as Yankee Stadium.
>
> Ask Don Newcombe how Henrich is looking these days. He'll agree this is the most violent invalid on the Eastern seaboard.

The Dodgers won Game 2 by the same score, but one gets an idea of how cursed they were whenever they saw the Yankees on the same field when Pee Wee Reese, Luis Olmo, and Campanella each hit a home run in Game 3 and they still lost, 4-3, when the Yankees scored 3 in the ninth inning—2 on a pinch-hit single by Johnny Mize. Good as they were, the Dodgers could read the tea leaves and they went quietly, going under in five games.

Ted Williams, who also hit .343 and lost the Triple Crown because that was .0002 behind Cleveland's George Kell, won another MVP in '49, his last. After the season he was given a raise as well, to $120,000, the highest salary in baseball at the dawn of the 1950s, and for years afterward. As the new decade would pan out, however, the game would only taste more bitter to Williams, who loved baseball so much it probably killed him that the game didn't seem to want to love him back.

The Yankees, meanwhile, would take yet another dynasty into yet another decade, easily able to replace the broken-down DiMaggio with yet another brawny, over-hyped superstar of epic and tragic dimensions, whose yin-yang symbiosis (yin-yang-yin, actually) within the city limits of New York City would be the pluck and dash of that most placid of decades.

10

Baby Boomers

Oasis of Calm

The '50s began with a seemingly sanguine America facing global challenges and domestic paranoia that had Communists hiding under the beds of, well, everyone. For baseball, which would contribute players to the Korean conflict and to army hitches all during the decade, the mission was to insulate the game from the roiling outside world, keeping it an oasis of calm and conventionalism. Thus, the first thing its chieftains did in 1950 was to implant an appropriately obsequious commissioner to uphold the owners' feudal system.

Rock 'n' roll may have been in the wind in the early 1950s but baseball was still lost in a minuet of old-world values and hypocrisies. Which is why there was a problem when the man they had appointed after Kenesaw Mountain Landis's death in 1945, Kentucky senator Albert "Happy" Chandler, didn't know the dance. Chandler's worldview was far too tolerant to suit the neanderthal owners, which cost him his job—though the revisionist spin that Chandler's obeisance about integration got him sacked is pure drivel, since his role in the fall of the color line was at best passive-aggressive. Chandler's bigger perceived sin was his "subversive" sympathy for player concerns, read by the owners as a willingness to eliminate the last bastion of baseball autocracy, the reserve clause. In truth, all Chandler did was institute a player pension fund and suggest that owners listen to the players more. Oh, and by the way, he ordered investigations of several owners' gambling activities.

And so at the winter meeting in 1950, the old line came up with the seven votes needed to deprive Chandler of another term. In his place, a year later, came a friendly establishment face—Ford Frick—whom earlier was one of Babe Ruth's ghostwriters. Frick was very good at swathing the game in apple-pie optimism, and he parlayed that skill into jobs as the NL's PR director and then NL president in 1935. But at least Frick was a baseball guy, not a judge, a politician, or the scourge of latter-day baseball, a CEO. Frick had deftly handled the tension of Jackie Robinson's rookie year, playing it like a walk in the park, and as the game began to swell with black players in the '50s Frick neatly fit this transition into the game's country-fair-light traditions. Frick even had the foresight to suggest interleague play—the NL shot him down—but his defense of the sport's elite (such as his refusal to allow the players to unionize) won him a nickname he adored—that of baseball's "Czar."

Soon enough, when tradition and old loyalties would clash with simple fairness, the home run would feel the sting of the Czar's most infamous fiat.

Let's make Chandler happy, though, by giving him his due; at his urging teams dropped their resistance to providing free local radio coverage and then a national game of the week on the new medium of the cathode ray tube (correctly realizing that a rising tide of appeal would lift up all the boats). And just in time for a decade that would offer perfect, made-for-TV moments and icons.

The home run, of course, would be featured front and center in that big picture, its history and myths riding the wind with a new generation of long balls—including those of four men whose careers were birthed in the '50s and who would venerate Ruth by chasing his home run numbers, his home run distances, and his home run persona.

The baseball barons were by then head over heels in love with the long ball. In 1950, they even showed their appreciation by strictly redefining the strike zone in its favor. A strike now could only be called from the batter's armpits to the top of his knees, making it even tougher to deliver a called strike and get ahead of a hitter, the single greatest strategy against the home run. Except they forgot the usual dynamic of helping the hitters: that smarty-pants pitchers adjust and do different things than they're supposed to do. What they did, beginning in 1951, was to stop thinking that the only thing they could do to avoid the home run was to throw wildly, either walking or striking out hitters in between dingers. In the '40s, pitchers tried to be Bob Feller, with very erratic results. Bill James cites as the archtypical hitter of the later 1940s' Pat Seerey, who in

'48 with the Indians and White Sox struck out 102 times and walked 90 times while hitting 19 homers (4 in one extra-inning game).

By three years later, the control pitcher had made a comeback, nibbling at the corners, swapping speed for location, and getting ahead on the count. Suddenly, that tide of walks abated, strikeouts rose, and averages and home runs drooped—in the NL from 1,100 to 1,024 to 907 between 1950 and 1952, and in the AL from 973 to 839 to 794. One of the great control pitchers of all time, Robin Roberts, led the Phillies, of all people, into the thick of a pennant race in 1950 that climaxed in heart-thumping fashion on October 1, the season's final game, when the "Whiz Kids," as the media dubbed them, met the Dodgers at Ebbets Field.

Brooklyn smelled Phillie blood on that day. The Kids had lost much of their Whiz during a late September collapse, and the Dodgers pounced, cutting a seven-game deficit with eleven to play to one game. If they won now, they would force a three-game playoff for the flag. On the hill, Roberts faced off against Don Newcombe, 2 nineteen-game winners, who were both airtight. The game was a 1-1 tie as the Dodgers came up and made a bid to end it in the bottom of the ninth. They got the first two runners on when Duke Snider lined a single to center, sending Cal Abrams around third and heading for home—but Richie Ashburn's throw from center nailed him. The Dodgers still had men on second and third with one out, and then the bases loaded after Roberts intentionally walked Jackie Robinson, but Roberts retired Carl Furillo and Gil Hodges without harm. Then in the top of the tenth, Roberts and Eddie Waitkus singled, and after a botched bunt, up came Dick Sisler.

No, not George Sisler, the wondrous hitter of the 1910s and 1920s (who, ironically, was in the stands on this day, as Branch Rickey's chief scout). This was his son Dick, an unheralded first baseman who got a chance to play the year before only because Waitkus, then the first baseman, was shot by a woman in a Chicago hotel room. Dick was not in George's class, but he did hit .296 with 13 homers in '50, his career high, and he'd had three singles in this game. Newcombe, though, paid him scant respect. He tried to blow Dick away with heat, getting two quick strikes before wasting one high and outside. Both he and Sisler knew the deal: the next one would be another fastball. When it came in, a bit high and away, Sisler cut loose and yanked it over the left field wall for a 4-1 lead that Roberts preserved in the bottom of the tenth—amazingly, the Phillies didn't go to their big closer, Jim Konstanty, who would win the league's MVP award for that season—for the first Phillie pennant since

1915. And for Dick Sisler, an eternal ray of light. As Sisler recalls, echoing at least a thousand other commoners touched by the baton of the home run, "If it hadn't been for that homer, I don't think people would have remembered me. I was just another ballplayer."

Roberts, who finished 20-11, would win 21 or more over the next five seasons (going 28-7 in '52) and lead the NL twice in strikeouts while never walking more than 64. In '57, though, by which time baseball was taken back by the home run hitters, Roberts would *lose* 22 games, giving up the most runs in the league, and well on his way to surrendering more home runs than any other pitcher in history, 505.

The moral of this story: you can defuse the homer, but you can never beat it for long.

So don't fret when I tell you that the leading home run men in the early '50s bore progressively lighter numbers. That from 1950 to 1952, Ralph Kiner's league-leading totals dropped from 47 to 42 to 37. That the AL became a free-for-all, the leaders changing each year, from Al Rosen (37) to Gus Zernial (33) to Larry Doby (32). And that even the Yankees could only squeeze out 2 homers (to the Phillies' 0) in their sweep of the 1950 World Series. (The AL MVP that year? That renowned slugger Phil Rizzuto.) Because if the Dick Sisler dinger wasn't enough to make the point or Sid Gordon's 4 grand slams for the Yanks in '50—or even that year's All-Star Game, when 2 stunning blows saved the NL's hide, 1 by Ralph Kiner for a 3-3 tie in the top of the ninth and 1 by Red Schoendienst to win it in the top of the fourteenth—it was also during this home run lull that the most celebrated dinger of all time was hit, and the biggest home run argument of all time began to rage.

Virgin Spring

Has there ever been a more meaningful year than 1951? Of course not. Not only for one particular home run but for who came through the baseball and pop culture doors that season—and who went out. As spring training that year fairly crackled with the arrival of "The Natural" times two, one in the Yankee camp, one in the Giants', nearly overlooked in the commotion was Joe DiMaggio, who was now more of a relic than a clipper.

He was 36 that spring, more brittle than he cared to admit to himself. While he had become the first player to earn $100,000, beating Ted Williams by a few weeks before the '49 season, Joe D was the last to know he was washed up. So the Yankee brass kept dropping hints to that effect.

This included Casey Stengel, who realized both that DiMaggio could no longer play center field and that nothing could be done to move him out of there. While Stengel tried in vain to prod him to lighten his load, DiMaggio was set on his own plan for '51: banging the long ball.

As noted before, in DiMaggio's last few seasons, when he was bigger and slower, he reverted to the early Joe D, before he began aiming for the gaps. He swatted 32 homers and had 122 RBIs during his healthy-again 1950 season. But he was eaten alive by Death Valley—23 of his dingers came on the road—and his average slipped to .301, his lowest ever save for his rusty postwar .290.

Still, Joe D enjoyed using the bulk he had gained. On September 10, 1950, he crushed three homers in one game at *Griffith Stadium*, something no one had done before. He also beat Robin Roberts with a homer to win Game 1 of the World Series, 2-1. But in '51, he was merely mortal and became enmeshed in ungodlike petty squabbling with Stengel, who let him play no more than 115 games. When DiMaggio misplayed a fly ball in a July 8 game against the Red Sox, the old man unceremoniously yanked the living legend from the game—after he had already gone out to center for the next inning, an unconscionable slight. In another game he absent-mindedly jogged off the field, head down, with the ball he'd caught for the third out—except it was the second out and a run scored. That time Stengel let him be and he atoned by hitting a game-winning homer.

DiMaggio also hit some key homers as part of the Yankee drive to the '51 pennant, finishing with 12 homers, 71 RBIs, and a .288 average. But he was eclipsed by the new Yankee vanguard led by the gnome-like existential philosopher Yogi Berra, who won the MVP that year, with a team-high 27 homers, bulldog-faced ex-Marine Hank Bauer, and a certain pubescent blond bombshell rookie from Oklahoma. In fact, Joe D only played as much as he did because the latter, Stengel's pet project, nearly washed out as a monumentally over-hyped stiff.

This, of course, was the kid with the stranger-than-fiction name of Mickey Mantle, who had been touted as DiMaggio's replacement even before he wore his first Yankee uniform—which, as trivia freaks know, had the number "6" on it, foreordaining him in the line of succession after Ruth, Gehrig, and DiMaggio. Indeed, Mantle's arrival was like a Broadway opening after two years of summer-stock-building anticipation. Born in Spavinaw, Oklahoma, in 1931, he was a bulging myth already, the New York media having knitted every detail into a fairy story. How he was groomed to play by his father, an obsessive failed ex-ballplayer known as Mutt, who named his boy after Mickey Cochrane. How while other scouts scrupulously waited for him to graduate high school before moving in on him, Yankee scout Tom Greenwade inveigled the school to graduate him early and then signed the kid in his father's car after a sandlot game when he blasted two long homers.

Mantle, given a $1,100 bonus and a $140-a-month contract with the Independence, Missouri, team in the Kansas-Oklahoma-Missouri league, hopped up the bush-league ladder as a star in waiting. Tales of his booming homers made headlines in the New York papers. It wasn't only that he hit balls into the next county; because of his Tobacco Road origins, he was a real-life Li'l Abner, a wire-coiled 6-foot, 180-pound man-child with a golden buzzcut and a Bunyanesque upper body made powerful by long hours slamming sixteen-pound rocks with a sledgehammer in the lead and zinc mines he worked with his father back home. He would come up swinging a tree stump and blithely hit pitches out of sight—from either side of the plate. And if he wasn't doing that, he'd just as easily drag a perfect bunt and run like a jackrabbit to first, within 3.1 seconds.

The ingenuous caricature, while essentially accurate, did nothing but invite failure, not least of all because he was really not another Ruth, just an enormously gifted athlete and a painfully shy goober with a breakable ego. While he had a big year with the Class C Joplin, Missouri, team in the Western Association (26 homers, 136 RBIs, .383), when he came to the Yankee camp in '51 and converted from a sorry shortstop to an unsure outfielder, he stepped in to a crock pot of pressure. Being given that No. 6 didn't help. Neither was the endless pursuit of every "agent" in town once he got to New York, the same as Ruth. One maggot duped him into signing a contract giving the guy a *50 percent* cut. Mantle also awoke after a boozy night with a showgirl to find he'd signed away 25 percent more to *her*. The Yankees were able to extricate him from those compacts, and hook him up with a legit agent, Frank Scott. Boozy nights, that would be another matter.

Mantle mashed some unbelievable shots (two reputed to be over *600 feet*) in his first spring training—exactly as Ruth had—and generated much the same breathless ink in the papers. When the Yankees hit town for their season opener at Yankee Stadium against Boston on April 17, Mantle, playing right field, went 1-for-4, the hit being a single off Bill Wright in a 5-0 win. But he was still the story. Red Smith, for one, couldn't resist stoking the folk-hero angle in his column the next day:

> An hour and a half before the New Year dawned, Mickey Charles Mantle . . . was standing on the top step of the Yankees' dugout. . . . Sitting on the bench, Casey Stengel could see his newest outfielder only from the chest down.
>
> The manager grunted with surprise when he noticed that the sole of one baseball shoe had come loose and was flapping like a radio announcer's jaw. He got up and talked to the kid and came back shaking his head. . . .
>
> "Who is he?" a visitor asked.
>
> "Why, he's that kid of mine," said Mr. Stengel, to whom proper names are so repugnant he signs his checks with an X.
>
> "That's Mantle?"
>
> "Yeh. I asked him does he have any better shoes and he said he had a new pair, but they're a little too big." . . .
>
> When he came up for the third time the Yankees were leading 2-0, with none out and runners on first and third. Earlier, Joe Dimaggio had started a double play with an implausible catch of a pop fly behind second, as if to tell Mantle, "This is how it's done up here, son." Now Joe, awaiting his turn at bat, called the kid aside and spoke to him.
>
> Mantle nodded, stepped back into the box and singled a run home. . . . When the kid raced home from second with his first big-league run, the whole Yankee bench arose to clap hands and pat his torso. He was in the lodge.

Stengel's mantras about "that kid of mine" and his intention not to let the press overlook anything good Mantle did made it even tougher for Mantle to cope with the reality of existing as a raw rookie. As obsequious as the writers were to him, Mantle had no idea what to say to them, and eventually said nothing, stoking a simmering boil that would come to a head down the road. For now, Mantle simply tried to somehow live up to his notices. He hit his first big-league homer on May 1 against Chicago's Randy Gumpert in an 8-3 win; a 450-footer in St. Louis on May 4 off Duane Pillette; his first right-handed shot on May 13 in Philadelphia off Alex Kellner; and three days later his first Yankee Stadium tater off Cleveland's Dick Rozek. And though Mantle was hitting .321 and right in the thick of the home run race, he began to tank. Pressing more, he began to overswing and strike out—a lot, five times in a May 30 doubleheader loss to the Red Sox, three times in the opener and his first two times up in the nightcap, whereupon Stengel pulled him from the game. He also made bonehead plays, such as missing second base on a hit. And right field was always adventureland. (In a spring training game, Mantle tried to catch a ball only to have it bounce off his head.)

Then, too, Stengel's maneuvers aside, the fans still loved DiMaggio. Blinded by loyalty to the fact that Joe D was getting to very few balls not hit straight at him, many fans blamed Mantle—the obvious center fielder–in–waiting—for undercutting DiMaggio. Mantle felt the sting in his first taste of Yankee Stadium booing, and came to deeply resent DiMaggio by proxy for it. Unprepared for DiMaggio's iceberg manner, he took it personally, feeling that Joe D wanted him to fall on his face. Very soon, that fear would play out in a terrible scenario.

Worse, Mantle fell into controversy when it got out that he'd been classified 4-F by his Oklahoma draft board due to a congenital bone disease, osteomyelitis. The condition had flared when Mantle suffered a high school football injury, nearly costing him his leg. While it had abated enough for him to play ball, under military regulations, the condition disqualified him from serving. The deferment lit a brushfire of criticism. Mantle, wrote one columnist snidely, was let out of the service because "he couldn't kick anyone in Korea." Soon letters began to appear in the newspapers questioning his patriotism, and when vitriolic fan mail poured in to the Yankees, the team arranged, with Mantle's open assent, for him to be reexamined by his board, though the verdict was the same.

In time the contretemps faded, but Mantle was so offended by the slurs on his patriotism that he kept a distance from both the writers and the fans, though in truth the press never stopped giving him his props even during the draft business. And after he struck out three times on July 13 and had sunk to around .260, Stengel knew he had to get the kid out of town for a while. Mantle's violent bat and helmet-throwing tantrums after strikeouts had become scary, but scarier still was his uncontrollable crying in the clubhouse after his five-strikeout day. Any day, the Yankees believed, he would have a nervous breakdown. And so on July 15 he was sent down to Kansas City in the American Association. Crushed by the demotion, an aimless Mantle pouted, went hitless in twenty-two minor-league at-bats, and wanted to quit. What transpired next, of course, is the, ahem, mantelpiece of Mantle lore: how Mutt Mantle, dying of Hodgkin's disease, drove to see him, called him out—"I thought I raised a man, not a coward!"—and gave him his other career option, working in the zinc mines.

Because Mantle was slapped out of his self-pity, and went on a tear, Mutt Mantle's piece of reverse psychology is now regarded as a great moment in Freudian history. Just as Mantle's morbid fatalism about dying an early death is the gateway—and the pity factor—in all of his self-destructive tendencies all through the ensuing years. A more mature Mantle returned to the Bronx on August 20—wearing, at his request, the less-stomach-bubbling No. 7—for what would be a sixteen-year melodrama of power, courage, and pain—a run that Baby Boomers would take as the reification of bent-but-unbreakable manhood but which would for Mantle himself be a parade of too many wasted days and wasted nights, squandering his incredible natural gifts.

And yet on the many days and nights that weren't wasted, the breadth of Mantle would make people swallow their gum in awe as they watched his home runs soar high and far and higher and farther. Mantle wanted it no other way. His stance and swing—his entire gestalt—was built around the home run. Even when he was still on the skinny side, his broad back, thick neck, and muscle-padded forearms immediately located him in a crowd. When Mantle grabbed a bat—a rather light one for the times, at $35\frac{1}{4}$ inches, 34 ounces—the home run had its living, breathing billboard. Mantle, from either side of the plate, used no frills. He just bent deeply at the knees, generating raw power from his bullock thighs as he rose up and swung. And what a swing it was, often taking him down on one knee at the point of contact. This did not, however, drain any power from that swing. If he made contact, the transfer of momentum was nuclear. His problem was making contact, and it would forever be a problem. In fact, Mantle's arrival and the telegenic appeal of his swing and home runs probably was when the art of hitting homers by being a good fundamental hitter began to melt away into the homer-at-any-cost ethos, and with it the end of the strikeout as a cause for shame among hitters everywhere, on every level from crib to weekend beer-belly softball league.

For Mantle, who wound up with 13 homers, 65 RBIs, and a .267 average in '51, the ethos was the macho strut that was fused into the concept of American malehood during the '50s—the same ethos he still wore around his neck many years later when he wrote in his autobiography *The Mick*, "[I]f I had played my career hitting singles . . . I'd wear a dress." This was to be Mantle's corona on the field and off, but as with many other male icons of the era, it offered little sanctuary when real men tried to drink each other under the table without realizing the toll they'd have to pay for it.

Mantle, though, wasn't the only melodrama in town. Right across the Harlem River, a similar one was unfolding at the Polo Grounds, where another teenage phenom of humble origin, from the backwaters of Alabama, was also working through early failure. And in retrospect, Willie

Mays had an even greater burden, since he was being touted as the first African American superstar of the Boomer generation. The rub was that while Jackie Robinson, Larry Doby, Roy Campanella, and Hank Thompson had made it safe for young black men to realistically ponder big-league careers, few teams were in any great hurry to accommodate them. Even Branch Rickey, after leaving Brooklyn in 1950 for Pittsburgh, seemed to lose interest in the movement he had stuck his neck out for, signing only one non-Caucasian player, Roberto Clemente, in 1954. Even with Mays, it came down to an either-or choice.

Born in Westfield, Alabama, five months before Mantle in 1931, Mays also had a father with a goofy nickname—Kitty Kat—who when not picking and baling cotton for a living was a backwater baseball legend, and his wife the holder of local records for the 100-yard dash. Mays came through the now-dying Negro League pipeline, starting his career at age 17 with the Birmingham Black Barons—who, in a common scenario of the times, was signed by the Giants for $5,000 in 1949 without regard or compensation for the black team that held his contract. The big leagues' attitude was that if you found a player of uncommon ability, you just took him. And Mays was most uncommon, a postmodern type of power hitter—an organically perfect player who didn't have to swing for a dinger to get one. Where Mantle looked bigger than he was, Mays, at 5 feet 11 inches and then around 170 pounds, looked smaller, but only because he was a tight coil of a man, every sinew in him concentrated TNT and as flexible as a rubber hose. People said Mantle could do everything, but Mays really *could* do everything—meaning he had it all over Mantle as an outfielder, including being able to run down any ball and gun down a runner at 300 paces.

Most of all, he did everything with an elan that could steal one's eyes and wouldn't give them back. In the batter's box, Mays' knees jittered and his bat wiggled, just dying to explode, which happened with a long, sweeping stroke that seemed to come by way of Alabama—yet rarely left him vulnerable to breaking stuff or inside stuff or *any* stuff, because he was just too damn quick for biology to explain. Again, I'm talking organics here. To be sure, part of Mays' tintype was his pure joy for the game and his pure showmanship—he wore his cap a size too big so it would fly off as he ran the bases or the outfield, and that of course would be the most deeply etched image of his career. That and the basket catch—a creature cursed by all managers and coaches as the wrong way to catch a fly ball and which marked the start of baseball's now–de rigeur showboating—though for Mays it was entirely purposeful: it was easier to get the ball out the glove at belt-level to make a throw. So let's draw a big, thick line between Mays' medium-cool style and, say, Barry Bonds posing at the plate lovingly watching his home runs—something Mays never did, and with reason: it might have cost him an extra base. Simple, right? So tell Bonds, Mike Piazza, and Ken Griffey Jr.

But Mays didn't have it made. The Giants in 1951 had four black players—Monte Irvin, Hank Thompson, Artie Wilson, and Rafael Noble—one more even than the trailblazing Dodgers—and held to a one-black-a-year quota. When Mays was assigned to the Giants' AA team in Minneapolis in '51, his competition for promotion was 37-year-old Ray Dandridge, arguably the finest third baseman in the Negro Leagues whom the Giants had signed that season. The choice turned out to be Mays only because he hit .477 with 8 homers and 30 RBIs in his first thirty-five games. Dandridge? He played the entire season, hit .311, and was the league's MVP. But for this future Hall of Famer, the call never came. Ah, baseball. Cherish the tradition.

Mays arrived with only a fraction of the delirium that surrounded Mantle, and at the time the Giants were a dismal 6 and 20 so the pressure quotient was low. Still, Mays was rushed into the starting lineup by Leo Durocher, who was to Mays as Stengel was to Mantle, a courtier, protector, and flack—but in a far more fatherly sense. Not that Leo wasn't a crude, even loathsome lout, but his sensitive nurturing of a barely literate black man far from home was a critical 1950s' racial signpost. Of course, it also put heat on Mays, to reward the man he reverently called "Missah Leo." And it didn't happen.

In his first at-bat, against the Phillies' Bubba Church, he struck out. After five games, Mays was still hitless after 22 at-bats. Like Mantle across the river, Mays was coming unglued, and he tearfully told Durocher he wanted to be sent down. Leo's reaction, like Mutt Mantle's to his son's blubbering, was to tell the kid to be a man (this was evidently the emerging theme of the new decade) and that he was staying in center field at Coogan's Bluff. Mays never looked back. On May 28 he stepped up against Warren Spahn at the Polo Grounds and kissed it good-bye.

As charted by Red Smith, the ball "cleared the fence in left. It cleared the seats in the lower seats. It cleared the tall upper deck. It cleared the roof above that, and disappeared."

A meatball pitch? Hardly. Spahn, who's never talked about any of his 363 career wins as much as he has about giving up that epochal dinger, recalled the pitch as "one of the best curves I ever threw in my life. It must have broke a foot." His reliable one-liner about the homer goes like this: "I'll never forgive myself. We might have gotten rid of Willie forever if only I'd struck him out."

Once in the groove, Mays really never lost it. He blasted 2 homers to break up extra-inning games that season and in late July had 3 in six days. There were rookie boners, too. Like Mantle, a ball bounced off Mays' head in the outfield for a double. He was picked off second base. He blew an inside-the-park homer when he failed to touch third base. But, oh, the things he could do. On August 5 against Brooklyn, in the eighth inning of a 1-1 game, he ran down a long drive hit by Carl Furillo into the right–center field alley, pivoted on a dime counterclockwise completely around, and threw out an incredulous Billy Cox trying to score after tagging up. Wes Westrum then hit a 2-run shot off Ralph Branca in the bottom of the frame for a 3-1 Giant win.

"I'd like to see him do that again," said the Dodger manager, Chuck Dressen.

If only he knew.

Dressen, though, was prone to such cracks. After sweeping a July 4 doubleheader from the Giants, he told the press, "They'll never bother us again." In fact, even after the incredible Mays play, punctuating a mid-season Giants' revival, the Dodgers still led them by 10½ games. On August 11 it was 13½. And Mays, who would bag 20 homers, 68 RBIs, and hit .274 that season, had become a sidebar. While Durocher would later turn up the hyperbole, calling Mays no less than "Joe Louis, Jascha Heifetz, Sammy Davis and Nashua rolled into one," neither Willie nor Mickey were icons yet. But then neither were Marilyn Monroe, James Dean, nor Lucy. They all would be in the turn of a page, but in the summer of '51 it wasn't Mays or Mantle who stood as the best young outfielder in New York.

That was Duke Snider's turf.

As well it should have been, since the Duke—so nicknamed by *his* ballplaying father as a teenager growing up in Los Angeles—had a head start roaming center at Ebbets Field since 1947. Just as Mantle's father had him learn to switch-hit nearly at birth, Edwin Donald Snider, who threw right-handed, was ordered to bat left-handed, the better to see those predominant right arms in motion from the batter's box. But after the Dodgers signed him, Snider did little as he bounced around the bushes for five years and lost another year to military service. It wasn't until Branch Rickey hired George Sisler to, as Rickey said, "establish a relationship with the strike zone" for Snider that he arose. The Duke became a superb hitter with power to all fields. Sisler's method was to put the young man in the batting cage without a bat and tell him to recite what each pitch was. Snider thus learned to read pitches and gear his swing accordingly.

Snider also had the benefit of being couched in an All-Star lineup with Robinson, Campanella, Reese, Furillo, et al., both easing the pressure and netting him better pitches. And of course, he had Ebbets Field, that magnificent mash of fences, beams, advertising-graffitied walls, jutting scoreboard corners, overhanging second deck, and wack-job fans—all right on top of him on the field. Dead center field was only 384 feet, right field a mere 297 feet, very similar to the Polo Grounds where Mays, not a strict pull-hitter, would become adept at punching shots over the shallow right field wall.

In fact, this bizarre infrastructure spawned some of baseball's most insane homers, which was only logical in a place where the motif was early cuckoo's nest (its rotunda lobby was accented with tiling to look like the stitches of a baseball and featured a chandelier with twelve baseball-bat-styled arches propping twelve baseball-shaped globes). In 1946, a big fly by the Braves' Bama Rowell smashed the right field scoreboard clock, giving Bernard Malamud the idea for Roy Hobbs' similar literary clout in *The Natural*. Another shot by the Reds' Lonnie Frey landed on top of the right field wall and bobbed around in the chicken wire as Frey came all the way around the bases. To prevent other such funhouse homers, the Dodgers put up slanted boards between the wall and the wire to funnel the ball down. Well, they tried. Only a few years later, in that last-day loss to the Phillies in 1950, Pee Wee Reese hit one that bobbed around in the same chicken wire as Reese came all the way around.

The 6-foot, 200-pound Snider, hitting out of a closed, crouching stance, was able to either pin-ball shots rattling around the nooks and crannies out there, or belt ones over the wire that would come to rest in the used car lot across Bedford Avenue. In '49, when he had 23 homers, 92 RBIs, and a .292 average, it kicked off an eight-year streak in which he had fewer than 30 homers only twice, under 100 RBIs only once, and hit under .300 only three times. (Oddly, he actually hit more taters away from Ebbets in '49, 15 to 8, the only time in that span he did that; in 1951, the breakdown was 21 home, 8 away.) From 1953 to '57, he had 42, 40, 42, 43, and 40 homers. In 1950, he hit 3 homers in a game.

Snider hardly prospered alone at Ebbets. Gil Hodges, the Indiana-born catcher-turned-impeccable first baseman, who like Lou Gehrig was beastly strong and almost eerily quiet, smacked 4 dingers (and drove in 9 runs) on August 31, 1950, against the Braves at Ebbets. The year before that, Hodges became the first Dodger to rack up four extra-base hits in a game. It was Hodges' 27th homer of the season on July 4, 1951, that sunk the Giants and emboldened Chuck Dressen to pronounce the Giants DOA. By the end of the season, Hodges would have 40 homers (second to Ralph Kiner's league-high 42, though Hodges did whiff a league-high 99 times—still low by today's standards) with 103 RBIs. He also had a 2-run shot in the All-Star Game—which sparked a record 6 homers by both leagues.

Snider added 29 homers and 101 RBIs. Campanella had 33 and 108 and won the first of his three MVP awards. The Dodgers led baseball with 184 homers, a .275 team batting average, 249 doubles, and 693 strikeouts by their pitchers, and led the NL with 89 steals and 192 double plays in the field. Preacher Roe won 22 games, Don Newcombe 20.

They had everything. But in the end they didn't get everything. Because in the end they didn't have the fickle home run gods on their side.

A Shot Heard 'Round the World

Remember that 13½-game Dodger lead on August 11th? From the next day on, the Giants didn't lose a game the rest of the month, ripping out 16 straight wins and shaving the lead to five games. Now, as they closed in, the early-season Brooklyn tactics, such as Dressen's hubris and Jackie Robinson stealing home with an 8-run lead in a game, created a thirst in the Giants for payback. By the last weekend of the season, both teams stood 94 and 58. And while the Giants' .250 team average was 15 points below Brooklyn's, the core of Mays, Irvin (.312, 24 homers, league-high 121 RBIs), and Bobby Thomson (.293, 32, 101) was white-hot. They also would have two 23-game winners, Sal "The Barber" Maglie and Larry Jansen. They just would not lose.

But neither would the Dodgers. On Saturday, September 29, when Maglie blanked Boston 3-0, that night Don Newcombe shut out Philadelphia. On Sunday, Jansen beat the Braves 3-2, the Giants' thirty-seventh win in the last forty-four games. When it ended, the Dodgers were down 8-5 in the fifth inning. A frantic Dressen tried to survive by using seven pitchers in the game, including Newcombe again, and by the ninth the Dodgers had battled back to a tie. Then Robinson, who'd saved the game in the thirteenth with a fabulous bases-loaded defensive play, came up in the fourteenth and slammed a homer to win the game and square the pennant—which came down to the NL's playoff format, a best-of-three series, for just the second time. (The Dodgers were in the first one, too, losing to the Cards in 1946 in two straight games.) Dressen won the coin toss for home field, though in this nutty format if a team chose the home field for the first game the other team got it for the next two. Chuckles took it anyway, hoping Ralph Branca would register a quick win. But Branca gave up 2 home runs—a 2-run blow by Thomson and a solo by Irvin—and lost, 3-1.

A little setup: even at that point, Thomson had emerged as the unsung hero of the season, though it was surely a bumpy ride. If this long and lanky cabinetmaker's son—the best major leaguer who was ever born in Glasgow, Scotland, before being raised in Staten Island—had a date with destiny, it could only have seemed like a blind date back in early July when, coming off his great 1950 season—which also included an inside-the-park grand slam—he was benched by Durocher so that Mays could play center field. Then, on July 20, third baseman Hank Thompson was spiked at third and Durocher put Thomson at the hot corner. There he stayed, hitting .307 from then until the end of the season.

Still, things went bad for the Giants when the playoff series shifted to their home park and the Dodgers rode dingers by Robinson, Andy Pafko, and Rube Walker to a 10-0 wipeout win.

So now it came down to the third and deciding game played on Wednesday, October 3, 1951, under a dull gray afternoon sky. Looking back, much of what is assumed about the events of that day is fallacious. One common assumption is that the Polo Grounds must have been filled to the bursting point by supportive Giant fans. In truth, attendance that day was 34,320 (although it included Frank Sinatra and J. Edgar Hoover), who had plenty of leg room in the 55,000-seat park. So the next time someone tells you they, their father, or grandfather were there, ask them to produce a ticket stub and an affidavit. Another was that Bobby Thomson was some sort of nobody who fell dumbly into the arms of fate, instead of being arguably the Giants' best hitter at the time.

Still, as the plot thickened, Thomson seemed to be dug in as the goat of the series. And how the plot thickened. With Maglie—the chin-aiming "Barber"—on the hill, the Dodgers put up a marker in the first inning and it stayed 1-0 until Thomson, who already had a single and a double, tied it with a sacrifice fly in the seventh. But this was only part-redemption for Thomson, who in the second game had made two errors and a base-running blunder—and then made another blunder in this game, when after he singled he rounded first, failed to see that Whitey Lockman had held second, and was tagged out in a rundown. Then in the eighth, Andy Pafko's hard grounder glanced off Thomson's glove to score a run, and another playable ground ball by Billy Cox got by him to net another run. By the time the inning was done, it was 4-1 Brooklyn.

As Newcombe struck out the side in the bottom of the eighth, up in the press box the writers composed running leads about the Dodgers' heroic refusal to buckle, and some began the long trek through the stands to the center field clubhouse. Giant owner Horace Stoneham was already there, and when Maglie came out in the top of the ninth he put his arm around the Barber and told him he was magnificent in defeat. Meanwhile, out on the field, Jansen retired the Dodgers in the ninth and now the Giants came up for last licks in a tranquil silence as many fans were shuffling to the exits. Leading off, Alvin Dark hit a bouncer wide of first that both Robinson and Hodges went for. Normally, it would have been fielded by Robinson and thrown to Newcombe covering first. But the ball ticked off Hodges' glove, ruining the play and leaving Dark on first with a scratch single. Now the time was at hand for Chuck Dressen to royally screw up, neglecting to tell Hodges to play off the bag at first instead of holding on a runner who wasn't going anywhere. That left Don Mueller with a hole to shoot for and he pounded one through it to right field—a sure doubleplay if not for Dressen's funk, but now putting runners on first and third.

Newcombe did get Irvin to foul out, but Lockman sliced a double to left, sending Dark home and Mueller to third where he slid so hard he broke an ankle and during a long delay was carried off the field and replaced by Clint Hartung. Critically, during the pregnant pause, Dressen got to thinking, concluding that Newcombe was out of gas. Dressen usually set up his exact order of pitchers before games, but at this extraordinary moment he had three pitchers warming up. He called bullpen coach Clyde Sukeforth and asked, "Who's ready?" Sukeforth noted that Clem Labine and Carl Erskine didn't seem as fresh as Ralph Branca. Nowadays, managers would pay greater heed to the fact that in Game 1 the latter had given up a homer to Bobby Thomson—the next batter. Dressen didn't care.

"Then send me Branca," he ordered.

Neither did Dressen care to intentionally walk Thomson to load the bases, set up a force at any base, and pitch to a struggling Willie Mays—a notion that Mays later said made him feel sick to his stomach as he kneeled in the on-deck circle hoping not to have to bat with the game on the line. And so Branca came in on the crest of destiny, to face a man very much like himself. Just two years apart in age—Branca, 25 and Thomson, 27—both were from sturdy immigrant stock and both had hawk-like beaks, bushy brown hair, and excellent if unspectacular careers that would in an instant be all but forgotten but for one pitch and one swing.

As Branca, wearing No. 13, threw his warm-up pitches, Thomson swung a bat near the on-deck circle. "If you've ever hit one," Durocher barked at him, "hit it now." But he was so zoned he said later he didn't hear anything or even know how many outs there were. Just wait on the pitch, he said to himself. Wait, wait, wait.

He waited so long on Branca's first pitch that he let a fastball go down the middle for a called strike. Branca had a wonderful plan: throw another fastball high and inside to set up a low and away curve. Thomson's own plan was not to let another hittable pitch get by him. And so the most unctioned hit of all time came on a bad pitch, a ball. Indeed, when Thomson pulled it hard to left field, it was a fluke; he never hit an inside pitch like that anywhere near as solidly.

You already know how much of baseball's home run history has been shaped by fortuitously shallow walls. When Thomson laid wood on horsehide, there was a match-strike of great expectation in the air because the 17-foot left field wall at the Polo Grounds was just 315 feet away. At Yankee Stadium, or even Ebbets Field, it would have been out number 2, a sacrifice fly, maybe a double. When the ball flew over the infield, Billy Cox, the third baseman, screamed at it, "Get down! Get down!" And Thomson, who hit it just above the sweet spot, wasn't sure the trajectory was right for a homer.

At first, Thomson said, "I thought it was headed for the upper deck. But I'd gotten on top of it and it started to sink [and] I didn't think it would be a home run. I thought it might hit the fence."

So did Pafko in left. He went to the wall thinking he might even catch it, and Snider raced over from center looking for a carom. Not on this day. The home run gods willed that sucker into the lower grandstand about five feet over the wall.

The single greatest artifact of that home run to end all home runs—still the only one of its kind, the ultimate turn-on-a-dime, defeat-turned-to-victory lightning bolt to ever win a pennant or World Series—is of course the frenetic and fabled radio call by Giants announcer Russ Hodges—"There's a long drive, it's gonna be, I believe . . . ," punctuated by a shrieking five-time repetitive chant of "The Giants win the pennant!" and followed by, "And they're going craaaaaazzzzzy *whooooooooooaaaaa*!" Don't underestimate the power of this unusually over-the-top call for the times in pumping up the homer's mythic value

The Sultan of Swat: Babe Ruth takes the majestic swing that transformed both him and the home run from urchins to royalty. Ruth's 60 homers in a season and 714 in a career have been bettered, but the "big monkey" stands alone.

All photos are courtesy the National Baseball Hall of Fame library

Jimmie "The Beast" Foxx looked like, drank like, and hit homers like Ruth, hitting 534 overall. And he outdid Ruth by winning a Triple Crown in 1933.

Hank Greenberg and Ralph Kiner: Mentor and student in the scientific method of hitting the dinger. Greenberg hit 58 homers in 1938 to tie Foxx's record by a right-handed hitter, while Kiner won an unprecedented seven consecutive home run crowns between 1946 and 1952, and was the first National Leaguer to have successive 50-homer seasons.

Ted Williams and Joe DiMaggio were grand masters in the now-lost art of hitting home runs while almost never striking out. Williams hit 521 and DiMaggio 361 despite losing a combined 10 years while serving in the military. Had they not missed those years and had they played in each other's home parks, DiMaggio might have hit 700 and Williams 800.

As strong as Ruth and just as mythic, Josh Gibson was the home run king for a race barred from the American pastime in the 1920s, '30s, and '40s. Gibson was reputed to have hit over 800 home runs in the Negro Leagues—over 70 in a season *four times*—and may have hit a ball or two out of Yankee Stadium. He lived hard and died young, at 35, the year baseball's color line was broken.

October 3, 1951: Bobby Thomson connects with the most famous homer of all time, the "Shot Heard 'Round the World," to send the New York Giants and not the Brooklyn Dodgers to the World Series. To some, it is also the most famous case of sign-stealing of all time.

Country boy turned city slicker Mickey Mantle strikes the pose that launched 536 home runs and made him the idol of Baby Boomer boys. Mantle hit the longest homers of the 1950s and won the Triple Crown in 1956, but for all his power and swagger he could never overcome the pain and frustration of endless injuries and a weakness for the bottle.

Willie Mays: Simply the best all-around player ever, and the most electrifying, the Say Hey Kid exuded pure joy on a ballfield and swatted 660 home runs—including four in one game—playing most of his games in the worst stadium ever, cold and windy Candlestick Park.

October 13, 1960: Unheralded Bill Mazeroski romps home along with half of Pittsburgh after ending the wild and wacky World Series against the mighty Yankees with one swing. Mazeroski's first-pitch blast in the bottom of the ninth is still the only seventh-game walkoff home run in baseball history.

October 1, 1961: Roger Maris sends home run number 61 into the right field seats at Yankee Stadium to set a new record. The first to challenge the sacred Ruth, he came through despite enormous pressure—only to see his feat cheapened by an asterisk placed next to his record. The asterisk was removed in 1971, but resistance to Maris being in the Hall of Fame endures to this day.

April 8, 1974: With one historic swing against the Dodgers at Atlanta Fulton County Stadium, Hank Aaron replaces Babe Ruth as baseball's all-time home run king, sending number 715 into the record books. With grace and grit, Aaron endured months of racist hate mail and death threats before setting the new standard and didn't stop swinging until he had hit 755 homers over 22 brilliant seasons.

Always in the eye of the storm, Reggie Jackson admires his work after getting hold of his third home run on three pitches to put away the Dodgers in the sixth and final game of the Yankees' 1977 World Series victory. It was the signature highlight of a career that produced 536 home runs, a record strikeout total, and tons of controversy.

A moment that lives in Beantown infamy: Light-hitting Bucky Dent comes home to a hero's welcome after his shocking, sudden three-run homer over Fenway Park's Green Monster turns the playoff game of October 2, 1978, around, putting the Yankees in the postseason and making the Red Sox go home losers yet again.

The youngest man to reach 400 homers in a career, the sweet-swinging Ken Griffey Jr. put the Seattle Mariners on the map by racking up 56 dingers in both 1997 and 1998, and at least 40 each in five out of six years. But after forcing a trade to his hometown Cincinnati Reds in 2000, Junior has been ravaged by injuries and nearly fallen out of sight.

The buddy act of Californian Mark McGwire *(right)* and Dominican Sammy Sosa invigorated baseball and captivated the country in 1998, as they drove each other to unheard-of home run heights. McGwire belted 70 and Sosa 66, and they followed up in 1999 with 65 and 63 respectively, becoming the only players ever to reach 60 twice. McGwire also reached 500 career homers faster than anyone in history and cleared 50 in a record four-straight seasons (1996–99), while Sosa cleared 60 three times between 1998 and 2001.

The enigmatic and polarizing Barry Bonds made few new friends but converted many old critics in 2001 when he broke McGwire's record and set a new one—73 home runs in a season. In 2002, he joined Aaron, Ruth, and Mays in the 600-homer circle. Arguably the most feared slugger ever, Bonds was walked a record 198 times in 2002, yet still hit 46 homers during the season and four cannon shots in the World Series.

It only became *the* call because a Dodger fan was recording the game with a rudimentary reel-to-reel tape machine. Had it not been preserved, the other options were calls by Ernie Harwell on NBC Radio ("It's gone!") and Red Barber in the Brooklyn booth ("It's in there for the pennant!"). Somehow I just don't think either would have echoed and elevated the bedlam that accompanied that magic dinger.

Be glad that baseball filmmakers learned how to cover a big home run since Babe Ruth's days, because the newsreels of Thomson's victory tour of the bases are a priceless public record. In them we see Thomson jumping up and down and carried as though on a zephyr, weeding his way through Giant fans and Dodger players on a death march to the center field clubhouse—and how Durocher in the third base coaching box never got to embrace him because coach Eddie Stanky tore from the Giant dugout, grabbed Durocher in ecstasy, and wouldn't let go of him as Thomson bounded home, leaped on the plate, and was swallowed by an enormous mass of bodies, then lifted onto teammates' shoulders and paraded around the field.

It was the delirium as much as the homer that built a shallow line drive into an ecclesiastic happening—earning its canonization as "The Shot Heard 'Round the World," in the phrase arguably used first by *New York Post* columnist Jimmy Cannon days later. Hell, we even forgive the normally tempered Red Smith for waxing a tad purple in his next day's column, which began:

> Now it is done. Now the story ends. And there is no way to tell it. The art of fiction is dead. Reality has strangled invention. Only the utterly impossible, the inexpressibly fantastic, can ever be plausible again.
>
> Down on the green and white and earth-brown geometry of the playing field, a drunk tries to break through the ranks of ushers marshaled along the foul lines to keep profane feet off the diamond. The ushers thrust him back and he lunges at them, struggling in the clutch of two or three men. He breaks free and four or five tackle him. He shakes them off, bursts through the line, runs head on into a special park cop who brings him down with a flying tackle. . . . At heart, our man is a Giant, too. He never gave up. . . .
>
> Ralph Branca turned and started for the clubhouse. The number on his uniform looked huge. Thirteen.

This juxtaposition, of course, would become the most visited and revisited theme of all—Thomson and Branca, two commoners caught in a combine that dwarfed them both. In fact, that one swing began a five-decade commercial partnership between the two protagonists in the drama, living off the glow of the home run. Four days later, they appeared on the *Ed Sullivan Show*, singing, sort of, gag lyrics written for them about the confrontation to the tune of "Because of You." For Branca, bearing the scarlet letter must have bore a hole into his soul—there is no better piece of American photography than the AP shot taken of him in the locker room, head bowed, staring at the floor between his cleats—but apparently as time wore on, being yoked to the hero of Armageddon, and sharing the battle's glory, allowed Branca to ease the wound. Thomson, too, has struck the theme. "Let's face it," he once said, "without that moment we'd both be long forgotten." Branca can even get evangelical about it. That night, he asked a logical question—"Why me?"—of his wife's cousin, a Jesuit priest at Fordham University, who told him, "Ralph, God chose you because He knows your faith is strong enough to bear this cross." And Branca has often called the homer "my salvation," with the matter of who won and who lost nothing more than dust to dust, ashes to ashes.

"The guy just hit a home run," he once said. "He was better than I was that day. Life goes on. You don't go through it undefeated." And, proudly, "I don't care what anybody says, that's the most famous home run of them all."

Even the savage Dodger fans let him off easy, sparing Branca from booing the next season, their sympathy serving as a cathartic effect in a widening legacy of losing the big ones.

As permanently epoxied as it is to the status of baseball's all-time greatest home run, however, even this magical dinger has taken abuse from pickle-puss revisionists. The *Washington Post*, in a crabby editorial on October 7, 1999, harpooned it on grounds that size matters: "Mr. Thomson's heroic blow, had it been hit in just about any other ballpark on earth, would have been a routine out and the object of little more than a scornful paragraph in the next day's papers." In other words, just like that paragraph.

A far more serious threat to the homer's near-biblical standing came in January 2001 when Joshua Harris Prager in a front-page *Wall Street Journal* story blew the whistle on the Giants for stealing pitching signals, an operation that apparently was more sophisticated than Hank Greenberg's binoculars-in-the-bleachers scam.

Actually, suspicions that the Giants copped signs had surfaced before through the years. In a 1991 book, *The Home Run Heard 'Round the World*, Branca not only put the claim on record, but Sal Yvars, who was the Giants' backup catcher, confirmed it. Still, for lack of detail, the charge didn't make a ripple until Prager provided the detail after interviewing twenty-two surviving Giants. It seems that from late July on, little-used infielder Hank Schenz had sat at a window in the team's office in center field with a telescope, his finger on a buzzer system (rigged by a Polo Grounds electrician from *Brooklyn* named Abraham Chadwick, who later had severe guilt about what he did to the Dodgers) connected to the Giants' left field bullpen. One buzz was for a fastball, two buzzes a curve. In the pen, Yvars would then relay the info to the hitter, crossing his legs for a fastball or tossing a ball in the air for a curve. It was Yvars who became a kind of Joe Bananas for the plot, telling *The New York Times*, "I was the guy. I relayed the signals to the batter. . . . [I]f you ask me if we could have won the pennant without stealing the signals I would have to say, 'No way.'"

But the touchier matter was whether Thomson got the sign when he hit in the ninth. While Yvars didn't pull his punch—"I gave him the sign," he said—Thomson has hedged, implying that signals may have been stolen but that he didn't get one before his historic swing. "It would take a little away from me in my mind if I felt I got help on the pitch," is how he puts it. And you can't blame him. After living in a vesper serenade for fifty years, you wouldn't want it to be changed to the theme from "Dragnet," either.

But need he even worry at all? Despite Branca's assertion that the revelation vindicated him, Thomson still had to hit that inside fastball on the nose. Moreover, the Giant hitters may have been better off when they *didn't* get the signs. An analysis of the Giants' season by SABR's Stan Jacoby indicates that not only did four regulars hit worse from late July on—including Mays—but that the team hit *fewer* home runs (49 in the last 48 games, compared with 130 in the first 109). So if they were cribbing signs, maybe they read a lot of them wrong, or maybe it took them out of their normal hitting mind-set, making them lazy. In any case, Jacoby concludes that the Giants' pitching, and the Dodger collapse, were bigger factors in the comeback.

The squall over the sign stealing faded fast, anyway. Among even casual fans, the notion that players cheat would evoke the same reaction as Claude Rains had as Captain Louis Renault in *Casablanca*, biting his lip as he insists, "I'm shocked to find that gambling is going on in here." What's most fascinating about the tale is that such cheating was actually *legal* in '51, albeit not very nice; it wasn't until ten years later that espionage with mechanical devices was prohibited by baseball law, not that it had much effect in the real world. So Thomson's mind can relax. The Shot remains sacrosanct. Say amen.

11

The Shape of Things to Come

Tearing Into the Breath of God

The problem for the Giants was that they still had to play ball that year, because everything about the pennant victory was like Jason's *Argo* conquering fire-breathing bulls and dragons. Most unfortunately for them, they had to play the Yankees in the World Series the very next day, at Yankee Stadium. The Giants awoke that day to a town that had gone slightly cuckoo over them. *The New York Times* duly noted their wondrous triumph on front page left, with a headline reading GIANTS CAPTURE PENANT, in type as large as a story across the page about a Russian nuclear bomb test. All over town, people cheered them, many simply because New York had a winner that wasn't the Yankees or Dodgers—especially the former. (How ironic was this given that the Yankees came of age as a "fun" alternative to Muggsy McGraw's never-lose, regimented Giants?)

But this was also the '50s, when entrenched institutions bred unease and angst but in the end would come down hard on any rebels. And the Yankees, in this morality play, did their establishment part by crushing baseball dreamers, as the Phillies had learned. The Giants even got Game 1, winning 5-1 behind Al Dark's 3-run homer, and led two games to one after Whitey Lockman crushed a 3-run job to break open Game 3, a 6-2 win. Now, though, it was time for Joe DiMaggio's valedictory. In the first three games, the creaky Joe D was nearly invisible, going hitless. He was also unwittingly responsible for Mantle suffering one of the worst baseball injuries ever seen.

In the fifth inning of Game 2, Willie Mays lifted a soft fly to right-center. In years past, no one but DiMaggio would have moved for it. But before the Series Stengel told Mantle to take any ball he could, because "the big Dago can't get there anymore." Mantle made for it, but DiMaggio was unwilling to recede—the same problem Mantle had the whole season. When Joe D called, "I got it," Mantle had to make a sudden stop and his spikes impaled on the rubber sheath of an in-ground sprinkler, ripping every ligament from his right knee with a noise Mantle later compared to a tire blowing out. He crumpled to the ground in unbelievable pain and was carted off on a stretcher. Mantle's season wasn't only finished, so was much of the speed he came up with. The injury, repaired by surgery the next day, healed in time for the next season but it would be just the first of an endless chain-link of infirmities that would render him a one-dimensional player. With Mickey Mantle, it pretty much would be over the wall or nothing at all—and with a sense of desperation that heightened over the winter of his recuperation, when Mutt Mantle died of Hodgkin's disease, an affliction common to many men in his family for generations. At the time, Mantle was not yet 20 years old and a newlywed. And here he was counting down the minutes of his own life.

As for Joe D, the minutes of his career drew to a close covered in—what else?—glory. In Game 4 at the Polo Grounds, he slammed a 2-run homer and single to help beat Maglie 6-2, evening the Series. Then the new guard sewed up Game 5. Trailing 1-0, third baseman Gil McDougald, the AL Rookie of the Year, came up with the bases loaded against Larry Jansen and spanked a grand slam—the third in Series history and first since Tony Lazzeri in '36—setting off a 13-1 laugher. The Giants, out of miracles, expired in Game 6, 4-3, with a cold slap in the face that stung Bobby Thomson hardest—he hit only .143 in the Series, with no more round-trip excursions.

U.S. Steel whirred on to win two more championships in '52 and '53, while the Giants dissipated, primarily because Willie Mays got his draft notice thirty-four games into the '52 season and was gone until '54. Without him, the team's home run production fell by 26 to 153, topped by Thomson's 24, and they finished fifth in '53. (But there will be nice things to say about what they did in '54.)

Until then, commencing with DiMaggio's fateful announcement after the '51 Series that "I've played my last game of ball," the center field concession in New York meant Mantle and Duke Snider—though '52 was a holding pattern for each and for the home run. That year, as hitters were still adjusting to those cunning control pitchers, Snider hit a modest 21 with 92 RBIs and a .303 average (Gil Hodges had the heavy wood with 32 dingers and 102 RBIs) and Mantle rang up 21 with 87 RBIs and a .311 average (behind Yogi Berra's 30). So, of course, against all logic, when the Yankees met the Dodgers in the World Series, it was a home run orgy. Game 1 saw 4 of them at Ebbets Field, 3 by Brooklyn including Snider's key 2-run blow in a 4-2 win. Game 2 was owned by the pugnacious Billy Martin, who after hitting just 3 all year took Carl Erskine out of the park with a 2-run shot, icing a 7-1 victory. Then, when the Series came to Yankee Stadium, out of the shadows of glory past stepped Johnny Mize.

Now 39, Mize had hit only 4 homers in seventy-eight games mostly as a pinch hitter, and was a year away from hanging 'em up, but Mize still had his cat's eyes. "Your arm is gone, your legs likewise," wrote Dan Parker in a sonnet to Mize, "But not your eyes, Mize, not your eyes." And the big, craggy-faced Georgian must have seen the ball as big as a cantaloupe in the Series. In Game 3, a 5-3 Dodger win, he hit a pinch homer in the bottom of the ninth. Leading Casey Stengel to play a hunch. With first baseman Joe Collins in an 0-for-12 slump, Mize started Game 4 and in the fourth inning he put the Yankees ahead 1-0 with a scorching homer and they won 2-0. Then in Game 5 he yanked another with two on in the fifth for a 5-4 lead. Mize thus became the first to hit 3 homers in a Series since King Kong Keller in '39—and did it in three straight games (in which he also had 6 RBIs), one of the great overlooked home run spurts.

The Dodgers, though, came back to win 6-5 in the eleventh and stood one game from their first-ever title, with two games at Ebbets to do it. Enter that Yankee voodoo they do so well. In a Game 6 pitching duel, Snider went yard off Vic Raschi in the sixth for a 1-0 lead, *his* third of the Series. But the Yankees tied it in the seventh on Berra's second and went ahead on a single, a balk and a Raschi single off Billy Loes' knee. An inning later Mantle crashed one over the chicken wire for a 3-1 lead. Snider then rocked his *fourth* Series shot in the eighth to make 3-2 but Allie Reynolds came on to get the last four outs.

If the Ebbets crowd thought that was frustrating, there was more in Game 7 when Mantle broke a 2-2 tie with a tater in the sixth and the Yankee pen got the last eight outs in a row.

In all, both teams cranked 16 homers, a Series record then. The message of it all was clear: the dinger was back in style. And while Snider and Berra and many others would carry the message, the home run's gold standard for the foreseeable future was going to be the decade's golden boy. Indeed, Mantle personally reinvigorated the home run market with one titanic swing in the Sahara of homers.

It happened on April 17, 1953, when the Yankees played the Senators in hoary Griffith Stadium. In the fifth inning, with 2 out and the Yankees up 2-1, Mantle, hitting right-handed—his natural, more powerful side—against southpaw Chuck Stobbs, met a letter-high fastball and sent it on a merry journey toward the left–center field stands 391 feet away. The shot seemed to have a second life. Just as it appeared to be descending, the ball shot deeper as if propelled by a booster rocket and vanished after scraping a beer sign atop a 60-foot-high back wall of the bleachers.

The mythical properties of such a blow in such a place were immediately clear to the Yankees PR man, Red Patterson, who in the tradition of tape-measure fiction, subsequently announced he had found the ball in the backyard of one Perry L. Cool (this is not a joke) at 434 Oakdale Street, which he paced off as being 105 feet from the park. Added to his other calculations—391 feet to the fence, 69 feet to the back wall—the blow was put at 565 feet, which he reckoned was the longest home run of all time.

Dutifully accepted by the sportswriters, the number 565 quickly became the story of the Yankees' 7-3 victory in the next day's papers—when history records the first usage of the term "tape-measure home run," in the *Daily News*, which initiated another future cliché by tracing the path of Mantle's home run with a perforated arrow imposed on an aerial shot of the stadium. Other pictures showed Mantle kissing the ball he had so punished. But perhaps there is less to all this than meets the bat. First is the matter of a 565-foot home run being the longest ever—after all, hadn't Babe Ruth mashed that alleged 600-footer at Forbes Field in his last game, as well as another reported 600-footer in Detroit in 1926? There is also the singularity issue. Not that any other major leaguers matched Mantle's blast, but Josh Gibson was said to have hit *two* balls over the bleachers at Griffith Stadium, where he played most of his home games. Then, too, can one really buy Red Patterson's backyard baseball story? Not according to David Falkner, who in his Mantle biography *The Last Hero*, writes that "Mantle said years later that Patterson confessed that he had actually never left the park—he just announced that he had after jotting down the name and address of the youngster who returned the ball."

Such is why, in *The Home Run Encyclopedia*, William J. Jenkinson writes:

> [R]egular references over the years to 500 and 600-foot home runs were born out of scientific ignorance, misinformation, or even deliberate exaggeration. . . . Seeing great drives land atop distant upper-deck rooves, sportswriters observing from a press box would resort to their limited skills in mathematics without any regard for the laws of physics. . . . [W]e know that once a batted ball has reached its highest point and lost most of its velocity, it falls in a rapidly declining trajectory. [A reported 550-foot homer] could have been re-created at that length by historians for years thereafter, when in fact it traveled about 100 feet less. Hyperbole has always been part of the phenomenon of long-distance home runs.

Of course, it is also possible Mantle hit the damn thing 565 feet—or longer. Besides, physicists are singles hitters.

Face it, without our sportswriter-induced worship of the longest long balls, the homer wouldn't be quite the party animal it is, or inspired so much pulpy prose—and homage poetry penned by otherwise sane people. Another Mantle Moon ball that 1953 season, which soared over the Briggs Stadium right field roof, engendered an ode *46 years* after the fact, Robert L. Harrison's "1953 Young Mantle Hits One." It goes:

> It was a shot like no other
> tearing into the breath of God,
> leaving earth and grass and fans.
>
> A sphere for the ages racing along
> casting no shadow in frozen space
> finally arching for the great fall.
>
> Described on the radio as a new star,
> a stellar moment of freedom expressed
> bright and clean as a summer's dream.

For us, the real poetry of Mantle was the distinct thickening of the air in anticipation when he batted, and he kept the beat going with a string of bombs. He may have had at least three other 500-foot homers, one each at Municipal Stadium, Comiskey Park, and later in Minnesota's Metropolitan Stadium. And, of course, there were the three mortar shots that nearly wound up outside Yankee Stadium. The first two of those came in 1956 when, as you'll soon see, any county on the map seemed within his reach. Still, on the grand scale of 1950s events with a bang, the big three are Sputnik, nuclear tests at Yucca Flats, and Mickey Mantle's 565-foot home run against Chuck Stobbs.

5 O'Clock Lightning and a 5 O'Clock Shadow

As they had with Ruth and DiMaggio, the Yankees would grow utterly dependent on Mantle, further affixing his own dependency on the long ball. In turn, they as a team paid less attention to other ways of scoring as the decade progressed. But from 1952 through 1954, the Yankees were still operating on DiMaggio time—building runs with solid, timely hitting that put them near the top in nearly all offensive categories but leading in none. In home runs, for example, they finished behind the Indians all three years.

During that interim, the real home run theater was the National League, where the long ball flourished wildly despite the decline of one of the great home run machines of all time, Ralph Kiner, whose 37 dingers in '52 tied him for the league lead with a guy who was built in his image: snail-slow and trapped by fate to hit home runs for a seriously awful team. This was Hank Sauer, a first baseman who hadn't found a home in the majors until he came to the Reds in 1948 at age 31. Traded to the Cubs in '49, he was to Wrigley Field what Kiner was to Forbes Field, unleashing 11 homers in his first month with the team. In '52, he also led the NL with 121 RBIs and batted .270, good enough to win the MVP award toiling for the fifth-place Cubs. Sauer also authored one of the oddest home run anomalies ever. On August 28, 1950, he became the first to hit 3 in one game off the same pitcher, the Phillies' Curt Simmons. Then on June 11, 1952, Sauer hit 3 in *another* game against one pitcher—none other than Curt Simmons.

For Kiner, the co-homer title in '52 was his record seventh straight home run crown, but his run ended there. Like his mentor Hank Greenberg, Kiner's bad back was worsening and Branch Rickey saw no upside in Kiner's homers, and salary, on his team of losers—a quote widely attributed to Rickey at the time, apocryphally, was his telling Kiner, "We can lose just as easily without you as we can with you." On June 4, 1953—nine days after Kiner hit his 300th career home run—he was traded with three other Bucs to the Cubs for six players and $150,000. The idea for the Cubs was to pair the two veteran sluggers, Kiner and Sauer, in the heart of the order. And Kiner turned in quite a season, playing a combined 158 games and racking up 35 homers and 116 RBIs. But Sauer broke a finger, hitting only 19 and screwing up the equation, and while he did rebound in '54 to hit 41, with Kiner adding 22, finishing seventh for the second straight year ended Kiner's excellent Wrigley adventure. Sauer would go, too, in '57, to the Giants, where he hit 26 homers.

Kiner's curtain call was staged by Hank Greenberg, who as the Cleveland GM traded for a barely mobile Kiner in '55 for $60,000, giving Kiner one year with a decent team. Kiner gave it all he had—18 homers in 321 at-bats—and though the Tribe followed up their '54 pennant year by coming in second, being in a pennant race and on a team that won ninety-three games must have tasted like nectar to Kiner, who retired contented after the season leaving 369 homers, a NL record 12 grand slams (tying him with Rogers Hornsby), and a ratio of 7.1 homers per every 100 at-bats—second only to Ruth's 8.5—and 1 every 14.1 times up. Our advice: Don't ever forget Kiner in any round table home run debate.

With Kiner's dim-out, the home run center of gravity became Brooklyn, where the Snider-Hodges-Campanella axis solidified into the first great power trio, years before Cream. In '53, Duke had 42, Campy 41, Hodges 31, and the Dodgers notched 208, 32 ahead of the Giants, who themselves had five guys with more than 20 homers—and 69 more than the Yankees, who were led by Berra's 27 (Mantle had 21). Even so, in the '53 World Series—another home run festival—the Yankees had the edge, 9 homers to 8. More important was *when* the Yankees went yard. In Game 1, three Dodger dingers paled when Joe Collins' homer in the seventh put New York ahead to stay. In Game 2, Mantle did the same with an eighth-inning blast. After Brooklyn evened the Series at two games all, the Yankees belted 4 homers in an 11-7 win at Ebbets Field—including Mantle's grand slam. Then back at Yankee Stadium, they traded power for a well-timed single by Martin in the bottom of the ninth to win Game 6, 4-3, and go home champs again, for a record fifth straight year.

The writers had a name for the way the Yankees would wait patiently before ripping a team's heart out with a late-inning homer—"5 O'Clock Lightning," and by the mid- and late 1950s it became baseball's most ominous weather forecast. Indeed, only as late as 1954, the last year of Mantle's slow-growth period, could anyone pull home run rank on the Yankees—the Indians, who outhomered them 156 to 133. But then the Tribe pretty much did everything right that year in setting a record with 111 victories. Larry Doby led the AL with 32 homers and 126 RBIs, ex-Yankee Al Rosen had 24 and 102, and second baseman Bobby Avila hit a league-best .341. They also had baseball's best pitching (2.78 ERA), as Early Wynn, Bob Lemon, and Mike Garcia alloyed for 65 wins. In the All-Star Game, fittingly played at Municipal Stadium, Rosen slammed 2 home runs and had 5 RBIs, and Doby's pinch homer in the eighth tied the game the AL would win 11-9. The Tribe came to the World Series expecting to be crowned—and they were, with a pick ax.

History, of course, has engraved the '54 Series as Willie Mays' finest moment, though not for his bat, and the Series did in fact cap off Mays' triumphal return to the game after two years in the Army. He hit .345 with 41 homers and 110 RBIs, and the Giants' 186 homers, with the Dodgers the most in baseball, carried the club to 97 victories and the pennant by five games over Brooklyn. Mays' sizzling numbers made him the man in the New York center field war, by a whisker over Snider (.341, 40, 130) and by plenty over Mantle (.300, 27, 102). Mays broke Mel Ott's extra-base hit record that season and led baseball by slugging .667.

But his World Series props are based on one play, because that play may be baseball's most famous—the back-to-the-infield, over-the-shoulder snare of Vic Wertz's 440-foot cannon shot to the warning track just in front of the bleacher screen in right–center field. And the catch was only half the story. When the left-handed-hitting Wertz hit the ball off southpaw reliever Don Liddle, the game was tied 2-2 in the eighth, men on first and second. Though it was crushed, Doby, on second, saw the ball tailing back to the left and figured Mays would catch up to it—indeed, the newsreels show that Mays nearly overran the ball—and so he tagged up, figuring he'd go not just to third but all the way home. But, defying physics yet again, Mays caught the drive, spun on a dime and threw a rocket back to the infield, holding Doby at third, and there he stayed as the Giants got the next 2 outs.

In the tenth, Mays walked with 1 out and stole second. Thomson was then walked and now, with Monte Irvin due up, Leo Durocher called on his answer to Johnny Mize—James Lamar "Dusty" Rhodes. A tall, bony man, Rhodes was only 27 yet because of severe alcoholism he looked like he was at death's door, his sunken cheeks buried under a perpetual five o'clock shadow. But his left-handed uppercut made him very dangerous at the Polo Grounds, where he had hit 11 of his 15 homers that season, when he also hit .340 with 50 RBIs in 164 at-bats. While Rhodes' drinking would curtail his career four years later, the '54 season was a gift from the gods. And they kept giving when he came up to hit for Irvin.

Facing Bob Lemon—no weak sister—Rhodes got a high curve on the first pitch and wafted a lazy pop fly down the right field line that got caught in the wind and carried, oh, all of 258 feet—the distance to the lower grandstand at the foul pole. Right fielder Dave Pope, who thought it was a can of corn, moved back, then leaped against the 11-foot-high wall, but the ball plopped into the first row for a stunning walkoff home run. Lemon was so disgusted by this, the very definition of what the more enlightened baseball people called a "Chinese" or "Chink" home run, that he threw his glove in the air as Rhodes circled the bases.

"In our park," Lemon snarled later, "the right fielder would have moved *in* to catch that ball"—though of course the fences in Cleveland that had been shortened by Bill Veeck in the '40s had been most kind to the Indian hitters all that year.

Rhodes rejoined with the long-ball (or short-ball) hitters' favorite piece of existential philosophy. "A home run is a home run," he said with a shrug.

Rhodes' whimsical flight of fancy wasn't over. In Game 2, his fifth-inning pinch single off Early Wynn tied it 1-1. Then, left in the game, he whacked a "real" homer against the façade of the Polo Grounds' right field roof in the seventh for the last run of a 3-1 win. In Game 3 he pinch hit a bases-loaded single to break open a 6-2 win. The Giants put the Series away in Game 4, 7-4. And yet, sweep and all, Mays had little to do with the last three wins, hitting .286 for the Series. It was Rhodes who hit the Giants' only 2 homers, and he batted .667 with 7 RBIs.

Because Mays didn't get back to the World Series for another eight years, while the Yankees got there the next four years, as great as Mays was for the rest of the '50s the decade belonged to Mickey Mantle. And here's the kicker on that—Mantle would wind up as a less productive long-ball king than four others, including Mays, who began their careers in the '50s. Hang on. I'll have more to say about this in a bit.

Ernie's Whip

At first, it seemed the best of the new wave was the biggest and certainly hardest to miss, a Reds' first baseman with the best blue-collar name ever, Ted Kluszewski, who was an obvious reflection of baseball's Neolithic Era, when men were men and the bigger the better. (While everyone talks about the grand size of today's players, according to Bill James there were more 250-pounders in the game in the '50s.) Kluszewski, a onetime Indiana University football player, was a frightful sight at 6 feet 2 inches and 240 pounds. His bulging arms evidently so strained his uniform sleeves that he had to cut them off (the sleeves, not the arms) to let them breathe. Oh, and maybe he wanted to scare the sap out of pitchers, too. Which he did, primarily because in '52, after five seasons of decent numbers, Big Klu went from 16 dingers to 40—the kind of leap that today would bring cries of "steroids"—then a baseball-high 49 (with 141 RBIs) in '53, and 47 in '55 (second to Mays' 51), each time breaking his own club record. No lumbering oaf, he also led the league in fielding five straight years, a then-record for first basemen. As well, from '49 to '56, he hit over .300 five times, over .320 twice. In 15 seasons he had 279 homers and a .298 average. And he would make a loud noise in the '59 World Series.

Because injuries burned out Big Klu's power, however, other titans would have more staying power. There was, to begin with, Kluszewski's polar opposite, a lithe, 170-pound shortstop who scared no one physically and swung with the unhurried cadence of a violin bow. In fact, Ernie Banks' near-apologetic power unearthed a whole new long-ball genre: the Everyman home run hitter. Banks' power came from steel-hinged wrists, though he was a deceptively strong man who had been a high school star in all sports and ran a 52-second quarter-mile.

That he was an African American made him more significant, auguring that the look—and the color—of the prototypical home run king was changing. The Cubs' first black player, Banks needed no minor league break-in after being signed off the roster of the Kansas City Monarchs (who, like most Negro League teams dishing up big leaguers, got no compensation) in '53. With his hair-trigger swing, he could squarely lay into any pitch, seemingly plucking the rare ones that got by him right out of the catcher's mitt. On September 20, he hit his first homer off Gerry Staley in St. Louis. In '54, his first full season, he banged out 19 homers, 79 RBIs, and hit .275. Then in '55 he changed the fundamental philosophy of long-ball hitting.

I told you that bats began getting slimmer and lighter since Babe Ruth's tapered lumber in the 1910s. But in early September of '54 Banks created a new demarcation line (especially on the Cubs, given that Hank Sauer's bat was a whopper, 46 ounces) when he began using a really, really light bat, around 30 ounces, and which at 34 inches had almost all of its weight in the barrel head. Its handle was so thin—about an inch in circumference, compared with the 1.2 inches of most bat handles of the day—that it gave the feel and illusion of lashing a bull whip. Banks made the effect greater with a little wiggle of the barrel to set his swing in motion. (Incredibly, even Banks' bat is thick by today's standards, when handles are as thin as .7 inches around.)

Banks hit the last 7 of his dingers with the bat—within two weeks. Using it the entire '55 season, he strafed the league, pounding 44 homers, a record for a middle infielder. On August 4, Banks hit 3 against three

Pirate pitchers—the first shortstop to go yard thrice in one game (it's been done by two others since, Fred Patek and Barry Larkin). He hit 5 grand slams, then a big league record and still the NL standard. He drove in 117 runs and batted .295. Injuries cut him to 28 homers in '56 but from '57 through '60 he hit 43, 47, 45, and 41 (leading the league in '58 and '60), won two RBI titles (as many as 143 in '59), twice hit over .300, and was the MVP in '58 and '59. From '55 to '60, he hit more homers than Mantle, on a club that didn't finish higher than fifth. And all the while, and until he hung 'em up in 1971, this sunny Texan had a ball and a simple wish: Let's play two.

Of course, his success bred imitation. Those whip-handle bats swept through baseball, to the eternal benefit of many, none more so than the next, and last, Negro League expatriate to shape home run history.

Hammer Time

Henry Louis Aaron was an unlikely candidate for the home run pantheon in the early '50s. If Banks had a smooth swing, it was barbaric next to Aaron's, which seemed hard enough only to break a thin pane of glass. But, swinging one of those bull-whip bats, Aaron combined timing with enormous wrist and forearm power to move the wood through the hitting zone so that it gathered a torque that peaked precisely at the moment of contact. Again, it all comes down to science—that point of contact is always the same, but there are a million ways to get to it. Like few others, Aaron was born to get to it.

Aaron's way was the height of economy and conservation, the same laws that governed how he ran the bases and across the outfield. Like Mays, at 6 feet 1 inch and 190 pounds, he seemed smaller than he was and at first sight he appeared apathetic, even lazy. At second sight, he would beat out grounders, take extra bases, and run down balls in the alleys. He also had a strong, accurate arm. Like Banks he rarely took days off.

How amazing were Aaron's wrists? Playing ball as a teenager in Mobile, Alabama, he found it easier to swing while holding a bat cross-handed—a long-outdated grip in which the hands are reversed, which fell out of favor because it punished the wrists. But Aaron hit a ton and was signed by the Negro League Indianapolis Clowns in 1950 at age 16. Instructed to use a normal grip, he became the object of a big league bidding war that was won by the Boston Braves when they signed him for $7,500. Aaron laid waste to the Southern Atlantic League and in '53 was promoted to the Braves as their first black player.

This was the year the Braves jumped to Milwaukee, the first time any of the original sixteen major league teams had abrogated the unwritten taboo of cuckolding the towns they played in. For years owners quietly broached the topic, and seriously once the postwar flush of excitement and easy money gave way to a tighter economy that crimped attendance all over baseball, particularly for the "other" teams in Boston and St. Louis. In March 1953, Bill Veeck, his bottom-feeding Browns—having drawn an AL-low 518,796 in '52—planned a jump to Milwaukee, but was blocked by Braves' owner Lou Pirini, whose team owned the minor-league team in that city. A week later, in the middle of spring training while Veeck dickered with Perini for the territorial rights, Perini—whose own moribund team had drawn less than half what the Browns did—had an announcement: the *Braves* were moving to Milwaukee. By opening the door, Perini made it inevitable that baseball's future would be played to the sound of musical franchises, not to mention ill-timed expansion. Veeck, denied Milwaukee, sold his club to owners who took them to Baltimore in '54, to play as the Orioles.

In Milwaukee, the Braves flourished in the box office and on the field as Aaron joined a hard-hitting team that solidified when he complemented another young turk, left-handed-hitting third baseman Eddie Mathews, whose rise was nearly a rerun of Mickey Mantle's. Mathews too had a Svengali father, Ed Sr., and he too was signed the day of his high school graduation, one state over, in Texarcana, Texas. He signed with the Boston Braves because Ed *pere* scanned big league rosters for the most vulnerable third baseman, and found it in Bob Elliott, whom Ed *fils* displaced when he came up in '52 and hit 25 home runs with 58 RBIs. In '53, in Milwaukee, the dead-pull-hitting Mathews—at 6 feet 1 inch and 195 pounds a near clone of Mantle—was baseball's top home run man, with 47, along with 135 RBIs and a .302 average. Also like Mantle, he was an insular guy who hammered tape-measure balls all over the league—including 3 on September 27 at Ebbets Field.

Because of Mathews, arguably the most underrated slugger of all time, the Braves stopped being a doormat. On August 30, 1953, they tied the '39 Yankees' mark of 8 dingers in a game in the first of a doubleheader against Pittsburgh, when Jim Pendleton hit 3, only the second rookie to do that. They then hit 4 more in the nightcap, breaking by 3 the old record for homers in a twinbill. Mathews had 4 that day. And I haven't even mentioned first baseman Joe Adcock, a menacing 6-foot-4, 230-pound monster who came from the Reds in a trade that year. On April 29, Adcock merely hit one into the center field bleachers at the Polo

Grounds—475 feet away, where no home run had ever gone and where only 2 went thereafter—one by Aaron. Adcock had 18 homers and 80 RBIs. And the Braves went from seventh place to second, winning ninety-two games and drawing two million fans.

Aaron's arrival in '54 lit no fires. The Braves won three fewer games and came in third. Getting his shot when Bobby Thomson broke his leg in spring training, the rookie went 0-for-5 in his debut on April 13. Homer No. 1 was hit 10 days later against Vic Raschi, then with the Cardinals. By September 5, Aaron had 13 homers, 69 RBIs, and a .280 average when a broken ankle ended his season. Mathews crashed 40 homers, now well on his way to notching 190 homers in his first five seasons—and to hitting 200 at a younger age than anyone has except Mel Ott. Adcock added 23, catcher Del Crandall 21. Was it because County Stadium was a homer magnet? Hardly. The power alleys there alone were nearly 400 feet. Of Mathews' 47 dingers in '53, *30* were hit on the road—a record, then—and only three times in his thirteen years there did he hit more at home than away. Of Aaron's 13 in '54, *12* were on the road. And Adcock? On July 31, 1954, he hit 4 homers and a double at Ebbets Field—for those eighteen total bases that Shawn Green bettered forty-eight years later. Adcock had 15 dingers that July, something achieved only by Greenberg and DiMaggio. In '56, he jacked 38, one more than Mathews and second in the NL to Duke Snider's 43.

Aaron? He wouldn't bloom until '57, when the Braves ruled. By then, the yin to *his* yang had come along.

Rockin' Robby

The game's first African American superstar not incubated in the Negro Leagues, and its first postmodern racial lightning rod, was a man who shared Jackie Robinson's surname and molten sense of moral outrage, contempt, and confrontation about the bigotries baseball tried to glaze over but couldn't hide. But the second Mr. Robinson was no ready-made cause celebre. Instead, Frank Robinson was a complete unknown when the Reds signed him off the sandlots of West Texas in 1953 at age 17. Physically, Robinson was nearly identical to Aaron, at 6 feet 1 inch, 190 pounds, but his incendiary style and willingness to challenge anything in his way—from inside pitches to fielders trying to tag him to outfield walls—added gravitas to a spindly frame that was all arms and legs.

After a year in the minors, Robinson was brought up in mid-April of '56 and on the 28th he blasted his first homer, off the Cubs' Paul Minner at Crosley Field. With Robinson, the Reds now had their own home run firing line, with holdovers like Kluszewski and right fielder Wally Post, who had combined for 87 homers in '55. Now they went from 181 dingers to a then-record *221*. Robinson led with 38, tying Adcock for second in the NL home run derby, Post had 36, Kluzsewski 35, center fielder Gus Bell 29, and catcher Ed Bailey 28.

Robinson, the unanimous Rookie of the Year, was an astonishingly dangerous player, conceding not an inch even as a rookie. He stood towering on top of the plate, his elbows halfway across the dish, meaning he was able to mash outside pitches while daring pitchers to come inside—and brushing off the pain of being tattooed from chin to ankles for his impudence. Robinson was hit by a pitch 20 times, a rookie record that lived for forty-five years until tied, but as pitchers learned throughout his career (when he was struck 198 times), dusting Robinson did nothing to tame him or the blinding slash that was his swing. In the wilting heat of August he crushed 11 homers, another rookie record until broken by a latter-day Red, Adam Dunn, by 1, in August 1991. On August 18 he hit 2 of the Reds' record-tying 8 dingers in one game against the Braves at Crosley (also not a cheap home run paradise). On September 11 he tied Wally Berger's rookie homer record with No. 38 against the Giants. He finished with 83 RBIs, a .290 average, and a league-high 122 runs.

Over the next nineteen seasons, Robinson would fail to hit 30 homers only eight times, hit over .300 nine times, drive in less than 90 runs seven times, and score less than 90 runs eight times. He and Aaron would become baseball's longest-running stories, with Robinson's roiled in controversy and unfairly tied to the Reds' habitual failure to win a pennant. Even winning one in a few years wouldn't stop him being run out of town after some very ugly incidents.

And Aaron? He would win very fast, then not once ever again, yet play every day in a soporific calm until, well, you know.

The Case for Eddie Mathews

Mantle's preeminence was a self-fulfilling prophesy of the New York press. As early as 1952, Jimmy Cannon had written in the *New York Post*, "I believe he will be the greatest ballplayer in either league. There is no doubt about him. The Yanks and Ruth and DiMaggio. Now it's Mantle." But Mantle's good-not-great first four years, when his home run high was 27 and he struck out 100 times twice, showed him how quickly the writers could turn on him. An example was a column by Joe Trimble in the

Daily News, saying that Mantle "lacks the high professional pride which Joe [DiMaggio] possessed. . . . DiMaggio tried to analyze his trouble and licked it with a scientific approach. Mantle, bewildered and hurt, finds no solution but the physical relief of going up to bat until he finally gets the fat of the bat on the ball and can smile again."

This actually was a more trenchant critique than it seems because it tore at the heart of what the home run's problem would be in the near future—Mantle's high-visibility homers. Once, his "swing until you hear a loud crack" credo was a baseball sin. Now, it came with no shame as the price of a chance to make the bell go ding. This, more than anything else, would both inflate and subvert home runs—though it would take another three decades of fluctuations before the exponential increases in home run hitting and strikeouts would be fully felt. Indeed, by today's levels Mantle's high of 126 strikeouts in 1959 are modest.

Another related trend of Mantle-mania was the atrophying of the RBI. One of the great conundrums of Mantle's career was that he drove in 100 or more runs only four times in eighteen years. Mantle's amen corner made all kinds of excuses for it, such as injuries, other great Yankee hitters cleaning the bases, and his five times leading the AL in walks. Nice try, but Mantle drove in under 100 in seasons when he played 147, 144, 150, and 153 games, and once drove in 128 while walking 126 times. By contrast, Yogi Berra had 5, 100-RBI years. Aaron had 11, Mays 10, Mize 8, Banks 7, Hodges 7, Snider 6, Kluzsewski 5. The difference was, they came along before Mantle was king, and struck out less, far less.

The plain fact is, Mantle's strikeouts—five times leading the league, eight times over 100—cost him not only more homers and RBIs but in the end a .300 lifetime average, something he bitterly rued in his autobiography, *The Mick*. "[G]oddam, to think you're a .300 hitter and . . . find yourself with a lifetime .298—it made me want to cry," he wrote. It was his own fault, as with the RBIs. And it was the game's fault for getting sucked into his style, creating what SABR's John C. Tattersall calls baseball's "bases empty syndrome" in which so few runners got on that the power men had nobody to knock in much of the time. The syndrome affected smart hitters like the Tigers' wondrous Al Kaline, as close to the perfect player as possible who nonetheless had only three 100-RBI seasons with 399 career homers. I'll deal later with the not-so-smart hitters, such as the poster boy of baseball inefficiency, Reggie Jackson, who in twenty-one years had all of six 100-RBI seasons. Not by coincidence, Jackson surpassed Mantle as the game's most-struck-out man in history.

My vote for the best slugger of the '50s is not my boyhood idol Mantle but rather Eddie Mathews, who was never much of an average guy but what a home run hitter. Mathews had the most homers in the decade—338, 18 more than Mantle—and homered every 14.5 at-bats to Mantle's 15.6. Between '53 and '61, Mathews had 30 or more dingers all nine years, one more than Mantle's eight straight from '55 to '62 (and with Lou Gehrig and Mike Schmidt second to Jimmie Foxx's 12 straight). And he did this hitting nearly as few homers against southpaws as Ted Williams, 94 out of 512. Mathews was also a hell of a third baseman. How dumb was it that he didn't get into the Hall of Fame until his fifth try? Very.

It's a Mantle's World

In 1955, Mantle had his first 3-homer game, tied the record when he hit a homer from each side of the plate twice in a season, and netted his first league homer crown, with 37. But the season ended on a downer when a hamstring injury in early September—while running out a bunt, yet—limited him to 10 at-bats and 1 homer in the World Series against the Dodgers. That Series, of course, finally lifted the Yankee monkey off the Dodgers' backs, in part because of Johnny Podres' superb pitching, 4 home runs by Duke Snider (whose 3-run shot in Game 4 and two taters in Game 5 helped turn a 2-games-to-1 Yankee edge to a 3-to-2 break for Brooklyn), and the second most famous World Series catch in history in Game 7 at Yankee Stadium. Podres, leading 2-0 in the bottom of the sixth, faced Yogi Berra with 1 out and 1 on and when Yogi sliced one right down the left field line, it looked like a lock for extra bases, maybe a tie game. But Sandy Amoros, running a day and a half from left-center, reached the ball just before it plopped into the corner, stuck out his gloved right hand, and the ball nestled in it. When Amoros threw it to Pee Wee Reese who threw it to Gil Hodges for a double play, the air left the Yankees and Podres coasted to the Dodgers' sole championship in Brooklyn.

Mantle then ate everyone's lunch in '56, the year that made his reputation. Everything about '56 had Mantle written all over it, and not with false hype. The man was in another zone. He had a record 20 homers in May, switch-hit homers in a game for the fourth time (before Mantle, no one had done it twice in a *career*), and made the first two of his four metaphoric bids to clear the Yankee Stadium right field roof. The first time came on May 30 when against the Senators' screwball-throwing pitcher Camilo Pascual he took a pitch up, up, and away in the area between the foul pole and the bullpen alley. Most home runs begin to drop before they get to their destination. This home run kept rising until its flight was rudely interrupted by the classic art-deco frieze façade that hung just below the 108-foot roof, the ball smacking against it about 18 inches shy of leaving the park. Springing into action again, Red Patterson came up with math showing that had the ball not hit the façade, it would have flown 600 feet. He may have even been right.

Mantle also homered in the All-Star Game in Griffith Stadium—as did Stan Musial, Willie Mays, and Ted Williams (who connected right before Mantle). He hit his 50th on September 18th off Chicago's Billy Pierce, in the Yankees' pennant-clinching win, and clocked one 480 feet into the center field bleachers at Fenway Park three days later. Remarkably, hitting with the abandon he did, his three hits in that Boston game raised his average to .302, 4 points behind Williams in the batting race.

For the ageless Splinter—who had lost the batting crown in '54 and '55 because his abundance of walks shaved his official at-bats below the required 400—such frustration was typical. Throughout the decade, Williams had travails physical and psychological—after muffing a Mantle fly ball in that series, he was booed by the fans at Fenway and spit into the stands, drawing a $5,000 fine. ("The Splendid Spitter," one paper called him.) Mantle's emerging star was his final frustration. In the last two series between the teams in '56, Mantle went 7-for-14, Williams 3-for-20, leaving Mantle at .353, Williams .345—and a Triple Crown for Mantle, to go along with his league-high 52 homers (20 ahead of runnerup Vic Wertz) and 130 RBIs. Mantle also led the league in runs with 132 and slugging at .705, but not in strikeouts, whiffing only 99 times. The whipped cream was the World Series revanche against the Dodgers, as Mantle slammed 3 homers, as did Berra (the Yankees had a 12-to-3 edge in dingers). Mantle also played a large role in Don Larsen's Game 5 perfect game, with a homer and a nifty running backhand catch of a scorching Gil Hodges line drive into the left-center alley, though the Yankees' biggest blow was Moose Skowron's Game 7 grand slam salting away Johnny Kucks' 9-0 three-hitter.

In '57, when baseball changed the batting title criterion to plate appearances to right the wrongs done to Williams, The Thumper hit a no-contest .388 with 38 homers (second to Washington outfielder Roy Sievers' 42), and a .731 slugging average in a bravura performance at age 38. But again there was Mantle to gum it up for him. Even though Mantle's power numbers dipped to 34 homers and 94 RBIs, he batted .365, led with 121 runs, and had a stunning ratio of 146 walks to only *75* strikeouts (the last time for five years he fanned less than 112 times). And of course the Yankees won the pennant again. The MVP vote: Mantle 233, Williams 209. It prompted Tom Yawkey to sputter that the voters were "incompetent and unqualified" because two Chicago writers placed Williams ninth and tenth (though even had they voted him second Mantle still would have won).

Bill James, reflecting the still-strong Mantle cult, writes in the *Abstract* that "anyone who thinks Ted Williams in 1957 was a better player than Mickey Mantle is a lunatic." However, Williams got even in '58, with less impressive stats, winning another batting title with a .328 average, 26 homers, and 85 RBIs, while Mantle's 42 homers (a league-high) and 97 RBIs were devalued by his renewed bad habits—a league-high 120 strikeouts, helping him fall to .275.

Still, Mantle was baseball's Cicero, his status exalted. Even his infamous night-on-the-town brawl at the Copacabana nightclub on May 16, 1957, joined by Billy Martin, Whitey Ford, Hank Bauer, and other Yankees, hardly tarnished him, whereas Williams probably would have been drawn and quartered for such a thing. The Yankees, and in turn the press, dealt with it by diverting blame to the "bad seed," Martin, who was traded to Kansas City as a human sacrifice. On the other hand, having set an impossible standard to live up to with his Triple Crown, Mantle had his own travails. Even a second MVP didn't stop the tightwad Yankee brass from making Mantle grovel for a tiny salary increase to $80,000. He also began hearing boos at Yankee Stadium, usually after a big whiff, and he got into the old cycle of pressing and swinging harder, which only got him struck out more. And he was becoming increasingly unhelpful in the World Series, starting with '57 against the Braves.

The latter's ascension that year gave Walter O'Malley a break; as dastardly as he was in jumping Brooklyn for L.A. after the season, it was a lot easier to do as a third-place team. (But then again, how much more dastardly could O'Malley have been by finalizing his plans—which included taking Horace Stoneham's Giants along as leverage, with the bogus promise of milk and honey in San Francisco—a year before it happened?) The Braves did it the new-fashioned way—with home runs. They hit the most in both leagues, 199, and Aaron—in his lone MVP season—had baseball highs with 44 homers and 132 RBIs (his .322 average was behind only Musial and Mays and tied with Robinson). Mathews had 32 homers, 22-year-old outfielder Wes Covington 21, an injury-slowed Adcock 12. These figures dwarfed the Yankees' 145 homers. What's more, the Braves also made late lightning of their own. It was Aaron's eleventh-inning homer, for example, that clinched the pennant against the Cardinals.

Thus the Series became a duel of huge clutch home runs. After the teams split the first two games at Yankee Stadium, the Yankees rang up 3 homers—two by rookie shortstop Tony Kubek and one by Mantle—in a 12-3 pounding. Then in Game 4, with Warren Spahn working on a 4-1 lead with 2 outs in the top of the ninth, Elston Howard slammed an unbearably dramatic 3-run shot to tie it, and the Yankees went ahead 5-4 in the tenth. The Braves came up and were a breath from defeat when pinch hitter Nip Jones was nicked on the foot—or so the umpire said, and still said after a ten-minute ruckus by Casey Stengel. Johnny Logan then doubled and Mathews went yard against Bob Grim for a, well, unbearably dramatic win.

After Lew Burdette's Game 5, 1-0 win, the Braves went into the seventh inning of Game 6 trailing 2-1 when Aaron homered off Bob Turley to tie it, his third Series tater—before, in the bottom of the frame, Hank Bauer clocked one off Ernie Johnson for the lead and eventual win, 3-2. Now it was Game 7, Yankee Stadium, full house. Edge, Yankees? Never happened. Burdette, an ex-Yankee prospect, hurled *another* shutout, on two days' rest, to win 5-0.

The rematch came the following October, when the Braves were a little lighter (their home run total dipped to 167) and the Yankees a little heavier (an AL-high 164). This time Mantle led his league with 42 homers, and Aaron fell to 30, 17 behind league leader Ernie Banks and one behind Mathews. And talk about needing late lightning. For the Yankees, as Yogi Berra would say, it got late early. They lost the first two games in Milwaukee, wasting a pair of Mantle dingers in Game 2, and were down 3 games to 1. Now Bob Turley stepped into the Burdette role, winning Game 3, 7-0.

Now the last two games were back in Milwaukee. Game 6 was tied 2-2 after nine innings when Gil McDougald crashed his second homer of the Series for a lead that stood up in a 4-3 win. Game 7 also turned into a death match. Tied 2-2 after seven, Howard's base hit drove in the lead run, and Skowron came up and crushed a 3-run monster of a homer to put the game out of reach. The 6-2 victory made the Yankees the first team in fifty-three years to prevail when down 3 to 1 in a World Series—and it saved a few high-priced reputations in the Bronx.

For the highest-priced of them all, the one with the No. 7 on his back who had underperformed in the two Series, the pressure went on unabated. It wouldn't be until another harried home run hero came to town and got himself into an even bigger Crock-Pot of stress, that Mantle would learn to relax and live a little more easily with his immortality.

Homers That Weren't

Don't ask me to explain the '59 season, which was so wildly out of sync in the '50s maw of easy home runs that I'll go cosmic and say it could only have been a great unseen force dropping a hint that things were getting a tad out of hand again with home runs. In fact, at a time when the concepts of newness and youngness were on people's minds as the Einsenhower era was expiring, baseball's home run–or–perish ways now seemed sclerotic, too. Which is why the new concept became reinventing the very old concept of going one base at a time at top speed when, with that game plan, the Chicago White Sox broke out on top in the AL and stayed there.

The Sox, a constant contender through the decade with almost no one who could hit a home run, hit 97 homers in '59, the only team in the majors under 100. Their team batting average was .250, 3rd worst in the league, and they had two double-digit homer men, center fielder Al Smith (17) and catcher Sherm Lollar (22 with 84 RBIs). The Sox also picked up Ted Kluszewski on waivers in August and he kicked in a whole 2 more homers. The team's foundation was speed, led by the quicksilver keystone combo of second baseman Nellie Fox and shortstop Luis Aparicio, who between them amassed 8 homers but led baseball in putouts, assists, and fielding, and always were on the move. The Sox made a league-best 46 triples and were the only team to rack up more than 100 stolen bases, with 113. Worthy descendants of the 1906 "Hitless Wonders," these Sox had their own nickname—the "Go-Go Sox."

By August, they had disposed of the Yankees, who finished third, and eventually the Indians, with a 94-60 season—this in a year when the AL hit more homers than ever before, 1,091, and unveiled the newest ball-buster of note, the Senators' balding, doughy Harmon Killebrew, who had been signed as an 18-year-old "bonus baby" in 1954 at the urging of a U.S. Senator from Idaho, the kid's home. After bouncing to and from the minors for five years, Killebrew blasted 15 homers in May 1959 and a co-league-high 42 overall with a short yet muscular swing anchored by his tremendous leg and hip strength.

The Senators (who would move to Minnesota in '61 to play as the Twins just as they were getting good, and be replaced in D.C. by a rag-tag team that was very bad) never could find a position for the 6-foot-

1, 210-pound, fielding-challenged Killebrew. He would for the next two decades loiter at third, first, left, then inevitably his best position—designated hitter. But no matter where he played, this most gentle and well-behaved man proved to be an incongruous but aptly nicknamed "Killer," leading the AL six times in homers and, bucking the empty-base syndrome, clearing 100 RBIs nine times. Up until the mid-1960s, he was a threat to break Ruth's career homer mark. And, oh yes, caught in the Mantle tide, he walked a lot and struck out a whole lot—116 times as a rookie and over 100 times the next six seasons.

Killebrew's co-leader in '59 was the best home run hitter the Indians ever birthed, the tightly wound, Bronx-born Rocco Domenico Colavito, who had arrived in '56 with 21 homers in 101 games and increased his production to 25 in '57 and 41 in '58 with 113 RBIs and a .303 average. "Rocky" Colavito was a compelling figure who practiced a weirdly fascinating ritual at the plate. First, he'd wrap his bat around his upper back and stretch his torso violently as his eyes scrunched tightly and his face grimaced in pain. Next, breaching etiquette, he would balefully point the bat at the pitcher and stand frozen in that pose until the windup began.

Cleveland had a love/hate affair with the hirsute, manic Colavito, its first ethnic star, who hit 20 or more homers for 11 straight years (374 overall) and was a splendid right fielder with the game's strongest arm but who also fell into horrendous slumps. In '59, when he became the first Indian to have consecutive 40-homer years, on June 10 in Baltimore, he smashed dingers in four straight at-bats, something only Lou Gehrig and Bobby Lowe had done. Colavito also struck out far less than his generation's sluggers, never reaching 90 in a season, and drove in 100 or more runs six times. But his .257 average in '59 made the Indians GM, Frank Lane, nervous. Lane, called "Trader Frank" for his compulsion to wheel and deal, wheeled the Rock to the Tigers two weeks into the next season in a blockbuster deal for the '59 batting champ, Harvey Kuenn, who had hit .353. Bad move. By season's end—when Colavito had 35 homers while Kuenn, though he hit .308, was hobbled by injuries and was again traded, to the Giants—Lane could boast of having made the fourth-worst trade in history, behind Ruth to the Yankees, Foxx to the Red Sox, and, as you'll soon see, one involving Frank Robinson.

As providence would have it, the Dodgers recovered their groove in '59 in L.A.—though it was a rather different groove imposed by their temporary home in a football Parthenon, the cavernous Coliseum, where baseball became an arcade game. Shoe-horned into this wide oval, the outfield dimensions were comically staggered: right field, 300 feet; right-center, 440; center, 425; left-center, 320; and left field, *250*—the last necessitating the erection of a 40-foot-high screen from pole to alley, which didn't help. As hitters took turns trying to poke cheap shots over the screen, 193 homers flew out in '58—182 to left. In '59, right field was shortened by 60 feet but still 132 of 172 homers were hit to left, including 14 of *left-handed*-hitting outfielder Wally Moon's 19 homers that year, or "Moon Balls," as his opposite-field shots came to be dubbed.

Yet the Dodgers didn't benefit from such shots. In '58 they hit 172 dingers, second to the Cubs, but finished seventh. In '59, they traded some power and went go-go as well. By now Roy Campanella was in a wheelchair after a tragic car wreck in '57 and while Duke Snider—who'd hit the last home run at Ebbets Field and hit his 300th at the Coliseum in '58—and Gil Hodges each hit 25 homers in '59, the new sparkplug was the marvelous Junior Gilliam, who batted .282, walked a league-high 96 times, and had 25 of the team's league-best 84 steals. With 24 fewer home runs than the year before, and a .254 team average, the Dodgers stayed in a tight race with the Braves, who were done in by a homer that wasn't.

It happened on September 15 when the Braves visited the Coliseum holding a one-game lead. In the fifth inning, Joe Adcock hit one to the very top of the screen, where the ball hit a girder that secured the screen and became ensnared in the netting. Totally baffled, the umpires first ruled it a double, then when fans shook the screen and the ball fell into the stands the call was changed to a homer—then changed back to a double. This shades-of-Ebbets moment left Adcock stranded on second and the Dodgers ultimately won in extra innings—a huge factor in the two teams ending the regular season in a tie before the Dodgers won the flag by sweeping the two-game playoff.

(This wasn't Adcock's only homer that wasn't in '59. On May 26, the Pirates' Harvey Haddix pitched a perfect game over a remarkable 12 innings but no one could score on either side. Then in the thirteenth, Felix Mantilla reached on an error. Haddix then walked Aaron intentionally, and Adcock hit one over the wall to break up the game—only Aaron brain-locked and ran off the field instead of around the bases. Adcock circled the bases but because he had technically passed Aaron he was called out, as was Aaron for leaving, and the homer entered the record books as an official double. *D'oh!*)

The World Series figured to be a battle of the creampuffs, so of course when it began on October 1 at Comiskey Park, the Go-Go Sox went yard-yard—thanks to Big Klu, who turned back the clock by slamming a pair of 2-run homers in an 11-0 victory. This was a one-game illusion, though. Three of the next four games were nail biters decided by 1 run, the other by 2 runs. The Dodgers won Game 2, 4-3, when Charlie Neal hit two homers and went home to the Coliseum to ring up 3-1 and 5-4 victories, the latter clinched by Hodges' eighth-inning homer. The Sox would get one back, winning 1-0 before a record World Series crowd of 92,706 when three pitchers scattered nine hits and beat a young Sandy Koufax. That brought the Series back to Comiskey Park and the Dodgers unloaded, clocking 3 of their 7 Series homers, by Snider, Moon, and pinch hitter Chuck Essigian (who with his second pinch-tater in the Series tied a record). Staked to an early 8-0 cushion, Johnny Podres weakened and surrendered a 3-run shot by Kluzsewski in the bottom of the fourth—his 3rd, a record for a six-game Series—but the Dodgers closed it out, 9-3, on $5^2/_3$ scoreless innings of relief work by Larry Sherry, who with a win and two saves earned the Series MVP trophy.

So now the great anomaly of '59 was in the books, to be swept into obscurity in the giddiness of the '60s "New Frontier" leitmotif—one taken literally, too literally, by the baseball Brahmans who would soon expand its borders for the first time and unwittingly begin the distillation process that became epidemic, and nearly ruinous. In the overlap of eras, there would be four more years of Yankee home run melodramas—including one convulsive year that would mandate the fall of every long-ball standard imaginable, and in turn cheapen the home run beyond all recognition.

Part 4

AND THE WALLS CAME TUMBLING DOWN

12

Deconstructing Babe

The Long Good-bye

In keeping with the premise of renovation, the beginning of the new era was the end for baseball's hoariest senior citizen, Ted Williams. Teddy Ballgame went out in his usual way, with his tongue stuck out at his critics—which now included even his owner, Tom Yawkey, who after an injury-riddled Williams hit just .254 with 10 homers in '59 urged him to quit. "That burned my ass," recalled Williams, who came back in '60 at age 41 locked and loaded. On June 14 he banged a 2-run homer off Wynn Hawkins in Cleveland to become the fourth man to reach 500, and by September 1 he had 517—off Washington's Don Lee, whose father, Thornton, had given one up to Williams twenty years earlier. With great majesty, he would hit 29 homers with 72 RBIs and a .316 average, making his point that he would exit stage left on his terms.

He made sure of it with his last dinger, on September 26 at Fenway Park, a blow that delivered with poetic irony the first big homer of the '60s—and for Teddy Ballgame an elegy of triumph instead of pity. This was the Red Sox's last home game of a dreadful seventh place season. Williams told his manager, Mike Higgins, it would be his last good-bye. The team held a ceremony before the game, and an unrepentant Williams insincerely thanked the fans and sincerely insulted the press. Then he entered a game for the last time against the Orioles. He walked and flied out twice, the last a 400-foot drive caught at the warning track. Then in the eighth, with Baltimore up 4-2, he came up with one out as the crowd of 10,454 rose in an ovation for his putative final at-bat. "[N]o calling, no whistling, just an ocean of handclaps . . . a somber and considered tumult," wrote John Updike in his classic October 22, 1960, *New Yorker* homage to Williams, "Hub Fans Bid Kid Adieu." The Kid, in form, chose not to acknowledge it.

Facing right-hander Jack Fisher—remember the name—Williams tore at a 1-1 pitch and lifted a towering drive that landed 450 feet away in the right–center field seats. As he circled the bases in an unusually rapid gate ("like a feather caught in a vortex," said Updike), the cheers no doubt rang hollow because he never looked up from the ground. Disappearing into the dugout, he would not come out as chants of "We Want Ted" rang through the park, though he did consent to leave the game on this mythical plane; by pre-plan, he went to left field after the inning, to be replaced so the crowd could cheer him some more as he jogged in, head down, unyielding.

"I felt nothing," he said later when asked about the vibe. "Nothing, nothing, nothing."

Or, as Updike noted, "Gods do not answer letters."

With great anticlimax, the Sox pulled the game out 5-4, and the Williams era was over. Mercifully. Before anything else could go wrong. As for the Sox, they had a seamless transition. The Carl Yastrzemski era could now begin. As for Williams, let's just hope he's at peace in that big Frigidaire his son put him in when he died.

The other dinosaur still extant, Stan Musial, was also dying hard. In '57, at age 36, Musial hit .351, winning his seventh batting crown, and was second to Aaron in the MVP vote. At this point, Musial—who had set a record in May 1954 with 5 homers in a doubleheader—was still a potent long-ball threat, with 29 dingers. In fact, the All-Star Game had by now become a synonym for The Man going yard. In the '55 Game, in Milwaukee, Mickey Mantle's 3-run bomb off Robin Roberts helped mount a 5-0 AL lead. The NL squared it in the eighth and then in the home twelfth Musial led off with a rocket against Boston's Frank Sullivan to win it. That was his 4th All-Star dinger, even then a record. He then hit No. 5 in the '56 Game. But Musial's power ebbed along with his average over the next three seasons.

Then came 1960. That year Musial, who had become the NL's first $100,000-a-year player in '58, *gave back* $20,000 of it, which of course was nuts but it made him feel hungry again. That year he hit homers in both All-Star Games in Kansas City and at Yankee Stadium, elevating his

All-Star record to 6. And guess what? I still can't finish off Musial even now, so hang on.

A Maz-Ter Stroke

Speaking of dinosaurs, the Yankees lumbered into the new decade dismissing any notion that home runs weren't the way to Arcadia. Indeed, losing the pennant to the Go-Go Sox only made them more power-mad. After dipping to fourth in homers in '59, with 153, the Yankees traded four players, including the burned-out Don Larsen and Hank Bauer, to Kansas City in a seven-player deal that brought them a made-for-Yankee Stadium paradigm, Roger Eugene Maris. Compact and muscular at 6 feet 1 inch, 205 pounds, Maris was a left-handed-hitting right fielder with a fillip-quick uppercut swing and the personality of a damp sponge, and thus could lift some of Mantle's home run burden without stepping on Mantle's star power.

In 1960, the dynamic worked like a charm. Maris—whose previous high-water year was in '58 when he split the season with the Indians and the A's and had 28 homers and 80 RBIs—seemed to have a career year, and all was sweet and light in the Bronx. Hitting in the cleanup spot behind Mantle, Maris hit 2 homers, a double, and a single in an 8-4 opening-day win over the Red Sox at Fenway Park. On May 28, they homered back-to-back for the first time, and vied for the AL home run title the rest of the way. The Yankees, mired in third place on August 14, cranked out fifteen straight wins in September to win the flag by eight games—pounding 193 home runs, then an AL record. Mantle finished with 40, Maris 39. But Maris led the league with 112 RBIs to Mantle's 94, and in average .283 to .275. And with Mantle again hurt by his strikeouts, Maris beat him out for the MVP, 225 to 222.

Born on September 10, 1934, in Hibbing, Minnesota, and raised in South Dakota, Maris was a fabulously gifted athlete, a former high school star in many sports. But he was the world's worst candidate for stardom in New York, completely ill suited for the New York arc lights by his small-town upbringing and by his own brooding tendencies and sneering defensiveness. Even so, in '60 it was hardly noticed since Mantle was the only Yankee that really mattered and the team offered Maris blessed sanctuary. When they swaggered into the World Series against the Pirates, the matchup was most piquant for its contrast between U.S. Steel and the corner hardware store. The Pirates, who had one home run man—alleged first baseman Dick "Dr. Strangeglove" Stuart, who hit 23—

were built around their flashy double-play combo, shortstop Dick Groat and second baseman Bill Mazeroski. (Roberto Clemente was not yet a star.) But even in pitching and fielding they had inferior numbers next to the Yankees, and few expected a different outcome than the last time the Pirates got in the Series—as Yankee fodder in 1927.

Don't ask for an explanation of the '60 World Series, either, because it was just too wavy. The Yankees outhit the Pirates .338 to .256, outhomered them 10 to 4, outscored them 55 to 27, and lost.

Still, right up until the last swing of the seventh game, a good many people—many of them in Pirate uniforms—expected the Yankees to win. The Pirates were so awed with Mantle that when he blasted a 450-foot homer in Game 2, which flew over an iron gate behind the center field wall at Forbes Field and completely out of the park, Dick Groat raved like a schoolgirl, gushing to teammate Bill Virdon, "That was the granddaddy of them all! I never in my life saw a ball hit like that!"

Mantle hit 3 homers, had 11 RBIs, and hit .400 in the Series. Maris and Skowron had 2 homers each, and Skowron a Series-record 12 hits. Even the bantam second baseman Bobby Richardson—who had hit exactly 1 home run that season—drilled 1 over the left field fence at Yankee Stadium with the bases loaded in Game 3, in which he had a Series-record 6 RBIs. However, Pirate hurlers Vern Law and Harvey Haddix, aided by Elroy Face out of the bullpen, tamed the Yankee bats in Games 4 and 5, 3-2 and 5-2 Pirate wins. Ford's 12-0 whitewash in Game 6 at Forbes Field would set up yet another climactic Game 7. And what a Game 7!

No World Series game has ever risen to the punch-drunk battle royal that occurred on October 13, 1960. And leave it to those capricious home run gods to wake up the Pirates' bats that afternoon. After having gone without a dinger for five games, reserve first baseman Rocky Nelson (no, not Ricky Nelson), replacing Dr. Strangeglove, took one deep against Bob Turley in the first inning for a 2-0 lead. The Bucs added another deuce in the second and stayed ahead 4-0 until Skowron hit a solo homer in the fifth. But with Law tiring, Pirate manager Danny Murtaugh again handed the ball to Face, who immediately gave up a run-scoring hit to Mantle to make it 4-2. Then with two on, Yogi Berra—with an archetypal swing—golfed a pitch nearly on the ground and smacked it high and just fair into the upper deck in right field, a stunning 3-run homer to put the Yankees up 5-4—prompting the usually contained Yogi to leap up and down in ecstasy. By the bottom of the eighth, it was 7-4.

In that frame, however, the Bucs—not the Yankees—got the mother of all World Series breaks. First Gino Cimoli blooped a single to right. Then Virdon hit a routine double-play grounder to short, or so it appeared until Fate put a pebble in its way on the uncombed infield dirt. The ball ricocheted off the turf and toward Tony Kubek's face, striking him flush on the Adam's apple when he reflexively pulled his head back. Kubek collapsed as if he had been garroted. Clutching his throat, unable to breathe and coughing up blood, he was taken off the field and to the hospital. But as grotesque as the interlude was, it gave the Pirates life. A hit by Groat drove in 1 run. Then Stengel screwed up. He yanked Bobby Shantz, a good-fielding pitcher, and brought in lanky Jim Coates—who after a bunt put runners on second and third with 2 outs, forgot to cover first on Clemente's slow bouncer to Skowron, allowing another run in.

Now, at 7-6, backup catcher Hal Smith, who had come into the game for Smoky Burgess, crushed a Coates pitch 450 feet over the center field wall—another stunning turn of events that gave the Bucs the lead back, at 9-7.

Facing the grave in the top of the ninth, the Yankees were, well, the Yankees. They scratched out a run on a 1-out Mantle single, which put him on first and Gil McDougald on third. Berra then mashed a scorching shot just to the left of first base that Nelson snatched on a hop. But Nelson blundered. Instead of throwing right to second to begin a sure Series-ending double play, he stepped on first, taking off the force at second. That should have led to Mantle being caught in a rundown between first and second, likely allowing McDougald to score. Except that Mantle blundered, too. Thinking Nelson caught the ball on a fly, Mantle never took off for second and wound up slithering back to first on his belly. His hand just touched the base ahead of a belated tag by the startled Nelson as McDougald scored the tying run. It's a play no one can figure out to this day.

So now, after the Pirates retired the side a batter later, history awaited Bill Mazeroski, a a man who like Bobby Thomson has been downgraded by revisionists for the sake of a good story into a power pauper turned into a power prince at the witching hour. Only he wasn't. Still just 24 though in his fifth major league season, Mazeroski, who was bred in Ohio coal country, had hit 19 homers in '58 and in '60 he had 11 with 64 RBIs and a .273 average. His home run in Game 1 of the Series and his double in Game 5 were the deciding blows. But as he waited in the dugout before the inning began, Mazeroski's mind was elsewhere. As he recalled, the Yankees had freaked him out, bringing childhood memories of being a frustrated Indian fan into his head.

"All I could think of," he said, "was how the Yankees used to beat up on Cleveland for years and years, and how the Yankees would come back and how, just now, they'd come back on us with all that hitting." He was so lost in this dark retrospection that he didn't realize he was the leadoff hitter until Murtaugh yelled, "Maz, you're up!"

Mazeroski was a known high-ball hitter and when the Yankees got him out it was with low, swooping curves. He came to bat against Ralph Terry, the fifth Yankee pitcher that day, expecting to see nothing but low stuff. Terry's first pitch, though, was a fastball, high and tight, for ball 1. The pitch surprised not only Mazeroski but the Yankee catcher, Johnny Blanchard, who yelled out to Terry, "Get it down!" as he threw him the ball back. Terry then tried a slider, but it too stayed high. Chest high. Hittable.

Mazeroski stepped into the pitch, swung and drove it into the crisp autumn air, high and far to left field. At the crack of the bat, millions of TV viewers only saw the warthog-like image of Yogi Berra, playing in left, drifting back, his No. 8 to the infield, then sharply cutting away to play an angle on a ball he thought was sure to carom off the twelve-foot, brick and ivy-strewn wall at about the 406 sign just to the right of the left field scoreboard.

Instead, the force was with Maz, carrying the ball into the trees behind the wall—after, as Berra recalled, the ball had skimmed the very top of the wall. Mazeroski, who sprinted out of the batter's box anticipating the ball would hit the wall, didn't watch Berra but the left field umpire, Stan Landes. "He was holding up his hand and giving it this little circle thing," Mazeroski recalled, "and I knew it had gone out. From the time I hit second base, I don't think I touched the ground the rest of the way home."

Halfway through the trip, Mazeroski stripped the helmet off his head and ran home with it in the crook of his arm, sidestepping delirious Pirate fans pouring onto the field before he was inhaled by his massed teammates at home and toted into the dugout atop their shoulders—the blueprint of bedlam written by the Thomson homer, to be emulated after every big game-winning homer ever since. While the Pirates partied in eddies of champagne, the Yankees retired to a bleak and silent clubhouse. In his locker, Mantle buried his head in his hands and wept, just as Ralph Branca had in '51.

That Mazeroski was a perfect insignia of Pittsburgh's blue-collar sensibilities only drove up the metaphoric regency of his shot, which was at once spun in the media as a kind of populist uprising in a baseball class war. "It was a win for the poor little guys against the big rich guys swollen with past loot and overladen with records," was Jimmy Cannon's take in the *Daily News*. And yet, while it was also the death knell for the 70-year-old Stengel—who was fired five days later by the Yankee brass who believed his erratic moves cost them the Series—the Yankee hegemony kept the revolution at a safe distance. When sportswriters voted on the Series MVP, they gave it to a losing Yankee, Richardson, for his 12 RBIs and the "NY" on his uniform.

Such condescension didn't faze Pittsburgh, where the first championship in thirty-five years brought confetti raining from office windows and thousands of Pirate fans from Ohio and Pennsylvania driving toward the city, clogging the interstate. By midnight in the city, the bars ran out of glasses, because people took them to revel in the streets. "This was New Year's Eve, the Mardi Gras and Armistice Day jammed into one boisterous package," wrote Arthur Daley in the *New York Times*. And every year, on the site of where Forbes Field stood, fans gather on October 13 and at 3:36 P.M., the exact moment the ball left the yard, commemorate the only homer to win a seventh game of a playoff or World Series.

All of which fascinated Mazeroski to no end. "I never dreamed when it happened that people would still be talking about it 40 years later," he told *Sports Illustrated* in 2000. "It has seemed to grow and grow. Amazing, really amazing."

Which sounds a lot like Bobby Thomson. The only difference is that in 2001 Mazeroski's dinger for the ages landed him in the Hall of Fame. Sure, Mazeroski was the best defensive second baseman of his generation, a man called "No Touch" for his smoothness in handling a ground ball. But let's face it: the man got into the Hall because of one titanic swing. Unfair? Maybe. But if you can get to Cooperstown on one swing, that had to have been one damn good swing. A larger issue to use is why the subject of the next section isn't in the Hall with him, for sixty-one damn good swings.

1961

The two best teams in baseball history, the '27 Yankees and the '61 Yankees, were dominated by the same overarching image—Babe Ruth. Dead for thirteen years, Ruth arose like Lazarus just as the game seemed to be headed down a path the big monkey would have hated. Though the Pirates had won it all with a home run in '60, the dinger was falling out of fashion in the NL, seeming to necessitate a retro counterbalance in the

AL, back to the days when Ruth turned it into Home Run paradise. As soon as the Yankees hit their stride in '61 and Mickey Mantle and Roger Maris mounted a dual assault on 60 homers, Ruth's ghost was again alive and waddling.

Mantle was the first to make it thinkable that Ruth's record might really fall this time. He broke out of the gate blasting 9 homers in the first eighteen games. Maris got out slowly with only 3 in the first month, leading new manager Ralph Houk to drop him in the order as low as seventh and order him to get his eyes examined. In fact, Maris didn't consider himself a long-ball guy, telling a friend, "I doubt if I'll ever hit more than 25 or 30 homers a year." With the Yankees hovering around the .500 mark, both Maris and Houk were hearing boos.

But Maris and all the Yankees woke up in May, in no small part due to Houk asking of Mantle what the obsequious Stengel never had. In spring training Houk, a gruff ex-Marine, had challenged the pampered idol—now 29 and no longer the "hillbilly in a velvet suit," as Joe Trimble had dubbed Mantle—to show real leadership. Instead of using the clubhouse mainly as a drying-out tank, Mantle got there early and did what DiMaggio never did: talk to the players. He also agreed to move from his plush city hotel suite and live in a prosaic Queens apartment with Maris and outfielder Bob Cerv.

Houk also flipped Mantle and Maris in the order, with Mantle in the cleanup spot, à la Lou Gehrig, giving Maris the opportunity to see better pitches. On May 17 he hit his 4th of the year, and over the next thirty-eight games he would add 23 more (20 in 30 calendar days, tying Ralph Kiner's record, broken in '97 by Sammy Sosa). On June 19, he and Mantle went yard in the same game for the first time. On July 25 he hit homers in four straight at-bats over a doubleheader, tying an AL record. At the time, Maris had 40 homers, Mantle 38, and both were ahead of where Ruth was in '27—as New York fans knew because, every day now, the papers were running with this angle. A day later, for example, Dick Young wrote in the *Daily News*, "Roger Maris is running away from Babe Ruth like a scared kid in a graveyard. With 40 homers, Roger is 25 games ahead of Ruth's pace. . . . Oh, Clete Boyer had two homers and now is only 80 games behind Ruth."

Before I get into the payoff of this story, however, '61 must be placed in context. That year, expansion came to baseball, at a time when the game's weakened economy hardly demanded adding new markets. The AL made room for teams in Los Angeles and Minnesota (actually the second new team came to D.C., replacing the transplanted one now called the Twins), and hurried plans for two more in the NL, in New York and Houston, for '62. This made the AL, with its 162-game schedule and need to fill 20 pitching slots, a hitter's delight, and I don't mean singles hitters. That year, while the league's batting average rose only 1 point to .256, home runs rose from 1,086 to a record-and-then-some 1,534—or around *50 percent.* Deducting the dingers of the two new teams still brings the total to 1,226.

Another way to look at this is home runs–to–at–bats. In '60, it was 1 every 38.5 at-bats; in '61, it was 1 every 35.8. And homers per game rose from 0.88 to 0.95, which would hit 0.96 in '62, the highest it would be until 1985. If you're wondering, walks also increased, by a modest 500 but remained at 3.6 per game—but strikeouts rose by around *3,400*, and from 4.86 to 5.14 per game, and would only keep rising for another decade. Finally, the league's ERA rose from 3.87 to 4.02. Does this sort of make you think people were trying to go deep a lot?

People like Mantle and Maris. By July their mounting home runs were scaring the hell out of Ford Frick, who was so unprepared for the consequences of expansion that he never bothered to consider records that might be set in those extra eight games. For Frick, the matter had personal ramifications. He, of course, had been a Ruth lackey, one of his ghostwriters, and no doubt privately shared the open sentiment of Ruth's widow, who said, "I don't want the record broken. It's the one my husband loved best. Maris and Mantle are nice boys, but my husband wanted to be the home run king forever."

Frick, taking the cue from some old-line sportswriters, floated his solution to the threat to one of them, Dan Daniel, who wrote in early July that Frick "believes it would not be right to recognize the mark after 154 games [and] has strong backing in this attitude. If Ruth had gone to 162 games, he would have hit seven more homers if he had continued at his current pace. In the last eight games of 1927, Babe hit seven." The absurdity of this extrapolation was a sign that Frick needed to justify his plan to make 162-game home run records separate but equal from 154 game home run records. On July 18, Frick called a press conference and said, "There [will] have to be some kind of distinctive mark in the record book to show that Babe Ruth's record was set under the 154-game schedule."

Even more absurdly, Frick never even addressed whether non–home run records would be treated in this way. And it got worse: Ruth had actually played *155* games in '27, because of a seven-inning rainout. (The '61 Yankees, ironically, would play 163 because of just such a game.) There was also the possibility, as Maris pointed out, that he or Mantle could hit 61 in 154 games and the other would catch up and hit more in 162—leaving one as the all-time home run king and the other the all-time overall record holder.

And you thought Bud Selig doesn't know what he's doing.

Incidentally, Frick never suggested using the infamous asterisk to delineate records, and one was never used in the record book. That was the idea of Dick Young, the acerbic *Daily News* columnist. But asterisk or not, Frick's decision didn't spark much controversy. Most all in the media favored it, including those who later railed against Frick for it. And while Maris thought it was dumb and a direct slap at him, Mantle said, "I think Frick is right. . . . If I should break it in 155 games, I wouldn't want it."

And so the great race pushed on, in a new context of urgency. On August 16, Maris hit his 7th dinger in six games, tying another league record and putting him up on Mantle 48 to 45. On the 22nd, he got No. 50, the first to hit that mark in August. On September 9, when he hit No. 56, that and Mantle's 52 broke the record for teammates, 107, by Ruth and Gehrig in '27. As the race reached critical mass, both men, rather than feuding as the more inane rumors suggested, prospered by incorporating to consolidate endorsement deals. Maris, though, paid a price as well. As the new flavor, he got most of the media attention, wrecking his beloved privacy. In Tony Kubek's book about that season, *Sixty-One*, Yankee pitcher Bud Daley relates that "I saw Roger go take a crap and five reporters followed him right up to the stall." Virtually ignored in '60, Maris was so harried now that he began losing hair from his crewcut, and cowered in corners endlessly chain-smoking Camels. On September 14, he stood up to the press by not coming out of the trainer's room after a game, looking, as Trimble wrote, "like a culprit trying to hide."

Maris, in fact, was a culprit in New York, mainly for not being Mantle. With Maris now the whipping boy, Mantle was suddenly the favorite son. Gone now was the booing, which was transferred to Maris (though *not*, Mr. Crystal, after hitting home runs, nor as a target for any thrown stadium chairs). Not that Mantle wasn't as monosyllabic as Maris, but he had a practiced smile. Maris needed no practice to scowl.

Still, it was Mantle who ran down first. In early September, arm and hip injuries took him out of the race, and he sat out most of the last two weeks. Maris too was gassing out; it took him until September 16, in Detroit, to get No. 57. But the next day he hit No. 58 and, with impeccable dramatic irony, the next three games—152, 153, and 154—were in Baltimore, where, as Trimble wrote, "Babe Ruth's ghost, Ford Frick's edict, and the hard-to-scale walls of Memorial Stadium are all closing in on Roger Maris." And where, indeed, a Maris homer was taken away due to a July rainout. The first two games were a doubleheader on Tuesday, September 19, and 33,317, a mob by Orioles' standards, came to the games, braving the winds of an advancing Hurricane Esther. Maris, hitting into the teeth of those gusts, went homerless in nine times up. Concluded Dick Young: "Here in the monumental town where Babe Ruth was born, the chauvinist wind tonight whipped up a proud fury to protect Babe's homer record."

The next day, September 20, with another chance to see history in excelsus, 23,032 showed up on a damp and cold Wednesday night. In his first at-bat, Maris lifted a ball to right against right-hander Milt Pappas that normally would have gone out but was turned back by the still-stiff wind and became a fly out. Then in his second at-bat, Pappas dished up a 2-1 fastball—back then, when pitchers were men, there was no "wet your pants and walk him" stuff—that Maris sent slicing through the wind into the right field bleachers. No. 59.

Next time up, against reliever Dick Hall, everyone on both benches was up on the top dugout step. Fans were itchy with anticipation. The writers had their phones at their mouths, ready to scream to their desk men the magic number—*60*. Hall, whose stop-and-go motion and submarine delivery were a hoot, saw Maris overeager to swing and whiffed him on a high fastball.

Maris faced Hall again in the seventh and smacked one right down the right field line that made everyone's capillaries tingle—but it went foul by a few feet. Then on the next pitch he stroked a shot high and deep that the wind again turned into an out.

Now, in the ninth, the Yankees up 4-2, Maris got a last whack against Hoyt Wilhelm, the knuckleball master. With 2 outs, Maris stepped in, took a knuckler for a strike, then couldn't hold up on going after another one and hit a check-swing grounder to first. The race was over.

It was great relief for all those who believed Maris was the wrong man for veneration. One of those was a now-elderly Fred Lieb, who having shilled for Ruth wrote that Maris' squib was "my biggest sports thrill of 1961." Another, the *Milwaukee Journal*'s Oliver Kuechle nearly popped champagne: "Maris' failure . . . evokes no great regret here. . . . If the record is to be broken, it should be done by someone of greater stature and greater color and public appeal. [Maris] is nothing more than a good big-league ballplayer [who] is often surly. There just isn't anything deeply heroic about him."

This sophism—which was something like demanding to choose one's own parents—was rot, of course. Aside from the canard that a merely "good" player could go where only a god had gone, two men who'd hit 58 homers, Hack Wilson and Jimmie Foxx, were alcoholics, ferchrissakes, as was Ruth. Maris may have been a social misfit, but was it unheroic to perform in a fishbowl under intense pressure? On the contrary, it may have been baseball's most heroic crusade. Now back to the story.

With eight games to play with, Maris got in an overswinging rut and came up empty in five. Then, on September 26, in the second game of a series with the Orioles at Yankee Stadium—attendance: a sickly 19,401—Maris came up in the fourth with 2 outs and none on against Jack Fisher—I told you to remember the name—and crushed a 2-2 pitch into the right field upper deck six feet inside the pole. Now he was breathing the rarefied air of owning 60 homers.

Blame Maris, but only a little, for the obscene modern vogue of posing in the batter's box watching a big fly because he stayed put to see whether it would go foul—something he felt he had to explain later. Maris also did what Ted Williams was too stubborn to do. After rounding the bases with business-like crispness, he came out of the dugout to wave his cap at fans so suddenly on his side. Maris then got two more at-bats and had a single in the 3-2 win.

The writers were now with him as well—Joe Trimble called the homer "the Golden Gopher"—though Kuechle's *Journal* harumphed, "60 Too Late," in its headline. But when Maris, who told Houk, "I can't stand it anymore," sat out the next game (the Yankees, who won 109 games, had long since clinched the flag), the writers made it into an outrage, which after endorsing the Frick formula was rank hypocrisy. He was back in for the final three games against the Red Sox and went hitless in the first two, before 29,182 and 19,061 fans.

Now, still sitting on 60, the last shot at immortality was on Sunday, October 1, a brilliant sunny day that failed to bring out more than 23,154. Maris stood in against rookie righty Tracy Stallard and in his first at-bat he flew out to center on a change-up.

Now came the third. Maris dug in. Stallard threw one pitch high, another in the dirt. But, again, a pitcher didn't wuss out then and Stallard—who went 2-7 that year but would knock around for seven seasons before alcohol dissipated *him*—came in with a fastball, a little out over the plate, down at the knees. Maris couldn't have asked for it any better. He put his thirty-five-inch, thirty-five-ounce lumber on it and after a high flight it came down in Ruthville, into a cotillion of reaching arms before being finally plucked out of a guy's coat by a Brooklyn teenager named Sal Durante.

Maris ran, head down, on his historic excursion around the bases, encountered a trespassing fan who he shook hands with, did the same with Yogi Berra at the plate (Mantle was in the hospital with the flu that day), and sat down in the dugout, leaned his head back against the wall and sighed loudly. As with Williams, the crowd wouldn't quiet and Maris didn't move until several Yankees pushed him onto the field for another wave of the cap and a forced smile.

If the fans were belatedly supportive, not so for Frick and Mrs. Ruth. Neither the commissioner nor anyone from the baseball office was there, and Claire Ruth, who had been in the house for No. 60, couldn't bear to see the Babe lose his crown, asterisk or not.

Actually, it was not. Maris, who made out his last two times up in a game in which his monumental homer was, aptly, the only run, went into a record book that now read:

61 Roger E. Maris, AL : NY, 1961 (162 G/S)
60 George H. Ruth, AL : NY, 1927

The Yankees went in, too, with 240 homers, as Mantle wound up with 54, Skowron 28, Berra 22, Howard 21, and *third-string* catcher John Blanchard 21. Maris's other numbers were a .269 average and a league-best 142 RBIs. Mantle's were .317, 128, and a league-high 132 runs and 126 walks. And for all of Maris's wrangles with the writers, he took the MVP from Mantle again, 202-198. (Imagine being the Tigers' first baseman Norm Cash, who in just his second big league season that year led the league with a .361 average, had 41 homers and 132 RBIs, and came in a distant third.)

Not that Maris would ever really be accepted, long term, as shown by his Hall-of-Fame embargo. Maris might have owned '61 but in the long lens of history, '61 itself wears a taint—especially home runs hit in '61, a season when five men hit over 45 homers, including Baltimore first baseman Jim Gentile, a home run–or–strikeout crap-shooter who finished 1 RBI behind Maris, and on May 9 against Minnesota smacked grand slams in consecutive at-bats. Even the expansion Angels hit 189 home runs. It was, said *Newsweek*, "the year everybody hit home runs."

By contrast, in the NL, power had less impact. The Braves led with 188 dingers, 5 more than the Giants, playing their second year at windswept Candlestick Park. That season, Willie Mays had 40 taters, 123 RBIs, and hit .308, but suddenly played second banana to a muscular, sweet-swinging first baseman, 24-year-old Orlando Cepeda, the son of a great Negro Leaguer, who went from 24 homers and 96 RBIs in '60 to a league-best 46 and 142, and hit .311. And not far behind was an ectomorphic outfielder, 23-year-old Willie "Stretch" McCovey, who raked 18 homers and 50 RBIs in 106 games. Still, the flag went to the Reds, a timely hitting bunch with a modest 158 dingers—37 by Frank Robinson.

The AL model offended a lot of people, all of whom seemed to take it out on Maris thereafter, but really took it out on the home run. Even National Leaguers who hit them were guilty by association. Arthur Daley, sounding like a church deacon in the *New York Times*, decided that "This is a time for appraisal of values. Maris wasn't the only homer-hitter in the big leagues, he was just part of an epidemic, a contagion that reached its most virulent form in the American League."

Neither was Jimmy Cannon overly impressed with the author of 61 homers. Acting as a self-appointed spokesman for the game's rotary club, he averred, "The community of baseball feels Mantle is a great player. They consider Maris a thrilling freak who batted .269."

Thus did Cannon betray the real reason for Maris's eternal damnation: It wasn't that '61 was so cheap. It was that he wasn't Mantle. In the end, the wrong guy hit 61 home runs.

What of the arguments of the anti-Maris faction that he had a free ride in '61? In truth, they're so weak that, had Mantle hit the 61, it's doubtful they would have even been raised. For one thing, the ball wasn't much livelier in '61 than it was in '27, so don't even go there. The bats were more whippable, but if only two guys hit over 50 homers that year, was it so unfair to Ruth? Or was it more unfair to Maris that Ruth played only in the sparkling clear daylight, with no day games after night games, and never had to stand in against fastballs after a cross-country plane ride? Ballparks? Didn't Ruth aim for the same fences at Yankee Stadium? And the newer ones in the AL were actually bigger than the ones in Ruth's day. Forget Yankee Stadium being an aid at all, since Maris hit 31 of the 61 on the road, Mantle 30 of 54 (just as Ruth also had more away homers in '27, 32 to 28).

To be sure, the 20 new pitchers in the league included a lot of dogs—and Maris hit 9 homers against the Senators, 4 against the Angels. *But*, the pitchers Maris faced overall had a *lower* aggregate ERA than the pitchers Ruth faced in '27. Maris also hit 36 homers off pitchers who won at least ten games; Ruth hit 33. And while Maris hit just 1 off a future Hall of Famer (Early Wynn), the Babe hit 1 off just two (Ted Lyons and Lefty Grove).

And what of his much-reviled .269 average? Well, consider that Maris's lifetime average is actually lower, .260—which is the same or better than Killebrew and Mazeroski, 2 points lower than Reggie Jackson, 5 lower than Brooks Robinson, Mike Schmidt, and Johnny Bench. His 5.39 home run percentage is better than those of DiMaggio, Williams, Bench, Berra, Doby, and Billy Williams. All of these other names are in the Hall, as are all but one of the eleven men who have won consecutive MVPs. The lone exception: Roger Maris.

What am I trying to say?

Put the man in the Hall of Fame already!

The Forgotten King

It took only thirty years before the non-asterisk asterisk was removed from Maris's home run record by another commissioner, Fay Vincent, whose divergence from Ford Frick was immediately obvious by his logic in stating, "I'm inclined to support the single record thesis, and that Maris hit more home runs in a season than anyone else." However, neither Frick nor Maris would live to see the good guys win. In fact, for the rest of Maris's days, he was dissed, ignored, insulted, even forgotten. And for what?

"Do you know what I have to show for 61 home runs?" he once asked. "Nothing, exactly nothing."

The '61 World Series was an anticlimax for Maris—who hit .105 with 1 homer and 2 RBIs—and for Mantle, whose hip injury held him to six at-bats and one hit. Amazingly, the Yankees didn't *need* them; everyone else ground the Reds into the dirt like Maris's cigarette butts in a five-game farce, with Blanchard stroking 2 homers and Whitey Ford breaking the record of 29⅔ shutout innings—a record held by Babe Ruth, who clearly had better years than '61.

For Maris, '62 was an even bigger migraine than '61. Even before it began, the Yankees chose to reward Mantle with a raise from $75,000 to $100,000 (though they announced it as $82,000) but played nutcracker with Maris, refusing to hike his $60,000 salary to more than $67,000. After months of acrimony, Maris settled for $72,500 and played the season amid reams of negative reviews such as one from Rogers Hornsby, the old redneck, who said Maris "couldn't carry Ruth's jock."

It didn't help that Maris, who'd resolved not to reprise the home run grind, took a more level swing and was no doubt much happier hitting 33 homers—*sixth* behind Killebrew's league-high 48—though his RBIs fell to 100 and his average to .256. An injury-occluded Mantle eroded, too, with 30 homers and 89 RBIs but he batted .321 and that won him the MVP this time. As a team, the Yankees lost 41 dingers and finished second in homers to the Tigers' 209, but they had fresh blood—such as shortstop-outfielder Tom Tresh who had 20 homers and hit .286—and in October they were in the World Series again, facing the heavy artillery of the Giants, who had blasted an NL-high 204 homers.

Although the NL's bats got their turn at expansion pitching and banged a league-record 1,449 homers, Frick was spared playing the fool again when the home run race between Mays and Aaron stayed within reason, with Mays ending up at 49, Aaron 45. Indeed, the homer was no panacea. The Giants, echoing 1951, again cut out the Dodgers' hearts, coming from four games back with seven to play to tie for the pennant on the last day, but the Dodger method was on its way to changing the game. They hit only 140 homers but they had Drysdale and a maturing Koufax and a stunning 198 steals—including a record 104 by quicksilver shortstop Maury Wills (in Ruthian fashion, Wills had more steals than any other *team* in baseball). While the Giants followed the '51 script and won the playoff by scoring 4 runs in the bottom of the ninth in Game 3, the Giants wouldn't return to the World Series for the next seventeen years, a span that saw the Dodgers get there eight times.

The '62 Series was showcased as the long-awaited Mantle versus Mays foxtrot, but both were reduced to bit players—Mantle hit .120, Mays .250, and each went homerless—in yet another classic seven-game death match. Maris too came up small, hitting .174 with 1 homer, while lower-wattage bats came up big. Clete Boyer's dinger won Game 1 for the Yankees, Chuck Hiller hit the NL's first-ever World Series grand slam to put away Game 4, and Tresh's 3-run shot did the same in Game 5. In the end, though, the most compelling figure of all was Ralph Terry. Talk about the trials of redemption. Terry, two years post–Bill Mazeroski, was on the hill in Game 7, which was delayed three days by rain. On that October 16, Terry too came up big. Entering the bottom of the ninth, he'd given up one hit and led 1-0, and though he gave up a single to Matty Alou he stood an out from victory when Mays came up. Here is where Maris made arguably the second most magnificent defensive play in Series history. Mays lined a double to right, but Maris cut off the ball before it ran to the wall and got it back in so fast Alou held up at third.

Now, with the weight of the world once more on his neck, Terry, against Houk's wishes, chose to pitch to the mountainous McCovey—who'd homered off him in Game 3—instead of Cepeda in a bases-loaded, force-at-any-base situation. (Today, of course, Terry would have been long gone, replaced by a relief pitcher.) McCovey made the tension even more unbearable by smacking a long drive just foul. Then on the next pitch he hammered an ostensible game-winning hit to right. People rose to their feet. Eyes looked to right field. It was a blur, a flash—and, in the end, an out, snagged by Bobby Richardson for the third out on its way to Xanadu. But for a few inches either way, Terry would have been the ultimate goat. Instead, he was the Series MVP.

This heart-stopping victory seemed to drain much of the Yankees' karmic reserve. Consider Mantle's fate in '63, when he got off to a torrid start. On May 22, the Yankees had blown a 7-0 lead to the A's when Mantle stepped in against pitcher Bill Fischer in the tenth inning and ripped the ball so hard that it rose nearly on a straight line before crashing against the Yankee Stadium right field roof façade, for the third time. Mantle would recall, "That was the only homer I ever hit that the bat actually bent in my hands—the hardest ball I ever hit." That blow, calculated a noted physicist, would have gone *620 feet* if not obstructed. Imagine what Mantle would have done in June had not on the 5th of the month he run into a fence trying to catch a fly ball in Baltimore and broke a bone in his foot and tore up a knee, a horrifying injury that held him to sixty-five games and 15 homers that season.

Maris, too, was crippled, with a bum wrist, and the M&M Boys would sink to 38 homers combined. And while the Yankee slugging void was filled by Elston Howard and Joe Pepitone, and they breezed to the pennant by ten games, their stodgy power game was suddenly an anachronism by comparison to baseball's new paradigm—best embodied by the Dodgers, who raced to the NL pennant with only an occasional dinger (the most, 28, by humongous 6-foot-7, 250-pound outfielder Frank Howard, who made Ted Kluzsewski look like a pygmy). The Yankees were goners in the World Series after Koufax vaporized them in Game 1 at Yankee Stadium, striking out a then-record 15. The Dodgers would win four straight games, by scores of 5-2, 4-1, 1-0, and 2-1. They hit .214, the Yankees .171. It wasn't exactly the wave of the next two decades, but neither was it out of context.

Not by surprise, the Cardinals would rise to the top in '64 using the same formula. They hit just 104 homers and stole 73 bases, led by Lou Brock, who came from the Cubs in midseason and hit .348 for the Cards with 43 steals. Sadly ironic, however, was that they got to the World Series in Stan Musial's first year of retirement. But what a run it was for The Man, who in '62 at age 41 had drawn from an inner tap and hit .330

with 19 homers—including 4 in one game, the oldest human to do that. (In '63, he sagged to .255 but on September 10 he hit a homer in his first at-bat as a grandfather, which we're pretty sure is a record.) When he hung 'em up, Musial had 475 homers and, at the time, records for most hits and extra-base hits, and the most runs and RBIs in NL history.

The '64 season was Mantle's vindication. Still only 32, he was dissipated by endless injuries and alcohol, yet if he could stand without wobbling, he was dangerous—and could be so even if he couldn't stand. This was a man who in 1963 was kept out of a game for that reason, yet when he was put in to pinch hit, blasted a game-winning home run. Jim Bouton, who later told of that great moment in sports in his grandly subversive book *Ball Four*, recalled Mantle's reaction to the wildly cheering crowd. "Those people," he said, "don't know how hard that was." In '64, Mantle had homers from each side of the plate for the tenth and last time. He also hit his 450th homer and, alas, broke Ruth's lifetime strikeout record of 1,330.

That season, the Yankees were mired in mediocrity until, after a doubleheader loss to Chicago in July, Yogi Berra—who had been promoted to manager when Houk moved into the front office that year—ordered Phil Linz to cease playing a harmonica on the team bus. Relieved of the pressure by that absurdist drama, they went on to win the pennant by one game. In the World Series against the Cards, Mantle was magnificent. In Game 3 at Yankee Stadium, he came to bat in the bottom of the tenth in a 1-1 game. On the mound was knuckleballing reliever Barney Schultz, who'd given up exactly 1 homer during the season. In a frame borrowed from Ted Williams against Rip Sewell, Schultz fluttered a knuckler on the first pitch and Mantle whacked it into the right field upper deck for the win and a 2-to-1 lead in games.

However, in Game 4, a fifth-inning grand slam by Ken Boyer off Al Downing—remember *that* name—turned a 3-run deficit into a 4-3 lead, and win. Now who had the home run kavorka? In Game 5, Tom Tresh stepped in with two outs in the bottom of the ninth, St. Louis up 2-1. The pitcher? No less than Bob Gibson. And out of nowhere Tresh slammed a homer to tie it. But then in the top of the tenth, Tim McCarver went yard against Pete Mickelson and the Cards won 5-2.

The old homer voodoo shifted back to the Yankees in Game 6, as Maris and Mantle hit back-to-back taters and Pepitone a 3-run shot in an 8-3 win. This brought Gibson and Mel Stottlemyre out to face each other for the third time in Game 7. The Cards got ahead 6-0 before Mantle popped a 3-run homer in the sixth. Then in the ninth, a withering Gibson gave up 2 more dingers but held on for a 9-5 victory.

And that was that for the Yankees until the next decade. A mummified Mantle would hang on for another four battered seasons in the dusk of second-division misery, averaging 20 homers, 50 RBIs, and a .260 average. He racked homer No. 500 on May 4, 1967, and tied Jimmie Foxx for third all-time in '68 when on September 29 he faced Detroit's Denny McLain, who with his thirty-first pitching victory of the year in the bag, gave Mantle a going away gift. McLain told him he would groove a pitch, whereupon a grateful Mantle cracked No. 535. He retired after that season with 536 taters, and 18 in World Series play—a number still inviolate for postseason play, even throwing in latter-day league division and championship playoff rounds. Mantle's records (did you know he played more games than any other Yankee?) live on, and Mantle did, too, far longer than he ever expected. The pity is he would have had more years in him, but his alcohol abuse turned his liver cancerous and killed him on August 13, 1994, at age 63.

"If I knew I was gonna live that long," was his well-practiced line late in his life, "I would have taken better care of myself."

As for Maris, he was excused by the Yankees after the '66 season, traded to St. Louis for middling third baseman Charlie Smith. Playing part-time, Maris clanged 14 homers over the next two seasons, both pennant-winning and blissfully carefree years. Providence smiled on Maris when late-season Cardinal injuries made him a full-timer again. Starting all seven games of the '67 World Series against Boston, Maris had a vital role in the Cards' conquest, hitting .385 with a Game 5 homer. A year later, after the losing '68 World Series against the Tigers, Maris called it quits, with zero fanfare. For all his help, the Cards' beer-magnate owners, the Busch family, gave Maris a beer distributorship—until his death from cancer on December 14, 1985, at age 51, when the Busches took it back from his wife and children. The Maris family sued and won a $50 million judgment in 2001. That's how bad Roger Maris's timing was. In order to be rewarded, he had to die first.

Flower Power

By the mid-1960s, the home run again reflected a cultural change. After November 22, 1963, the country receded into a numb ennui that let a military escalation in Vietnam sneak in through the back door. And in baseball's own new frontier, widened with limited enthusiasm by expansion, the once-bold pluck and dash of the homer had become lost in an endless, and at times stupefying, churn of 2-1 and 3-2 games.

Prime among the reasons for this trend was the rise of the power pitcher. Where Robin Roberts could take a scalpel to the edges of the plate, now so could pitchers with near-100 mph fastballs, elastic-band curves, and hard-biting sliders. But every pitcher benefited in 1963 when the baseball nabobs tinkered with the strike zone again, this time restoring it to pre-1950 dimensions by expanding the limns from shoulders (instead of armpits) to the bottom of the knees (instead of the top). Hoping for fewer cheap homers, and maybe a little more offense once hitters turned to getting simple base hits, the game instead got what Bill James calls "the second dead ball era." While the smart teams played more for speed, the dumb ones—all but three or four—just kept swinging harder, at invisible pitches, while falling behind deeper in the count. Result: a dramatic fall in overall offense. In '63, homers fell 10 percent, runs 12 percent (to 3.9 a game), and batting averages by 12 points—.245 in the NL, .247 in the AL. Not to take anything from Koufax, but his 382 K's in '65 were a bit of a gimme.

How fearless were pitchers now? In '65 Mickey Mantle told *Sport*, "I still get a kick out of hitting a home run, maybe a bigger kick than ever. . . . [But in] the early 1950s, when the count was 3-and-0, or 3-and-1, you could look for the fastball, because they didn't want to walk you. Now they throw the slider 3-and-0. I have even seen knucklers, 3-and-0." Mantle and the great sluggers also saw something else then that hitters today don't—pitches high and tight.

Add in one more dampening factor: new ballparks, which for pitchers backed up strike zones with comfort zones. The '60s saw a stadium real estate glut necessitated by new teams and old ones that desperately needed replacements for the rusty bowls that had become tied to big-city urban decay, causing fans to stay away from them. So now came the attack of the modern parks, with the first one taking the prize as the worst stadium ever hatched. Completed in 1960, Candlestick Park sat beneath Bay View Hill in an icy wind tunnel, yet instead of buffeting the elements the place was cold enough to be Ted Williams' current home. And with its prosaic architecture and obstructed views it was no place to play or watch a game. While Willie Mays learned to inside-out his swing to steer the ball into the wayward wind blowing to right, playing in this mausoleum probably cost him at least 80 homers in 13 seasons.

As putrid as "Windlestick" was, its Sahara-like dimensions—397 feet to the alleys, 420 feet to center—signaled the new wave in ballparks, the real model for which was Dodger Stadium, which opened in 1962. The immaculate, Oz-like mien of "Taj O'Malley," with its perfectly symmetrical baby blue grandstand and oil-painting backdrop of palm trees and the Hollywood Hills beyond the pavilion-capped bleachers could not be recreated anywhere else. But spurred by the Dodgers' success on the field, and at the box office, virtually all the new parks were cookie-cut copies in style and dimensions, which were slightly more agreeable to hitters than Candlestick—330 feet down the lines, 380 feet to the alleys, 410 feet to center. Within three years, baseball sent in the clones: the Astrodome (designed by Buckminster Fuller), Shea Stadium (designed by Ray Charles), Anaheim Stadium, Busch Stadium II, Jack Murphy Stadium—and in the '70s three gray tombs—Three Rivers Stadium, Riverfront Stadium, Veteran's Stadium—and two more for the expansion Kansas City and Montreal clubs, Royals Stadium (which reversed the trend of the miserable too-big and too-drafty parks) and Olympic Stadium (which didn't).

Most of these edifices were built for baseball and football games, saving urban communities money. The circular configuration left grossly excessive foul-grounds areas. Many also had Astroturf surfaces that begged for speed, not power. And the early ones had pitching mounds that laughed at the unenforced 1950 rule that decreed the mound couldn't stand higher than fifteen inches—Dodger Stadium, it was said, may have had a *twenty*-inch hill, making Koufax and Drysdale seem to be throwing overheated fastballs from a second-story balcony.

Of course, the home runs hardly went away in the '60s. It's not as if Aaron, Killebrew, and Mays suddenly started bunting their way on. Proof? Killebrew hit the most homers in the '60s, 403 (ahead of Aaron's 373, Mays' 349, and McCovey's 326)—only the third time anyone had hit 400 in a decade. The other two people who did it were named Ruth (462 in the '20s) and Foxx (414 in the '30s).

In '64, Killebrew's Twins blasted an AL-best 221 taters—second in history at the time to the '61 Yankees—and went to the World Series the next year, though they capped the power a bit (150 homers) to ratchet up speed (92 steals). The Twins, in fact, scared the pants off the Dodgers in the Series, beating Koufax and Drysdale once each and squaring the affair in Game 6 on a 3-run blow by *pitcher* Mudcat Grant. It took another of those inexplicable random-selection Series homers, by the Dodgers' Lou Johnson, to finally pacify them in Game 7.

Then there was Frank Robinson, whose midlife rebirth increased his home run productivity. That happened in '65 after he hit .296 with 33 homers and 113 RBIs and was judged to be an expensive albatross by the Reds' owner Bill DeWitt. With the prescience of Harry Frazee, DeWitt—famously saying that Robinson "is not a young 30"—shopped him and closed a four-player trade with the Baltimore Orioles, mainly in exchange for Milt Pappas, who'd never won more than sixteen games in a season.

In reaction, people in Cincinnati demanded a public hanging of DeWitt. Failing that, they boycotted Reds' games. Attendance fell by 300,000 in '66, and on the field the team went to seed. Pappas that year went 12-11, then 16-13 the next. In June 1968, he was sent packing to the Braves. But Pappas outlasted poor DeWitt-less, who sold his devalued team in December 1966 for $7 million. As for old man Robinson, all he did in Baltimore was to rewrite history and raise attendance in '66 from 780,000 to 1.23 million. In his first game in Baltimore, he slammed a homer to beat the Red Sox. On May 8 he tacked a 450-foot homer off Cleveland's Luis Tiant that climbed over the Memorial Stadium left field bleachers—the only time that was ever done. On that day, the Orioles went into first place and they never dropped out, winning ninety-seven games and the pennant by eight games over the defending league champs the Twins. Robinson led baseball with 49 homers (besting Aaron by 5) and the AL with 122 RBIs and a .316 average—thus becoming the first and still the only man to win an MVP in each league.

The Orioles had 175 homers that season, 4 behind the Tigers. Buick-sized first baseman Boog Powell was third to Robinson with 34. In the World Series against the Dodgers the Orioles' two Mr. Robinsons—Frank and Teflon-gloved third baseman Brooks—set the tone with back-to-back homers in the first inning of Game 1 against Drysdale. Baltimore's "Baby Bird" pitching staff (Palmer, McNally, Bunker) threw a Series-record thirty-three scoreless innings and yielded 2 runs, 17 hits, and 1 homer in a four-game sweep. The Orioles didn't hit much either, batting .200, but of their 4 dingers, Robinson had 2—the second off Drysdale in a 1-0, Game 4 win—and he hit .286. Completing his personal sweep of honors that year, he was named the Series MVP.

The Orioles proved that not everyone had renounced the long ball. They hit 4 in one inning on May 17, 1967, the eighth AL team to do that—and seven different players hit 1 in that game, a record. Then, in '67, the Red Sox returned to the Series after twenty-one years with an AL-high 158 homers. That, of course, was Carl Yastrzemski's Triple Crown fantasia.

Now in this seventh season, "Yaz" finally rose out of Ted Williams' still-vibrant shadow, though nobody knew how to spell his name right. Reared on a farm on Long Island, he had been signed off the Notre Dame campus and from the start was a curiosity: a nervous coil whose face was set in a permanent grimace and whose stance was wacky; "Yaz" held his bat at a 90-degree angle above his head, then lowered it in an instant to tear into the pitch. As a left-handed power hitter, he was groomed to replace Williams, but soon proved to be a far better left fielder who by intuition played the angles of balls caroming off the Green Monster. He was also a more utilitarian hitter than Williams, gearing himself to drive outside pitches the other way—Yaz could seemingly pepper the Monster for extra-base hits at will—until someone tried to slip a fastball by him inside; then he'd turn on the ball and pull it like lightning to right.

In '67, with four teams battling for the flag, Yastrzemski was outrageous down the stretch—over the last twelve games he had 23 hits in 44 at-bats (.523), with 5 home runs, 14 runs, and 16 RBIs. The Red Sox needed to win the last two games with the Twins to avoid a three-way tie between those two and Detroit, and in those games he went 7-for-8 with 5 RBIs, nailing a 3-run homer in the first game. Yastrzemski tied Killebrew with 44 homers, but his Triple Crown has been devalued because of his other numbers—.311 average, 94 RBIs. But why hold the times against him? Nobody could hit much then—as '68 would prove, with a thud.

Indeed, but for Yaz, the Sox were not far off the baseball bell curve. The second-highest home run total on the team was 20 by Tony Conigliaro, and just as vital as Yaz was pitcher Jim Lonborg, who went 22-9. Their opponents in the '67 World Series, the Cardinals, were an organic match for the era, living off Bob Gibson's arm and Lou Brock's feet. And yet, as always, homers held the key, though in Game 1 Boston's starting pitcher Jose Santiago went yard only to lose 2-1. The Sox squared it in Game 2, 8-1, with a 1-hit masterpiece by Lonborg and 2 dingers by Yaz. The Cards came home to Busch and came alive. In Game 3, third baseman Mike Shannon jacked a 2-run shot in the second inning to put the Cards up 3-0, and they won 5-2. Next Gibson won his second game, a 6-0 gem, but Lonborg answered with a 3-1 Game 5 win to keep the Sox alive.

In Game 6 at Fenway, the Sox were trailing 2-1 in the fourth when, in succession, Yaz, Reggie Smith, and Petrocelli cleared the wall, a World Series first, and Petrocelli later cracked another in an 8-4 victory. So now came Game 7, Gibson against Lonborg. But the latter, on two days' rest, had no zip and gave up a homer to Gibson, who won the 3-hit, 7-2 clincher and the Series MVP.

A year later the Tigers came back to lead baseball with 185 homers, led by Willie Horton's 36 (no, not *that* Willie Horton) and 25 by Norm Cash and Bill Freehan. And in the World Series they put no less than Denny McLain and his 31 wins against Gibson twice—and lost both games; Gibson, a phenomenal athlete, even hit *another* homer in Game 4. But now a Tiger savior appeared—Mickey Lolich, who also won two games to keep Detroit in it. In Game 6, down three games to two, McLain faced someone other than Gibson and won one, 13-1, with help from Jim Northrup's grand slam.

Another year brought another dramatic Game 7, now between Gibson and Lolich, both of whom went the route in a tingling contest scoreless into the seventh. Then Gibson—who whiffed a Series-record *35*—laid one in too fat to Northrup who tripled beyond a stumbling Flood in center for 3 runs, and Lolich closed the deal, 4-1. A year before, Detroit had been cleaved by race riots. Now, blacks and whites united by a ball team reveled on those same ravaged streets.

Despite the loss, Gibson had now congealed as the symbol of the times—the power pitcher. For all of the big World Series homers of the '60s—and those in All-Star Games, including Johnny Callison's 3-run, ninth-inning bolt to win the '64 Game at Shea Stadium and Tony Perez's fifteenth-inning jack to win the '67 Game in Anaheim—baseball's offenses had clearly gone along with the late '60s spirit of flower power. Remember those homer totals in the 1,500s in '61 and '62? By '68, they had atrophied to 1,104 in the AL, *891* in the NL. That was the year that Yastrzemski would again catch historical heat for leading the league with a .301 average, the lowest since Elmer Flick hit .306 in 1905. The AL's composite average was .230, the NL's .240. Gibson's ERA was that unfathomable 1.12, and Tiant wasn't far behind at 1.60. Four others in the AL were under 2.00, too. And Gibson had an incredible 13 shutouts. Both leagues had sub-.3.00 ERAs, the first time that had happened since 1918.

You know what's coming. Baseball always gets nervous again about imbalance and stagnation, so the tinkering began again. The first target were those high-rise mounds. By law they were hacked down to no more than ten inches. And for good measure, baseball yet again redrew the strike zone, which now ran from *armpit* to *top* of the knees.

Change was really the name of the game. In '69, baseball split each league into two divisions, accommodating four new teams, in Seattle (which would jump to Milwaukee the very next year), Kansas City, Montreal, and San Diego. Aptly, all this alteration happened as the country had shaken off the ennui and was damn near tearing itself apart over the

Vietnam War. And while baseball contributed almost none of its players to this war, the brass knew the game was surely losing its country-fair innocence. In '69, too, Curt Flood filed his historic lawsuit against the reserve clause, which though rejected by the courts would become the genesis of a hundred-years' war that within just three years would bring the first player strike.

In the confusion and uncertainty, however, baseball could at least be comforted that hitting in general and the home run in particular were prodigal sons come home. In '69, runs ticked up by 15 percent. The NL hit .250, the AL .246. The overall ERA soared to 3.59. And homers? They soared to then-historic levels—1,470 in the NL, 1,649 in the AL. Even so, in a year that saw humans leave footprints on the moon, baseball's version of an Arthur C. Clarke novel was that a team with a paltry 109 homers and a .242 average won the World Series. After only seven years of futility and comically tragic losing, the Mets had gone from bumbling harlequins under Casey Stengel to a pitching-rich, gritty clutch-hitting winner under Gil Hodges. They made fools of an overconfident, bigmouthed Cubs team chipped off of Leo Durocher to win one hundred games and the East Division, then swept Hank Aaron's now–Atlanta Braves and sand-bagged the mighty Orioles in a five-game World Series.

The home run was kind to the Mets that October. They out-homered the Braves 6 to 5 and the Orioles 6 to 3, and in the Series, first baseman Donn Clendenon copped the MVP with 3 muscular bombs. In Game 5, the home run gods got loopy again—when a key blow was struck by second baseman Al Weis, who'd hit all of 2 homers during the year, and 6 in eight years, and whose bat was as lethal as a feather duster.

The moral: the home run gods were ready for some seriously deranged business in the years to come.

13

Hammering into History

Reggie's Rising

In 1970, Frank Robinson was 35, Harmon Killebrew 34, Hank Aaron 36, Willie Mays 39, Ernie Banks 39. But for Aaron, the game was moving past the home run generation seeded in the '50s, though Robinson could only be stopped, it seemed, with a stake through the heart at midnight. With him as their anchor, the Orioles won the first two pennants of the decade and a championship the first year when they blew past the Twins in the playoffs in three straight and then the Reds in a five-game World Series—hitting 10 homers to the Reds' 5, with a pair each by Robinson and Powell.

Robinson had 2 more dingers in the next year's World Series against the Pirates. But this was the Series that codified the long-simmering legend of Roberto Clemente. Now 37 himself, Clemente, a .317 career hitter with 240 homers, had won three batting titles in the '60s and was the NL's MVP in '66. He was renowned as a Michelangelo in right field. But not until this pulse-pounding seven-game Series was his grousing and habitual missing of games eclipsed by his will to win. Hitting safely in every game, as he had in the '60 Series, Clemente batted .414 and led the Bucs back after they dropped the first two games to Baltimore—a team with four 20-game winners, no less. He hit a homer in Game 6, a 3-2 loss, and another in Game 7, a 2-1 win that made him the Series MVP.

Clemente got his 3,000th hit in his final at-bat in '72, days before hopping that ill-fated plane bringing relief supplies to Nicaragua that went down in the ocean, the only player to ever perish as the Greek gods did, in terrible and glorious death.

A certain mythological force seemed to be tracking Willie Mays as well. After seventeen years of famine, the Say Hey Kid was given a final shot at a World Series as a Giant in '71 when the team won the NL West flag. But, alas, they lost a four-game playoff slugfest—which saw 8 homers for the Pirates (a record 3 in one game and 4 overall by first baseman Bob Robertson), 5 for the Giants, including 1 by Mays. Still, Willie had gone where only Babe Ruth had, and had the canceled checks to prove it—a record $165,00 salary. In '66, Mays hit home run No. 512, bypassing Mel Ott as the NL's all-time homer leader, and later that year passed Jimmie Foxx as the all-time right-handed-hitting slugger, with No. 533. He popped No. 600 off San Diego's Mike Corkins on September 22, 1969. Then on his first at-bat of the '70s he blasted No. 629, and homered in each of the first four games, a record Mark McGwire would equal in '98. On June 6 he hit No. 638, in the process passing Musial with 1,950 runs.

However, the most perfect player ever created sank to .271 that '71 season and, seeing him deteriorate, the Giants went along with a feel-good plan for Mays to finish his career in New York, with the Mets. On May 11, 1972, with a nearly decrepit Mays hitting .184 with 0 home runs, the deal was made, with the supernova moved for rookie pitcher Charlie Williams and $50,000. Three days later, wearing "NY" on his cap again, Mays came to the plate at Shea Stadium in the fifth inning of a 4-4 game against . . . the Giants. Lord, what mythic people can do at times like those. Mays merely stroked one over the left field fence for a 5-4 lead that would hold up as the final score. Mays managed to hit .267 in sixty-nine games with the Mets, with 8 homers in sixty-nine games. It made him think he had more in him and he came back in '73, when the Mets would give him yet one more shot to go out a winner, against baseball's first '70s dynasty.

This, of course, was the Oakland A's, who confounded their owner's unending attempts to make them into buffoons. Among other things, Charles O. Finley dressed his players up like jockeys in green and gold uniforms and white shoes, tried to have them use yellow baseballs, and made a jackass the team mascot. As big an ass as Finley was, much of this played into the '70s new individuality, and the A's went with it, wearing mustaches and long hair and fighting among themselves. Most of all, they had the perfect new-era baseball avatar in Reginald Martinez Jackson—the prototype for every A-List slugger for the last thirty years. And I don't mean this necessarily as a compliment.

Jackson's buff and rippling 6-foot, 200-pound frame came wrapped around an inner fission that blew sky high when he took his left-handed swing. The age of hitters aping the Aaron-Banks method of letting the wrists move whip-handle bats in an easy arc was lost on Jackson. In fact, no less than Joe DiMaggio had tried in vain to shorten Jackson's cut when Joe D was an ad hoc A's hitting coach. Jackson ignored him, as that bestial swing had already gotten him the attention he craved, first as an All-American at Arizona State. Signed by the Kansas City A's in '66, he was sent a year later to Birmingham and led the Southern League with 17 homers, while hitting .293. Called up late in the year, he hit under .200 with 1 homer, but tore the cover off the ball the next spring training, and when the A's began play in Oakland in '68 he was in the outfield.

He was surely an odd sight: a half-black, half–Puerto Rican kid with big glasses who was impossible to take one's eyes off of. His drives were Mantle-like, beautiful parabolas that became little specks in the air, and for the year he slammed 29 dingers with 74 RBIs and a .250 average. Not incidentally, he had also a jaw-dropping 171 strikeouts, a record then and not far from it now. Old-time ballplayers would have died of shame if they had done that. Wally Berger, who had set the rookie record of 38 homers in 1930 and had 242 over eleven seasons, many years later recalled that "In 1933 I struck out 77 times, leading the league in that department. It was my most embarrassing experience in baseball." Now, Jackson's booming homers and the style with which he hit them turned his strikeouts into a windy bugle presaging his next boomer.

Thus was the new ethos of the home run born and walking: If you had to whiff six times to buy a home run, it was a nice trade-off. If you lost RBIs in the process, hey, you'd make 'em up on the dingers. If you lost base hits? So freaking what? Those were for singles hitters.

Jackson led the AL in strikeouts his first four seasons, but by his second year—the one when hitting returned—he hit 47 big flies, with 118 RBIs, third to Killebrew's 49 and second to Frank Howard (now with the expansion Senators), who had 48. Jackson would never hit as many as that again, and would bat .300 exactly once, in 1980. Yet none of his flaws seemed to matter. By '71, the A's won 101 games and went to the playoffs (Jackson's two-game 3 homers off Jim Palmer couldn't stop the Orioles' sweep). The next, they were in the World Series—though without Jackson, who injured his hamstring while stealing home in the A's Game 5 victory over the Tigers.

The ironies about Jackson are many. He was no more powerful than

Killebrew, who hit 10 more career homers. He was a lot less humble than Mantle. He had speed that he used early in his career, stealing as many as 28 bases in '76, then all but stopped running hard, period. Though he had a strong arm, for his entire career he was a dreadful, uncommitted right fielder. His batting average, again, was 3 points higher than the reviled Maris. He was inferior as a ballplayer to every major star of the '50s and '60s. And yet maybe only Mantle and Mays had a greater impact on modern baseball. The only way to explain it is timing and the dumbing down of cultural standards for stardom—something, I'm mortified to report, the home run has had a whole lot to do with, but only because self-promoting hucksters such as Jackson and Barry Bonds co-opted it.

Smarminess became ingratiating in the '70s, and nothing was smarmier than Jackson's million-dollar smile or his lack of loyalty for every team he played for, which at the time seemed cool to many because it reflected baseball's new era of "maverick chic" individual freedom and player enrichment after decades of servility. Jackson charmed the pants off a now-younger, entertainment-oriented media corps with his style and his habit of creating puerile pop philosophy like instant pudding, such as, "For a certain amount of money, [a player] will eat Alpo," or the ever-famous "Hitting is better than sex."

Actually, the hitting–sex metaphor was a running theme, which he once expanded for *Time* thusly:

> I'd rather hit than have sex. To hit is to show strength. It's two against one at the plate, the pitcher and the catcher versus you. When I'm up, try everything you want. Rub up the ball. Move the fielders around. Throw me hard stuff, soft stuff. Try anything. I'm still going to hit that ball. God, do I love to hit that little round sum-bitch out of the park and make 'em say, "Wow!"

After himself and sex, a favorite Jackson topic was race, though his thoughts carried about a half of Frank Robinson's wisdom and a third of its sincerity. In these constructions, *he* was the object, not the cause. Referring to himself in the third person, which he often did, he once blathered, apparently seriously, "After Jackie Robinson, the most important black man in baseball is Reggie Jackson. I really mean that."

In time, the media that enabled him would turn on him, leading him to sulk in self-pity. Indeed, as impregnable and centered as he wanted everyone to think he was, Jackson's ego was as brittle as a twig. Hubris was his best defense. And I really mean that.

Undeniably a fascinating case study in excess, Jackson, more than even Mantle, took the home run ethos back full circle to Ruth. Mantle, after all, could not have been as narcissistic and theatrical in the baseball of the '50s. Jackson could, and did, getting the most out of it before those who emulated his arrogance—such as Bonds—seemed yawningly derivative.

For Jackson, one swing made his reputation, and fortuitously it came early, in the '71 All-Star Game, which itself was a major laying on of hands for the home run. As it happened, this All-Star Game, on July 13 at ancient Tiger Stadium, was the perfect venue for baseball's home run–based renaissance, as one of the few parks left that were hitter-friendly. The Game itself carried a swell of anticipation. The year before, the contest became a prime-time attraction, ensuring a large TV audience, as did the fact that the fans had also begun choosing the starters. The 1970 Game, which ended with Pete Rose nearly dismembering Ray Fosse in a home-plate collision, further sold the '71 Game, which drew a crowd of 55,559 and a gate of $435,134, both All-Star records.

The home run gods took notice. In the second inning, Johnny Bench hit a dinger off of the A's flashy lefty Vida Blue for a 2-0 lead. Hank Aaron hit his first All-Star homer in the third to make it 3-0. Then, in the bottom of that frame, with a man on first, Earl Weaver pinch-hit Jackson for Blue. The Pirates' mouthy righty Dock Ellis sailed in a dead fastball and Jackson simply crushed its remains. In Mantle-style, the ball kept ascending without end, up and over the right field roof and into the night until it struck a one-hundred-foot light tower atop the roof, then crashed back down to Earth, finally ending its ride on the outfield grass. The calculus said the ball traveled 520 feet but, like Mantle's façade shots, might have landed on the moon without obstruction.

Nobody could quite recall a ball hit like that, not even Mantle's shot against Chuck Stobbs, and for many it was the first they'd seen of Jackson—who stood at the plate to admire his flying object and, unlike Roger Maris, didn't apologize for it. A trend was born. And a reputation, for better or worse.

The fireworks that night weren't over. Two batters later, Robinson took poor Ellis over the right field wall for another 2 runs and a 4-3 lead. In the sixth, Killebrew bashed a 2-run shot off Fergie Jenkins, and in the eighth Clemente hoisted a solo shot off Mickey Lolich. For those not counting, that made a record-tying 6 homers, each by a "Hall of Famer to be" (bettering by 2 the '56 Game's home run count by future Cooperstown residents). The AL won 6-4, its first win since '64 (and last until '83). But while all this was interesting, and Robinson—who became the first to hit an All-Star homer for each league—won the Game's MVP, three decades later all most really remember clearly is Reggie's light-tower show. So imagine how deeply it was etched back then.

That Jackson figuratively towered over his era's home run hitters dimmed the exploits of many other sluggers. Take Richie, or as he insisted, Dick Allen, for instance. As a stone-handed third baseman, he broke in with the Phillies in '64 and won Rookie of the Year with 29 homers, 91 RBIs, 201 hits, and a .318 average. Brutally powerful and impossibly obnoxious, Allen delivered resounding numbers for six years—including 40 homers, 110 RBIs, and a .317 average in '66—playing for resoundingly bad Phillie teams, all while being savaged by fans. One time, Allen scratched the word "BOO" in the infield dirt with his spikes, and famously uttered that Phillies fans "would boo funerals." Allen habitually showed up late, or not at all, for games and in '69 he was suspended for twenty-eight games and fined $500-a-day, and in succession, was traded to the Cardinals, Dodgers, and in '72 to the White Sox. That year, he had a huge comeback, leading the AL with 37 homers, 113 RBIs, 99 walks, .603 slugging, and was named MVP. The next, he was putting up similar numbers when in midseason he decided to "retire," though he returned to play two more seasons in Philadelphia and Oakland.

Like Jackson, Allen wore glasses, was a toxic presence in the clubhouse, and made tons of money—a baseball record $250,000 in '73. He hit 351 homers and drove in 1,119 runs. In seven more seasons, Jackson had 563 and 1,702. On a per-season basis, that works out to 25 and 80 for Allen, 27 and 81 for Jackson. Both had the same number of All-Star homers (1) and MVP awards (1). Allen's home run percentage is 5.5, Jackson's 5.7. Allen batted .292, Jackson .262. While Jackson played for great teams that he made better, and was a first-ballot Hall of Famer, Allen played for losers, was a loner, had the charm of a rottweiler, and needs a ticket to get into the Hall. There's a lesson in this somewhere.

Jackson's absence from the '72 World Series must have hurt Jackson a lot worse than his hamstring. In that gut-churning seven-game Series against the Big Red Machine of Bench, Rose, and Perez, pitching ruled—each team hit .209 with just 8 homers between them. Still, the A's had the home run voodoo. In Game 1 at Riverfront Stadium, Gene Tenace—a second-string catcher who had hit 5 homers all year—started. He came up in the second inning against Gary Nolan and spanked a homer for a 2-0 lead. Then he came up in the fifth and did the same thing to make it 3-1—the first time anyone had gone yard in their first two Series at-bats. The A's won 3-2.

In Game 2, lanky outfielder Joe Rudi cracked 1 off Ross Grimsley to put the A's up and saved the 2-1 win with a backhanded catch against the left field wall. Tenace then hit another dinger, at home, in the A's 3-2 Game 4 squeaker, putting them up 3 games to 1—and *another* in Game 5, a 2-run shot in the second inning for a 3-1 lead. But in a wondrous game, Rose—who had hit the first pitch of the game from Catfish Hunter for a rare homer—won it, 5-4, with a single in the ninth.

At this point, each of the first five games was a 1-run acid reflux. The Reds staved off another match point, winning 8-1 at home behind a Bench homer. But in Game 7, another Maalox moment, Tenace cemented his Series MVP status with 2 hits and 2 RBIs in a 3-2 win.

The A's would be back at the summit the next two years, with Jackson. And while Rudi would outhit him both times, Jackson made nearly everyone else next to him invisible. That, of course, was what he did to other home run hitters. Which is why, by the mid-1970s, the home run wasn't only back, but dripping with flamboyance, narcissism, and psychodrama.

High-Risk Bonds

Quick. Besides Jackson and Allen, name one other AL home run champion from 1971 through 1976, and besides Jackson and Jim Rice, any other one until 1987. Bet you can't.

There were others, for sure, though the numbers—even those of Jackson and Allen during the former period—didn't knock anyone out. In '71, as homers leaguewide fell by nearly 300 to 1,484, the leader was White Sox third baseman Bill Melton, who hit 33 for the second straight year. In '72, Allen had 37, beating the Yankees' post-Mantle center fielder Bobby Murcer by 4.

The other league, by contrast, was a long ball playpen, particularly for one veteran slugger—Willie Stargell—and one young turk who had quickly disposed of the nostrum that a catcher could not withstand the physical rigors of the job and be able to pound homers consistently. More remarkably, Johnny Lee Bench pounded homers despite giving so much of himself behind the plate that it's a wonder he didn't leave a kidney back there. That the Reds had something special was made clear in '66 when he was 18 and hit 22 homers for Peninsula in the Carolina League. The home fans loved the burly, part–Native American kid from Oklahoma so much that the team retired his number when he was called up in '68.

That year Bench set rookie records for games (154) and doubles (40) and hit 15 homers with 82 RBIs and a .275 average—Rookie of the Year numbers. After a 26-homer, 90-RBI year in '70, he had a season like no other catcher has ever had—45 homers and 148 RBIs (both records for the position still) with a .293 average. MVP numbers. Arising from the rubble of the Frank Robinson trade, the Reds rode Bench, hard. The club now had a murderer's row on their hands, boosting its home run total from 106 in '68 to a league-high 171 and 191 the next two seasons. In '70, first baseman Tony Perez ripped 40, outfielder Lee May 34. In '71, those two had 25 and 39. Pete Rose and Joe Morgan set the table, and solid pitching staff and bullpen choked the opposition. But mostly, there was Bench.

In '72, he had 7 homers in five games and three 3-homer games, notching 40 for the year with 125 RBIs and leading the Reds to the NL West flag. In the climactic fifth game of the playoffs, the Pirates took a 3-2 lead into the ninth inning. Bench led off against Dave Giusti and, *whomp*, the game was tied in an instant. Three batters later, a wild pitch put the Reds into the World Series, only to suffer heartbreak against Gene Tenace and Joe Rudi.

Stargell, meanwhile, had morphed from a freak-show attraction to steady home run terror. The heavily muscled Stargell broke in with the Pirates in '63 as a lumbering, one dimensional outfielder. Twirling his bat in a circular motion like an airplane propeller while awaiting the pitch, Stargell's swooshing left-handed cut sent tape-measure drives flying—including no less than 7 balls over the right field roof at Forbes Field and a 512-footer out of Dodger Stadium in '69. From '64 to '70, he pumped at least 20 homers and had two 100-RBI and .300 seasons.

An affable Okie, Stargell was hugely respected and probably the most well-liked man in the game. But not until '71 did he crash the home run elite. That year, he clocked 11 in April, then a record, and in May homered in the first game played at Three Rivers Stadium—where over the years he would bombard 4 monster shots into the distant upper deck. On August 1 he had 3 doubles and 2 homers, with 6 RBIs, tying the then-record for extra-base hits in a game. For the season, he led baseball with 48 and had 125 RBIs and a .295 average. (The MVP, though, went to the Cards' Joe Torre, who hit .363 with 24 homers and 137 RBIs.)

The next year, Clemente was martyred and at age 30, "Pops" Stargell was the Man in Pittsburgh, on a nearly all-black team playing at the foot of The Hill, where Stargell himself owned a popular chicken shack. In a victory for the good guys, Pops would get all the props a man could get before the decade was out.

The NL homer tide also buoyed another courtly slugger, the magnificent Billy Williams, whose smooth left-handed swing seemed to be coated with apple butter but had generally been lost in Ernie Banks' shadow since '64. In his first decade with the Cubs, Williams never hit less than 22 homers, 84 RBIs, or a .278 average. Twice he had over 30 homers, and in '68 he tied a record with 5 over two games. From '63 to '69, he played every game of every season and broke Stan Musial's NL consecutive-game streak of 896 and extended it to 1,117 (broken by Steve Garvey in '83). But in '70, Williams just detonated, ringing up 42 dingers, 129 RBIs, and a .322 average, with league highs in hits (205) and runs (137). In '72, he was still sizzling, winning the batting title at .333 with 39 homers and 122 RBIs.

Alas, like Banks—who became the eighth tenant of the 500-home run club when he strafed the Braves' Pat Jarvis on May 12, 1970—Williams was tortured by never getting to play in a World Series, though he was on a division winner in '75 after being traded to the A's. Two nicer men never played the game, and only two other pairs of teammates—Aaron and Mathews, Ruth and Gehrig—hit more homers than the 904 of Banks and Williams. But baseball isn't about being nice.

The AL had a lot be jealous about. The Nationals not only had power, they had speed. More impressively, they had people with both power and speed. In truth, the NL, through its early infusion of the best black and Latin talent, had brought this very dimension to the game. When Willie Mays cleared 30 homers and 30 steals in '56 and '57, it was the first time anyone had done that twice. (The only time it had been done at all was by St. Louis' Kenny Williams—remember him?—in '22.) In '57, in fact, Mays further broke the mold with more than 20 doubles, triples, homers, and steals. Hank Aaron then went 30/30 in '63, with 44 homers and 31 steals. And while the AL snuck in a 30/30 man, Milwaukee's Tommy Harper (31/38) in '70, the power-speed concession had been taken over by one of the most influential players ever, albeit one known today mainly for his procreational skills.

Of course I speak of Bobby Bonds, who at 6 feet 1 inch and 190 pounds possessed taut, rubber-band limbs and a habit of swinging at everything under the sun, and hard. Bonds came to the Giants on a thunderclap. In his first game, on June 25, 1968, against the Dodgers at Candlestick Park, he came up in the seventh inning for his third at-bat. Facing pitcher John Purdin with the bases drunk, he cranked a homer—

the first time anyone hit a grand slam in his debut since one William Duggleby of the Philadelphia Nationals in 1898. Bonds became a regular in '69 and spread out with 32 homers, 90 RBIs, 45 steals, a league-high 120 runs—and, need I add, a record 185 strikeouts, and just a .259 average.

This was New-Age baseball at its best, and worst. Because of his speed, Bonds was used in the leadoff spot and was a tremendous run producer, scoring more than 100 times five straight years. No leadoff hitter ever had his power, though through longevity Rickey Henderson would break Bonds' mark of 35 career leadoff dingers. But, good Lord, those strikeouts—*10* times over 120 in 14 seasons, including seven straight—were an obscenity. Bonds never walked more than 95 times (a level reached by his son halfway through the 2002 season) and his career on-base percentage was an abysmal .353.

In '70, he had 26 homers, 48 steals, and wrote those eyesore 189 strikeouts into the record book; in '71, he went 26-44-157; in '72, 39-43-137. And if you think the man should have had some shame about all those whiffs, consider Bonds' riposte to being criticized for not running out easy grounders. "If you get 200 hits a season," he said, "you're going to hit .333 and you'll still have 400 outs. I don't see why you have to run down to first base every time to make an out." This might explain why his son behaves as he does; lack of shame, like male-pattern baldness, can run in the family.

Bonds was reviled by many purists, but the game's strategic tethers loosened because of him. In the NL, the power-speed quotient was priority one, unearthing muscular, fleet players like Houston's Cesar Cedeno and San Diego's Dave Winfield. The AL could see the trend coming and recognized they were way behind the curve, having finished the '72 season 150 homers, 100 steals, and 9 batting points behind the NL. Not by coincidence, AL attendance was 4 million behind, 15.4 to 11.5 million. The solution wasn't to improve scouting or to run more. That would take work. Instead, the league elders opted for a cheap gimmick—keeping pitchers out of the batter's box.

Hello DH, Good-bye Willie

The designated hitter (DH) never would have happened had not traditionalist owners been replaced by new, more crudely mercantile ones needing a quick return of their overpriced investments—one of whom, an impatient shipbuilder named Steinbrenner—had annexed the Yankees that very year and shot off the immortal words, "I won't be active in the day-to-day operations of the club at all." Logically, putting another bat into the lineup seemed to ensure fat batting numbers. And, of course, it worked. Averages rose by 20 points to .259, runs by nearly 200 to 4.2 a game, homers by nearly 400 to 1,552, steals by 150 to 1,058—all higher than the NL. ERAs went up from 3.57 to 3.82. Attendance rose to 13 million.

But what *really* happened? Check the leader boards. Rod Carew hit .350 but nobody else broke .306. And the home run leader, Jackson, had all of 32, the lowest since Larry Doby's 32 in '54. And Jackson's league-high run total, 99, was 3 *less* than Bobby Murcer's total the year before. The entire difference in hitting, then, wasn't any synergistic effect of the DH but the work of the DH's themselves, most of whom were veterans like Boston's Orlando Cepeda (20 homers), Oakland's Deron Johnson (19), Minnesota's Tony Olive (16), Detroit's Gates Brown (12), and untried hopefuls like the best Jewish DH ever, the Yankees' Ron Blomberg (.329, 12).

The NL, meanwhile, didn't need gimmicks. In '73, Davey Johnson was traded from the Orioles—with whom his home run high had been 18—to the Braves, who had the only ballpark in baseball with its own Indian chief in a wigwam and an elevation one thousand feet above sea level. It was the latter, for aerodynamic reasons discussed already, that turned the typically spacious dimensions of Atlanta Fulton County Stadium into a gallery that was aptly dubbed "The Launching Pad." Since the Braves began playing there in 1966, they led the league in home runs twice, were second once, third once. Teams loved to play the Braves. On August 1, 1972, the Padres' Nate Colbert tied the major league record with 5 homers in a doubleheader—including a 3-run shot in the first game and a grand slam and two 2-run blows in the second—setting a league record in the process with 13 RBIs in the twinbill. In '73, the Braves again led baseball with 206 dingers—45 more than any other team. Three Braves had 40 or more, Aaron (40), third baseman Darrel Evans (41), and the 170-pound Johnson, whom Aaron convinced to switch from the heavy bat used by most Oriole veterans because of Frank Robinson's influence. Johnson's 43 are among baseball's strangest-ever enigmas—the next year, even at one thousand feet, he had 15 and he was finished as a player three years later.

The '73 season also re-inflated a real home run hitter, Frank Robinson. Two years before, Robinson hit No. 500 on September 13 against Detroit but even though he hit .281 with 28 homers and 99 RBIs, it was déjà vu all over again when the Orioles judged him to be an "old 36" and traded him to the Dodgers, where he hit just .251 with 19 homers in '72. Traded again after the season to the Angels, Robinson now rebounded, cranking 30 homers, 97 RBIs, and a .266 average. That season, too, Robinson bagged a homer at Arlington Stadium on September 19, bringing the number of parks he'd homered in to 32, then a record.

By then, Robinson was openly campaigning to become the first black manager and, by pre-arrangement, he was released on waivers in September of '74 so he could be signed by the Indians and named player-manager for '75. Robinson managed as he played, taking no bull. His ace pitcher in Cleveland, the hoary spitballer Gaylord Perry, derided Robinson's managerial qualities. On Opening Day, Robinson made Perry a winner with a homer to beat the Yankees. Days later, Gaylord, and his brother Jim, another pitcher of the staff, were traded. Eventually Robinson retired as a player in September 1976 and finished with 586 homers, then fourth all-time (now fifth), and 1,812 RBIs. He also managed with the Giants and Orioles before becoming a big-league executive (in charge of *discipline*). Last year, when baseball took over the Expos, he was named their manager until Bud Selig could figure out how to kill off the team.

The '73 campaign almost provided a warm and fuzzy denouement for Willie Mays, and for a while it gave Bobby Bonds a chance to be a team leader. With Mays gone from the Giants, Bonds, who was also a Gold Glove outfielder, contended for the MVP. He set a record with 11 leadoff homers (still the NL record, as are his 30 career leadoff taters, behind Rickey Henderson's big league mark of 79), and 39 for the year with 115 RBIs, 43 steals, and 131 runs. But for any of the 5 homers he had that were washed out by rain, he would have become the first 40-40 man. Finally, though, Bonds' high-risk game caught up to him. He slumped late in the season and his endless strikeouts—148 this time—left him with a .264 average. When he dropped off to 21 homers and 71 RBIs in '74, he was traded to the Yankees the next year for Bobby Murcer (who in '70 had hit 4 homers in consecutive at-bats over a doubleheader). Thus began a seven-year rent-a-Bonds tour in which he played for seven teams. In this game of Bonds roulette, he went 30-30 twice before the end of the line in '82—four years before the arrival of the son who made him forgettable.

The only other man besides Bonds to have hit 300 homers and steal 300 bases—Mays—was long past his 30-30 days in '73, when he had a last chance to go out a champion. Playing in sixty-six games with the Mets, he went yard 6 final times, the last on August 12 when he etched

No. 660 into the record book off the Reds' Don Gullett. At the time, the Mets were mired twelve games behind but made their push to win the division on the last day with a mediocre 82-79 record.

This was likely the worst team ever to win anything. They had 85 homers, *27* steals, and not one .300 hitter. But their pitching—and 3 homers by creaky outfielder Rusty Staub—humbled the Reds in a five-game playoff, overcoming Pete Rose's twelfth-inning homer that won Game 4. That deposited them in the World Series against the A's, the first two games of which were slapstick baseball, with Mays part of it. Given a start in the opener in Oakland by manager Yogi Berra, the world's most perfect outfielder fell down on one fly ball and misplayed another that scored the A's winning run in the 2-1 game. But this is Willie Mays, so with Game 2 tied 6-6 in the twelfth, he bounced a ground ball through the infield to score the lead run, before three more scored on two errors by second baseman Mike Andrews; the Mets won 10-7.

Andrews, of course, was fired on the spot by Charlie Finley, who was overruled by the equally bumptious commissioner, Bowie Kuhn. And Mays sat out as the Mets won two of three at Shea Stadium—with Staub pounding a first-inning 3-run homer in a 5-RBI Game 4—to take a 3 games to 2 lead back to Oakland. But now it became Jackson's Series. In Game 6 against Tom Seaver, he doubled twice for 2 runs and added a single in a 3-1 win to bring about a climactic Game 7. Up to now, the A's had not hit a single home run to the Mets' 4. They got on track in the third inning when scrawny shortstop Bert Campaneris—who had hit all of 4 dingers that year in *601* at-bats—popped a 2-run shot off Jon Matlack. Two batters later, Jackson came up with a man on first and crushed one over the right field fence for a 4-0 lead—ending his trip around the bases with a two-footed landing on the plate. With the 5-2 win, Jackson won the Series MVP. Of course.

And so Willie Howard Mays, the best ballplayer in history, went into the good night, 660 home runs in his quiver, a big-league record 63 games with at least 2 home runs, and an NL-record 6 straight games with a homer. Until the '90s, Mays would be the only NL player with multiple 50-homer seasons. Even now, Mays stands third in total bases (6,066) and runs (2,062), fourth in extra-base hits (1,323), ninth in RBIs (1,903), eleventh in hits (3,283). His legacy can be seen all over the game though with diminishing returns: what he did so naturally with his bat and legs, people strain to do by swinging only for home runs, and when they don't, running hard only when the spirit moves them.

If only he could have stayed forever as a counterbalance. But now he was gone, leaving only one '50s-bred home run hero, who was about to get really, really funky.

715

Late in 1973, baseball looked up and saw an amazing thing: Henry Aaron, who had run silent and deep in the game's veins for twenty years, was pushing Babe Ruth's consecrated lifetime record of 714 home runs. And, in typical baseball fashion, it didn't know quite how to deal with it.

For many casual fans, Aaron was really an interloper. Not that he wasn't given his props. When Aaron hit his second, and final, All-Star homer in '72—in his own park, Fulton County Stadium, a sixth-inning, 2-run blast off Gaylord Perry—he was given a long ovation and removed from the field at the start of the next inning to jog off to a curtain-call ovation. Still, while Aaron was well rewarded—his $240,000-a-year contract in '72 was the most lucrative ever—he had won the MVP only once, had never hit more than 47 homers in a season (but at least 30 in every one since '57), and as the Braves bounced to Atlanta without much success or local adulation, almost no one noticed his home runs.

Aaron's remarkable physical condition and Type-B personality cheated the calendar, but so did The Launching Pad. When Aaron played in Milwaukee, he had hit 213 of his 398 homers on the road. In Atlanta, 190 of 335 were at home—including 31 of 47 in '71. The next year, he broke Stan Musial's record for total bases, tied Gil Hodges' NL record with his 14th grand slam, and on August 6 slammed Nos. 660 and 661—the most ever hit for one franchise. Eleven months later, on July 2, 1973, he belted a 2-run screamer off the Phillies' Ken Brett—No. 700, though with a fraction of the fanfare when Barry Bonds hit No. 600. That gave him 27 homers for the year, and 14 shy of Ruth with nearly three months to notch 14 and tie Ruth, hardly a bridge too far, and suddenly, a news story.

As Aaron wrote in his 1992 autobiography, *I Had a Hammer*, "It was as if I had been running a marathon along lonely back roads all these years and then I burst into the crowded stadium." At least Aaron would not have to suffer the buffoonery Maris had and be held to account for *his* advantages over Ruth, namely, that time had brought him to bat nearly 12,300 times by mid-1974, compared with Ruth's total of 8,397. Still, Aaron felt no comfort from the game's top echelon, or its backbone of writers who had already begun to quibble that his homers were a different flavor than Ruth's because of his longevity—an argument Aaron felt he had to rebut by pointing out that Ruth hadn't competed against the best black players. If carried to modern times, he noted with brutal salience, the leading home run hitter of the '60s in the NL would have been *Ron Santo.* (Not so salient was his assertion that Harmon Killebrew played in the "nearly all white American League," which was a too-simple, and gross, distortion.)

Aaron was particularly offended by Bowie Kuhn, who had lifted Maris's "asterisk" but failed to congratulate Aaron after his 3,000th hit in 1972 and his 700th homer. About Ruth's 714 going down, Kuhn was silent.

"I believed he would have shown more interest in the record if a white player had been involved," Aaron wrote in *Hammer*.

For Aaron, who had rarely become involved in racial polemics before, such Frank Robinson–style screeds were caused by the polarization that spilled off his assault on Ruth. Maris, too, had felt the wrath of cutting the Babe down to size, but the race element—which again stripped off baseball's collegial, perfect-world façade—turned Aaron into a literal target. He began receiving virulent hate mail by the thousands, nearly a million pieces over '73 and '74, from America's open and closeted bigots (who of course were unaware of the irony that Ruth was taunted with the word "nigger" with which they branded Aaron). This prompted the Braves to hire a bodyguard for him and on occasion to roll the team bus right up to the dugout rather than have him move through crowds on the street. Aaron's daughter began getting death threats while in college, and a kidnap plot brought the FBI on campus. Even his parents were harassed.

When word of Aaron's nightmare broke, great numbers of Caucasians supported him—including Claire Ruth, who said the Babe "would have been pulling for Hank Aaron to break the record." Still, because some writers made threats at specific ballparks and dates, Aaron played in genuine fear, "always on the lookout," as he recalled. "To this day, I'm still that way." The good thing about playing in Atlanta was that if someone did take a shot at him, the guy would never get lost in a crowd, because there rarely was one there. But the small houses at Fulton County Stadium offended him, too, construing it that his home town fans didn't care about his home run pursuit. Worse, much racial invective came from the grandstand there. "The only thing that mattered [to Atlanta]," Aaron wrote of the record, "was that a nigger was about to step out of line and break it."

Like a sphinx, Aaron's placid demeanor never changed, but inside he was churning. And if the bigots thought that abuse might inhibit him, it had the opposite effect. To Aaron, the record was racially metaphoric in its own way; it meant that a black man, given the means to power, could achieve it. "When you grow up in the South," he wrote, "I don't think you can imagine the surge of freedom and power I felt just knowing that I controlled my own destiny."

In the penultimate game of '73, Aaron homered off Houston's Jerry Reuss and was sitting on 713, with 40 for the year. On the final day, 40,000 fans did bother to attend Fulton County Stadium when Aaron swung for the record. But while he had two singles, which put his season's average over .300, in his last shot, against Don Wilson, he popped out to second. He would have six months to think about No. 714. And so would the world, which only now seemed to realize what Aaron was about to do. In spring training 1974, a pack of three hundred media people began trailing Aaron. Bill Bartholomay, the Braves' owner, was thinking, too, about maximizing profits from Aaron. The Braves would begin the season with three road games in Cincinnati before their home opener, and Batholomay wanted to hold Aaron out of all three games—until Kuhn, posing as Solomon, decreed he had to play in two of the three games.

And so on Opening Day, April 8, 1974, a cold and raw Thursday in Cincinnati, Henry Aaron finally walked into the spotlight, his image dwarfing the mounting Watergate scandal as national news. He came to bat in the first inning at Riverfront Stadium against sinkerball pitcher Jack Billingham, two on, one out. The count went 3-and-1. Billingham threw a sinker and Aaron took his first swing of the season and hit a Hank Aaron drive, which is to say a non-Ruthian drive that took off hard, climbed in a low arc that peaked above left field, and fell a few safe feet beyond the fence. If Maris had tied a Ruth record seemingly without asking permission, Aaron broke another ever so politely. His trip around the bases was prim and proper as 54,000 kempt people sedately applauded. Aaron, toeing home plate, was first congratulated by Johnny Bench, then swept up by his teammates. He then went into the stands to hug his wife and father. Also in the box were Vice President Gerald Ford and Bowie Kuhn, whom Aaron had grown to loathe.

In fact, the maw of personal grudges and real and imagined slights did not end with this home run—though some writers tried hard to use it as a salve for baseball's petty squabbling. Red Smith, for one, used that angle in his *New York Times* column the next day, writing that "it isn't particularly important that this courteous, modest man has at last overtaken Babe Ruth's roistering ghost. What really counts is that when Henry laid the wood on Jack Billingham's fast ball, he struck a blow for the integrity of the game and for public faith in the game. With one stroke . . . he rendered moot two months of wrangling between the money-changers and the Protectors of the Faith."

While that take sounded uplifting, the home run had barely landed when Aaron was again dissed. Brought to a microphone, he startled many in the park and around the country by asking for a moment of silence for Dr. Martin Luther King, who was killed a good six years before. He was then forced to defend himself for doing it when sportswriters pushed him to explain why after the eleven-inning, 7-6 Reds win in which he went hitless the rest of the way.

(Here's one for the trivia geeks: Aaron's 714th was the first home run hit with a cowhide ball, which by Kuhn's discreet order replaced the venerable horsehide ball starting that season.)

There was more discord when Eddie Mathews, who was now managing the Braves, thought No. 714 was enough of a concession to Kuhn and said he would sit Aaron the next two games. He relented only when Kuhn threatened him with a suspension. Aaron played the Sunday game, and when he went hitless, striking out twice, some of the geniuses in the press box actually accused him of whiffing on purpose. (Question: would anyone ever say such a thing about a white man in Aaron's position?) Rather than feeling kingly, then, when Aaron got back to Atlanta he was chafing, and more so when Kuhn opted to skip being in the stands for the Monday night game to open a series with the Dodgers, sending—with magnificent condescension—Monte Irvin in his stead, hoping to mollify Aaron. It was, Aaron said, as if Kuhn "didn't want to dignify the record or . . . be part of the surpassing of Babe Ruth."

Thus is the real curse of the Bambino, that no one could crack his home run records without some kind of misery and hurt feelings induced by baseball, its commissioners, its scribes, or its fans. But Aaron made all that go away for another moment on that Monday night at Fulton County Stadium, which began with a very belated Hank Aaron Night ceremony and climaxed with an unforgettable swing.

Maybe no other single baseball act has been revisited more than the one captured on the grainy tapes of Aaron's fourth-inning cut against the classic schlemiel, southpaw Al Downing—fittingly, an ex-Yankee. A onetime hard-thrower, Downing was more of a nibbler now, and after being walked in the second inning Aaron crowded the plate with no fear when he batted with 2 outs and Darrell Evens on first. Downing's first pitch was a changeup in the dirt. He then tried a slider, but it came in exactly where he didn't want it—a smidge low and over the plate.

To 55,755 people in the stands—a record for the park—and millions nationwide on TV, it was a cue to start tingling. To Aaron, and his steel-cable wrists, it was candy. His deceptively casual swing caught the infra-red-stamped ball (used expressly for Aaron since late in the '73 season to scotch counterfeit claims to homers 714 and 715) on its sweet meat and lifted another low-riser to left. Downing, instinctively knowing he too was about to enter history, yanked his head up and his knees buckled as the cowhide rose, yet it was slow enough that shortstop Bill Russell had to reflexively spring upward for a catch. Indeed, Aaron, just like Bobby Thomson and Bill Mazeroski, was unsure he'd gotten all of it. But Atlanta's elevation and a warm, humid evening provided a carpet ride.

Left fielder Bill Buckner drifted back, scaled the Plexiglas fence near the 385 mark, perched atop the wall, and tried to snare it, but the charmed ball fell five feet beyond him, into the mitt of relief pitcher (and future author) Tom House as the scoreboard clock read 9:07.

Upstairs, in the Braves' radio booth, announcer Milo Hamilton's time came, too. Hamilton had agonized over how to make the historic call, and decided on, "There's a new home run champion of all time, and his name is Henry Aaron!" But in the flush of the act, Hamilton nearly forgot his script and wound up saying "It's gone! It's 715! There's a new home run champion of all time and it's Henry Aaron!"

On the field, House sprinted in from the bullpen with his precious cargo as Aaron deliberately circled the bases. At first base, Steve Garvey shook his hand, and second baseman Dave Lopes was about to do the same when two young fans who had jumped from the stands came at him. Aaron, who no doubt lived in fear of such a scenario, hardly flinched, and as the fans pounded him on the back he nudged them aside and completed this never-before accomplished journey, completing the ritual by wading into a wall of bodies at home plate. A beaming Aaron weeded through them, found his mother and hugged her, then again stepped to a microphone.

"I just thank God," he said wearily, as if the air had been squeezed from his body, "it's finally over."

As Aaron spoke, rain began falling. I wouldn't dare say it was Babe Ruth's tears, but it was a little eerie, and it set up the chance that the game—and home run—could be wiped away. So play quickly resumed, Aaron went hitless in two more at-bats and the 7-4 Braves win was in the bank. Of his feelings afterward, Aaron wrote in his memoirs, "I didn't feel a wild sense of joy and I didn't feel like celebrating." But as a black man who had faced down fire and brimstone, liberation had come, and with it, "I felt a stream of tears running down my face."

No. 715 was a rather ambivalent creature itself. The homer had one more day of shelf life as news. In fact, in Atlanta, it was over as soon as it was hit. The next inning, around 30,000 people had left the ballpark. Just as suddenly as Aaron had ascended the national stage, he returned to the baseball underbelly, albeit with rapidly eroding skills and no less angry at the world and in particular at the Braves. Halfway through the '74 season, the club fired Mathews and Aaron expected at least a courtesy offer to become manager—which would have made him the first black manager, not Frank Robinson. He didn't get it, and when the team's GM, Eddie Robinson, was asked if Atlanta was ready for a black manager, and dodged the question, it infuriated Aaron, who wanted no more to do with the team or the town.

The quiet man no longer, Aaron went ballistic when the *Atlanta Journal*'s Frank Hyland wrote that Aaron's second wife, Billye, had put militant thoughts in his head. Seeing Hyland in the locker room, Aaron shoved a plate of strawberries in the writer's face. (Hyland respectfully let the incident pass without complaint.)

On October 2, in his last at-bat of the season, Aaron hit No. 733 against the Reds and ran out the year with 20 homers, 69 RBIs, and a .268 average. There were no more Hank Aaron Nights, no more thank-yous, and on November 2 a long-planned deal to send Aaron back to Milwaukee was finalized. For outfielder Dave May and a bush-league pitcher, the Brewers got as a new designated hitter a 41-year-old home run champion of all time. And his name was Henry Aaron.

On May 1, 1975, he also became the RBI champion of all time, breaking Ruth's mark of 2,209. (Or so it was thought at the time. In 1976, Ruth's number was revised to 2,204, meaning that Aaron actually broke it on April 18.) Even a doddering Aaron could go yard. He had 12 homers in 137 games, and the next year banged out dingers in 3 consecutive June games, and a tenth-inning, game-winning shot against Texas on July 11. But 1976 was his farewell tour, and the unending home run argosy at last ended on July 20 when he belted his 10th of the year—No. 755—off California's Dick Drago. In his last big-league at-bat, on October 3, Aaron singled in his 2,297th run.

Then he was gone, with nary a peep, taking with him other records, for total bases (6,856) and extra-base hits (1,477). He is also second in runs and at-bats and third in games and hits. But Aaron also took with him something much more fundamental to baseball art and science: the lost concept of home runs as an incidental reward for hitting smart.

And while Aaron did make his peace with the Braves, for whom he has been a club vice president for the last two decades, whenever I see him I sense the man could be happier. It's the same thing I sensed with Williams, Mantle, and Mays, and if I were older, probably would sense with Ruth and Foxx. It's like I told you. This home run thing, like a Faustian bargain, can claim your soul.

14

Straws That Stirred the Drink

Fisk and Fate

You're wondering: Did the cowhide ball affect the home run? The answer—you bet. In the NL, dingers dropped from 1,550 in '73 to 1,280 in '74; in the AL, from 1,552 to 1,369. Interestingly, batting averages held about the same, in the mid-.250s, as did runs. More interestingly, while the AL would make its way back up to the 2,000-homer level by '77, and up its average into the mid-.260s, the NL became stuck in a holding pattern in homers and overall offense that lasted into the 1990s.

For baseball, the big development centered on speed. In '74, stolen bases leaped over the 1,200 level in each league, and would top the 1,500 level by the late '70s, 1,800 in the NL in the mid-'80s. Rickey Henderson would steal 130 bases in '82, Vince Coleman 110 in '85. Another 30/30 man arose in '83 when Atlanta's massive, free-swinging outfielder Dale Murphy notched 36 homers and 30 steals, presaging a crowd of 30/30s leading to the entrance of the first *40/40* man in '88, Jose Canseco—who even more than Bobby Bonds would represent all that went wrong with the home run and with baseball.

Until then, the homer remained untainted and habitually unleashed with almighty fury at the height of the drama. In '75, one of those became embedded in the Red Sox legacy of eternal hope and eternal damnation. That year, the Sox struck the mother lode with two cocksure rookies, center fielder Fred Lynn and left fielder Jim Rice. The comely Lynn hit .331 with 21 homers and 105 RBIs and won both the Rookie of the Year and MVP awards. Rice, brooding all the way, went .309, 22, and 102. Their numbers more than compensated for the aging Carl Yastrzemski (14 homers) and season-long injuries to catcher Carlton Fisk, gaining the team its once-a-decade World Series berth (though without Rice whose arm injury shelved him). Few, though, gave the Sox much of a shot against the Reds, who won 109 games during the season.

While I don't necessarily agree with the conventional verdict that the '75 Series was the best of all time (I'm not sure it beats '26, '30, '34, '40, '46, '47, '55, '56, '60, '62, '67, '68, or '72), it surely was melodramatic comfort food. Game 3 alone featured a Series-record 6 homers, 1 a pinch-hit shot by that Barrymore of batsmen, Bernie Carbo, and a 2-run blow in the top of the ninth by Dwight Evans to tie it at 5-5—before the winner came home in the tenth after an interference call wasn't made on a bunt that a jostled Fisk threw into center field. Two dingers by the ageless Tony Perez put away Game 5 to give the Reds a 3 games to 2 edge.

Then, of course, came the "Ride of the Valkyries" that was Game 6, a contest that began on October 21 at Fenway Park and would not end until October 22 because the Reds—who surged ahead after an early 3-run tater by Lynn—couldn't hold a 6-3 lead in the eighth. With 2 out and 2 on, Carbo, an ex-Red, pinch hit again. He also made the earth move again, whacking a pitch by reliever Rawly Eastwick over the center field wall to tie it. Each team then got a chance to win—the Sox in the ninth—but George Foster threw out Denny Doyle at the plate. In the tenth, Joe Morgan scorched a line drive to right, seemingly over Dwight Evans' head. Evans stumbled back, spun, leaped, and somehow gloved it, reaching blindly over the wall.

Finally, in the bottom of the twelfth, half an hour into the new day, came the biggest melodramatic nacho, served up by the patrician, granite-carved figure of Carlton Fisk. A highly educated 6-foot-2, 200-pound New Englander, Fisk had been around since '69, racking up solid numbers when he wasn't hurt, and had hit more than 20 homers twice. He was also his team's metaphoric point man in the revival of Red Sox–Yankee rivalry, based on his personal rivalry with his foil and polar opposite, the stumpy and irascible Yankee catcher Thurman Munson. Because people were always suspicious that Fisk was perhaps not tough enough, Fisk pointedly crowded the plate when he batted, braving knockdown pitches, and his quick bat allowed him to get around on inside pitches, such as when he nailed Gary Nolan for a home run in Game 3 of the Series.

Now, facing reliever Pat Darcy, the *eighth* Red pitcher in the marathon game, he took a ball. Darcy then let go a slider, down, in. Fisk was right on it, a little early in fact, cracking it on a hard line bearing down on the left field foul pole just 315 feet away. The next few seconds, when Fisk tiptoed out of the batter's box and began frantically waving his arms and shouting at the ball to stay fair, are baseball's most ingrained pantomime next to Ruth's Called Shot, preserved by endless TV replays that commenced as soon as the ball clanged off the pole for the win. Fisk flounced up and down clapping his hands on his trip around the bases, before touching down on home plate amid the obligatory mob.

As with Aaron's record home runs, the media again saw cosmic deliverance for the game in the wake of a single swing of a bat—with the kookiest exposition spilling from Boston sportswriter Peter Gammons' typewriter. Fisk's dinger, he wrote, "virtually altered the autumnal equinox" and Game 6 "captured all that baseball could be."

Not to quibble with that take, but the problem for the Red Sox was that even altering the autumnal equinox will never be enough for them to win a World Series. Having depleted their empyrean allowance, they fell in Game 7 on, of all things, a bloop single by Joe Morgan. And Fisk, who stayed around baseball diamonds for twenty-two seasons, setting catcher's records for home runs (351—24 more than Johnny Bench, who had 389 overall) and total bases (3,999), would fall out with the Red Sox in '80 and sign with the White Sox. While Fisk never again sniffed a World Series, I'll cut him some slack, since he was still catching at age 45. When he hit 2 home runs in a game on October 3, 1991, he became the oldest man since Cap Anson did that in 1897. One was a grand slam, to boot, making him the oldest to hit a slam. Eventually he became the all-time White Sox homer leader, with 214 (until passed by Frank Thomas in '96).

Fisk's "Body English" homer set off a yearly ritual of rhapsodic post-season homers. The next in line did no less than resurrect the dormant Yankee dynasty. So don't blame a moneybags owner or a psycho manager for that. Blame a mellow man with a superb sense of timing.

Rowdy Rebirth

In '76, after four years of playing home games at Shea Stadium, the Yankees returned to a renovated Yankee Stadium as a renovated team. The year before, when arbitrator Peter Seitz ruled that veteran pitchers Dave McNally and Andy Messersmith, having played out their contracts, could not be bound to their teams and thus were sports' first free agents,

George Steinbrenner played the good baseball company man and uttered more famous last words. "I'm dead set against free agency," he said. "It can ruin baseball." Within months, of course, he would be feeding his megalomania by shelling out $3.25 million for first star free agent, Catfish Hunter, thereby making baseball safe for dollar-snorting greed, the consequences of which would bring the game to the brink. For that, blame The Boss.

But in '76, the narcotic effect of finding a shortcut to success by renting players was clear as Steinbrenner, a nobody only three years before, preened like the cock of the walk. Of course, Steinbrenner used his money wisely all around, shoring up a bankrupt minor league system and trading for and paying still-effective aging players handsomely, such as Graig Nettles, Mickey Rivers, and Lou Piniella. All these pieces brought a pennant won by 10 1/2 games. Still, the Yankees faced a tenacious Kansas City team in the playoff, and this was a small, early clash of conflicting baseball IDs—mercenary versus lunchpail, big-town rich versus small-town frugal.

The Royals, who finished second to last in homers in the AL, with 65 (the Yankees had 170), thrived on speed, and in third baseman George Brett and DH Hal McRae had the league's top two hitters (.333 and .332). They also had no quit in them. Falling behind in games twice in the Series, they overcame 2 Nettles homers to win Game 4 at Yankee Stadium 7-3. Then in the climactic Game 5, they were down 6-3 in the eighth when Brett, a tremendous clutch hitter, spiked a 3-run homer to right field to square it. God only knows who Steinbrenner might have fired had the Yankees died a hard death and lost this game, but fans will never know because of that mellow man, Chris Chambliss.

For a big guy—6 feet 1 inch, 195 pounds—Chambliss, a left-handed-hitting first baseman, wasn't much of a home run hitter, nailing only 17 that year (he did hit .293 with 96 RBIs) and would never hit more than 18 in six seasons with the Yankees, nor more than 20 in any of 17 big-league seasons. Yet in Game 3 he'd had a 2-run homer and all 3 RBIs in the 3-0 win. Now, in Game 5, he led off the bottom of the ninth against reliever Mark Littell and on the first pitch got the pitch of his dreams—a high, inside, hittable fastball. Chambliss's swing met the ball about neck-high and powered a high drive that began falling to Earth in deep right-center. Right fielder Al Cowens ran back and braced against the wall around 350 feet away, then leaped with his glove outstretched over the top of the wall. But the ball landed three feet out of reach, into a cadre of New York policemen stationed in the gulley between the wall and the bleachers.

And so the Stadium was once more erupted by an epic home run, winning a pennant the way Bobby Thomson's won one. And the ritual begat by Thomson repeated once again, with Chambliss skirting dozens of fans, several of whom knocked him off his feet as he rounded second base—a sign that the ritual had now crossed over into something dark. "When I fell," Chambliss admitted, "I was very scared. I thought people might try to jump on me. Somebody tried to steal my helmet, so I took it off and put it under my arm." Looking much like the running back he had been in college, he lowered his shoulder and bulled through a few more fans. With bodies littering the field and a few cops trying to escort him, Chambliss couldn't find third base—it had been dug up and stolen—and forgot about home plate. Instead, he headed for the dugout, bowling over another crazed fan on the way.

This meant that, technically, it was not yet a home run, though the umpires who had run for cover were not about to press the matter. But minutes later, Chambliss (who hit a staggering .524 in the series with 8 RBIs), surrounded by a phalanx of cops, came back onto the field—which by now looked like bombed-out Beirut—to toe the plate, but found only its outline in the dirt where it had been until it too was pilfered.

Once, Yankee fans sat in suits trying to stay awake during championship games. Now, after causing $100,000 in damages, they made it necessary for cops on horseback to ring the stands at future clinching games, a procedure copied by many other teams. Who knows whether this was human evolution, or devolution.

The Yankees would have to wait a year to go all the way to the top. The Reds brushed them aside in four straight in the World Series, holding them to 1 home run (by weak-hitting shortstop Jim Mason) while banging out 4 of their own, 2 by Johnny Bench in the Game 4 clincher at Yankee Stadium. This underscored that the Yankees needed a big bat, and so Steinbrenner did what came naturally and wrote a check to get the biggest, bringing baseball's most self-obsessed manic-depressive other than himself to the big town. For better and for worse.

Reggie to the Third Power

From the moment free agency became a reality, Reggie Jackson's days in small-town Oakland were on borrowed time. Given an escape hatch from Charlie Finley's nut house, the A's stable of highly talented and meagerly paid stars began to drip away, with Finley in no legal or financial position to get in the way. And as Jackson's contract ticked down toward its end at the conclusion of the '76 season, he gave less and less to the team. During '74, Joe Rudi openly dissed him as "not mentally in the game," and in June of that season Jackson brawled with outfielder Bill North, injuring his shoulder. Still, Reggie being Reggie, he was indispensable. His second-inning home run in Game 1 of the '74 World Series against the Dodgers gave the A's an edge they never gave up in the five-game victory.

In '75, Jackson led the league with 36 homers, but hit .253, and the A's were swept by the Red Sox in the playoff. Jackson entered his option year in '76, with zero chance of re-signing with the team. Finley, knowing he'd walk, began the now-common practice of dumping a lame-duck player to get something for him. In April he traded Jackson to the Orioles for Don Baylor and pitchers Mike Torrez and Paul Mitchell. Of course, he had no intention of staying in Baltimore. He played to showcase himself for all those who would come on bended knee to sign him after the season—and damn near blew it. Held to 134 games by injuries, his numbers were 27 homers, 91 RBIs, and .277. Yet he needn't have worried. Both he and Steinbrenner had become aroused by the thought of Jackson pointing his bat at Ruthville, and quickly agreed on a four-year, $3.5 million deal.

Jackson needed only until his first Yankee spring training to say something stupid. Offended that many believed Thurman Munson was still the guts of the team, Jackson, after knocking back a few scotches-and-soda, famously told *Sport*'s Robert Ward, "It all flows from me. I'm the straw that stirs the drink. Munson thinks he can be the straw that stirs the drink, but he can only stir it bad." Billy Martin, who hadn't wanted Jackson on the team, needed this hubristic sideshow like a sebacious cyst, and in fact the cyst grew malignant rapidly when Jackson, injured early in the '77 season, started haltingly, was kept out of the cleanup spot held by Chambliss, and played as if in a hammock.

On June 18, in a nationally televised game at Fenway Park, when Jim Rice blooped a soft line drive to right field, Jackson made a half-hearted jog and let it drop for a double. After the inning, Martin—an angry and twisted gnat who at 5 feet 9 inches and a bony 165 pounds had spent his entire career kicking the tar out of bigger men—told him he was out of the game, whereupon Jackson mouthed off. Martin, neck veins bulging, bolted across the dugout, got in Jackson's face, and threw a punch that missed. Jackson, clearly more a lover than a fighter, tried to talk his way out of the situation as two Yankee coaches restrained Martin and things cooled off. Steinbrenner, in *his* hubris, reacted as only he could. Rather than backing up his manager, he backed up his investment. At first he wanted to fire Martin on the spot, but backed off and Martin versus Jackson became a simmering Cold War.

Drowning in self-pity, Jackson couldn't help but portray himself as a prisoner in a Gulag, nor to cast the situation in an absurd racial light. "It makes me cry the way they treat me on this team," he said, and rather than fitting in the chain-link from Ruth to Mantle, "I'm just a black man to them who doesn't know how to be subservient."

Credit Martin for forging a détente. On August 10, with the Yankees still floundering, Jackson came alive at the plate and Martin finally put him in the cleanup hole. The team then turned around, winning 40 of the last 53 games—during which Jackson had 13 homers and *49* RBIs—and won the pennant by 2½ games. Jackson, who didn't pulverize Ruthville after all, did finish with 32 dingers, second on the team to Nettles' 37, but had 110 RBIs and hit .286 (strikeouts: 129). But he was of little use against those pests, the Royals, in the playoff, held to a .125 average and 1 RBI. The Royals again had the Yankees on the brink. In the deciding Game 3, they had a 3-1 lead in the eighth, only to see the Yankees score four times over the last two frames to win 5-3 and clinch the series.

This set up a retro-matchup, Yankees versus Dodgers in the World Series. A very different Dodgers, who still had the arms and speed, but a defense that was like a sieve. The tradeoff was that they now could hit the long ball, clubbing 191 in '77, tops in the NL and 7 more than the Yankees. Four Dodgers nailed 30 or more homers, first baseman Steve Garvey (33), right fielder Reggie Smith (32), third baseman Ron Cey, and left fielder Dusty Baker (30 each). The Dodgers had made grinds out of the Phillies in a four-game playoff win, with Baker hitting 2 homers, and in Game 2 of the Series at Yankee Stadium they dished out 4 long balls to win 6-1 and even the set at one game apiece.

Still, Game 3 at Dodger Stadium showed that no matter the decade the Yankees had this team's number. After Baker's 3-run homer tied it at 3-3 in the third, the Yankees nickel and dimed 2 more runs to win 5-3. Then, in Game 4, Jackson's straw stirred up a homer and a double to pace a 4-2 win and stand a game from the championship. The Dodgers stayed alive with a 10-4 laugher in Game 5, but the omen was that Jackson, in his final at-bat of the game, in the eighth inning, went yard on Don Sutton's first pitch.

So now the Yankees could wrap it up at home. And on October 18, with the night air decidedly crisp and yielding, something other-worldly chose Jackson as its tool. The night was still young when Chambliss slammed a 2-run homer off Burt Hooton to tie the game at 2-2 in the second inning. The Dodgers went up 3-2 an inning later. Then, all the forces of nature and man channeled Reggie Jackson's bat. Not waiting a moment too long, Jackson, with Munson on first, cut at Hooton's first pitch and drove a hooking line drive over the right field wall for a 4-3 lead. Since he had walked in his first time up, that meant he officially had hit 2 home runs on the last two pitches thrown to him.

Now to the fifth inning. Mickey Rivers was on first, 5-3 New York, reliever Elias Sosa on the hill. First pitch, *bang*, and another drive over the right field wall.

Now, to the eighth, 7-3, Charlie Hough pitching. That's Charlie Hough, *knuckleball* pitcher, unfriendly to the home run hitter. Jackson led off, and fans who only months earlier couldn't abide him, stood and chanted his first name over and over. The game, even the Series, seemed superfluous in a scene described by Yankee second baseman Willie Randolph as "surreal." As Jackson would tell it, he came up in a state of extreme serenity.

"At that point I couldn't lose," he told *Sports Illustrated*. "All I had to do was show up at the plate. They were going to cheer me even if I struck out. So the last one was strictly dreamland. Nothing was going through my mind. Here it's a World Series game, it's going all over the country on TV, and all I'm thinking is, 'Hey man, wow, that's three.'"

And then, on the *first pitch*, he was dead solid perfect, lifting the ball into the night at very nearly a perpendicular angle, like a popup that instead of coming down, began to flatten out and shoot through the sky—"on a soaring arc . . . up the white speck climbed," wrote Red Smith. It kept climbing, climbing, then began falling, yet still cleared the center field bleachers by a good hundred feet before dropping into the vacant black batting-eye seats about a third of the way up, some 450 feet away. It wasn't the longest home run ever hit, but bathed as it was in World Series brilliantine, it will forever seem as if it was.

In the dreamy surrealness of the moment, Jackson firmly affixed his image, springing around the bases, dipping into the dugout, then reappearing to doff his cap to the screaming fans. At first base, Steve Garvey applauded into his glove. Even in retrospect, it's difficult to comprehend just how amazing an event this was: On 3 pitches, from 3 different pitchers, Jackson had hit 3 home runs in the clinching game of a World Series at Yankee Stadium. Only Babe Ruth had ever hit 3 homers in a Series game, twice, but that now seemed almost tame. No one, not even the Babe, had ever hit 5 homers in a single World Series, as Jackson had—the last 4 in official sequence, all on the first pitch! There's more: Jackson hit .450, he scored 10 runs—a record 4 in Game 6—had 8 RBIs, and set a record for total bases with 25, and the most in one game, 12.

After the 8-4 win was done and Jackson was unanimously named the Series MVP, he was transformed into baseball's Sun King. As reported by *Sports Illustrated*'s Ron Fimrite:

> For more than two hours after the final game he stood before his locker, entertaining and supposedly enlightening wave upon wave of newsmen with his philosophy, his theology and his analyses of the war-torn Yankee season, all the while quaffing champagne and exchanging pleasantries with those of his friends and teammates—they are not necessarily the same—who could get within shouting distance. . . . When Jackson was asked by a newscaster after the reception what his plans were, he replied with uncharacteristic brevity, "I'm going to bed." But he did not. He visited friends at the plush Cartier jewelry store, picked up his Rolls-Royce at the Stadium, bought some newspapers to confirm his own greatness, took a 45-minute bubble bath, watched television with the sound off, had dinner and retired finally at midnight after 40 hours of being more or less on his feet.

While the image of Jackson in a bubble bath is one I don't need, and while I may not like the man much for his odious effect on the evolution of the home run, let's give him his due for having the single greatest home run sequence in history. I'll even go along with the "Mr. October" handle, because in the '78 World Series rematch with the Dodgers he hit 2 more homers and again had 8 RBIs. But, to get back to the Series, the Yankees would need magic from somebody else—a man whose name you will hear in Boston spoken through locked jaws and gritted teeth.

Bucky-Freakin'-Dent

Jackson enjoyed little carryover from his virtuoso performance. In '78 he had fewer home runs (27), RBIs (97), a lower average (.274), and more strikeouts (133) than the year before. He also made Billy Martin more psycho, and soon after, unemployed. That chapter began on July 17 in a game against the Royals when Jackson came up during a budding rally in the bottom of the tenth inning. On the first pitch Martin gave his slugger the *bunt sign*. He did this to seduce the infield to move in, but

Jackson wasn't convinced. Hardly practiced in the art of the bunt, he awkwardly squared, then drew the bat back and took the pitch for a ball. When Martin then took off the bunt, a petulant Jackson tried to lay one down three straight times, the last a foul ball for a strikeout.

Martin didn't rush him in the dugout this time, but he seethed about it. After the game he went to his office and smashed glasses and a clock radio against the wall. He then suspended Jackson for five games but, again, got no support from Steinbrenner. Two days later, Martin had become unstrung, and after a few drinks quit the team, tearfully delivering his classic parting shots at Jackson and Steinbrenner to Murray Chass of the *New York Times*, saying, "one's a born liar and the other's convicted," referring to Steinbrenner's 1974 guilty plea to Federal charges of giving illegal campaign contributions to Richard Nixon's 1972 campaign, for which he was suspended from baseball for two years.

Of course, Martin didn't stay departed for long—he'd be rehired four more times and re-fired each time, a bad running joke that wore very thin after the Yankees stopped winning again. Indeed, with few exceptions, until the mid-1990s the last time the team could concentrate on the game in spite of the "Bronx Zoo" atmosphere created by the Boss's ego-driven meddling was the last two months of that '78 season, under the placid but resolute managing of Bob Lemon. Trailing the Red Sox by 14 games on that July 19 when Martin quit, the Yankees went 52-21 the rest of the way. The Sox, biting the big one, lost 14 of 17 in September, and when the Yankees came to Fenway and swept a 4-game series, they took over first place and went up by 3½ games with two weeks to play.

But now the Sox awoke, winning their last eight games to force a tie for the AL East lead on the season's final day. So now came a one-game playoff between two teams with not a wafer of difference between them. While the Sox had baseball's top slugger, Rice, with 46 homers and 139 RBIs, the Yankees had its top pitcher, Ron Guidry (25-3, 1.74, 248 strikeouts) and relievers Sparky Lyle and Goose Gossage. Each team hit .267. The Sox led in homers 172-125, the Yankees in steals 98-74, and ERA 3.18 to 3.54. If there was one edge, it seemed it might be 39-year-old Carl Yastrzemski, still aching for a ring and still dangerous as a DH, having hit 17 homers during the season.

The win-one-for-Yaz theme got a boost when he drew first blood in the game, going yard against Guidry for a 1-0 lead. A Rice single in the sixth made it 2-0. In the seventh, though, the Yankees put two men on against Mike Torrez. But for the vagaries of Fate, Lemon now would have pinch hit for the next hitter, taffy-hitting shortstop Bucky Dent. But

Lemon was boxed in because he'd already pinch hit for his second baseman Brian Doyle, who himself had replaced an injured Willie Randolph, leaving Lemon with no other infielders. And so up came Dent, seeming for all the world a gimme out.

Standing 5 feet 9 inches and 170 pounds, Dent—christened Russell Earl O'Day before his mother remarried and he was adopted by his new father—came to New York in a 1977 trade. He became a Yankee fan favorite for his spirited play at shortstop and for his swarthy, doe-eyed good looks. His bat, however, was purely incidental. He hit .243 with 5 homers in '78. Certainly Torrez couldn't have been worried, and was no doubt less so when Dent fouled a 1-0 pitch off his own foot, prompting the trainer to come out to check on him. Still, and this is eerie, that interregnum had the same effect as Don Mueller's injury right before Bobby Thomson's fabled at-bat. It altered the natural course of nature.

The day was cold and breezy, yet instead of throwing lightly during the delay, Torrez stood on the mound, losing some focus. "I should have thrown a couple of pitches," he recalled, "just to loosen up." Then came another fateful moment. Dent could be seen examining his bat, which had a small, uh, dent in it. At that point, he realized it wasn't his bat at all. He called time, went back for his own, and returned, making Torrez wait even more. And on the next pitch, Torrez left it out over the plate, chest high. Dent tore at it and in the blink of an eye the ball went up, not particularly far—anyone say Polo Grounds?—and likely an out in any other park. But in Fenway, it was ominous, and it ended its flight just clearing the top of the Green Monster and falling into the screen.

What anyone who was there that day remembers is the funereal, stunned silence as Dent came around the bases and gave the Yankees a 3-2 lead. Torrez in particular, who later admitted, "I was so goddamned shocked," fell apart, giving up another run that inning and a Jackson solo home run the next. But Goose Gossage nearly returned the favor, giving up 2 Sox runs in the eight. Then, in the bottom of the ninth, with a man on, Jerry Remy lined 1 to left that Lou Piniella lost in the setting sun, yet he somehow reached out blindly and gloved it on a hop before it could get by him and roll to the wall and bring home the tying run. Gossage still faced catastrophe, with none other than Yaz up, 2 outs, 2 on, the game hanging. With all of New England praying for merciful deliverance, Gossage went mano a mano. Heat, up and in. Yaz couldn't handle it. Jammed by the pitch, he popped up to Nettles off third. All of New England cried.

Dent wasn't through, either. The Yankees, sparked by Jackson's 2-run homer in Game 1, yet again disposed of the Royals, in a four-game playoff. Then they met the Dodgers in a rematch World Series. The Dodgers were coming off a four-game playoff victory against the Phillies in which they slammed 8 homers, 4 by Garvey. But they weren't prepared for Bucky Dent. Not even Jackson's killer Series didn't match Dent's .417 average and 7 RBIs, propelling the Yankees to a six-game conquest.

And that was it for Dent's walk on the Sun. He returned to Earth and played out a twelve-year career in which he hit exactly 40 home runs in 4,512 at-bats. Up in Beantown, though, by the agonies of fate, they will forever pay perverse tribute to Russell Earl O'Day by what they call him through those clenched teeth:

Bucky-Freakin'-Dent.

Top of the Pops

The aberration of Bucky Dent blew out the *Yankees'* store of karma. After a stumbling start in '79, Lemon was fired, Martin re-hired, and with a fourth-place finish, re-fired. That season, psychodrama wasn't in. Instead, the big theme in baseball was touchy-feely sentimentality for values clearly on the wane. And the main actor in the season's mawkish three-act play was Willie Stargell.

In the mid-1970s, Stargell, nearly immobile and moved to first base after knee surgery, seemed to be washed up. But in '78, at 38 and with arthritis creeping into his knee, he earned Comeback Player of the Year honors by hitting .290 with 28 home runs and 97 RBIs. In '79 his bat was still young—.281, 32, 82. And when the Pirates rose to the top in the NL East, Stargell became a kind of mother superior, doing things like issuing daily inspirational mots, passing out gold stars to the previous game's heroes to put on their caps, and adopting as the team's hymnal "We Are Family," which was played ad nauseum at Three Rivers Stadium.

Stargell, who had been robbed of the MVP award in '73 by Pete Rose, finally got his trophy, though he had to share it with the Cardinals' first baseman Keith Hernandez. With no Pirate pitcher winning more than fourteen games, the team's blend of power (148 homers) and speed (180 stolen bases, a league-high 77 by center fielder Omar Moreno) was lethal. And Stargell just killed in clutch situations. In the sweep of the Reds in the playoff, "Pops" hit a 3-run homer in the eleventh inning to win Game 1 5-2, a single and double in Game 2, a dinger and a double in Game 3. He hit .455 with 6 RBIs.

The World Series against the revived Orioles was a delayed rematch of

'71, and it ran along the same plot line, with the O's getting the early edge. This did not seem out of whack. The Orioles, who had won 102 games and beaten the Angels in a four-game playoff, were another Earl Weaver masterwork, without a hole in sight. They had a power trio composed of one veteran, ex-Yankee bust Ken Singleton (35 homers, 111 RBIs, .295) in right field and two precocious sluggers, left fielder Gary Roenicke (25 homers) and, most intriguing of all, first baseman Eddie Murray—that rarest of baseball commodities, a fence-busting switch hitter.

The Los Angeles–born Murray, one of twelve children, broke in two years before with 27 homers, 88 RBIs, and a .283 average. In '79, still just 23, he went 25-99-.295. In '80, 37-116-.300. What's more, his strikeouts *went down* each year. This gives you an idea of how his career, and it would be a *long* one, would progress, with remarkable consistency. Simply, he and Mike Schmidt were the best untainted power-hitters of the last twenty years. Now, if only the moody Murray—who spoke with few people and made the snarling Jim Rice seem like a cruise ship's social director—could have enjoyed it for even a few minutes.

Just as in '71, the Orioles got out of the gate fast, surging to a 3 games to 1 lead, winning Games 3 and 4 8-4 and 9-6, respectively. The Bucs took Game 5 7-1 at Three Rivers, but the O's had two games at home to win one. Then they had one to win one, because the Pirates won Game 6 4-0. Still, only three teams had ever won a World Series after being down 3 to 1. When game seven began on a bone-chilling night in Baltimore (where Game 1 had been *snowed* out), with bats and other extremities freezing more by the inning, a homer by light-hitting second baseman Rich Dauer put the O's up 1-0 in the third, and Scott McGregor held the lead into the sixth. With one out and a man on first, he faced Stargell—who had hit dingers in Games 1 and 4 and had already singled and doubled in this game.

On the first pitch, Stargell turned the game on its head. He mashed a high drive into the cold night, over the right field wall for a 2-1 lead—one of the most profound home runs in Series history. The Pirates tacked on 2 more runs in the ninth and three Buc relievers shut down the Orioles to win 4-1.

Stargell, in full preacher-man mode, stood in the locker room afterward—amid endless brain-corroding playings of "We Are Family"—and averred that "The Good Man above has given us the right to shed tears at this point." Given what had happened in Boston the year before, The Man was getting good at that.

Talk about fate. Stargell—who hit .400 with 12 hits, 3 homers, and 7 RBIs in the Series—came away sweeping all the MVPs available in '79, for the season, the playoff, and the World Series. And I'm not through. From '70 through '79, Stargell tolled more homers, 296, than anyone else, though he rapidly declined thereafter and was gone three years late with 475 lifetime taters, twentieth all-time. And when he was no longer sermonizing in the clubhouse, the Pirates stopped winning championships. They did, however, do some scoring. In '85 a cocaine scandal broke that reached from its star Dave Parker all the way down to the team's *mascot*. This happened a few seasons after revelations that a number of Phillies, including Pete Rose, had acquired amphetamines from a local doctor.

While these dark doings were again reflective of baseball's existence within the folds of American culture, it also indicated something else: pharmaceutical diddling was now in the game's mainstream. And pursuit of the home run at all costs would only make it worse.

Waiting on the Thunder

By the end of the '70s, the last of the great '60s homer kings were either gone or on the way out. Harmon Killebrew had retired in '75, finishing with 573, the most ever by a right-handed hitter in the AL, fifth all-time, third in home run percentage (one every 14.2 at-bats), and the most hit in the '60s, 403. And with the home run bouncing like an orphan from one master to another, no one racked up as many as 40 until the Reds' spindly George Foster, wielding a very sinister-looking tar-black bat, nailed 52, then 40 the next year before receding the rest of a vastly overrated career in which he hit 348 homers over eighteen years. He was also one of the most spectacular free agent busts after being signed by the Mets in 1982.

Foster wasn't nearly as overrated, however, as the towering figure of home run bastardization in the '70s and '80s, Dave Kingman, all 78 inches of him. Though leaner and more tapered than either Ted Kluszewski or Frank Howard, he had greater impact as a freak show attraction, hitting some of the longest, highest-soaring dingers known to man. The difference was that Kingman didn't care a whit about doing anything else on a ball field, which is why he wound up doing one thing better than hitting home runs—striking out. Swinging harder and harder in the general vicinity of every pitch, he struck out more than 100 times in *13* seasons, leading the NL three times, with a high of 156 in '82. Kingman also hit above .238 exactly four times, and he also couldn't get along with anyone he played with or for. This may explain why he played for seven teams in a sixteen-year career, including a record *four* teams in one season, 1977.

But I'm talking '70s and '80s here, when just about any moax could have a monster home run year, and Kingman had one in '79 with the Cubs when he hit 48 with 131 RBIs and a .288 average. That year, he had a .613 slugging average and hit a homer every 11 at-bats. He led the league again in '82 with 37 homers while with the Mets. Talk about modern-day muses. Kingman, with 442 lifetime homers, is fifth all-time in home run percentage (1 every 15 at-bats) and seventh in strikeouts (1,816).

Don't believe me about the '70s and '80s? Then I give you one of my favorites of the era, James Gorman Thomas III, who played thirteen seasons mostly with the Brewers. "Stormin' Gorman" hit 22 or more homers seven times and led the AL twice and also had 100 or more strikeouts seven times. In '79, when he banged out 45 homers, he hit .244 and struck out a league-worst 175 times; the next year, it was 170 times. Thomas, for whom fielding was a foreign concept, was used almost exclusively as a DH, yet hit under *.200* no less than *five* times. And this man collected big-league paychecks for thirteen years. I rest my case.

Actually, there were a few real players who emerged as home run protagonists before the cheap and dirty homers began to fly. The AL had its misanthropic twins, Murray and Rice (the latter of whom extended the Boston's aversion to him as a hero when he told this writer in a 1978 *Sport* interview, "I think race has been a factor in the way I've been used because the front office *lets* it be a factor. Race has to be a factor when Fred Lynn can hit .240 in the minors and I can hit .340 and he gets a starting job before I do. It's not [then-manager] Don Zimmer who decides who plays and where. It's the front office.") The NL's best was the Phillies' third baseman Mike Schmidt, who like Murray began as an untamed boar cranking homers between great gobs of strikeouts, then adjusted, learned pitchers' weaknesses, and wreaked holy hell on the league for eighteen years—all in Philadelphia.

A freckled-faced redhead born in Dayton, Ohio, Schmidt had been drafted out of Ohio University. He arrived in '73 and hit 18 homers as a student in the Gorman Thomas school of free-swinging, hitting just .198 and whiffing 136 times in *367* at-bats—prompting teammates to dub him "A-choo" for the drafts he created. We're talking some serious airing out of ballparks here, since Schmidt hit in the third hole in front of the abundant outfielder Greg "The Bull" Luzinski, himself a potent home run threat and easy strikeout victim (he cleared 30 dingers and 100 RBIs four times and hit below .280 only once in his first seven seasons—but struck out over 100 times in *10* of his 15 big-league years).

In '74, Schmidt struck out 138 times, leading the NL. But it was in 568 at-bats, and he doubled his homers to a league-high 36—the first of eight home run titles, a number bettered only by Babe Ruth—with 116 RBIs and a .282 average. The first three of Schmidt's homer crowns were from '74 to '76 (36, 38, 38), and he also walked more than 100 times each year. But don't get too excited yet because in '75, affected by a shoulder injury, he actually struck out 180 times, only 9 shy of Bobby Bonds' egregious record, and hit just .249. (Brace yourself: Luzinski that year fanned 151 times, and Richie Allen, back in Philadelphia, added another 109 K's.) The next year, '76, he walked back to the dugout a league-worst 149 times.

However, this season was his turning point, his imprimatur stamped by a record-shattering afternoon at Wrigley Field. Schmidt began the year feebly, then pulled into Chicago on April 18 just as face-slapping winds were whipping in the direction of left field. At first the Cubs drove Steve Carlton from the game and led 13-4 in the fourth inning. And then came Schmidt. Baseball physicists will tell you Schmidt had the perfect swing, from his smooth shifting of weight on his stride to the straightness of his extended arms through the hitting zone and even distribution of power between upper and lower body. At 6 feet 2 inches and 200 pounds he was built almost precisely like Eddie Mathews, whom he would replace as the top home run–hitting third baseman of all time. And against the Cubs on this blustery day, everything he hit was either given a lift by the wind or crashed right through it.

In the fifth, his third time up, he took Rick Reuschel deep for 2 runs. In the seventh, he hit a solo rocket to cut it to 13-7. In the eighth, a 3-run shot off Mike Garman to tie the game 12-12. The Phillies took the lead in the top of the ninth. The Cubs tied in the bottom. In the tenth, Allen walked and Schmidt came up against the other Reuschel brother, Paul. *Boom* went his fourth consecutive homer—the first time any human had hit 4 straight in the NL since Bobby Lowe in 1894. The Phillies won 18-16, Schmidt went on to tie the major league record with 11 homers in April, and the team never stopped winning. They racked up a club-record 101 games and the East Division before the ride ended with a three-game sweep by the Reds in the playoff. Schmidt, though, would anchor a run of five division titles, two pennants, and a championship from '76 to '83.

Schmidt would get ever more dangerous. By '79, he was slamming pitches to all fields, taking the sucker pitches and waiting for the meatballs. He clocked 45 homers that year, walked 120 times, struck out a reasonable 115 times, and scored 109 runs. No third baseman who could hit like that has ever been a better fielder than Schmidt, a perennial Gold Glove winner. In other words, the man was money in the bank, with an especially high interest rate when he got to Wrigley Field. On May 17, the Phillies and the Cubs staged yet another pyrotechnic show there, sending a record 11 homers flying over the ivy walls. Again the Cubs struck hard early. Kingman hit 3 dingers and had 6 RBIs. Third baseman Bill Buckner had a grand slam and 7 RBIs. The Cubs led 7-0, 15-6, and 21-9, but after nine innings it was tied *21-21*. Then Schmidt, who'd hit 1 out earlier, faced ace reliever Bruce Sutter and whacked 1 out for an absurd 23-22 win in a match that featured, get ready, *97* total bases on hits.

Then, on July 7, Schmidt homered his first three times up against the Giants—which, tacked on to the homer he'd hit in his last at-bat the day before—gave him *another* 4 straight homers. And he merely hit 3 more over the next three games, or 7 in five games, tying the record.

Schmidt was even better in '80, copping his fourth home run crown with 48, slugging .621, leading the NL with 121 RBIs, and hitting a solid .286. Down the stretch, the Phillies were locked in a tight pennant race with the Expos, a slick and speedy bunch with one power hitter, catcher Gary Carter. The teams met on the season's final weekend in Montreal. The Phillies needed to win the last game to clinch the division title. It was 4-4 through ten innings when Schmidt stepped up in the top of the eleventh and blasted a 2-run tater that won the game 6-4. And when the Phillies beat the Astros in a five-game playoff—in which, amazingly, only 1 homer was struck, Luzinski's 2-run blow in Game 1—Schmidt had a World Series date with baseball's other premier third baseman, who gave away nothing when it came to dramatic home runs.

Preparation H and Pine Tar

While the Phillies' entire history reeked of frustration—they'd not won a single championship in *98* years—the Royals' own futility was such that had they lost to the Yankees for the fourth time in the '80 playoffs they would have been placed on a twenty-four-hour suicide watch. Fortunately, they had a supernatural force that year—George Brett.

By that year, Brett had perfected and become chief avatar of a trendy hitting style, originated by the Royals' batting coach, Charlie Lau. A .255 hitter in the '50s and '60s, Lau's techniques as a coach centered on a kind of minuet at the plate—closed stance, weight on the back foot, even swing so dependent on the bottom hand that a core tenet was to allow the top hand to slide off the bat just after contact. It worked, too, though power hitting was traded for spray hitting, like the Royals did.

Brett, with his natural mechanics, likely would have hit 40 homers a year sans Lau, and 50 points lower, but never gave in to the long-ball temptation until after Lau's death in '85. That's when his homers jumped to a career-high of 30 and his average began to sink. When he finished up in '93 after twenty-one seasons, with 3,154 hits, his career average had leveled off to .305. Even as a minion of Lau, though, Brett was a severe home run threat when one was needed. In '80 he did it all, hitting over .400 until late summer and ending at .390, with 24 homers, 118 RBIs, a 37-game-hitting streak and a .664 slugging percentage—numbers that made the AL's MVP award a moot point. And he did all this even while missing 45 games with injuries.

Still, while the Royals won the West Division by 14 games, and led the league in hitting and steals, the Yankees won 6 more games, 103 in all, and Reggie Jackson co-led the loop with 41 homers. And yet that year's Royals-Yankees LCS was a walkover. Brett, who'd already hit 4 postseason homers, nailed 1 in the opening game in Kansas City to cinch a 7-2 win. The Royals took Game 2 3-2, prefacing some very sweet revenge at Yankee Stadium. Though the Royals trailed 2-1 through six innings of Game 3, Brett came to bat with runners on first and third in the seventh against Goose Gossage—who'd yielded a mere 5 homers all season in relief. One could hear Gossage grunt trying to blow a fastball by Brett on the first pitch.

Not on this night.

Brett caught the high, hard pitch and, oh happy day, the ball soared into the upper deck in right, symbolically, high over the head of Jackson. The Royals closed out the game, 4-2, lifting the pinstriped monkey from their back.

"We let down the [Yankee] tradition," Gossage said mournfully. "That really hurts."

Oh yeah? Then why were so many people in the world so happy that night?

So baseball's two MVP third basemen were in the World Series. And Brett again came up big. He hit .375 with a homer—but it was his butt, not his bat, that left an imprint on this Series when because of the most celebrated case of hemorrhoids in history, he had to miss Game 2, a 6-4 Phillies win. Brett, in fact, was to be overshadowed by unsung Royals' first baseman Willie Mays Aikens, who cracked 2-run homers in both Games 1 and 4. Aikens hit .400 with 8 RBIs. But Schmidt had the final word. With the Series tied two games apiece, his 2-run tater in Game 5—his second of the Series—put the Phillies up early and he scored the gamer in the ninth inning of the 4-3 victory. He then owned Game 6 with 2 RBI hits to put it away in the 4-1 Series clincher—a moment all Philadelphians had thought to be impossible. Schmidt, the Series MVP, hit .381 with 6 runs and 7 RBIs.

For Brett, there would be more memorable big clutch at-bats, and in '85 a world championship, when with Brett hitting .370 the Royals downed the Cardinals in seven games. However, one lunatic at-bat takes precedence, and a high rank, on all lists of epic homers. And all that's needed to relive it are the words "pine tar."

It happened on July 24, 1983 at—where else?—Yankee Stadium. The Royals trailed 4-3 with 2 outs in the top of the ninth when Brett busted another Gossage fastball into the right field seats for a 5-4 lead. But before he even came around the bases, Billy Martin was at the plate having a high legal colloquy with umpire Tim McClelland. The subject: Brett's bat. Martin had long suspected that Brett used too much pine tar on the handle. Case: Rule 1.10 (b), which stated that a material or substance could not be rubbed higher than eighteen inches from the handle; any bat caught in the act would be removed from the game.

McClelland nodded, picked up Exhibit A, and laid it across home plate to measure it, then concluded the eighteen-inch limit had been violated and, interpreting the rule like an activist judge, ruled that since Brett had already batted, his illegal lumber was cause to call him out and nullify his homer. Result: 4-3, Yankees, end of game.

Brett, who by now was on the bench, saw McClelland's arm go up to signal out—meaning he had hit the world's first game-*losing* home run—and was up and out of the dugout like a load of buckshot. He wedged himself against the ump as he bellowed, his face scarlet and his eyes about to pop from his head. Ejected as soon as he hit the field, Brett had to be all but carted back off it, and his manager, Dick Howser, also was ejected.

The Yankees, of course, crowed about how clever they were. But Judge McClelland's verdict underwent judicial review—and the patent unfairness of the call would not stand. After the Royals filed a protest with the league, AL president Lee MacPhail wasted no time in reversing the call, on grounds that the bat had not violated the spirit of the rule, and restored the "Pine Tar Homer." (Actually, MacPhail was incorrect, too.

Brett *did* violate the rule's spirit, but the rule only implied removal of the bat, not nullifying any hit by it, and the rule was rewritten to state that specifically.)

Steinbrenner, who no doubt expected MacPhail—the son of Larry MacPhail and a former Yankee GM—to throw out the appeal, reacted with his normal grace. "I wouldn't want to be Lee MacPhail in New York," he huffed. Steinbrenner also wanted at first to charge admission for the resumption of the game—with 4 outs left—on August 18, before relenting. And so, most bizarrely, on that day the Royals traveled halfway across the country and before around 1,200 people allowed in for free, played about five minutes of ball, minus Brett and Howser, whose ejections stood. They won 5-4 and went back home.

And they call this the National Pastime.

As for Schmidt, MVP awards accrued to him like coal dust. He won another in '81—the first season to be blackened by a midyear work stoppage, cleaving the campaign into two halves of around fifty games per team, followed by a two-tier playoff scheme. That shortened season, he hit 31 homers with 91 RBIs and a career-high .316 average. In '83 (48, 121, .286) came another World Series—a disastrous one, as it turned out, as he had just 1 hit in 20 at-bats in a five-game loss to the Orioles—and the highest salary in history to then, $2.1 million a year over four years. By '86, Schmidt had his third MVP and eighth and final home run crown (with 37).

By now, Schmidt had clearly won over the baseball media, both bourgeois and effete. There was, for example, the take of one of the latter, *The New Yorker*'s Roger Angell. "During a game." Angell wrote, "Schmidt brings such formidable attention and intelligence to bear on the enemy pitcher that one senses that the odds have almost been reversed out there; it is the man on the mound, not the one up at the plate, who is in worse trouble from the start."

At that point, as well, principally because of Schmidt, there was some hope that the pomp and circumstance of the home run was salvageable. But the tide of indignity was turning, fast.

Mr. May and Other Mr. Octobers

Yankee-haters still rejoicing over Brett's coffin-nail homer of '80 were rapturous in '81. While the team managed to get into the playoffs that strike-shortened season and slink by the Brewers and A's, Jackson clearly was fading, and Steinbrenner's new pride and joy, outfielder Dave Winfield—a sensational athlete who signed a ten-year, $20 million free agent contract—seemed capable of any feat except when it really mattered. At 6 feet 6 inches and 220 pounds, the Minneapolis-born Winfield—born on the day Bobby Thomson hit his Shot Heard 'Round the World—was a petrifying sight at the plate and desperately craved superstardom. Working off the Jackson blueprint, he smiled, jived, swung with volcanic force, and as a right-handed hitter at Yankee Stadium mastered hitting fly balls to the left field warning track. In the clipped '81 season, he hit 13 homers with 68 RBIs and a .294 average.

In the World Series, once more against the Dodgers, Winfield dug a hole for himself he never escaped from. Hitting cleanup, he amassed 1 hit, a single, in 22 at-bats. The Yankees won the first two games at home, then folded in the next four. By induction, Steinbrenner assessed the blame. "I wanted another Mr. October," he said, "and got Mr. May." It only got worse for Winfield. Steinbrenner's chronic obsession to destroy his own player led him in 1987 to pay a wormy gambler $40,000 for incriminating information, or gossip, about Winfield—the smoking gun in the subsequent "lifetime" ban given the Boss by Commissioner Fay Vincent. (Alas, Steinbrenner's lawyers backed Vincent down just three years later and he was reinstated.)

Leave it to a *schlemiel* like Winfield to bloom when the Yankees went back into the dumper in '82. That year, Jackson's turbulent Bronx stay ended when he signed as a free agent with the Angels and in his last big season led the league with 39 homers and 101 RBIs and delivered the team to the AL West flag. Winfield did nearly as well, with 37 big flies, 106 RBIs, and a .280 average, but the Yankees slid to fifth place. And while Winfield constructed solid seasons (and a superb one in '84 when he hit .340), banging out more than 20 homers and 100 RBIs six times, he receded as left-hand-hitting Don Mattingly took flight as the best all-around Yankee since, arguably, Joe DiMaggio. Mattingly, a Gold Glove first baseman, was the AL's MVP, hitting .324 with 35 homers. Over fourteen seasons he hit .307 with 222 homers. In '87 he tied the record by hitting dingers in eight consecutive games. He also struck out no more than 61 times in any year. Obviously, he was not a man for his times—which is why he's still waiting for a Hall-of-Fame plaque. Then again, he played only five games of postseason ball (in '95 when he hit .417 against the Mariners), and in the Yankee meritocracy this is not helpful.

Winfield might still be waiting, too, had he not hung on like a stubborn war horse for twenty-two seasons, through '95, fattening his home run total to 465. As late as '93, at age 40, he cleared 20 dingers. And let's give the man his credit. Big swinger that he was—and big run-producer, with 1,833 career RBIs, thirteenth-best all-time—his strikeout numbers also were remarkable for the modern era—only three times over 100, and just barely so each time. His 5,221 total bases are tenth all-time. So while Winfield may have, as Steinbrenner alleged, skimmed a few dollars for himself from the Dave Winfield Foundation, I'm still happy for the man that when he got a chance to do a make-good in a World Series, with the Blue Jays in '92, his 2-run double in the tenth inning of Game 6 against the Braves brought his team a championship.

Jackson, meanwhile, used his stay with the Angels to rack up milestones. On September 18, 1984, he popped career homer No. 500 off the Royals' Bud Black, moved past Willie McCovey with No. 522 on August 17, 1985, and past Mantle with No. 537 on May 14, 1986. He then went back to the A's to orchestrate a farewell season and left the scene he had molded in so many ways with 563 home runs—and those monstrous 2,597 strikeouts. And as obnoxious as his fame was, his exodus stripped the home run of much of its elan. Indeed, now the era of truly grotesque numbers proliferated, with not a trace of shame and in a warp when it seemed possible for just about anyone to be a home run king.

They look good on paper, too, all those 30/30 men in the mid- and late '80s such as Dale Murphy (Braves, '83), Eric Davis (Reds, '87), Darryl Strawberry (Mets, '87), and Howard Johnson (Mets, '87 and '89). However, I prefer to call them 30/30/100 men, because every one of them bought their 30 homers with over 100 strikeouts. Call it the Curse of Bobby Bonds.

The flawed home run hitter. That was the newest paradigm. Take Pedro Guerrero, who cranked out 30 or more homers three times between '82 and '85 for the Dodgers, and 215 overall in fifteen seasons, yet perfectly embodied the empty base syndrome, driving in 100 RBIs only twice. When he hit 33 homers in '85, he drove in just 87 runs. This caveat also applies to Andre Dawson, called "The Hawk" for the quick, barbaric sweep of his swing. Dawson, who played 21 years, cleared 20 home runs all but three times his first 16 seasons, peaking with a monster '87 when he was traded to the Cubs after a long tenure with the Expos and slammed 49 homers with 137 RBIs, both league highs. But that was only the second and last time he would reach 100 RBIs, and in two postseason series his average was .128.

Most home run hitters merely blended into a distilled culture of forgettable, interchangeable parts. To prove that, I give you Jesse Barfield, who had an AL-high 40 homers with the Blue Jays in '86, with 108 RBIs and a .289 average. Barfield, who would later go to the Yankees, hit an admirable 241 dingers in twelve seasons. He also struck out over 100 times in all but four of those seasons, as many as 150 times twice. I bet the name doesn't even ring a bell.

Tellingly, none of these souls had anything to do with any of the biggest homers of the '80s, which besides the picaresque shots of Brett and Schmidt unfolded like this:

- *October 19, 1981.* Olympic Stadium, Game 5 National League Championship Series (NLCS), Dodgers-Expos, top of the ninth, 1-1, 2 outs. Rick Monday strokes a game- and series-clinching home run off Steve Rogers.
- *July 8, 1983.* Comiskey Park, All-Star Game, bottom of the third, bases loaded. Fred Lynn hits a grand slam off Atlee Hamaker to plate four of the AL's 7-run inning en route to a 13-3 victory, the league's first since '71.
- *October 8, 1983.* Comiskey Park, Game 4, American League Championship Series (ALCS) Orioles–White Sox, top of the tenth, 0-0. Tito Landrum jacks a solo homer off Britt Burns. Orioles win 3-0 to take the pennant.
- *October 14, 1984.* Tiger Stadium, Game 5, World Series, Padres-Tigers, bottom eighth, 5-4 Detroit. Kirk Gibson hits his second tater of the game, a 3-run blast off Goose Gossage (what, again?). Tigers win 8-4 to take the Series.
- *October 14, 1985.* Busch Stadium, Game 5, NLCS (now a best-of-seven), Dodgers-Cardinals, bottom ninth, 2-2, 1 out. Shortstop Ozzie Smith, a 150-pound switch-"hitter" who in eight seasons had hit 13 home runs, takes one out against Tom Niedenfuer—his first-ever home run hitting left-handed in over *3,000* at-bats—to win the game and put the Cards up 3 games to 2.
- *October 16, 1985.* Dodger Stadium, Game 6, NLCS, top ninth, 2 out, 5-4 Dodgers. With runners on second and third, Tom Lasorda had Niedenfuer pitch to cleanup hitter Jack Clark, who takes the first pitch over the wall. Cards win 7-5 and go on to the World Series.
- *October 11, 1986.* Shea Stadium, Game 3, NLCS, Astros-Mets, bottom ninth, 5-4 Astros, 1 on, 1 out. Lenny "Nails" Dykstra hammers a homer to put the Mets up 2 games to 1. They lose the next two, then win two extra-inning thrillers to take the series.
- *October 12, 1986.* Anaheim Stadium, Game 5, ALCS, Red Sox-Angels, top ninth, 5-4 Angels, 1 on, 2 out. California is one strike from its first pennant when Dave Henderson crushes a pitch by Donnie Moore over the left field wall for a 6-5 lead. The Angels tie it in the bottom of

the inning and Henderson's sacrifice fly off Moore in the eleventh puts it away. The Sox then rip off the last two games at Fenway Park to win the pennant. Moore, unable to get over the stigma of the devastating home run, sinks into depression and is cut in June 1989. A month later, he critically wounds his estranged wife and shoots himself to death—another victim of a home run curse. Ironically, Henderson also homers in Game 6 of the World Series against the Mets, who down to *their* last strike rally to win on the famous Mookie Wilson dribbler that got through Bill Buckner's legs, setting up the usual Red Sox downfall in Game 7.

• *October 10, 1987.* Candlestick Park, Game 4, NLCS, Cardinals-Giants, bottom fifth, 2-1 Cards, 1 on, 1 out. Jeffrey "Penitentiary Face" Leonard cracks a homer in his fourth straight series game, a record, and ties the record of 4 LCS homers held by Steve Garvey and Bob Robertson, giving the Giants the lead in a 4-2 win. Leonard, one of those implicated in the cocaine scandals of the early '80s, enrages the Cards with his "one flap down" showboating around the bases. The happy ending is that his team loses in seven games.

• *October 9, 1988.* Shea Stadium, Game 4, NLCS, top ninth, 4-2 Mets, 1 on, 1 out. With the Mets about to go up 3 games to 1, Mike Scoscia rocks one over the left field wall against Dwight Gooden to tie it. Then in the twelfth inning Kirk Gibson smacks the gamer off Roger McDowell. The Dodgers will win in seven.

• *October 15, 1988.* Dodger Stadium, Game 1, World Series, A's-Dodgers, 4-3 A's, bottom ninth, 1 on, 2 outs. Gibson, reduced to little more than a flat tire by leg injuries, limps to the plate as a pinch hitter to face Dennis Eckersley, who'd had an AL-high 45 saves. Gibson barely fouls off three fastballs, each time nearly buckling when he puts weight on his front leg. Now, on 3-and-2, Ecklersley throws a slider—"a terrible pitch," he says later—and Gibson sends it into the right field seats and hobbles around the bases, yanking his arm back and forth in a victory mime, accompanied for the TV audience by Jack Buck wailing, in what would become this home run's epitaph, "I can't believe what I just saw!" Gibson doesn't get a single at-bat the rest of the Series, but his tide-turning tater sends the Dodgers on to a four-game sweep.

The Gibson homer, as it turns out, has another epitaph—as the last inspired breath of baseball's long life of home runs earned by men using nothing more than their natural abilities against mainly challenging conditions and rules. Because it was in the late '80s that the game hideously altered the old equations and institutionalized bad habits and bad baseball by coupling easy money with easy homers.

15

Foul Balls

Bash – Bang – Zoom . . .

It's tempting to say the bankrupting of the home run coincided with the retirement of Mike Schmidt in '89. And, to be sure, Schmidt's deified status among sportswriters isn't misplaced. "If Mike Schmidt had hit .320, he would have been the best *player* who ever lived," swooned Bill James in the *Historical Baseball Abstract*. "Even fifty points lower, he is the best third baseman [ever]." Schmidt left with 548 homers, passing Foxx and Mantle in '88, and sits ninth all-time. In May 1989, when he finally called it a career because of a shoulder injury, the fans still voted him the NL's starting All-Star third baseman. Schmidt had the most homers (295) and RBIs (839) in the '80s. His 1,507 walks is fifteenth all-time. And, oh yes, his 1,883 strikeouts is fourth. (But remember, I'm cutting him slack on this.)

Actually, the home run's subversion began in mid-decade, when the baseball nabobs decided, without telling anyone except the umpires, that fewer strikes should be called. According to Bill James, "From 1985 to 1987, baseball . . . wrestled with an unannounced, *de facto* redefinition of the strike zone, making the strike zone smaller and lower than it was." Result: by '87, those cowhide spheres were flying like Pennsy Pinkies over outfield walls—1,824 in the NL, up by 301, and—gulp—a record *2,634* in the AL, up by 344. This included the 49-homer performances that year by the league leaders, Andre Dawson and an elongated, moose-strong, 24-year-old rookie first baseman with the A's named Mark McGwire, who also drove in 118 runs, hit .289, and slugged .618—easily the best season by a rookie in history. He also struck out 131 times, not that such a thing mattered anymore.

The New York Times made the lava flow of homers in '87 an official trend when early that season it ran a Murray Chass column entitled "Home Runs Are Flying." In it, Chass noted that four players had already hit 3 homers in a game and 57 had hit 2 in a game. Ken Phelps and George Bell had done the latter *four* times, Jack Clark and Dale Murphy three times. By now, homers per game had risen from .90 to 1.40. Accordingly, attendance was booming. By season's end, the AL had jumped from 25.1 million to a record 27.3 million; the NL from 22.3 to 24.7 million. By '93, the numbers would be 33.3 million and 36.9 million. And while the dastardly player strike had eviscerated the '94 season and sank the gate in each league to around 25 million in '95, a year later—as several players seemed headed for 60 home runs—it was on the rise again. Three years later, when the NL featured a home run drama like no other ever before it, the league would set its all-time crowd record.

That the man who provided the, ahem, juice during that magical '87 was built for New-Age superstardom was already clear back in '81. That year, Mark McGwire rejected an $8,500 offer from the Expos to fry bigger fish; instead he went to USC, winning national attention with some ungodly home runs, and then on to the '84 U.S. Olympic team. McGwire's five-year plan worked handsomely. Signed by the A's in '86 for $60,000, he came up late in '86, fully formed. Though his beautifully feral swing would evolve greatly, its basic identity would remain intact: an unapologetic uppercut that seemed to begin at his back knee and end up, as with George Brett, with his top hand off the bat, which took the Charlie Lau philosophy into a new dimension—turning contact hitting into all-field power hitting.

McGwire hit his first home run on August 25, 1986, a mortar shot off Walt Terrell that screamed 450 feet over the wall at Tiger Stadium. In '87, first base was his, and on June 22 he jacked 3 out against the Indians, and on the next day 2 more to tie the major league record of 5 homers in two games. By the All-Star break, he'd rung the bell 33 times. No. 38, on August 10 against the Mariners, tied the rookie record of Frank Robinson and Wally Berger. Four days later, it was his alone when he clocked one off the Angels' Don Sutton. There was even a small window when it seemed he might get to 60, before concluding with 49—the first rookie to lead baseball in homers since Al Rosen in 1950.

The 6-foot-5 McGwire, who won the Rookie of the Year award by acclimation, weighed a good 215 pounds, and though in hindsight he seemed about half the man he would grow into, even then baseball heard for the first time whispers that just perhaps this new Bunyan had an edge, the kind that came out of a 100-cc syringe. And he wasn't the only one on the A's raising suspicion, since outfielder Jose Canseco—an extraordinarily well-muscled 6 feet 3 inches and 190 pounds, was also crushing the life out of baseballs.

Canseco had made nearly as spectacular an entrance as McGwire, hitting 33 homers with 117 RBIs—and *175* strikeouts—in *his* Rookie of the Year season of '86, then 31 and 113 in '87. Canseco, who whipped a bat around like a Q-tip and swung for the next zip code on every pitch, hit just .240 and .255 those years. Then, in '88, he was a revelation. When he spanked 2 homers against the Mariners on July 31, he became the first to hit 30 or more in his first three seasons. On September 23, when he cranked No. 41 and stole 2 bases against the Brewers, he stood as the first 40/40 player. He ended up at 42 and 40, leading the league in homers and RBIs (124), was fourth in steals, and hit .307.

This was the exemplar of the new New Age. For all that hefty hitting, Canseco also struck out 128 times and walked just 78 times. McGwire wasn't far behind: 32 homers (including 2 that won consecutive sixteen-inning games), 99 RBIs, 117 strikeouts, 76 walks. One June 20 McGwire hit a triple. His next, and last, triple, would come *11 years* later. What am I saying here? Simply that while Canseco put some steals into the mix, he and McGwire had taken one-dimensional baseball into its halcyon.

Canseco unanimously won the MVP award in '88, the first to do that since Reggie Jackson in '73. He cranked 3 homers in the ALCS against the Red Sox, tying Brett's record, and then hit a grand slam on his first World Series at-bat against the Dodgers, though he pulled a Winfield and went hitless the rest of the Series. And McGwire broke up Game 3 of the Series with a bottom-of-the-ninth homer. How scary was it that Canseco was only 23 at the time and that McGwire 24?

Still, the home run gods may not have been thrilled that their gift to mankind was in the hands of these precocious "Bash Brothers," as the media dubbed them, and voted to make the two of them pay some belated dues to test their characters. If so, McGwire passed and Canseco failed, both in epic proportions.

This could be predicted since the Brothers could not have been less alike. Born in Pomona, California, McGwire was red haired and freckle faced, a Bible-reading family man who was uncomfortable with the rituals of stardom such as, say, speaking in public. Canseco, born in Cuba and raised in Miami, was utterly self-absorbed, impossibly ego driven, insecure, paranoid, and had a fondness for driving flashy sports cars too fast, philandering, and raising his hands to women, mainly those married to him.

Both men, however, shared the common bond of being branded as suspects 1 and 1A in the then-nascent game of Who's Shooting Steroids. Whether they were or not—though Canseco says as much in his breathless recent admissions in hopes of selling his memoirs—they were in a sense crucified by their own desire to break free of the corroding strictures of past baseball generations by seriously training with weights. This was a practice always avoided; indeed, up until then, functional strength was regarded strictly an accident of birth or the product of young men having spent long hours in steel mills or coal mines before baseball called them away. The concept of conditioning generally meant running, jumping in place, and tossing around a medicine ball in spring training. (I love those old newsreels of Babe Ruth's belly nearly swallowing up one of those balls.) Weight training, so the thinking went, would only generate inflexible, musclebound lugs who would be slow, clumsy, and susceptible to injury. All that would change, though with grudging resistance among the old guard. When Tiger catcher Lance Parrish came to camp freshly muscled in the mid-1980s, his manager, the flinty Sparky Anderson, asked him whether he wanted to be a catcher or a member of the Russian weight-lifting team (a parallel that actually would have some resonance once steroids fully entered the picture). But all resistance would gradually evaporate and within just a few years *everyone* was suddenly bigger, wider, and buffer, and looking to get even more so—which could be accomplished only one way.

Enter the steroid solution, with the certain rewards and uncertain risks of ingesting testosterone derivates.

Baseball, of course, saw nothing but the rewards. By casting blind eyes to the obvious, it sowed the seeds of ruination—the main villain of which would be the escalating credibility problem of the home run. In baseball's defense, at least at the beginning, the subject of performance-enhancing drugs was virgin territory in the '80s and most people were naifs about it at a time when anabolic or muscle-building steroids were prescription drugs but not illegal, *per se*. Not until 1990 were they classified under the Controlled Substances Act as a Schedule III drug and yoked—absurdly—with cocaine, heroin, and morphine. Only then did possession without a prescription become a felony. But even as chants of "Ster-oids! Ster-oids!" greeted both McGwire and Cansceo in enemy ballparks, the baseball barons professed ignorance (very believably) and thrilled at the master race of *uber*men that had descended on the game. While other sports got hip and began drug testing their players, baseball simply sat back, allowed the players to broker greater leverage to resist testing, and spit tobacco juice in the face of every home run that has ever been hit.

Bash – Plop – Fizz . . .

More than any loose talk about steroids, the primary speculation for the state of the long ball was, as usual, the state of the ball itself. Was it the players who were juiced or the balls? To oldtimers, *something* was up with those cowhides. Hank Greenberg, a year before his death in 1986 at 75, saw the home runs screeching over walls and felt like he'd been cheated in his era. "I do know that the ball today is far more lively than any used in my time," he told Bill Starr in *Clearing the Bases*. His evidence: the opposite-field home run.

> In my day, a home run to the "off" field for most players was a rarity, I doubt I hit as much as a handful to the opposite field. During my career, it was quite an achievement to hit a ball on the roof of the outfield stands in any ballpark. I did it once at Comiskey Park. I recently saw an exhibition of long-ball hitting there. There were seven balls hit on the roof. There is no way than can be done without a juiced-up baseball.
>
> I don't believe players today have more natural power than [we] did. . . . I wish I could have had the same baseball to hit as they have now.

Once again, a round of tests was done that concluded the ball was not demonstrably livelier, manufactured any differently, or had any change in composition. But the players themselves swore it was. A recently retired Bobby Bonds, after taking some batting practice, said that the ball went farther than it did when he was 25. "And I'm not that strong," he noted. "I've never lifted a weight in my life. I hit balls really terrible and they [now] cleared the fence by 30 feet. I don't need tests on some machine. I go by contact." (For those wondering, I'll soon get to Bobby's little boy, who in the '80s was just getting used to the lay of the land and the possibilities of the home run. But first, this prophetic 1987 quote from Bobby: "The way this ball is going out of the ball park, it wouldn't surprise me if someone hit 80 home runs one day.")

This time, the rabbit ball theorems were correct, though it was *not* a secret plot by the baseball owners. (Trust me, they're not that smart.) Instead, we can chalk up the modern lively ball to the march of technology. Put simply, baseballs, like cars and TVs and underwear, are made a lot better than they used to be. What is different is the textile industry and the improvements in yarns and leathers, which are infinitely more durable, absorb far more shock, and have far more tensile strength than the balls that rolled off Ben Shibe's hide-stitching machines. And those cushioned corks could seal a Dom Perignon any time. Hit a ball on the nose today and that momentum transfer makes a little nuclear reactor out of its core.

Within a few more years, other ingredients would work their way into the long-ball soup like cheap food additives, with no nutritional value but lots of market value.

In fact, the tide of '87 receded in '88, dipping back to 1,901 in the AL and 1,279 in the NL. And Jose Canseco especially started to go adrift. He began '89 by being arrested for driving a Jaguar 125 mph and having a loaded handgun on the seat, and he missed the first half of the season with a broken wrist, though he did hit 17 homers in the second half to drive the A's to the AL West flag. During the ALCS against the Blue Jays, Canseco blistered a 480-foot meteor into the fifth deck at the Skydome, then hit .307 with a home run in the earthquake-interrupted World Series sweep over the Giants.

I still cringe thinking of Canseco then, the Lamborghini with the "40-40" plates, the "tell-all" rip-off 900-phone line, the dumb headlines about him and Madonna, the wrangles with the media and fans. Worse, in '90, he signed the fattest contract ever up to then, five years and $23.5 million. People wished hard for him to fall on his kiester, but he kept racking up homers, 37 in '90, a league-high 44 (with 122 RBIs) in '91. But the A's, having been swept by the Reds in the '90 World Series, dropped to fourth place in '91. And with Canseco's batting average reverting to the .260s, suddenly his power wasn't worth its weight in trouble. By then, too, Canseco had "trained" his way into a bloated 240-pound clod, a 40/40 man who after '91 would reach 20 steals exactly once.

The A's didn't wait for Canseco's cheesecloth veneer of superstardom to fall off. In August of '92, with Canseco slumping and scarified by home crowd booing, the team traded him to the Rangers—right in the thick of its late-season run to the AL West flag—for three middling players and cash. For Canseco, Texas was perdition. In two injury and apathy-ravaged seasons he still hit his long balls, but missed the train of high-visibility '90s sluggers. How metaphorically perfect is it that Canseco's major

1990s' highlight was the time he went back to catch a fly ball in May '93 only to have it bounce off his empty head and over the wall. Three days later, Canseco talked his manager into letting him *pitch* in a blowout loss, injuring his elbow and finishing him for the rest of the season. And if you think that is impressive, wait until the subsequent episodes of *Travels with Jose.*

McGwire, meanwhile, was hardly prospering himself. In '90, he clanged 39 homers with 108 RBIs, but his average withered to .235. The next year, unable to find his bearings from the start, he had 22 homers and 75 RBIs in 154 games and a dreadful .201 average. And though he rebounded in '92—42, 104, .268—he too was being plagued with injuries during a similar bulking-up phase that took him up to around 250 pounds. McGwire's chronic back and heel injuries made his windmill swing a hellish exercise and he would become little more than a spectator the next two seasons.

Now, with McGwire and Canseco seemingly falling off the Earth, it seemed that the Age of the Mastadons was short-lived. Other strongboys seeded in the late '80s were also on the way out, such as Wally Joyner, who hit 56 homers his first two seasons with the Angels, then got to 20 only once in his last fourteen seasons. And then there was Vincent Edward "Bo" Jackson, an ideal delegate of an eon when baseball players began to look like football players. Jackson *was* a football player, a damn fine one, having won the Heisman Trophy in '95 running the ball at Auburn. The 6-foot-1, 225-pound Jackson was built as solidly as sheet rock and could run like an antelope. Densely muscled from head to toe, Jackson's neck looked like a pedestal for his head. He was also business savvy—too much for his own good.

Marketing himself as the new Jim Thorpe, Jackson first signed to play baseball with the Royals and fit right in with the new power game. In '86 he banged 22 homers, many into the next galaxy—while hitting .235 and striking out 158 times in 396 at-bats, as well as playing left field like it was a minefield. His place thus set, he then signed with the Oakland Raiders, to play football as an "off-season hobby." By now, Jackson was starring in scads of "Bo Knows" Nike ads and raking in millions far above his $380,000 baseball salary. And, predictably, his football hobby began to take over just as he was growing into baseball.

In '89 Jackson hit 32 homers, had 105 RBIs, 26 steals, and a .256 average. At the All-Star Game in Anaheim, he led off the bottom of the first inning and crushed 1 off Rick Resuchel that flew like a tee shot over the center field fence around 450 feet away. The mammoth homer, which came just before Wade Boggs hit another dinger, earned him the MVP of the AL's 5-3 victory (a game also notable as Nolan Ryan's only All-Star win, at age 42). Five months later, Jackson was named to the NFL's All-Pro team. But Bo didn't know his body couldn't take two sports. In '91 he injured his hip on the gridiron, ending his football days. He lingered on in baseball, even after a hip replacement, but by '94 he was gone, an experiment in home run desperation gone awry.

Still, the home run readjustment hardly meant players with oodles of muscles were out of vogue. Beefcake was in, for good. Witness '93, when a specimen almost as big and ripped as Jackson and Canseco, and vastly more humble, accounted for nothing less than the second most profound World Series home run of all time.

A Good Joe

If Canseco was too self-serving for his own good, Joe Carter was too civil for his. Carter, one of the plethora of 30/30 men from the '80s, was his generation's Ralph Kiner—or was up until October 23, 1993. At 6 feet 3 inches and 215 pounds, with a physique out of *Gray's Anatomy,* not a syringe (unlike Canseco and McGwire, he almost never missed a game with injury), and a wonderfully leveraged swing, Carter had only one debit: not getting in step with baseball's culture of arrogance. I'm shocked it didn't ruin him.

The college player of the year with Wichita State, Carter, a right-handed-hitting outfielder and first baseman, was the second draft pick in '81, taken by the Cubs who then traded him to the Indians in a seven-player deal—the kind of thing he'd get used to. In '86 he matured, collecting 29 homers, a baseball-high 121 RBIs (and an AL-high 121 strike-outs), and a .302 average. After doing the 30/30 thing in '87, he had a career-best 35 homers two years later, though his average had begun to slip (he would never again hit .300) and his salary demands grated on the Tribe brass who traded him to the Padres for three players in '90. There Carter hit 24 homers with 115 RBIs, but was packaged *again* after the season, in a four-player deal to the Blue Jays.

Carter, a man habitually overlooked by the media, was by now the game's highest-paid player, pulling in around $3 million a year in '92 and '93. And he was money in the bank for the Blue Jays, building three straight 30-homer, 100-RBI seasons, and in '93 compiling a record five 3-homer games, as well as hitting 2 homers in one inning. He also was the last cog the Blue Jays needed to become an elite team, winning three straight AL pennants and two championships. In '93, they were the league's best hitting team (.279), stole the most bases (170), and were sixth in homers with 159. And Carter was their center of gravity, slamming 33 homers with 121 RBIs, while hitting .254. How great a clutch slugger was Carter? In the thick of the empty base home run era, he had *10* 100-RBI years—one in the 111-game strike season of '94. In 41 post-season games, he hit 6 homers, including 4 in twelve World Series games with 11 RBIs. One of the taters clinched the '92 ALCS against the A's, another the pivotal Game 3 of that year's World Series against the Braves. And then, of course, there was the Big One.

Let's not equate the clout that made Carter famous with Bill Mazeroski's—it didn't happen in a seventh game and it was against the Phillies, not the Yankees. Also, unlike Bobby Thomson's shot, it's not burned into the hearts and minds of its generation. Still, as with both of its forerunners, it is the very essence of the home run, a microcosm of life and sudden death. So, in their way, Carter and *his* foil, Mitch Williams, matter just as much.

To baseball purists it mattered a lot, because its secondary effect was to slap down the subversive blot presented by the burp-and-fart Phillies (two words to prove the point: John Kruk), even if it did take a team from Canada to restore the game's bogus veneer of antique Americana. This seemed to be in jeopardy when the Blue Jays marched to a three games to one lead but failed to close it out in Game 5—a 15-14 Phillies win. Then, in Game 6, the Phillies erased a 5-1 lead and went up 6-5 on a 3-run homer in the seventh by Lenny Dykstra—his fourth of the Series. They held the lead for two innings, then gave the ball to Williams, a hard-throwing but erratic character who had 43 saves during the season but often needed a compass to find the plate, thus earning the nickname "Wild Thing." Williams also liked to taunt hitters, which isn't the brightest thing to do if you live on the edge of death.

He did get the first out, but then gave up a single to Paul Molitor—who himself was writing a remarkable story. Now 37, Molitor, who had played through fourteen years of injuries and comebacks with the Brewers before coming to the Blue Jays as a DH, was a World Series animal. In '83, when the Brewers lost to the Cardinals in seven games, Molitor cranked 2 homers, hit .355, and rang up a record 5 hits in one Series game. A career .306 hitter, Molitor hit a sizzling .500—12 for 24, with 2 homers and 8 RBIs—earning him the Series MVP award, which was no small feat given what happened right after he got his ninth-inning single and Carter stepped in.

Williams, who was clearly burned out and laboring from heavy Series duty, went 2-and-1. Then he threw a slider that Carter swung badly at and missed for strike 2. Still, Carter had seen all he needed. The fact that Williams was throwing a slider at all, he recalled, was the tip-off. "His velocity was not good," Carter said, "and the only pitch he was throwing for strikes was a slider."

To a hitter as deadly in the clutch as Carter, it was a gift.

Predictably, Williams tried to get him to bite at another slider, but the one he threw in next was a meatball, low but very hittable. And Carter smoked it deep into the left field seats. End of game. End of season. Once again, the ritual of the big-game-winning walk-off home run set into motion the ritual of a man rounding the bases in exhilarating glory, in the midst of delirium all around him and carried off a ball field by a swelling crowd of teammates. It's a rerun that never grows tired.

Aftermath: Carter, the good guy in this set piece, enjoyed belated attention as one of the game's best players and kept hammering balls. In '94, he set a record with 30 RBIs in April and also became the tenth player to accumulate 300 homers and 200 steals in a career. He finished in '98 after stints with the Orioles and Giants, having authored 396 home runs and a .306 average. And Williams? Over the ensuing winter, his house was egged and his life threatened by outraged Phillies' fans. Then before he could toe the rubber again, he was traded. Not surprisingly, he never pitched effectively again, and after playing with three teams in three years, he was gone, to live in shared misery with Charlie Root, Ralph Branca, Goose Gossage, Tracy Stallard, and the ghost of Donnie Moore.

Branca may be right that being part of epic history, even as victim of the hero, is a saving grace. But I doubt the pain of surrendering an epochal gopher ball ever goes away.

Beef on the Hook

In typical fashion, baseball dimmed the glow of Carter's dramatic homer by following it with more demented labor-management posturing that led to the strike that killed half a season and the World Series in '94, and the first month of the '95 season. Also dimmed was the buzz being made by yet another new home run generation shaking out, unearthing new league leaders nearly each year. These included Fred McGriff and Kevin Mitchell in '89, the pachyderm-like Cecil Fielder (who blasted 51 for the Tigers), and Ryne Sandberg in '90, Juan Gonzalez in '92, and for the first time, one Barry Bonds, who after seven seasons with the Pirates came to the Giants in '93 and rang up 46 homers, 123 RBIs, 29 steals, a .336 average—and his third MVP in four years.

Though the two sides "resolved" the rift by agreeing to do exactly nothing about runaway salaries and rich-market imbalance for another six years, the game teetered, at least for a little while, until crowds began streaming back in even greater numbers. Obviously, the players and owners didn't save the game. So what did?

One guess.

Indeed, had the '94 season played out in full, upper-case, home run history might have been made right then and there. Consider that with no team playing more than 118 games that year, the league leaders both cleared *40* home runs (the Mariners' Ken Griffey Jr., 40, and the Giants' Matt Williams, 43), with six others hitting over 30. There were more hits and runs that year than in '87, and in the NL more homers per game, too, .95 (and a near-record 1.11 in the AL). Need I even tell you that strikeouts per game were stratospheric—6.03 and 6.32, easily new records.

When baseball returned in '95, the hitting wasn't quite there—it was actually a pitcher's year—and still one man hit 50 homers, the Indians' scabrous Albert Belle, and three had 40, the Mariners' Jay Buhner, the White Sox' Frank Thomas, and the Rockies' Dante Bichette.

Conspicuously absent from the party, however, was the duo that begat much of the new home run obsessions, the Bash Brothers. Mark McGwire was doing penance on the injury list. And by '94, Jose Canseco was a DH and a semi-joke, dealt to yet another team, the Red Sox. Now almost any move he made caused an injury to his overburdened body—his back, rib cage, groin, elbow. Recurring ligament and joint injuries, one should know, are classic markers of steroid use. The return for the Red Sox was 24 and 28 homers, chump change, and in '97 he was gone again, traded back to the A's—only to miss half of *that* season with a back injury. Goodbye, Oakland, again. Hello Toronto, where Canseco did register 42 homers and 107 RBIs, hitting .237 with a league-high 159 strikeouts and just 65 walks.

In the degraded baseball parlance of today, this meant Canseco had a "comeback" season. And the chance that he might hit some long homers would keep him in the game another three seasons, with three teams, slogging away in vain to try to reach 500 career homers and ending up with 462. (A Hall-of-Fame number? Forget it. Cooperstown would sooner enshrine Osama bin Laden.) But Canseco never lost his real talent—

adding another domestic abuse arrest in '99 and an aggravated battery charge in a street fight in 2001.

Unlike Canseco, McGwire truly was born again. In '95, while playing only 104 games, he clocked 39 homers with 90 RBIs in just 317 at-bats—or 1 homer every 8.3 at-bats, the best one-season ratio ever until then. On June 11, McGwire hit homers in three consecutive at-bats against the Red Sox. Combined with the 2 he had hit the day before, that made him the only man other than Ralph Kiner to rack 5 in two games twice in a career.

Then came '96. On June 25 he hit No. 300. A month later he blasted 1 into the fifth deck at the Skydome, joining Canseco and Carter in that achievement. On September 14 he hit his 50th, against the Indians' Chad Ogea; eight days later he homered twice in the same inning against the Mariners, and finished with a league-high 52—in only 423 at-bats, or 1 every 8.1, breaking his own record for home run efficiency. McGwire also drove in 113 runs and hit .312. With his free agency impending in '97, the timing could not have been better.

Or the pitching worse. The capitulation to hitting now complete, in '96 the two leagues set records for most runs (5.4 AL, 4.7 NL) and home runs per game (1.21, 0.98) and highest ERA ever (5.00, 4.23). Oh, and for the most strikeouts ever (6.38 per game in the AL, 6.7 in the NL), but how much does that matter now? That season, as well, no less than *eight* men in the NL hit at least 40 dingers, led by the Rockies' Andres Galarraga who hit 47. Another, lightly regarded Mets catcher, Todd Hundley, hit 41, tying Roy Campanella's one-year record for a catcher. In the AL, the Orioles shattered the '61 Yankees one-year team record of 240, with 257—one of *seven* teams that hit over 200 home runs. One Oriole—*leadoff hitter* Brady Anderson—at age 32, with a previous home run high of 21, and coming off 16 homers in 554 at-bats in '95, now went deep 11 times in April alone, tying the AL record, set a major-league record late in the month with leadoff homers in *four* straight games, and in all poked 50 in 579 at-bats, with 110 RBIs and a .297 average.

Anderson, who had been known as a slap hitter with great speed (53 steals in '92, and over '94 and '95 a then-league record 36 in a row), had once before hit 20 homers and stolen 50 bases in a season, becoming the first ever to do that. Now, he reversed the numbers: 50 homers, 21 steals. And with all that, he came in ninth in the MVP vote won by Gonzalez, who hit 47 homers, drove in 144, and hit .314 with the Rangers. How do you hit 50 homers and get lost in the shuffle? Easy, when everyone else and his brother is hitting home runs by the boatload. Indeed, while our man Brady would revert to the land of singles and doubles, the man who beat him out for the league lead was, at age 34, just getting started on his *real* home run hitting.

The Pendulum Swings

Advances in yarn and cork go only so far in explaining this bandolier of home run hitters. By '96, many factors all came due like a maturing Treasury bill. First, there were the bats—both the ones used in the big leagues and those what weren't.

Remember what Hank Greenberg said about those effortless opposite-field homers? Forget about steroids and the weight room for a minute. Just as critical was the use of aluminum bats that came into vogue in high school and college games in the late '80s to save on costs but which were prohibited in the majors. The whiny "ping" of a ball meeting a metal bat may be a sacrilege, but schoolboy hitters love the tin-foil bats because they're such a shortcut. Hit a ball solidly with one and, even if you shank one with a terrible swing, the ball will go far, most notably to the opposite field with a swing that reaches across the plate.

Big league coaches at first believed this intrinsically flawed illusion of all-field slugging would retard hitters when they came up and would have to adapt to the real world, in which good hitters didn't swing at outside pitches. But guess what? By hitting the "wrong way," the new crowd had actually programmed their mechanics to go deep the other way even when they switched to wood bats. And because they did, they began crowding the plate to jump on those outside pitches—without fear of being dusted by increasingly timid pitchers.

Why? For the same reason. Because aluminum bats are so light, and hitters get around with them so quickly, young pitchers eschewed the venerable philosophy of pitching inside, taking their chances on the outside corner. A whole generation of pitchers got to the majors in the '90s and fell into a new culture in which striking a batter with a pitch, *any* pitch, was a must to avoid—bringing the game full circle back to the 1840s when pitchers said, "Please, hit this ball, sir."

Surely the days of Drysdale and Gibson owning the inside corner and clanging one off a batter's skull with impunity if he dug in too close were over. For old-timers scarred with seam indentations, the World War III brawls touched off by a ball nicking an oversensitive hitter on the sleeve with a change-up are a farce. Another is seeing Barry Bonds, Mo Vaughn, and others step to the plate wearing armored plates on their forearms as they lean over the plate and merrily pound outside pitches. The upshot: according to Bill James, while opposite-field home runs have nearly tripled since the big home run year of 1987, hit batsmen have merely doubled. (For reference, triples and steals have declined, as have intentional walks—except for Bonds—since there are just too many damn power hitters in any lineup to face with men on base.)

Wood bats, meanwhile, keep getting lighter, thinner-handled, and have more weight in the barrel. In no particular order, here is a cross-section of bats that have been swung by the heavy hitters over the last decade, in ounces and length in inches:

Mike Schmidt: 35.7, 34.4
Ken Griffey Jr.: 34, 32 (1990), 34, 29 (1998)
Alex Rodriguez: 34, 31
Jose Canseco: 35, 32
Cal Ripken Jr.: 35, 36
Eddie Murray: 35, 32
Juan Gonzalez: 36, 35
Rafael Palmeiro: 34, 32
Barry Bonds: 34, 31.8
Shawn Green: 34, 32
Dave Winfield: 36, 33
Frank Thomas: 34.5, 32
Mo Vaughn: 36, 36.5
Mark McGwire: 34.5, 33
Sammy Sosa: 33.75, 32

Babe Ruth could have used most of these bats to pick his teeth. (After the 2002 Mets debacle, we would advise Mo Vaughn to lighten up his gut and his bat.) Babe wouldn't know what to make of today's hollowed-out barrel ends, either, a nuance that adds velocity to a swing. For Ruth, corking the bat was high-tech. (The proof that Ruth corked was discovered in 1983 with a patch of different wood affixed to one of his bats on its top end.) But today's bats are so easy to split open and reveal alien matter that corking has become passé. Instead, hitters have taken to the legal embellishment of slathering layers of lacquer on the wood for more heft. Who needs corking anyway when fences are so reachable to begin with?

Which brings me to another immense factor—the new round of ballparks built in the '90s, which blessedly moved away from the homogeneous 60,000-seat salad bowls and toward intimate curios. These publicly funded parks coincided not only with the decade's economic boom that revived their inner-city environs but also with the home run boom—and in fact most of them were consciously designed to be home run emporiums, or would become one, like the first of the new stadiums, the second Comiskey Park. When that park opened in '91, it had already-shallow dimensions, 375 feet in the right field alley and 400 feet in center; in 2001, these were shortened to a ridiculous 335 and 372.

While the concrete-slab parks of the '70s and '80s were often derided as "cookie cutter" edifices, the truth is that the varied architectural styles of most of the parks that followed—Camden Yards (Baltimore), Coors Field (Denver), Jacobs Field (Cleveland), The Ballpark in Arlington (Texas), Minute Maid Park (nee Enron Field, Houston), Comerica Park (Detroit), Miller Park (Milwaukee), PNC Park (Pittsburgh)—house nearly identical narrow dimensions. They also, as baseball-only parks with no need to accommodate a gridiron, have narrow foul ground areas that deprive pitchers of easy outs they used to get. In fact, the only spacious areas in the new parks are right–center field in San Francisco's Pac Bell Park—no less than 420 feet (though this is more than counterbalanced by the little-league-ready 307 feet to dead right, just in front of the bleacher porch that could be called Bondsville)—and all of Safeco Field, which ironically won public funding because of Ken Griffey Jr.'s home runs at the Kingdome, which helped set a record 264 team homers in '97.

The real windfall of homers, of course, came at Coors Field, where dimensions don't matter nearly as much as the 5,200-foot altitude. This was apparent in the Rockies' inaugural year, 1993, when as a rag-tag bunch of nobodies they hit the seventh-most homers in the NL, 142—and their pitchers gave up the most, 181. In the time since, they have led the league four times—toting up a then-league record 237 in '97—and given up the most four more times. In '96 they set the record for home-field home runs, 149. The Rockies regularly average around 8 runs a game—both for and against. In '95, their third year, they had four men with over 30 dingers, and three over 40 in '96 (Andres Galarrage, Vinny Castilla, Ellis Burks) and '97 (with Larry Walker taking Burks' place). Up until then, only the '73 Braves had three men over 40. The Rockies also had two 30/30 men in '95, Burks and Dante Bichette.

At high altitude, a commoner can become a king. Witness Castilla, a gaunt third baseman projected no more than a 15-homer hitter, who raked over 40 homers and 100 RBIs for three straight years, with a monstrous 46 and 144 in '98, when he also hit .319. In '95 he hit 3 homers in the National League Division Series (NLDS) against the Braves. Among third basemen, only Eddie Mathews, Mike Schmidt, and my man Vinny have hit 30 homers five straight years. And yet never during that span did anyone consider him anything but a fluke of Coors Field, where he hit over 60 percent of his homers. Nor did the Rockies feel overly compelled to keep him, and they let Castilla go in the 2000 expansion draft to the Tampa Bay Devil Rays, with whom he was once again a pauper, sliding to 6 homers in an injury-jinxed season. He was traded to the Astros in '01, hitting 23, then went to the Braves this past season and hit 12, in near-obscurity.

As for the Braves, baseball's other high-elevation team, they also enjoyed an advantage. Even after moving to Turner Field in '76—a park built in the round for the Olympics that year, resulting in a baseball configuration with deep power alleys—they've been at or near the top of the pack in homers each year. And unlike the Rockies, in pitching as well.

So, given all these propitious power conditions, you are no doubt asking why is it that when the Yankees were yet again resurrected in the mid-1990s, the home run was not their modus operandi. Or at least so it seemed. The new Bronx Bombers were a patient, conservative lot, grinding down pitchers by fouling off borderline strikes with defensive swings to get to the fat strikes—a vintage approach that struck younger fans as radically new—and driving balls into the gaps. In '96, their first pennant season in 15 years, the Yankees' 112 homers were twelfth in the league, and the best on the team was Bernie Williams' 29.

Still, these are the Yankees, so the homer—the killer homer—was always a hair-trigger away. Even of course when it's not really a homer.

In Game 1 of the '96 American League Championship Series (ALCS) against the Orioles, the Yankees trailed 4-3 when Derek Jeter hit a deep fly ball to the Yankee Stadium right field wall that seemed to be falling directly into the right fielder Tony Tarasco's glove when a 12-year-old fan—the now-immortal Jeffrey Maier—reached his glove out inches above Tarasco's and intercepted the ball. This was surely fan interference—except that a myopic umpire, Rich Garcia, with emphatic stupidity, ruled it a home run and a tie game that the Yankees won in the eleventh on a dinger by Williams.

Breaking rules at Yankee Stadium has its rewards. The snot-nosed kid became a fleeting celebrity, and appeared on the *Today Show* the next morning. Eventually the Yankees would clinch the climactic fifth game of that series with a 6-run third inning during which they cracked 3 bona fide homers, though we assume some umpire or other would have helped them, if needed.

Then came the World Series against the Braves, when they lost the first two games at home. Then, after taking Game 3 in Atlanta, they were down 6-3 in the eighth in Game 4. They got two men on with two outs when backup catcher Jim Leyritz—a man who was born for this moment—took reliever Mark Wohlers out of the park to tie it. The Yankees won 8-6 in ten and two games later they put the Series away. The Leyritz homer was exactly half their home run output in the six games (to the Braves' 4). But then, as we know, there are homers and there are *homers*. For half a decade, the Yankees hit *homers*.

Ah, but a *homer* can cut both ways. A year later, the Yankees had the American League Division Series (ALDS) won against the Indians, up two games to one and leading 2-1 in the eighth inning of Game 4, and they had the ball in the right hand of their godhead reliever, Mariano Rivera. But Rivera laid his "cut" fastball in too far to Sandy Alomar Jr., who punched it over the right field fence at Jacobs Field for a tie, and the Tribe won an inning later, and the next day, to salt away the series. Still, that was the last time until Luis Gonzalez came to bat in the ninth inning four years later that anyone beat the Yankee formula for victory.

The moral of the story is that all the cheap home runs in the world won't do much good in the postseason, when despite the overall worsening of major league pitching—and especially those woeful middle-inning relievers—the pitching usually dominates. The most prolific power team in history, the '97 Mariners, hit 264 homers and won ninety games and the AL West title—and lost the ALDS to the Orioles, who held them to a draw in homers at 6 apiece. The pennant winners that year, the Indians, were second to the Mariners in home runs, with 220—and lost the World Series in seven games to the Florida Marlins. During the season, the Marlins had hit a puny 136 homers, tenth in the NL. In the Series, they held the Tribe even, with 8 homers for each. The Braves, with their 11 straight homer-fueled NL East titles, have gone to five World Series yet won just one—mainly because they suck at getting, well, the *homer*. The last one they had was David Justice's shot in Game 6 of the '95 World Series to beat the Indians 1-0 and win their championship.

Of course, timing is everything. Kirby Puckett is in the Hall of Fame because he had it—his walkoff homer in Game 6 of the '91 Series against the Braves a game before the Twins won it all. Puckett's career stats are no better than those of Don Mattingly, who didn't have it. And while Barry Bonds' Hall-of-Fame status was never in doubt, his reputation was until he finally stopped stinking up his postseason appearances in October 2002.

Speaking of Bonds, in '97, five years after signing his six-year, $43.9 million contract with the Giants, he was diligently constructing rather impressive home run totals, with the swagger of a Hall-of-Fame player—and a Hall-of-Fame jerk. Bonds, of course, inherited more than a few of his father's boorish habits, such as treating grounders to infielders and non–home run fly balls as non-running plays; to this day, he's good for a dozen singles a year that should be doubles or triples after those forsaken fly balls wind up bouncing off the wall.

Still, don't even try to pretend this man isn't among the top five players of all time—only Ruth, Aaron, Williams, and Mays were better—or that he isn't the right kind of long-ball hitter, in that he strikes out relatively little (Bonds as a rookie fanned 102 times in 413 at-bats, the only time he's ever hit the hundred mark), doesn't swing at pitches he can't drive, and walks—a lot. He has also stolen a lot of bases and won a lot of Gold Gloves in left field. And as he reached his mid-30s, he got even better at these disciplines. (Remember DiMaggio and Mantle flailing away for homers late in their careers?)

But Bonds clearly had a problem—he just couldn't make his team win, or even much better, and the one time he did with the Giants, in 1997 when they won the NL West title and Bonds tied his father's record of five 30/30 seasons, he went 3-for-12 with no homers and 2 RBIs against the Marlins in the NLDS and the team was swept in the three games. (In three previous playoff series while with the Pirates, he had hit .167, .148, and .261, with 1 homer, 3 RBIs.)

As late as that year, in fact, while Bonds' ongoing statistics were stunning—in '96, when he reached the 40/40 level, he joined his father, Willie Mays, and Andre Dawson as the only men to reap 300 homers and 300 steals—he was not the big noise in home runs. Far ahead of him, for one, was Albert Belle, the greatest waste of talent in history. No one in the modern era has hit the ball as hard and long for as sustained a period. Yet Belle, like Canseco, will be waiting a *long* time for a call from Cooperstown because he too made it so easy to loathe him.

Even when he was a star at LSU, and called Joey Belle, he was bad news, a guy with an attitude and a drinking problem. As 1989 pro draft neared, Braves GM Bobby Cox told his staff, "If you pick Belle in any round, you're fired." When Indians GM John Hart held his nose and chose the renamed Albert Jojuan Belle in round two, the kid was in alcohol rehab. When he came out in '90, he refused to run out ground balls and was sent down—sowing a peevish relationship with, well, the world. In '91, the bull-strong, 6-foot-2, 210-pound outfielder hit 28 homers with

90 RBIs and a .282 average. Next year the numbers were 36, 112, and .260, then 38, a league-high 129, and .290. In '95, he led baseball with 50 big ones and 126 RBIs, hit .317, and slugged .690. He scored 121 runs. He became the first to have 50 homers and 50 doubles in a season. He tied Ruth with 17 homers in September and set a record with 31 over two months. He tied the record of 5 homers over two games. He had 13 over 16 games. He had 8 straight hits that were home runs, then a record. He struck out only 80 times.

And he lost the MVP to Mo Vaughn, who had 39 homers, 126 RBIs, and a .300 average.

Why? It may have had something to do with Belle's never-ending fines, suspensions, and attacks on fans (one of whom he hit in the chest with a thrown ball) and media people (one of whom, a woman, he chased around the locker room in anger). Then there was the time he was caught using a corked bat, drawing a seven-game suspension in '94. Belle by mid-decade was in the baseball Gulag. In '96 he had 48 homers, a baseball-high 148 RBIs—most in the game since 1949—and a .311 average. He had 2 World Series homers against the Braves. And he came in third in the MVP vote to Juan Gonzalez (47, 144, .314) and Alex Rodriguez (36, 123, .358).

A free agent in '97, Belle signed with the White Sox for five years and $60.5 million, and after a bad year rebounded to 49 homers, 152 RBIs, and a .328 average in '98. But he was a self-made caricature of villainy. During these years it came out that he lost $40,000 gambling on sports (apparently not baseball, so Bud Selig did nothing about it) and he was charged with domestic battery. And he wasn't through doing damage yet.

Even so, at the time, Belle was seen as a greater threat to Maris's record than Bonds. As was White Sox first baseman DH Frank Thomas, a frighteningly large fellow at 6 feet 5 inches, and 260 pounds who had passed up a potentially lucrative football career while at Auburn to convince people he could play baseball. Thomas was unusually shy and deferential, traits that belied the nickname that grew on him, "The Big Hurt." When he said things like, "I'd have signed for $5,000, that's how bad I wanted to play baseball," he could actually be believed. And he proved it, signing as a seventh-round draft pick and working up from Double-A ball. In '91 he set off on seven straight years with at least 28 homers, a .300 average, and 100 walks, RBIs, and runs—an unprecedented run. Thomas swung hard and level, and with care. He struck out admirably little for a modern-era slugger—as few as 54 times even while hitting a White Sox–record 41 homers in '93.

As with Bonds, as Thomas matured his homers escalated without damage to his other stats—hitting as high as .349 in '95 with 40 homers. He won consecutive MVP awards in '93 and '94. The former year, he drove the Sox to an AL West title and hit .353 in the ALCS in between being pitched around by the Blue Jays, who walked him 10 times. A year later, he was tearing up the league when the strike hit, having hit 38 homers with a *.729* slugging percentage, the highest since Ted Williams' .731 in 1957.

When Belle signed with the White Sox as a free agent in '97, he had the luxury of having Thomas hitting behind him. So leave it to Belle to screw up, sinking to 30 homers and a .274 average, leaving Thomas to do the heavy lifting—35 homers, 125 RBIs, a .347 average—and keep the team in the race all year before finishing second.

By now, however, both Thomas and Belle were ebbing in the home run wars, losing rank to Juan Gonzalez and Rafael Palmeiro. From '91 on, this Latin tandem has hit at least 40 homers a combined eight times, driven in at least 100 runs eight times *each,* and hit over .300 five times each, all without much panache or fanfare—although people did learn more than they needed to know about Palmeiro when he began appearing in TV commercials for another kind of performance-enhancer, Viagra.

The Rangers had dibs on both men from '90 to '93, Gonzalez as a stone-fingered outfielder, Palmeiro as a sure-handed first baseman, but even after the latter clanged 37 homers in '93 the Rangers leaped at the chance to import free agent first baseman Will Clark (who was Palmeiro's teammate at Mississippi State). Livid, Palmeiro, himself a free agent, jumped to the Orioles and helped make them a wild-card team in '96 and a division winner in '97, and hit 3 homers in the team's two losing playoff series. In three seasons in Baltimore, he slammed 39, 39, and 38 homers and drove in 142 RBIs in '96.

Gonzalez, meanwhile, remained in Texas for eleven years as an RBI man like few others in history, though this is not well known. Gonzalez hit 43 homers in '92 and 46 in '93 (when he also struck out 143 times), but his first monster year came in '96 when his 47 homers, 144 RBIs, and .314 average netted him the MVP award. The following season, despite a thumb injury that cost him 24 games, he drove home 131 runs in 133 games, along with 42 homers. And wait 'til you hear about what he did in '98, because you probably overlooked it at the time.

Gonzalez is the classic '90s-era slugger, buying his dingers by swinging at anything in the surrounding neighborhood, almost never walking, and striking out in great gobs. In '92, he had a truly ugly ratio of 143 strikeouts to 35 walks. As I said, this is MVP stuff these days, and Gonzalez has won two of them. But give him *his* due; he was about the only Ranger player who didn't melt when the team rolled over for the Yankees in the '96 ALDS, hitting .437 with a record-tying 5 homers and 9 RBIs in the four-game defeat. (He waited until the '98 and '99 rematches before rolling over with everybody else on the team.) Gonzalez still hits gobs of homers and drives in gobs of runs. But how ironic is that even during that career year of '98, he fell off the home run radar screen?

Even by '97, the lay of the land had again changed, primarily because of baseball's other fortunate son, Ken Griffey Jr. The seed of the Reds' outfielder during their glory years, Griffey had been an habitue in the Riverfront Stadium clubhouse as a kid and like Barry Bonds parlayed the family name into an early big league paycheck—right after graduating from Cincinnati's Moeller High School, he was made the top pick in the '87 draft by the moribund Mariners; a year and a half later, at age 19, he was a big leaguer. Griffey was a left-handed power hitter, too, but where Bonds' swing was short and scythe-like, the extraordinarily gifted 6-foot-2, 210-pound "Junior" had a huge metronomic sweep to his that seemed to begin at his ankles and end there after a great whoosh of a backswing.

The first time he came up, April 3, 1989, Griffey doubled. The first pitch he saw at the Kingdome, a week later against the White Sox, he went yard on Eric King in a 6-5 victory. Only a hand injury kept him from the Rookie of the Year award; in 127 games he had 16 homers, 61 RBIs, and a .264 average. He then crashed into the elite in '90, when Ken Sr. finished his career with a gimmick stop in Seattle, making them the first and only father-son teammates in history, and to hit homers in the same game. Over the next four seasons, his power numbers inclined, from 22 to 45 homers, and from 80 to 109 RBIs. From '93 to 2001, only once, when he broke his hand in '95, did he fail to yank at least 40 homers. (I am still agog at his 40 homers in 111 games in the strike-savaged '94 season.) Take out '95 again and he also hit over .300 every year from '90 to '97. In '93 he homered in eight straight games, tying the record—and missed by inches of making it nine straight games the next day when he doubled high off the wall.

Griffey was an All Star for ten straight years, and his debutante ball was the '92 Game in San Diego—surely an All-Star Game for its time, meaning that the AL won and the hitters ruled. In the first inning, the junior circuit popped 7 straight hits for a 4-0 lead that grew to 6-0 in the third when Griffey jacked a home run off no less than Greg Maddux. Ruben Sierra jacked another in the sixth to make it 10-0. In all, the AL had a record 19 hits and won 13-6, and Griffey's single, double and homer earned him the game's MVP—twelve years after Ken Sr. had won the same honor.

Though not a prolific base-stealer like Bonds, Griffey covered more ground from his post in center field. He won his first Gold Glove in '90 and one every year through '99. Unlike Bonds, too, he made his team better, lugging the Mariners out of baseball's gutter and to the AL West crown in '95—whereupon he helped derrick the Yankees in the five-game ALDS conquest with 5 homers, 7 RBIs and a .391 mark, as well as scoring the series-ending run. (Funny how these things tend to balance out; in the '97 ALDS against the Orioles, he tanked, going 2-for-15 with no homers.)

Up until then, Griffey was a humble young man sanguine in his leadership role. But the rise of another precocious superstar on the team, shortstop Alex Rodriguez, would hit a nerve in Griffey that changed the locus of his career.

The dashing "A-Rod," son of a New York City shoemaker who shuttled his family to and from the Dominican Republic and then to Miami, was attracting big-league scouts' attention at Westminster Christian High School. A willowy 6 feet 3 inches and 190 pounds, Rodriguez quickly fused into a triumvirate of hunky AL shortstops, with Derek Jeter and the Red Sox's Nomar Garciaparra, any of whom can do about anything on a field—though what sets Rodriguez apart is a buoyant swing that seems unhurried yet at the point of impact turns the ball around with astonishing force.

To be sure, Rodriguez is a big, solidly built man, and because Cal Ripken Jr. had broken the mold for lanky and muscular men to play shortstop it was easy to overlook just how much heft Rodriguez packed. Still, he was of the sinewy, lean genotype, and like Willie Mays seemed smaller than he was. Indeed, Rodriguez relied little on brute strength for his power, as he told this writer in a 2000 *Sport* interview:

> It's all leverage. I'm tall, wiry. I have good mechanics, good wrists. I get my hands and the bat through the hitting zone real quick and lift the ball up in the air. It's funny, when I came up, people said I was a great defensive shortstop and my hitting might never catch up. I thought I'd be a 15–home run guy.

Talk about your miscalculations. In '96, his first full year with the Mariners, Rodriguez raked 36 homers with 123 RBIs, a .358 average, and 379 total bases, a record for shortstops. These numbers placed him second in that MVP race behind Gonzalez. When he dipped to 23 homers, 84 RBIs, and a .300 average in '97, people assumed he had reached his natural level. Bad assumption.

But a good assumption was that Griffey would be the best bet to break Maris's record. In the home run carnage of '96—when in the then-record avalanche of 4,962 homers 17 of 45 players who had hit 20 or more homers by September had established new career highs, and 14 hit over 40 and 39 over 30—Griffey, now baseball's highest-paid player, having signed a four-year, $34 million deal, bested his personal-best from 40 to 49, even missing 20 games to injury. (By the way, one other name in the personal-best group was a late-blooming Cubs' right fielder, Sammy Sosa, who had 40.)

In '97, Griffey was in a sweet groove. He pounded 13 homers in April and 23 through May, both records. By September 10, he had climbed to 50, and with seventeen games left, 61 was doable, and even logical, given that Griffey was on a ridiculous hot streak—reaching the 50 mark with 7 homers in seven games since August 31, and 17 in thirty-one games from August 7. Bar graph comparisons with Ruth and Maris were in the papers and *The New York Times* ran a sports section page-one piece subtitled: "For Griffey, So Little Time With So Much At Stake: Home Run Mark."

As it turned out, that was prophetic, only a year early. Griffey blasted Nos. 54 and 55 on September 22 and finished with 56, the fifth-best total in history. He also hit .304 and had a career-high 147 RBIs, more than earning him his second MVP—this one by unanimous selection. However, in the last two weeks of the season he was passed in homers by the reincarnated Mark McGwire, even though he was playing for his second team and in his second league that year.

With McGwire's free agency looming and the A's out of the pennant race and in money straits, he had been dealt on July 31 to the Cardinals. When he left Oakland, he had 34 homers in his pocket. But in his first ten games in a new league, he looked lost, going deep not once. Then he found his way and tacked 24 dingers in the last forty-one games, ending with 58 big flies—tying Jimmie Foxx and Hank Greenberg for the most homers ever by a right-handed hitter. (Over '96 and '97, he hit a total of 110, beating Foxx's old record by 4.)

Think of the bizarre anomaly—and the asterisks—of McGwire breaking the home run record that year, which he would have accomplished while not leading *either league* in the category. And he had a shot at it, too. On September 6—the day he signed a three-year, $25.8 deal to stay in St. Louis—he hit a 517-foot meteor against the Dodgers, the longest home run ever hit at Busch Stadium. That one tied him with Griffey at 52. But he missed, as well, by 4, so Bud Selig caught a break.

Still, for McGwire, who became the first since Ruth to ring up consecutive 50-homer seasons, the promised land was in sight. And while Griffey would himself get closer still to Maris, Home Run Mark indeed would be the overriding theme of the wildest, freakiest home run season of 'em all.

16

Records Meant to Be Broken

70 (and 66)

The '98 season was "McGwire-ized" from start to finish. But before I begin laying on hands about the home run cannonade that for many fans demarcated baseball's alleged new "Golden Age," I'd like to say a huzzah for a man who was gone from the game that year after a much-underrated twenty-one-season run.

When last I left Eddie Murray, he was blasting through the '80s, leading the Orioles to a championship in '83 (when his 2 homers in Game 6 against the Phillies clinched the World Series), and among other things collecting a 3-homer, 13-total base-game against the Angels on August 26, 1985. You'll recall, too, how unlovable Murray was. Well, that never really changed. Even his own owner, Edward Bennett Williams, couldn't abide him and when Murray was slow to recover from a hamstring injury, Williams implied he was a slacker.

Murray, who by all accounts opened his mouth only once in the decade—to demand a trade—got it in '89, when he was shipped to the Dodgers. He hit a career-high .300 in '90, signed a two-year, $7.5 million free agent deal with the Mets two years later, and rang up his 400th homer on May 3, 1992. A month later he beat Mickey Mantle's RBI record for a switch hitter (1,509) en route to his sixth 100-RBI season.

But at age 36 he was on the slide, and when he signed with the Indians in '94 it looked like he was on the make for personal records. And he got them—including hitting homers from each side of the plate for the eleventh time to pass Mantle and notching his 3,000 hit in '95. And how happy must he have been under that hard-staring face when in his first game against the Orioles, at Camdem Yards, he smacked one off the foul pole. But Murray was no hanger-on. He hit .323 with 21 homers in '94, a vital cog in the Tribe's World Series berth that year.

For a guy with no personality, Murray's leadership was undeniable. In mid-1996, he consented to return to the Orioles, who were under new ownership that wanted to do a make-good for his exile. In his first game, he hit a homer, No. 493 lifetime. On August 10 came his 18th career grand slam, tying him with Willie McCovey for second all-time behind Lou Gehrig's 23. On September 6 he sent No. 500 on its way off the Tigers' Felipe Lira, becoming the second to rack 500 homers and 3,000 hits, with Mays and Aaron. He hit 10 homers down the stretch to help put the Orioles in the playoffs, and hit .400 in the ALDS against the Indians. The end for Murray didn't come until he played his 3,000th game and hit his nineteenth grand slam playing the next season with the Angels.

Longevity was also McGwire's ally. At 34, he seemed just then to be at his peak and cruising on a second wind. Coming off 58 homers, he was surrounded by media from spring training on in '98. His batting practice turns, when he sent rockets into distant seats, were must-see events. And McGwire set the theme in stone on Opening Day when he pounded a grand slam at Busch Stadium off the Dodgers' Ramon Martinez, and homered in each of the first four games, something only Willie Mays had done in '71. On May 8 he hit No. 400 against the Mets at Shea Stadium—doing that quicker than anyone in history, in 4,726 at-bats. When he collected his twentieth of the season on May 19, it was one of 3 that day, the second time he'd done that within two months. (Only twelve men had previously had two 3-homer games, over a full season.) It was also the fastest anyone had ever gotten 20 homers.

By June 30, McGwire had 37 bombs, tying Reggie Jackson's mark for most homers at the All-Star break. When he got 43, on July 20 against the Padres, down went Johnny Mize's 1940 club record. Things clearly were getting crazy with McGwire—who didn't drive in a single run from July 7 to August 7 with anything *but* a homer, which few found to be out of whack, though Allen Barra, writing in *The New York Times,* seemed to say as much obliquely, noting, "McGwire's swing is designed to produce home runs (and strikeouts)," and that "anything else—doubles, singles, the occasional ground ball—is an accident."

But then, this *wasn't* really out of whack in baseball as it stood. As

McGwire's home run stash burgeoned, he was hardly alone. Griffey, for example, with a homer against the Indians on April 13 reached *300* faster than anyone except Jimmie Foxx, at 28 years, 143 days (180 days behind), and would crack his fiftieth on September 7 against the Orioles, becoming the second to hit 50 in consecutive seasons. Bonds (who on May 28 was walked intentionally with the *bases loaded* by the Diamondbacks, for only the fourth time in history) hit *his* 400th on August 23 off the Marlins' Kirt Ojala—becoming the world's first 400-homer/400-steal man, and also set an NL record in September by reaching base 15 straight times. And Juan Gonzalez achieved his own All-Star break masterpiece—*101* RBIs, matching Hank Greenberg's 1935 output. While bar graphs in the papers tracked McGwire's home runs vis-à-vis Ruth and Maris, Gonzalez was challenging a far more long-standing record, Hack Wilson's untouchable 191 RBIs.

But it was another lesser-known slugger who got the most attention by staying closest to McGwire. This, of course, was Sammy Sosa, who even with his previous 40 and 38-homer seasons now seemed to come out of nowhere in '98. In truth, Sosa had traversed a long and at times trying career. And yet this *was* a very different Sosa than the 6-foot, 170-pound pipecleaner who arose from unspeakable poverty in the Dominican Republic to sign with the Rangers in '87. Sosa had played in San Pedro de Macoris using a milk carton as a glove, and when he went to the minors a Rangers' scout filed a report that called him "malnourished."

The Sosa seen in tapes from those early years appears to be an impostor, a gaunt stick figure taking windy swings at terrible pitches. The swing would stay the same; it was Sosa's body and hitting sensibilities that changed, but over time. In his rookie year, 1989, he played twenty-five games and hit his first dinger, off no less than Roger Clemens, on June 21. A month later, it was still his only extra-base hit. Batting .238 with 3 RBIs, with 20 strikeouts in 84 at-bats, he was traded—with the consent of the Rangers' majority owner, a fella named George W. Bush—to the White Sox in a five-player deal. Sosa did marginally better, with 3 homers, 10 RBIs, and a .273 average, then evolved, haltingly. In '90, he was the only hitter in the AL to put up double-figures in doubles, triples, homers (15), RBIs, and steals. He also struck out 150 times, made 13 errors in the outfield, hit .233, and was charged with beating his wife.

Although Sosa was still only 22, the Sox had no patience for him. In '91, after he hit 10 homers with 33 RBIs, a .203 average and 98 strikeouts in 116 games, he was demoted to the bushes, and in '92 deported to the Cubs. At this point, Sosa was close to washing out. That season, playing only sixty-seven games because of injuries, he hit .260 with 8 homers. The Cubs, though, stuck with him and in '93 came that different Sosa, one that had somehow attached twenty pounds of muscle on himself over the winter. He was different at the plate, too. The swing was still hungry and erratic, but with his new, thick forearms and cinderblock legs, he didn't have to leap and lunge at pitches. Hanging back in a crouch, he could release his power all at once, in a smooth and cohesive surge that, when he made contact, sent balls screaming to all fields. Even he seemed a tad surprised, taking a giant bunny-hop out of the box as he followed the arc of those long balls—a reflex that soon became extended into a marketable trademark.

Indeed, Sosa, playing for awful Cubs teams, became immensely popular at Wrigley Field before the country as a whole knew him. That '93 season, he cracked 33 homers with 93 RBIs, a .261 average, and the requisite 135 strikeouts, second in the league. He stole a career-high 36 bases, making him a 30/30 man for the first time (he did it again in '95) and began a skein of what has been eight straight 100-RBI years.

However, until '98 Sosa hit .300 only once, in '94, and was usually mired in the .250 to .260 range, leading Cubs manager Jim Riggleman to openly grouse after '97 that his impressionable and self-promoting cleanup hitter was perhaps too stat obsessed and too little team centered. Thus, as Sosa came in for the '98 season, he was walking on eggshells again. The Cubs did bring him some help, trading for left fielder Henry Rodriguez and third baseman José Hernandez, who would combine to hit 54 homers. Sosa was expected to get to a higher level.

And through the first two months, he stiffed. Through May 24, Sosa had 9 homers, *15* behind McGwire. Then he unchained, banking 2 against the Brewers the next day and went on to hit 21 homers over a thirty-day span, and 21 in twenty-four games through June 23—including 20 in June, a record for homers in any month. On July 27 he broke an improbable streak when he hit his *first* grand slam after a record 247 homers without one; the next day, he hit another, his second slam in four at-bats. When Sosa smacked No. 48 against the Cardinals on August 19 he was actually one up on McGwire—but only until Big Mac hit 2 later in the game. The next day, McGwire pounded another pair during a doubleheader against the Mets at Shea Stadium, Nos. 50 and 51—and was now the first to hit 50 in *three* straight seasons. Still Sosa kept on his tail. On August 31 each man had 55.

Up to now, Sosa had begged off inviting any rivalry with McGwire. "I'm not Mark McGwire," he said in July. "He's the man. If anyone is going to break Roger Maris's record, it's going to be him. Me, I'm just another kid on the block having a pretty good season."

Of course, Maris had said much the same thing in regard to Mantle in '61, and Sosa was just as eager to deflect any pressure on himself. Besides, all the attention was on McGwire anyway. As late as August 28, when Sosa hit No. 53 against the Rockies—two days before tying McGwire at 55—*The New York Times* finally got around to running a puff piece on Sosa, headlined "Hacker Becomes Hitter: Sosa Has Finest Season," and asked a good question: "He's chasing records, too, but where is Sosa-mania?"

In truth, Sosa was hardly without guile or conceit. His slavish praise of McGwire was sincere. It also helped to immunize him from the sophism attached to many Latin players as angry and sullen, or excessively carefree. These stereotypes were engendered mainly by Americans' impatience with the language barrier. Sosa, though, used his own language, with a contrived hand-sign routine that must have been cribbed from Sammy Davis Jr.'s peace and love gesticulations. As the *Times* described it:

> After every homer, Sosa unerringly finds a camera, grins and displays a flurry of taps and kisses. First he puts two fingers to his lips and kisses the sky. That's for his mother. Then he pats his chest and holds up a "V" sign. That's for Harry Caray, the late Cubs broadcaster.
>
> Fans could also learn Sosa's mantras. "Oh, what a country" is popular. And, "Making the playoffs is more important than hitting home runs." And, inevitably, "Mark McGwire is the man."

Concocted as all this was, Sosa became America's favorite foreign pet, and forced McGwire to buff his own public image and his crabby relationship with the media, lest he be swept away by "Sosa-mania." Indeed, that the great home run chase of '98 shared none of the dark, unpleasant side effects of the earlier ones in '61 and '74 had everything to do with the two men involved. Long treatises have been written about the racial détente that settled on the nation through the sunny symbiosis of one very white Southern Californian and one proud Latin. (Sosa, in San Pedro de Macoris, became a deity for keeping his home in the *barrio,* albeit with 10 automobiles and a mountain of gold jewelry dangling from his body; even some accounting discrepancies with the foundation he set up for Dominican hurricane victims didn't dent his standing.)

The glorified home run derby also counterbalanced the partisan stench coming out of The Capitol all that year. As the *Christian Science Monitor* headlined on September 18, "Sluggers Saving Graces: McGwire and Sosa Help Take the Nation's Mind off Clinton's Scandals."

Alas, the good vibrations lasted only as long as that one season, which is why it's almost quaint to re-read the overoptimistic takes in the media such as "Ballplayers For All Americans: McGwire and Sosa Rise Above Race" (*Washington Post,* September 12), and my favorite, the pithy "A Ball And A Bat: Exclamation Point Of Our Time. The Home Run Mystique Invokes The Power Of One Dramatic Blast To Pull People Together" (*Christian Science Monitor,* October 1).

There were other salubrious conditions stamping the race, including the simple fact that no one was stalking the holy ghost of Babe Ruth, and that Bud Selig, seeing dollar signs on each home run, played cheerleader. Selig faced one glitch in the serendipitous scenario in August when a reporter skulking around the Cardinal clubhouse peeked in McGwire's locker and found a bottle of something with a long, nearly unpronounceable name. Upon further inspection, it turned out to be an over-the-counter "food supplement" called androstenedione, which had found a market among the bodybuilding crowd because its chemical structure was only one small step removed from testosterone and thus believed to build muscle. The resulting furor in the media engulfed McGwire for a good week, though this whole episode was a comedy of ignorance. Because while "andro" is putatively a steroid, the difference from the real item was like Chicken of the Sea and caviar. While andro may or may not be dangerous to use, it is in fact next to useless in increasing muscle mass, though enough of it may grow a pretty nice rack of boobs on a man because of its conversion to *estrogen.*

McGwire clearly didn't gain an ounce of muscle or an inch on his home runs from andro, and not a dime from the booming sales that resulted from his identification with it. (The same could be said of another so-called "anabolic" supplement he was using, creatine.) But the "cheating" angle was a distraction that kept McGwire on the defensive, explaining that the andro was merely a recovery aid from the rigors of the game (which it isn't, either) and that it indeed did nothing to help him hit homers. "Mark McGwire's hand-eye coordination," he said, "was given by the Man upstairs." Still, dogged by the issue for another year, he had to publicly renounce the use of andro during the summer of '99.

Besides breasts, the only other side effect of andro is that it opened the door on the game's real dirty little secret—that management's bowing to the players on labor issues had precluded in the game's collective bargaining agreement the banning not just of andro, as the NFL, NBA, and International Olympic Committee had, but of *any* substance under the sun, and any testing other than on players who had been caught in *flagrante delecto* with drugs (and even then, they could only be sent to rehab as punishment). This meant players had a free pass to pop, shoot, and snort whatever they wanted, and of course to use real steroids.

Selig, of course, wanted this very awkward subject—and the corresponding question of whether the baseball lords were too smitten with the home run to *want* to ban anything that made balls fly—to stay submerged. The baseball culture did Selig's bidding. McGwire's bulk, said Mets manager Bobby Valentine, was incidental. "He's learned the strike zone better, his swing is more compact, and he's much more disciplined." Added McGwire's manager Tony Larussa, "You can't teach hitting a baseball. . . . [I]f it was just muscle and strength generating those home runs, then you'd have every weight-lifter and offensive lineman come off the street and start hitting balls over the fences." These nostrums effectively fudged the matter of whether McGwire or anyone else *was* using steroids, and the andro controversy died without branching out. "The bottom line on Mark David McGwire," concluded *The New York Times'* Ira Berkow, sternly, "is that he is legitimately the most astonishing home run hitter the world has ever known since George Herman Ruth ambled to the plate."

And so the American Way was saved, and Selig could for now dispense with the matter by getting the players union to sign off on a blue-ribbon study on andro. In other words, both sides agreed to do nothing.

To Selig's great relief, McGwire and Sosa kept up their frantic homer pace, letting him come out of his office again. On September 1, McGwire again put 2 balls over the wall, in Miami's Pro Player Stadium, the second tater breaking Hack Wilson's NL record of 56—then the next day hit *two more* in a 14-4 rout of the Marlins, and with 59 broke the record for a right-handed hitter he had tied the previous year. That made McGwire a bit giddy. "I passed myself," he said. "I feel pretty good about passing myself."

And still he couldn't shake Sosa, who three days later strafed the Reds for No. 56 and on September 4 the Pirates for No. 57. A day after, he'd do No. 58, but it would be minor news, since this was the day McGwire came up in the first inning at Busch Stadium facing the Reds' Dennis Reyes and sent No. 60 on its way to the seats in a 7-0 victory.

While both sluggers were driving homers at a clip not even Ruth had ever achieved, Sosa's were more impressive since his Cubs were in a dogfight for the wild-card playoff berth, while McGwire's Cards were dead in the water. Sosa's blows were winning games that mattered, not just for a personal rub. However, when fate brought the two teams together for a series beginning on Labor Day, Monday September 7, the Cubs may have been the only people in the world who cared about the outcomes of the games. Before the opening match, McGwire and Sosa sat side by side in a giggly joint press conference, with each saying the other was the greatest player and humanitarian on Earth, and Sosa getting off the best line by gently tweaking McGwire's andro mini-scandal. His own performance-enhancer, he said, was Flintstones vitamins. (Never mind that Sosa's physical transformation was no less sudden or dramatic.) Sosa also ventured that McGwire would hit 70 homers. McGwire said it would be "beautiful" if the two ended up tied. At what number?

"Seventy is a good one," he agreed.

"I will take it," Sosa said.

Hours later McGwire, before a sold-out Busch Stadium and a nationwide TV audience on ESPN, came to bat in the first inning against veteran right hander Mike Morgan. Little has been said about McGwire's mental state during his run, probably because it seemed so inevitable and because he seemed so sanguine and so immune to pressure. Actually, McGwire, like Maris and Aaron, began to fray at the edges. He later posited that "I don't think there's ever been another athlete to be singled out [for attention] like I was the last two months of the season"—though in reality he had faced nothing like Maris and Aaron had. For inner comfort, he got, well, to be kind let's call it metaphysical. He began looking for encouraging signs from above. The day he hit No. 60, for instance, the balls had been coded with a number "3" (to prevent counterfeit home run ball claims). Reflected McGwire, "No. 3 was Babe Ruth . . . and I hit [No. 60] on the third pitch. If that's not Fate, I don't know what is."

September 7, as it happened, was McGwire's father's birthday—his 61st birthday. Oh, and one last thing. McGwire, somewhat hauntingly, said he was looking forward to speaking with Ruth and Maris after he died. This is what home run pressure can do to a man.

But against Mike Morgan, he was sharp eyed and clear headed. "I told myself to just stay calm," he recalled later. "I was very relaxed today. Sometimes you might get caught up in the moment and you might be shaking a little bit. My heart was beating a thousand miles a minute, and I was just telling myself get a good pitch to hit."

Sosa, in right field, knew his opposite number meant business. "He went to the plate with such concentration. He was ready," Sosa thought.

On the mound, Morgan seemed less than ready. Amid the din of the crowd, he shook off two signs, insisting on using his best pitch. "I went to what I felt I could control off the plate," he would explain about the fastball he meant to arrive up and in but stayed up and over the heart of the dish. McGwire took his signature cut—that seeming half-swing, top hand impatiently leaving the bat. Ringed by thousands of flashbulbs going off at once, the ball climbed into the sky and crashed into the left field stands.

McGwire's tour of the bases was a love fest. He touched elbows with first baseman Mark Grace and high-fived third baseman Gary Gaetti. Sosa stood in right applauding into his glove. McGwire touched home, lifted his 10-year-old son from his broken marriage, Matthew, a Cardinal bat-boy, off his feet. He then looked toward right field and pantomimed Sosa's hand jive.

The unseen presence in the milieu, of course, was Roger Maris, the man synonymous with the number 61. The Cardinals had brought Maris's six children and their families to sit in a front-row box, though the families' emotional ambivalence could be understood. While McGwire graciously said later that it was criminal that Maris wasn't in the Hall of Fame, Bud Selig as usual was a bowl of oatmeal with glasses, refusing to concur.

McGwire, now only the second man to ever bat in a game with 61 homers, had three cracks at No. 62, but he singled and flied out twice. Sosa, meanwhile, was nearly lost in the McGwire corona, fouling out and striking out three times in the Cardinals' 6-2 win. The next night, he was no more than a retainer as McGwire walked onto the field having not just tied the home run record but in the guise of Moses bearing stone tablets. His first time up, the chosen sacrificial lamb for the evening, Cubs pitcher Steve Trachsel, was as reticent as Morgan had been. He threw three balls nowhere near the plate, but an eager McGwire, not looking for walks, swung at the next and grounded out to short. But he had seen enough of Trachsel's fastball to know where it would cross the plate when he stepped into the batter's box in the fourth, two outs, no one on, the flashbulbs turning Busch electric white. On the first pitch, McGwire tore into a low fastball, and rather than the usual McGwire mile-high trip into the clouds, the ball took off on a low, flat line, not rising 100 feet over the turf. It curved toward the foul line but made it over the left field wall, fair by around 15 feet—a drive that at 341 feet was his least prodigious homer of the season (when his *average* of the previous 61 was 426 feet). The enchanted four-ball skidded into a deserted walkway behind the wall, to be retrieved by a 22-year-old groundskeeper named Jim Forneris.

It happened so quickly that McGwire was barely out of the box when it landed. Stunned by the abnormal nature of the homer, McGwire weaved to first base, where he missed the bag and had to go back and touch it before making the trip no human had ever made—"a sweet, sweet run," he would say. Red and white streamers unfurled from the rafters, fireworks exploded, and as both teams emptied the dugouts to meet him at the plate, Sosa sprinted in from right. McGwire, with a leap, toed home plate, kissed and hoisted his son, and jogged to the first-base box seat where the Maris children sat applauding and weeping and hugged each of them.

When he turned back around, Sosa was standing before him and the two men showily embraced and took turns doing Sosa's heart-tapping riffs. Outside, car horns blared and downtown the streets filled with people. Forneris found his way to McGwire to give him the ball, which was bundled with McGwire's bat and flown to the Hall of Fame and encased with Ruth's and Maris's record-setting balls and bats. As McGwire made a short speech at home plate, a huge "62" banner was erected in center field. But if Forneris had no desire to cash in the biggest piece of instant McGwire memorabilia, others who did immediately sprang into action—within an hour, "commemorative" items of the occasion were being hawked on the Internet, including ticket stubs, scorecards, and 300 copies of the *St. Louis Post-Dispatch* with "62" splashed in scarlet ink on page one, which was bought up by one industrious entrepreneur.

McGwire had two more at-bats and was walked on both, once intentionally, in a game won by the Cards 3-2. Sosa, all but forgotten, was a trivial 1-for-4 in the Cards' 6-3 win.

When Henry Aaron had hit No. 715, its context was that it "saved" baseball. Now, twenty-four years later, that theme was appropriate yet again. As *San Francisco Chronicle* columnist Steve Keltmann phrased it, "The thrill the record-setting homer unleashed was universal, starting at the Busch Stadium epicenter and rolling in every direction like some California-into-the-Pacific monster quake. The party was for everyone. But the accomplishment had a more pointed purpose: it was for baseball."

Unbelievably, McGwire had eighteen games left to expand the record, and indeed the '62 Corvette with "62" license plates the Cardinals gifted him with was *jejune* within days. It took Sosa only until September 12 to get untracked again and pound his 60th, off the Brewers' Valerio De Los Santos at Wrigley Field—and *his* 61st and 62nd a day later also against the helpful Brewers—his tenth multi-homer game of the season, tying Ralph Kiner's NL record.

McGwire, who was in a weeklong post-*coital* home run slump, now faced the possibility of having broken Maris's record first and actually *losing* the home run race (an updated version of Maris's nightmare scenario of '61 vis-à-vis Mickey Mantle). And though he did rack No. 64 on September 15 against the Pirates, Sosa whacked a grand slam the next day in San Diego—a dramatic eighth-inning blast that gave the Cubs a big 6-3 victory. Then, after McGwire popped Nos. 64 and 65 in two games against—who else?—the Brewers, Sosa two days later tied the multi-homer season record of Hank Greenberg with a pair in—of course—Milwaukee.

So now, on the season's final weekend they were dead even—until, on Friday night in Houston, Sosa cracked No. 66, moving him ahead. McGwire came up 47 minutes later in St. Louis against the Expos and tied the race again, effectively taking the air out of Sosa's dream. His homers were done for the year. McGwire, though, teed off on Montreal's mincemeat arms, hitting 2 homers on Saturday. Sitting on 68, McGwire's coronation was the Sunday finale at Busch, its 58,000 red-draped fans making the place look like a raspberry sundae in the bright sunshine. In the third inning, 2 outs, none on, McGwire took rookie Mike Thurman 377 feet deep into the left field seats. And in the seventh, 2 outs, 2 on, against another accommodating rookie, Carl Pavano—who had given up No. 66—he turned another lame fastball around and deposited it in nearly the same place, 371 feet deep.

"I was going to go right after him," Pavano explained, "but he went after me."

McGwire had it right. Seventy big ones. And if he spoke with Babe Ruth while rounding the bases, we're sure he must have told the big monkey, "Let's see some sumbitch match *that*."

For the public, McGwire was rather ambivalent. "I know how exhausted I am mentally," he said. "Do I ever want to be in this position again? I don't know."

If there's anything more astonishing than McGwire's and Sosa's final home run numbers, it is the frequency of their homers. During the season, one or the other homered on more days—90—than not, 88. One or the other had a dinger on 26 of the last 40 days, with no more than a 2-day respite between them. And McGwire's 23 in that span alone would have led the Cardinals in 22 of the previous 32 years.

For McGwire, the sour ending was that Sosa was voted the MVP over him—and by a thumping margin, 30 first-place votes to 2, 438 points to 272. McGwire, in fact, was only 57 points ahead of third-place Moises Alou. This was the ultimate victory of Sosa's canny charm offensive, and of political correctness. Of course, it helped Sosa a *lot* that his team made it to the postseason, winning a one-game playoff against the Giants (though they were then swept by the Braves in the LDS, with Sosa batting .182 with no homers). Was McGwire hosed? Here are the stats:

	G	AB	R	H	2B	3B	HR	RBI	BB	K	BA	OB	SLG	TB	EXB
McGwire	155	509	130	152	21	0	**70**	147	**162**	155	.299	**.470**	**.752**	383	91*
Sosa	159	643	**134**	198	20	0	66	**158**	73	**171**	.308	.377	.647	**416**	86

bf = led majors; * = led NL.

Personally, I'd go with McGwire—after all, how many times does a human being hit 70 homers? And I cringe a little at Sosa's walk-to-strike-out ratio (73 walks? Oh, come now), whereas McGwire set a new league record for walks and had only a bit more than twice as many K's as homers. His slugging percentage was second all-time in the NL (behind Rogers Hornsby) and his home run percentage of one every 7.27 at-bats was a new record—for the time being.

In any case, it doesn't matter. The year was McGwire's, inspiring this kind of breathless prose from Daniel Okrent in *Time:* "No one could gainsay Mark McGwire. Nor could we have invented him; he was that close to perfect. He assaulted the most textured record in the most apposite sport—the sport closest to the American bone [and] remained at once focused on his goal and joyful in its pursuit. . . . He knew he was good, and knowing it made him even better."

Not that benedictions of this sort registered on McGwire. Being *Time*'s Hero of the Year didn't faze him. Nor did all the sociological shades of his homers, which in *Time* came out with the title "A Man For All Seasons" and read "Mark McGwire's 70 home runs shattered the most magical record in sports and gave America a much-needed hero." Only when McGwire visited the Hall of Fame after the season and saw what he had done in context did he melt a bit.

"The thought of television changing the games to go prime time. The thought of almost every reporter in the country and almost the world watching one player—it's unheard of," he said, adding that he was "in awe of myself."

And in three years, all of it would be old hat.

73 and Beyond

So what was the damage done in '98? In all, 5,064 home runs left the premises, breaking the '96 record by 98. For the first time ever, homers in the NL went out at a 1-per-game clip. (The AL rate was over 1-per-game for the fourth straight year.) Lost in the nebula of McGwire and Sosa, the Padres' Greg Vaughn hit 50. Eight AL players and five NL ones hit 40 or more. Griffey and Gonzalez had what otherwise would have been epic seasons. Griffey, at just 28, had 56 homers, 146 RBIs, and a .318 average, in the process clearing milestones suited to a 35-year-old—the third to hit 50 homers in successive seasons, third to have 50 homers and 20 steals, fourth-youngest to reach 1,000 RBI's, and the third to clear 140 RBI's three straight years.

Though Gonzalez came up short of Hack Wilson's RBI standard, he still delivered 157 runs, most in the AL since 1949—with a .318 average, 45 homers, and his second MVP trophy. (Like Sosa, though, he died in the LDS, going 1-for-12 against the Yankees.) Don't overlook other old friends who were rendered suddenly second-rate. In the case of Albert Belle, this meant that his good, bad, and evil sides were now all less compelling. In '98, Belle again had MVP numbers, with almost as many RBIs (152) as Gonzalez and more homers (49), a better average (.328), and fewer strikeouts (84 to 126). And he finished *eighth.*

At the same time, Frank Thomas, who played good cop on the White Sox to Belle's rogue cop, was hitting the skids. The Big Hurt showed up a little *too* big in '98 and unable to get around on the fastball. Thomas's average fell to .265, his homers to 29. The next year, Belle would be rewarded with a five-year, $65-million free-agent deal with the Orioles. Thomas, meanwhile, would hit .308 but manage only 15 homers and 77 RBIs, and the talk show chatter around Chicago that he was done sent this once-affable man into a Belle-like cavern. His mood didn't improve any when he hurt his ankle and the Sox brass believed he was babying it.

Thomas would come back big, detonated by a spring training shout-out with manager Jerry Manuel over Thomas's insistence on giving up first base to be a full-time DH. He began the season scalding and stayed so, finishing with 43 homers, 143 RBIs, a .328 average, 114 runs, and a second-place tally in the MVP vote behind Jason Giambi. And Belle? He hit a 3-run homer in his first game as an Oriole, then tanked. He gave the finger to a fan and in June team owner Peter Angelos was trying to somehow void the no-trade clause in Belle's bloated contract. Belle's fealty to the club was seen in a sign he hung from his locker in midseason reading "1/2 year down, 4 1/2 years to go, so don't fight it and show me some love!! AB."

He didn't quite make it. After a 37-homer, 117-RBI year in '99 that made him the fourth player with Ruth, Gehrig, and Foxx to go 30-100 for eight straight seasons, a degenerative hip condition slowed him in 2000 (27-103) and wrote finis to his career in 2001. He retired, at 35, with not a tear shed for him. To appreciate what a waste of talent Belle was, consider that his 381 homers break down to 37 per 162 games, the same as Mantle, Mays, and Schmidt, and 1 behind Foxx. He also left with 1,239 RBIs, a .295 average, and a don't-call-us message from Cooperstown. There's no such injunction on Thomas, who had a Lazarus rising comeback in 2002 when he hit 29 homers with 92 RBIs. I only wish he would retire. He's proven he can play baseball more than enough.

Gonzalez and Rafael Palmeiro are still raging if graying bulls. Gonzalez followed up his MVP season with 39 homers, 128 RBIs, and a .326 average in '99. Sadly, though, he too had morphed into a lower-case Belle. Curdled by a messy divorce and obsessed with getting a fat free-agent deal in 2001, for two years he was a brooding mute who refused to go to the All-Star Game when not chosen to start, or to play in the Hall-of-Fame Game because, he said, his pants were too big. I'm inclined to think it was his head.

The Rangers—who in '99 had five men with more than 20 homers but not one dependable pitcher—eagerly traded Gonzalez to the Tigers in 2000, whereupon he hurt his knee and was useless for the year. Instead of being contrite, Gonzalez said that if the Tigers hoped to sign him they'd have to move the deep left–center field fence in for him. Their answer: they traded him to the Indians, who signed him for one year—a very big year for Gonzalez, who hit 35 homers with 140 RBIs, a .325 average. Gonzalez hit .348 with 2 dingers in the five-game ALDS loss to the Mariners, then went poof, back to the Rangers.

As for Palmeiro, he returned to Texas in '99 and slammed 47 homers with 148 RBIs and hit .328. Over five years he hit more than 40 homers four times—the one time he didn't he had 39—and had 100-plus RBIs for eight straight years and nine out of the last ten, all while being next to unnoticed. Check those '99 numbers and tell us why Palmeiro, who's also been a perennial Gold Glover, finished fifth in the MVP race won by his teammate, catcher Ivan "Pudge" Rodriguez, who hit .332 with 35 homers and 113 RBIs. You probably had no idea that Palmeiro hit his 400th career home run two years ago and is currently 10 short of 500.

Blame much of that on McGwire and Sosa, who assumed ownership of the home run concession in '98, though it was inevitable not only that they would find it impossible to recreate the vibes of that year but that the home run itself was never going to be quite as cosmic an experience again. Indeed, their encore was nearly as riveting a shoot-out, with each man again firing round after round—again, without pitchers caving in to them. McGwire walked less, 133 times, second on the NL, but also struck out less, 141 (sixth), while Sosa walked only five more times (78) and struck out exactly the same number of times, 171, to again lead baseball.

It was as if the pitchers said, "Here, let's see you do that again"—and they damn near did. On August 5 McGwire nailed career No. 500 against the Padres' Andy Ashby, the first time anyone had hit Nos. 400 and 500 in consecutive seasons, and the fastest to 500 ever, in 5,487 at-bats. On August 22 he hit two against the Mets to reach 50 in a season for a record fourth straight year. But now it was McGwire doing the chasing. By September 1 Sosa had him, 56 to 52, and on September 9 he hit No. 59. But then he went dry. By the time McGwire got his 59th on September 17, Sosa, who had ten multi-homer games during the season, was mired in an 9-for-37 funk. The next day, though, he sent No. 60 in to the center field bleachers at Wrigley Field against the Brewers' Jason Bere to become the first to rack 60 twice.

In the end, however, Sosa again had to settle for second place (the go-figure fact of all history is that Sosa has hit over 60 *three* times, yet the only time he led the league was when he hit 50), because McGwire caught fire. His 60th came on September 26 against the Reds and he passed Sosa in the final week. When the Cardinals and Cubs closed out the season at Busch Stadium, with nothing else on the line since both teams were awful, McGwire knocked 1 out in the first inning of the finale off his old patsy Steve Trachsel—No. 65. Sosa then blistered one in the third—No. 63. No small taters.

And yet this time, the streamers and the fireworks were kept in the can, the media checked in only from time to time, and nobody wrote about the humanity-advancing properties of the home run while holding hands and singing "Kumbaya." The Cards did set a club attendance record, 3.23 million, and baseball's gate receipts were still way up there, 38.3 million in the NL, 31.8 million in the AL. And home runs were still incredibly plentiful—5,528 were hit that year (2,893 in the NL), which seemed staggering until the next year.

Even so, the team baseball revolved around, and by far its biggest draw on the road, the Yankees, finished no higher than seventh in home runs with 193, and their top man was Tino Martinez with 28. Being the Yankees, of course, they always saved their dingers for *the* moment (Chili Davis's 2-run blow in Game 5 of the '98 ALCS against the Indians; Tino Martinez's grand slam and Chuck Knoblauch's 3-run shot in Game 1 of that year's World Series against the Padres; Bernie Williams' tenth-inning walkoff homer in Game 1 of the ALDS against the Red Sox in '99; Chad Curtis's tenth-inning walkoff in Game 3 of the World Series against the Braves).

On the subject of walkoff homers, I'd like to note two of the unlikeliest, both hit by the Mets during the '99 postseason. One was by their catcher—and I don't mean Mike Piazza but backup Todd Pratt, who drove the ball over the center field wall at Shea Stadium in the tenth inning to end the NLDS against the Diamondbacks. The other was by Robin Ventura with the bases loaded against the Braves in the LCS. Grand slam? Well, no. Ventura stopped running between first and second when his teammates began jumping on him, and left the field right there, passing up a home run for an official single. I'm surprised his union dues weren't raised.

The '99 season was notable as well as Ken Griffey's last in the sun. That year he hit 48 homers to lead the AL, with 134 RBIs, but he tailed off after the Mariners moved in July from the Kingdome to the broad dimensions of Safeco Field. For Griffey, whose average had slipped as his homers—and strikeouts—zoomed upward, the move alone may have led him to walk on the team when he became a free agent following the 2000 season. But what clinched it was that his uneasy alliance with Alex Rodriguez had turned him paranoid as he brooded that A-Rod was usurping his grip on the team and the town. This came to a head after Rodriguez had reached his *real* level in '98, nearly doubling his homers to 42 (a record for an AL shortstop), with a .310 average, 14 RBIs, and 46 steals—to become the first and still only infielder to go 40/40. In '99, even missing five weeks with a knee injury, he hit 42 again, with 111 RBIs. With some reason, Griffey believed he was responsible for the team rising to big-league standards—with his influence, the Mariners had set the record for team home runs in '97, with 264—and the prime force behind the public funding of Safeco Field. Now, with his free agency nearing, Griffey was loath to share that new palace with the younger A-Rod.

The irony, of course, is that neither man's future was in Seattle. Rodriguez too would be a free agent after 2000, and for the frugal Mariners keeping both, or either, was a pipedream. But while A-Rod shut off discussion of free agency and played steady ball, Griffey let it interfere with his game, which in turn made him surly and openly critical of Rodriguez, calling him "calculating" and "manipulative" and inferring that A-Rod's mild-mannered disposition was a front designed to make Griffey look bad. Rodriguez's rejoinder—"I have nothing but good things to say about Junior"—did just that.

Everyone assumed Griffey wanted to force his way to his home town, Cincinnati, where Ken Sr. was a coach, and the Mariners wanted to get it done so they could acquire players for him before he walked. But Griffey wavered over the winter, first leading on the Mariners, then listing teams he'd consent to be traded to, then rejecting a trade to the Mets. By now he looked absurd, and feeling he had to justify leaving, he claimed he and his family had received death threats. The clumsily staged charade finally ended in early February 2000 when he was dealt to the Reds for four players—including Mike Cameron.

Because Griffey's ham-handed exit took his leverage away, he wound up with a relatively pallid nine-year, $116 million contract, which he professed he cared little about. "I'm finally home," he said. "It doesn't matter how much you make. It's where you feel happy." True to form, some in the media bought this spin that Griffey was a selfless soul who "took less to play at home." Within three years, the same folks would be reporting that Griffey, feeling less than happy, was perhaps seeking new trade routes out of town.

Rodriguez knew the score about Griffey all along. "I don't think [the notion that Griffey took less] is admirable if you sell yourself short," he told this writer. "I don't know if I would have done it the same way."

He didn't. In 2000, as speculation about what team he'd sign with after the season roiled about him, he took over Griffey's cleanup spot and calmly shredded the league with 41 homers, 132 RBIs, 134 runs, and a .316 average. While the Mariners fans were shocked that a goody-goody like Rodriguez could be mercenary to the extreme, A-Rod left tire marks in his haste to leave Seattle for the highest bidder—which turned out to be a high bid to the extreme: the stupefying ten-year, $250 million bounty offered by the Rangers' fatuous owner Tom Hicks, who needn't have paid that much but would have thrown in his first-born to get Rodriguez.

These numbers, of course, stunned even the most feckless of spendthrift owners, many of whom—during their downtime from inflating their own payrolls beyond all sanity—predicted impending Armageddon if salaries weren't capped for them by the players (whom they always want to stop them before they spend again). More irony is that the Rangers, with a payroll that also now embraces Gonzalez, Palmeiro, and Pudge Rodriguez, have been one of baseball's worst teams the last three years—while A-Rod, at the very least, has been its second-best player.

And Griffey? Here is a man who when he left Seattle was 30 years old and had hit 398 homers. An average of 36 homers over the next decade would mean Griffey would have had 758 at age 40. The math held up his first year in Cincinnati when he clocked No. 400 on April 10, 2000, against the Rockies—the youngest to get there—and finished with 40 homers and 118 RBI. But the hint was that he missed 17 games to injury, hit just .271 and struck out 111 times. Take a good look at those power numbers. That may be the last time Griffey will have them.

To repeat: the home run is a capricious creature. It was great to Mark McGwire while his team spit the bit. Then in 2000, when the team got good, the sun began to set on Big Red. McGwire finally had another long-ball hitter in the lineup, Jim Edmonds, who came in a trade, and both were pounding the ball until McGwire's knee started to hurt and never got better. The second half of the season McGwire sat as the Cards won the NL Central, ending up with 32 homers in 231 at-bats, behind Edmonds' 42. (The team hit 235, 12 more than in McGwire's 70-homer season.) When the team swept the Braves in the NLDS, then lost in five to the Mets in the LCS, McGwire's role was four pinch-hit appearances, with one hit—of course, a homer.

He was gone after a teetering farewell 2001 season when his homer-or-bust approach produced, in 299 at-bats, 29 homers, 64 RBIs, and a .187 average. He left, at age 36, his 583 homers a tease for what could have been 700-something if he had stronger ligaments. You'll have to figure out what that might mean.

The NL leader in 2000 was the redoubtable Sosa, with 50, 1 up on Bonds, 3 on Houston's Jeff Bagwell. With a great yawn, the season set yet another record for dingers, 5,603, and an NL-record 3,005. Records were also set for runs per game (5.3 AL, 5.0 NL) and for strikeouts (over 30,000 with an NL-record 5.5 per game), and walks continued in the near-20,000 range. Attendance went over 70 million for the first time, with an NL-record 39.7 million. But although nine men cleared 40 homers in the NL and 7 in the AL, suddenly the leaders had reasonable totals. (The AL top man, the Angels' Troy Glaus, had 47.)

Had the long ball gone egalitarian? After vesting itself on a few, it now seemed to share its wealth with, well, just about everyone with a bat.

Inarguably, the homer was entrenched as the game's single-minded objective. When McGwire, the '90s home run leader with *405,* had more homers in '99 than *singles,* nobody said, *"Huh?"* This is called being blasé. Or spoiled. Or blind to something being out of whack. Still, some observers felt not quite comfy with the situation. One, *Washington Post* baseball writer Thomas Boswell, addressed the cheapening effect of so many dingers in a July 5, 2000, column entitled, "Home Run Frenzy Is Taking the Clout Out of Long Ball."

Indeed, if you go position by position, the top home run hitters at nearly all of them are or will soon be someone who played in the '90s—Piazza at catcher, McGwire at first base, Ryne Sandberg at second, Rodriguez at short (he's 47 behind Cal Ripken Jr.), Edgar Martinez at DH (nearing Harold Baines' mark of 225), and possibly Bonds in the outfield. The guy Rodriguez will replace, Ripken, is one of my favorite all-time players, but was not really a home run hitter; he got to 345 on longevity. Only in the '90s could a Cal Ripken have hit a home run in the game when he broke Gehrig's consecutive-game streak, in his final All-Star Game, and in his final big-league game.

Which brings me to the definitions of blasé home run chic—when 70 home runs weren't enough to stand as a record, and the adventure that bettered it was met by stifled yawns and even contempt.

Of course, I'm talking about Barry Lamar Bonds, who in 2001 at age 36 was older than McGwire when his body gave out. And even though Bonds was a far better athlete than McGwire and always in condition, he too looked to be breaking down. As recently as '99, just two years after going 30/30 for the fifth time, he was beset with elbow and wrist injuries that put him on the disabled list for just the second time in twelve years. He hit just .262 with 34 homers and 83 RBIs that season, and had knee surgery in the winter.

If he were to survive, Bonds knew, some fine tuning was required. First, to his anatomy. That is when Bonds joined the bulk-up crowd, applying a good twenty pounds of insulating brawn. Because he was as solid as coaxial cable, it wasn't noticeable at first but the man was now *big.* And his bat was still *quick.* Bonds, who like all other sluggers was free to crowd the plate without reprisals from cowed pitchers, also came upon a biomechanical blasting cap for that sweet swing, a nimble, delicately timed two-step—he tapped his front, or right, foot just as the pitcher released the ball, then another tap a split-second after. This kept his stride short and economical, while allowing him the leverage to drive every ounce of his weight into the pitch.

Obviously, only a human with puma-quick reflexes could possibly do this, but look around baseball today and you'll see even lummoxes acting like Greg Hines at the plate trying to, uh, tap into Bonds' mystical power source. Similarly, hitters are also trading in their old ash bats for the newest trend in wood—maple, which Bonds made his choice of lumber in '98. With his bats shattering when he was jammed, Bonds found a carpenter from, of all places, Ottawa, Canada, named Sam Holman who had been marketing the harder, denser Maple Rideau Crusher, a model that tested to have a life span of around a month rather than the week or so of the typical Louisville Slugger—which for the first time since Pete Browning brought *it* into the game, is in decline.

More than three hundred big leaguers use the Crusher, including the vanguard of the most recent Generation X in the game, the immensely talented Vladimir Guerrero and Albert Pujols (who in his first two seasons with the Cardinals has compiled 71 homers with 257 RBIs and a .321 average). Guerrero—a long, lean, and utterly remarkable player who has amassed 197 homers since 1998, and displayed the game's strongest throwing arm in the outfield, playing in virtual obscurity with the moribund Expos—has refined batsmanship even more, by using the thinnest barrel ever seen, sacrificing a meatier sweet spot for an even quicker swing.

Bonds, the progenitor of these new ideas, benefited in 2001 from the final piece of the puzzle—being able to escape Devil's Island (a.k.a. Candlestick Park) for Pac Bell Park, with that custom-made 307-foot right field sliver of stands shoehorned into the waterfront landing dubbed "McCovey Cove." Wielding his red-handled, tar-black-barreled maple Crusher, Bonds had renounced speed to hit home runs, tilting his swing into a decided uppercut. (His groundball-to-fly ball ratio decreased from '97 to '99 like this: 0.76, 0.63, 0.57, 0.56, 0.59). In 2000, Bonds, who on May 1 against the Mets hit the 1st of what has become a string of 21 "splashdown" homers into the Cove, cracked 49 homers with 106 RBIs, a .306 average and slugged .688, good for a second-place MVP finish behind his teammate—and, progressively so, his nemesis—second baseman Jeff Kent, a reborn ex-Met bust who as a right-handed-hitting bullwark then batting behind Bonds in the order had 33 homers, 133 RBIs and hit .334, allowing Bonds to see better pitches. For only the second time as a Giant, Bonds' Giants won their division (small consolation for Bonds after his usual October humiliation—he went 2-for-17 with 1 RBI in the four-game NLDS against the Mets, updating his career postseason average to .196).

Bonds entered 2001 as the same old enigma, a man of incalculable talent held in incredibly low esteem, who reacted to being so unloved by whining in arrogance and wallowing in self-pity. Bonds practiced such tunnel vision that he no doubt was bewildered that with his free agency impending after the 2001 season, the Giants seemed in no great rush to sign him. But then, they never paid him kingly money—in 2000 he was making $10.6 million, no higher than seventh in the majors, way behind other sluggers like Sosa, Piazza, and Larry Walker. During that year, too, he wasn't among ten outfielders chosen during a bit of promotional nonsense intended to name a baseball All-Century Team.

Bonds began the season locked into a zone, though it was only mildly noted in the media that on April 17 he hit his 500th career home run into McCovey Cove against the Dodgers. Indeed, the response among his own teammates underlined Bonds' acceptance problem. Only the batboy was waiting at the plate when he arrived; the rest of the Giants could barely rouse themselves to shake his hand when he returned to the dugout. Bonds brooded about that, too, and inside the clubhouse walls he had some choice words for them, especially Kent, worsening the already-tenuous relationship between two vain and difficult men. For the sake of public appearance, it was agreed that Bonds would not be embarrassed on future milestone homers. Attendance at home plate would be mandatory—making the Giants surely the only team to have to be ordered to appreciate its big star.

In May he hit 9 homers in six games, and already had hit dingers in six straight games *twice,* though these feats were barely noted. There was a small stir when at the All-Star break he had nailed a new record of 38. By August, people had begun to sit up. On August 9, Bonds reached No. 49 faster than anyone ever had, followed three days later by No. 50, and on August 16 No. 53—beating Johnny Mize's NL record for a left-handed hitter. On August 23 he passed Mike Schmidt on the all-time list with No. 549. On September 1 came No. 60 against Arizona. On September 8 he hit 3 shots and with 63 stood as the top left-handed-hitting home run hitter of all time.

Three days later, of course, any growing interest in Bonds' rampage was forgotten in the smoldering rubble of the World Trade Center and the Pentagon. As the nation mourned the dead and steeled to raze a shadowy enemy in their name, baseball was shelved for a week. When it returned, the rites of spring had become blackened. But again baseball played a role in the rising of public spirit, and if Bonds' homers were seen now through that prism, he responded magnificently.

On September 23 came Nos. 65 and 66, breaking Ruth's two-year record of 115. With two weeks left, McGwire's 70 was a vulnerable target. The next day Bonds crushed No. 67 in Dodger Stadium. And now, unlike with McGwire and Sosa, pitchers were so intimidated by Bonds that they stopped pitching to him. Not that they had ever been eager to do so. Bonds had led the league in walks a record five times from '92 to '97, and in '99 he broke Aaron's all-time record for intentional walks with his 294th. Back on May 28, with Arizona leading the Giants 8-6, Bonds was walked *with the bases loaded,* the first time that has happened since Swish Nicholson in 1944. Even so, during those final weeks of 2001, Bonds' walks burgeoned like crabgrass. To his credit, he didn't swing wildly to feed the home run drive. Always possessed of a keen batting eye—even that year he would fan only 93 times—he simply waited for a hittable ball and pounced when he got one, such as on October 28 and 29 when he hit homers 68 and 69 against the Padres.

Now, with Bonds one away from McGwire, the Giants were barely hanging on in the wild card race, one game from elimination when they visited Enron Field for three games with the Astros, who were leading in the race but beginning to crumble. As with McGwire in '98, Bonds overshadowed a mere team race, and the Astros wanted no part of him. For three games they pitched around or outright walked him, gifting the Giants with an extra base runner that helped build rallies. The Giants won the first game, and in the second Bonds was walked three times to move past Ruth's 1923 record of 170, and scored all three times in an 11-8 win.

In the series ender, Thursday, October 4, Bonds still didn't see one good pitch, drawing three more walks all on four pitches—the last time with the Giants up *8-1*—and each time the Houston fans filled the park with booing for their timid team. After eight innings, the Giants led 9-2. When Bonds led off the ninth, the Astros—who would not recover from this dreadful series—finally agreed to pitch to him straight up, leaving it to rookie pitcher Wilfredo Rodriguez, in his second big-league game.

Result: on a 1-1 pitch, a 93-mph fastball was turned around and went like a rocket into the night. Bonds, as is his custom, stood at the plate admiring the flight of the ball, flipped the bat with two hands, and took three paces up the line, his silver cross earring dangling and dancing. Before he got to first, No. 70 had come to rest in the upper deck in right, 454 feet away—the kind of blast people used to call Ruthian but which Bonds made to seem common. He toured the bases to a loud ovation by the 43,734 fans who had booed their own team so they could see this moment.

Bonds, who often makes his round-trip trots seem like a bothersome *schlep,* for once had a spring to his step. Like McGwire, he had arranged for his son, Nikolai, to be at the plate when he arrived. Bonds shot his arms triumphantly into the air, hoisted his son, and turned to be greeted by the Giant players who had dutifully gathered to go through the motion of patting him on the back before hastily going back to their dugout seats. Bonds then pointed to his wife, Liz, and two daughters in the stands and waved his cap to the crowd.

Still, as warm as this scene was, and while Bonds later modified his usual sourpuss monosyllabic patter to call the moment "electric" in the clubhouse while sitting between his father and his godfather Willie Mays, there was none of the McGwire glitter-fest to it. Because as hard as the Giants tried to stage-manage Bonds' crusade, he was still Barry Bonds. As *Sports Illustrated*'s Tom Verducci pointed out, "Bonds is a moody, unembraceable presence" who "despite his unsurpassed skills [has] engendered no simpatico emotions or even a nickname." Yet the unembraceable Bonds would make it necessary to repeat these staged celebratory routines in the days to come.

The homer in Houston, Bonds' 564th, displacing Reggie Jackson for seventh place all-time, was merely antipasto for the following night, Friday, October 5, 2001, when the still-alive Giants went home to a packed Pac Bell Park to play the hated Dodgers, who having been eliminated from the race were dying to boot out the Giants—and apparently did in the top of the first when they scored five times, quickly defusing the festive air in Frisco.

Even before Bonds had taken a turn at bat, Verducci wrote in *SI,* "The emotion of No. 70 never returned." And when Bonds stepped up in the bottom of the frame with two outs, none on, facing right-hander Chan Ho Park, Verducci reported, "There was a buzz, but not a buzz. The crowd was loud, but not loud."

Bonds himself was tired now, running on fumes. After the team plane had gotten in late from Houston, he slept four hours before getting up to attend the funeral of his former bodyguard who had died suddenly. In fact, as with McGwire in '98, Bonds had become somewhat morbid about fate and mortality, as an uncle and a cousin had also died during the past year. Retrenching in his prodigal personal life, Bonds had drawn closer to his second wife, his daughters, and son. As well, he did some soul searching, until he could actually admit publicly that "I can always improve. I can be a better father, husband, friend. . . . Life is work on an everyday basis." He also admitted that under his many layers of distance and disdain, he was "scared" that entire season, as like Aaron, he received scary death threats and hate mail, and from the time he was 7 homers from 70 he traveled with a convoy of FBI agents.

"You begin to think that if you walk out on the baseball field," he said, "someone could take your life."

As with Maris, Aaron, and McGwire before him, at the witching hour Bonds was suffocating.

"Every time I had the opportunity to exhale or breathe," he reflected a year later, "something came up that made it difficult for me."

Of course, part of Bonds' problem was that his normally smarmy nature rendered such allegedly heartfelt thoughts nothing more than vacuous, self-serving whining to a great many people. This even applied to Bonds' repeated insistence that, as a good company man, any home run record paled in importance next to winning games and pennants. So it was no shock that his crowning moment that night of October 5 was hardly an unconditional victory. Bonds got a quick edge when Park fell behind him 1-0. Then he came in with a fastball designed to tail away from Bonds. Good idea, bad guy to do it with, since Bonds stands so close to the plate he can put a hurting on a pitch *before* it has a chance to skirt his bat. And this pitch he hurt all the way to the arcade above McCovey Cove, 442 feet away, where it was smothered by a fan named Jerry Rose.

As it happened, just as the ball cleared the wall, McGwire was coming to bat in Houston for one of his last career at-bats. When McGwire made out, the Enron Field scoreboard lit up with the news of Bonds' 71st.

At Pac Bell, Bonds was now going around the bases. The crowd was exploding and the Giants were on their way to home plate. But, again, it was a party without pizzazz. The Dodgers remained fixed, offering no extended hands. As with many others, they held their known grudge against Bonds—whose 500th homer earlier in the season against them left them to stew on the field when the Giants stopped the game for a long ceremony. And Bonds himself seemed on the subdued side, "rounding the bases with little glee," wrote Verducci.

Bonds put his foot on the plate, pointed to the sky in honor of the late bodyguard, picked up his son, milled with his teammates a while, then went into the dugout and spoke briefly on a cell phone with his father who passed up the occasion to play in a celebrity golf tournament in Connecticut. In the outfield, banners reading "Bonds" and "71" ringed the scoreboard video replays of the homer. It all had a familiar, even tired ring to it, as if people were following steps on a learn-tomambo chart, and now that the new king had ascended the world could go back to its business.

Wrote Verducci: "Bonds' teammates gathered, patted him on the head and quickly dispersed. There was one semi-noisy, extended curtain call. Bonds hugged several family members seated behind home plate. Then—nothing. 'Now batting, number 21, Jeff Kent . . .'"

A more caustic take was offered by Dave Kindred in the *Sporting News*: "After Bonds' 70th and 71st homers, we had communal festivities with everybody out of the dugout—there to be seen in the historic gathering, there as proof of camaraderie, there with batboys, sons and daughters, wives and mothers, maybe even an Amway sales rep in the scrum. It seemed not contrived exactly, but contrived sort of."

Don't blame Bonds for the sour taste left by his record. All of baseball conspired to undercut it. You can blame Bud Selig for paying almost no attention to Bonds' chase—rather than attend the games at Pac Bell, the Inspector Clouseau of commissioners chose to be in San Diego for Tony Gwynn's final big league game—but then you would have to blame Bobby Bonds for missing his boy's date with destiny for the more pressing business of golf. In the end, the real blame goes to the home run, for getting so cheap and easy.

For Bonds, the man who cares so much more about winning than home run records, the day was surely a downer. Even though he blasted No. 72 to dead center field against Park in the third inning that cut the score to 8-4, the Giants went on to lose a gruesome heartbreaker, 11-10, in what is the longest nine-inning game ever—4 hours, 27 minutes of agony—and thus was deprived of yet another chance to get to his first World Series.

After a day off, save for a pinch-hit single, Bonds coup de grâce was in the season's last game, when he hammered a first-inning, 3-2 knuckleball from Dennis Springer 380 feet into the right field seats—No. 73. I hate to sound overly shrill, but for all the fireworks that streaked the sky that Sunday afternoon, something was missing. Bonds' record may be among baseball's most negative achievements. I'd call it the most overrated—but in fact few gave a hang about it to begin with.

Again, Bonds has a lot to do with it, but not everything. McGwire could have hit 73 that year and it would have been more redundant than impressive. In fact, McGwire felt compelled to defend the sanctity of '98 by saying he had faced much more pressure than had Bonds. That contention, wrote Dave Kindred, was "small-minded and wrong-headed." Bull. McGwire was right—and even Bonds agreed.

to wake from a bad dream and see the ball caught in front of it. He stared so long that some of his infielders came over to snap him out of it, and Kim got the belated third out.

Logically, that should have been it for Kim, a one-inning guy at best, but manager Bob Brenly kept him in for a *third* inning when the game went to the tenth. And Kim looked strong, getting two quick strikeouts. Next was Derek Jeter, a big-game monster. Kim tried his slider, hoping for it to bite hard. Instead, it hung. And Jeter sliced a high drive over the right–center field fence for the gamer. As Jeter thrust his arm into the air at first base, Kim looked like a lost child, his eyes wide and confused as he left the field in a daze.

Now, in Game 5, the Series tied 2-2, came part two of "Same Time, Same Series" starring Byung-Hyun Kim as himself. On the talk shows, Kim was being called "Byung-Hung Slider" and people were seriously wondering if he needed to be kept from sharp objects. None of it sunk in on Brenly, who took so much heat in the media that he seemed eager to go to Kim again in spite. And in the bottom of the ninth, his team up 2-0, he again gave the ball to Kim, who gave up a leadoff double but then got the next two outs. Now, the hitter was Scott Brosius—need I say it? Another tough out in the clutch.

Kim threw his up-draft slider, Brosius got his arms quickly extended through the hitting zone, and slammed a high drive to left. As it rose, seemingly lifted by a squall of crowd noise, Kim sunk into a helpless squat and watched the ball fly over the fence for a tie. He sat in that pose, head hung as pitifully as his slider, while Brosius twirled around the bases. On TV, a shot of an incredulous Brenly came on, his eyes glassy, refusing to blink. After a minute of standing frozen in shock, he trudged to the mound and with the infielders nearly lifted Kim to his feet, trying to end his catatonia by screaming encouragement into his face.

"You just wanted to go over and hug him," said first baseman Mark Grace in an Oprah-like moment afterward.

Kim this time got out of the inning, but the D'backs were on a death watch and three innings later, in the twelfth, Alfonso Soriano's hit ended it, 3-2.

Never in a World Series had a team trailing in the ninth inning—much less trailing with two outs in the ninth inning—come back to win on a home run. Kim had allowed it to happen twice, *back to back*. But perhaps not even Christy Mathewson in relief could have slain the home run beast on those two nights. After the second defeat, Kim sat near his locker, eyes moist, repeating how sorry he was. And Brenly, who will never make anyone forget Earl Weaver, was even more adamant about wanting to throw Kim to the lions again. Luckily, he didn't have to. Back in Arizona, the D'backs crushed the Yankees in Game 6, 15-2. In Game 7 Schilling took a 1-0 lead into the seventh.

But now came some more of that old Yankee lightning. Martinez singled in the tying run that inning. Then in the top of the ninth, Schilling left an 0-2 pitch over the plate for the frighteningly young and gifted Soriano—a leadoff or No. 2 hitter with so much pop in his bat that I guarantee he will be hitting cleanup any year now. Soriano lashed the ball into the left field stands and just like that the Yankees were three outs from a fifth title in six years.

That, of course, is when irony did an Olga Korbut flip. All but salivating, the Yankees rushed in their own nonpareil closer, named Rivera Mariano—the one with the "cutter" fastball that, gripped with the index and middle finger on the two-seam side of the ball becomes an optical illusion of a hittable pitch when it's anything but. Baseball announcers refer to the "two-seam" and "four-seam" fastball when they're trying to sound like they know what they're talking about. The simple science of it (getting to the molecular level of pitching) is that a two-seam grip makes the ball break because pressure from the top causes it to spin, letting air friction force it down. (The four-seamer, with the thumb and ring finger on the bottom seams as well, creates equal pressure forces, making the pitch sail and not drop, increasing velocity.)

The whole dynamic is called the "magnus effect," and is influenced by the drag coefficient.

Whatever the coefficients and drag, Rivera is usually not hittable, and had not been in twenty-three straight postseason appearances when he came into the game. But he got himself in dutch when on a 1-out bunt he threw wildly to second base, putting runners on first and second. A double tied the game and after hitting a batter, Rivera threw a cutter to Luis Gonzalez, whose broken-bat bloop single over Jeter's head at short rendered all those massively profound home runs into nothing more than the Yankees' last meal before their execution.

To carry this theme out a bit, Gonzalez's bloop can be seen as the end of '90s excess. Indeed, Bonds was a victim not just of his own irritating nature but of changing economic times and attitudes. You don't think a lot can change in three years? Then explain Enron, Worldcom, the budget surplus, and the stock market. In '98, in the shank of the Roaring '90s, money was so easy that fans could get all warm and fuzzy about baseball without hoarding its little treasures. Most of McGwire's record-setting home run balls were returned to him for the price of a handshake or a photo with him. No one returned Bonds' homer balls to him. Return? The two guys who grappled with each other for No. 73 were *still* in court a year later suing each other claiming possession of the golden egg—which will in any case fetch only about a third of the $3 million paid for McGwire's 70th. (A judge ruled in December 2002 that they would have to split the profits.)

Even Bonds himself wasn't above a little profiteering. Every time he homered, he took the maple Crusher he had used out of commission so it could be sold at auction. Maybe Bonds could see it coming that his name and image would carry less than Midas value when he looked to the commercial market over the winter. While he did sign to do a few ads, *Business Week* reported that "Bonds is striking out on endorsement deals. [His] image keeping fans, the media and even his own teammates at arm's length is combining with the nation's balky economy to limit offers. Compare that to Sammy Sosa, the convivial slugger who has consistently fallen short of then home-run record but garners an estimated $10 million a year from [years-old] off-the-field endorsements."

No one had to hold any fund-raisers for Bonds. But neither did anyone empty any vaults for him. Bonds' free agency after the season met diffidence by GMs who no doubt had a hearty laugh when Bonds' agent Scott Boras—who had to work so little in scoring up Alex Rodriguez's $250 million deal the year before—floated a price tag of $20 million a year for Bonds, who of course had been so underpaid at $10 million. Bonds quickly aborted his free agency when the Giants offered him more than they had to—five years, $90 million, tying Bonds with Sosa at $18 million a year but on the whole no higher than fourth behind Rodriguez, Manny Ramirez, and Jeter. When he signed the deal, an unctuous Bonds put on a straight face and said, "No amount of money would make me leave San Francisco." Are you still wondering why this man makes people cringe?

And also go *aaaahhhhh*. In 2002 Bonds created a quadrangle of the 600-homer circle. He joined Aaron, Ruth, and Mays on August 9 by torching a pitch from the Pirates' Kip Wells into the center field seats at Pac Bell Park, and if you don't think Bonds' late-career numbers are outrageous enough, try these: the at-bats required between home run Nos. 500 and 600 by this foursome:

Bonds	710
Ruth	1,121
Aaron	1,402
Mays	1,981

You know of course that Bonds' followup to one storied season was a storied season of a different stripe—leading the NL in hitting with a *.370* average, and doing it with such ease and consistency that the batting title and his fifth MVP award was ceded to him by mid-June. The bottom line of the season was that Bonds had reached the point where his dingers were now no more crucial than the *threat* of the dinger. Bonds saw even fewer hittable pitches and was walked an unimaginable 198 times, breaking his own record by 21. This worked out to one walk roughly every three at-bats. (Ruth's best year was 24.3 percent, Williams' 25.8.) He also had a record *68* intentional walks, busting the old record by 23. More ridiculous, when Bonds batted with runners on base, he was walked nearly *half* the time. With the first base open and runners on second and/or third, he was walked—grab hold of something—*66 percent* of the time. Bonds, wrote Tom Verducci in 2001 in *SI,* "gets more passes than J-Lo. . . . Clearly, the numbers and anecdotal evidence suggest that Bonds is too good for this league. Getting such respect from opposing pitchers is unprecedented in this league." We're not sure why Verducci narrows this to one league. No one in any league—even Ruth at his height—has ever been more feared, though part of the fear factor has to do with the pitchers' wimp factor.

One final reason to marvel: with just *47* strikeouts, Bonds BB/K ratio was the best by far in history (would you believe *4:1*?), and his HR/K ratio a DiMaggio-like 1:1.

The second-half success of the Giants in 2002 had Bonds written all over it. Though I appreciate players like Kent and Rich Aurelia, that team was all Bonds, all the time; they scored either directly or indirectly because of him, again aided immeasurably by pitchers who wet their pants at the mere sight of him, and if they have to pitch to him, have no stomach for running one under his chin to back him off the plate. Between the walks, Bonds, at 38, constructed the very definition of perfection: a modest 46 homers, 3 behind Sosa's NL high, 110 RBIs, 117 runs, a .799 slugging percentage, and—unbelievably—a *.582* on-base percentage, burying Williams' 1941 record of .553. He did all this hitting against various permutations of the old Ted Williams Shift, and during a season in which the mutual loathing between he and Kent boiled over in an ugly dugout pushing match.

Well, he *is* Barry Bonds, isn't he?

And what of the wide continent of baseball? Well, much of it was written in home run Helvetica. There were the record-shattering days of Mike Cameron and Shawn Green, and the near 40/40 seasons by Vlad

Guerrero and Soriano, whose 39 homers, from the leadoff spot, were a record for an AL second baseman. (He also hit .300 despite the fact that his 137 strikeouts took down his on-base percentage to a dreadful .332. Remember, this is the modern age, when a nonentity like Brewers' shortstop José Hernandez can hit 24 homers while striking out *188* times, as he did in 2001, and call it a successful season.) The immaculate A-Rod hit 57 homers with 147 RBIs and a .300 average. The Indians' Jim Thome hit 52.

But only eight men cleared 40, with Green just making it, at 42. Luis Gonzalez came back with 28. The Cubs' 38-year-old Fred McGriff, a long-overlooked home run giant (478 lifetime, eight seasons with 30 or more, and a record for homering in 42 different big-league parks), just slid in at 30. Juan Gonzalez got hurt, played 70 games, and hit 8 home runs. The two leagues' totals dropped below 5,000.

Signs of a new skew were all around. The Rockies, fed up with their pitchers giving up 8 runs nearly every home game, found a way to beat the Colorado altitude by putting the game balls in humidifiers. (It didn't have quite the desired effect; the Rockies dropped to 152 homers, but the pitchers still gave up 225.) The Yankees, after signing jumbo first baseman Jason Giambi, the 2001 AL MVP with Oakland, abandoned their smart, balanced attack to go deep, and hit 223 dingers, second in their history to the '61 club—and were promptly pasted in the ALDS by the Angels, who hit merely 152 but like the Yankees used to do, like to hit them to complete a kill. (To wit, second baseman Adam Kennedy, after 7 homers for the season, going yard a record-tying three times to beat the Twins in the climactic Game 5 of the ALCS.) And Bonds' Giants hit 198 for the season, 37 fewer than in Bonds' record-setting year—and went to the World Series.

As the issue of too many cheap homers faded a bit, so did that of steroids. Not because they weren't still being used but because they seemed somewhat trite, as they may have become judged less necessary in an everglade of more "in" drugs like growth hormones. 'Roid rage peaked early in the summer concurrent with overdue exposes in *Sports Illustrated* and *USA Today,* and the endless inane mutterings of José Canseco, only to go cold all at once. That happened because the players union, as usual, outfoxed management by using steroid testing as a bargaining chip as the deadline drew closer for their horrific strike that would have murdered the game for good. Thus, when the strike was averted and age-old differences settled (for six years, anyway), the luxury tax for richer clubs (construed as a salary cap by the players) was kept lower in exchange for a watered-down steroid-testing regimen.

This illusory "concession," requires ongoing testing only if 5 percent of players fail easily fooled testing methods, and no testing at all for drugs like GH, Ecstasy, GBH, amphetamines, cocaine, heroin, and marijuana. (I have a feeling the Mets players voted unanimously on that last one.) In other words, a Bud Selig non-solution solution.

You can decide whether it was felicitous or not that Barry Bonds finally—after a record 2,439 games without playing in a World Series—made it in 2001 when the Giants this time won a wild card berth and dispatched the Braves and Cardinals in the league series. But he definitely made it worth the wait. Bonds slammed 4 resounding homers in the playoffs and when he got to the World Series against the Angels—the first Series between teams not to have won their divisions—it wasn't the Fall Classic as much as a Fox TV miniseries, *Barry in Wonderland,* complete with Thunderstix, rubber chickens, and rally monkey. Shots of Bonds, doing mostly nothing, seemingly popped up between each pitch. And, let's face it, the man deserved all the attention. He was the story.

Has anyone since Ruth ever dominated a World Series agenda the way Bonds did? The Angels turned inside out at his very presence, which provided a deadly conundrum. When they pitched to him, he hit whatever they threw him, and long, with a homer in his first Series at-bat, in each of the first three games, and 4 in all (the 8 postseason homers were a new record). When Bonds put one into orbit some 485 feet into the right field pavilion at Edison Field in the ninth inning of Game 2, Angels outfielder Tim Salmon, who had played there for years—and hit 2 dingers of his own that night to cinch Anaheim's 11-10 win—could be seen mouthing in almost the same words Dick Groat used about Mickey Mantle in the '60 World Series, "That was the farthest ball I've ever seen hit in this ballpark." It wasn't just the dingers, though. In Game 5, when Jarrod Washburn bravely pitched to Bonds with runners on first and third and one out, he pulled a double down the line for a 1-0 lead, sparking the 16-4 blowout behind two subsequent homers by Kent and one by Aurelia that gave the Giants a 3 games to 2 lead.

When they didn't pitch to him—which was most of the time, since Bonds drew a record 15 walks in the Series (and a record 27 over the postseason)—the Angels paid for it, too. Batting behind him, the ancient catcher Benito Santiago hit .348 after the six intentional walks given Bonds. (In Game 4 of the NLCS, in a 2-2 game in the eighth, the Cardinals walked Bonds intentionally to *lead off* the frame—ceding the Giants the potential go-ahead runner, a move that would have given Connie Mack a coronary. Santiago then smacked a 2-run homer that was the gamer of a 4-3 win.) Whenever the Giants were scoring runs, Bonds was in the middle of things.

I know. The 2002 World Series punctures the theory about the home run being in decline. Through only five games, the Giants had already tied the team record for a *seven-game* Series with 12 homers, as did both teams overall with 17. In Game 6, with the Giants a win away from their first title since moving to San Francisco, longtime baseball itinerant Shawon Dunston went yard in the fifth inning to put the Giants up 2-0—his first dinger since April 15, 147 at-bats ago. "He waited 39 years to get the biggest hit of his life," said Tim McCarver on the air as Dunston circled the bases.

In the sixth, Bonds, who earlier had been intentionally walked with a runner on first—again gifting a runner into scoring position—came up against the Angels' 20-year-old flamethrower Francisco Rodriguez, and made the ball disappear somewhere into Orange County for a 4-0 lead. That led TV crews to begin erecting platforms in the Giants' locker room for the post-game victory interviews. Champagne cases were unpacked. Bonds' first championship ring was to be theme of the evening.

The Angels, however, never stopped slashing away at the Giants' mediocre pitching. In fact, never has big-league pitching been more inept than in this Series, when both teams combined to hit .318 and scored *85* runs, both records for pitching futility. Through five games the starting pitchers' combined ERA was *8.93*. Only from the middle of Game 5 to the middle of Game 6 did the Angels not hit. In all they batted around *seven* times in the playoffs—and did it in *consecutive innings* in Game 3 of the World Series. And, just as the Giants appeared to be home free, leading 5-0 in the seventh inning of Game 6, Scott Spiezio, on the last of a gritty, eight-pitch at-bat, pounded a 3-run homer against reliever Felix Rodriguez to make it a 2-run game. Darin Erstad went yard leading off the eighth and it was 5-4. Then, after a key Bonds' error, Troy Glaus doubled over his head for 2 more, a 6-5 lead, and the game—the second the Angels had won after trailing 5-0. How bad was the Giants' pen? Every Angel win in the Series, they came from behind.

Yes, the home run was a mighty big player in the Series. And a player that came up small when everything was on the line.

After all those bombs bursting in the California air during that week, there was nothing close to a home run in Game 7. In fact, the championship of the world was decided when a 24-year-old rookie pitcher, John

Lackey, after giving up an early run, shut down the Giants for five innings, revealing the secret to stunting Barry Bonds—keeping the people who hit before him off base. With Keny Lofton and Aurelia 0-for-12, Bonds came up four times with no one on, leaving the Angels far less risk pitching to him. Bonds went a quiet 1-for-3 with a walk, the Angels ran up 4 runs, and their bullpen choked the Giants to death to give the Angels their first-ever championship since Gene Autry founded the team in 1961. (This, of course, in typical bad-taste baseball fashion, did nothing to stanch the Disney Corporation's eagerness to sell it.)

In winning, the Angels validated my theory. Because while Bonds' homers were a beautiful thing to watch, none of them were critical to the outcome of any game in the Series. Which is why the great Bonds adventure ended the way all Bonds adventures seem to, in great frustration. The man hit .471 (8-for-17) with 6 RBIs. His 4 homers and 8 runs tied World Series records. He had a .700 on-base percentage, 1.294 slugging percentage, 13 walks, and 7 intentional walks—all new World Series records. And the Series MVP award went to Glaus, a man twelve years his junior, who had 3 homers of his own. Bonds left the stage for the year being, well, Bonds.

"I went 1-for-3 with a walk, that's a good day," he said. "Am I supposed to go 3-for-3 with 3 home runs? What do you want from me?"

Actually, nothing; I've seen enough. And if you ask, the future of the home run does not lie with him. The best bet to break Hank Aaron's career home run record isn't Bonds, who is 142 short and needs at least three more years of 40-plus homers to get close at age 42. Rather, it will be Alex Rodriguez, whose home run average per 162 games is 43. (For reference, Ruth's is 46, Kiner 41, Aaron 37, Sosa 43, McGwire 50, Bonds 41, Juan Gonzalez 42.) A-Rod's advantage is his age. Should Rodriguez, who has 298 homers, hit 43 over the next 11 years (a very conservative number), he will have 728 when he's Bonds' age, or 115 more than Bonds has now. (God knows how many small countries Rodriguez will own by then—his contract requires that he always be the highest-paid player in baseball.)

If things should happen this way, something wonderful will happen. The home run legacy will be kept warm by someone who doesn't preen, pose, or pout; act bipolar; stand and check out each ball that springs high off his bat; who actually runs hard to first base; avoids steroids, earrings, and body armor; and talks nice to the media, who is not all bat and no cattle.

Just as those wily old home run gods planned it along.

Appendix

The Top 100 Home Run Hitters of All Time

(Active players in 2002 are in lower case.)
* denotes Hall of Famer.

1. HANK AARON 755*
2. BABE RUTH 714*
3. WILLIE MAYS 660*
4. Barry Bonds 613
5. FRANK ROBINSON 586*
6. MARK McGWIRE 583
7. HARMON KILLEBREW 573*
8. REGGIE JACKSON 563*
9. MIKE SCHMIDT 548*
10. MICKEY MANTLE 536*
11. JIMMIE FOXX 534*

T12. TED WILLIAMS 521*
T12. WILLIE MCCOVEY 521*
T14. ERNIE BANKS 512*
T14. EDDIE MATHEWS 512*
16. MEL OTT 511*
17. EDDIE MURRAY 504*
18. Sammy Sosa 499
19. LOU GEHRIG 493*
20. Rafael Palmeiro 490
21. Fred McGriff 478
T22. WILLIE STARGELL 475*
T22. STAN MUSIAL 475*

24. Ken Griffey Jr. 468
25. DAVE WINFIELD 465*
26. JOSE CANSECO 462
27. CARL YASTRZEMSKI 452*
28. DAVE KINGMAN 442
29. ANDRE DAWSON 438
30. CAL RIPKEN JR. 431
31. BILLY WILLIAMS 426*
32. DARRELL EVANS 414
33. DUKE SNIDER 407*
34. Juan Gonzalez 405
35. AL KALINE 399*
36. DALE MURPHY 398
37. JOE CARTER 396
38. GRAIG NETTLES 390
39. JOHNNY BENCH 389*
40. Andres Galarraga 386
41. DWIGHT EVANS 385
42. HAROLD BAINES 384
T43. FRANK HOWARD 382
T43. JIM RICE 382
45. ALBERT BELLE 381
46. Jeff Bagwell 380
T47. ORLANDO CEPEDA 379*
T47. TONY PEREZ 379*
49. NORM CASH 377
T50. Frank Thomas 376
T50. CARLTON FISK 376*
T52. Matt Williams 374
T52. ROCKY COLAVITO 374
54. GIL HODGES 370
55. RALPH KINER 369*
56. JOE DiMAGGIO 361*
57. GARY GAETTI 360
58. JOHNNY MIZE 359*
59. YOGI BERRA 358*
60. LEE MAY 354
61. Greg Vaughn 352

62. DICK ALLEN 351
63. CHILI DAVIS 350
64. GEORGE FOSTER 348
65. Mike Piazza 347
66. Ellis Burks 345
67. RON SANTO 342
T68. Gary Sheffield 340
T68. JACK CLARK 340
T70. BOOG POWELL 339
T70. DAVE PARKER 339
72. DON BAYLOR 338
73. JOE ADCOCK 336
T74. Larry Walker 335
T74. DARRYL STRAWBERRY 335
76. Jim Thome 334
77. BOBBY BONDS 332
78. HANK GREENBERG 331*
T79. Mo Vaughn 325
T79. WILLIE HORTON 325
T81. GARY CARTER 324*
T81. LANCE PARRISH 324
83. Ron Gant 320
84. CECIL FIELDER 319
85. ROY SIEVERS 318
86. GEORGE BRETT 317*
87. RON CEY 316
88. REGGIE SMITH 314
T89. Manny Ramiriz 310
T89. JAY BUHNER 310
T91. GREG LUZINSKI 307
T91. AL SIMMONS 307*
93. FRED LYNN 306
94. David Justice 305
95. ROGERS HORNSBY 301*
96. CHUCK KLEIN 300*
97. Alex Rodriguez 298
98. Rickey Henderson 295
99. KENT HRBEK 293
100. RUSTY STAUB 292

Index

Aaron, Henry Louis "Hank," 190–92, 243–49, 307; stats, 70, 71, 109, 194; swing, 73; 1957, 197–98; 1962, 220; 1969, 229; 1970, 230; 1971, 234; 1972, 243; 1973, 243–45; 1974, 245–48; 1975, 248
Abrams, Cal, 162
Adams, Franklin P., 50
Adams, Sparky, 99
Adcock, Joe, 191–92, 197, 201
A.G. Spalding & Brothers, 15, 25
Aikens, Willie Mays, 268
Air density, home runs and, 72
A.J. Reach & Company, 44–45, 57
Alexander, Grover Cleveland, 55, 88, 93
All-Century Team, 318
Allen, Dick, 235, 236
Allen, Lee, 14
Allen, Richie, 149, 265
All-Star Games: 1933, 111; 1934, 111; 1941, 139–40; 1946, 147; 1950, 163; 1954, 186–87; 1955, 206; 1956, 196, 206; 1957, 206; 1960, 206–7; 1970, 234; 1971, 234–35; 1983, 272; 1989, 280–81; 1992, 294–95
Alomar, Sandy, Jr., 290
Alou, Matty, 220
Alou, Moises, 309
Aluminum bats, 286
Amoros, Sandy, 195
Anderson, Brady, xii, 285–86
Anderson, Red, 139
Anderson, Sparky, 277
Andrews, Mike, 242
Androsenedione, 303–4
And the Crowd Goes Wild (radio broadcasts), 106
Angell, Roger, 269
Angelos, Peter, 310–11
Anson, Adrian "Cap," 13, 15–16, 18–22, 252
Aparicio, Luis, 199
Armstrong, Neil, 117
Ashburn, Richie, 162
Ashby, Andy, 312
Ashford, Tucker, 109
Auker, Eldon, 119, 139
Aurelia, Rich, 328, 330, 332
Autry, Gene, 332

Babe (Creamer), 104
Babe Ruth Story, The (movie), 106
Bagby, Jim, 139
Bagwell, Jeff, 315
Bailey, Ed, 193
Baines, Harold, 316
Baker, Dusty, 256
Baker, John Franklin "Home Run," 45–47, 50, 77, 83, 93–94
Baker Bowl, 49
Ball Four (Bouton), 222
Balls, 8, 15, 30, 57, 76–77; cork, 44–45, 98–99; dead, 30–31, 100, 116–17; doctoring, 48–49, 63; live, 66–67, 278–79
Baltimore Orioles, 30
Banks, Ernie, 70, 189–90, 194, 198, 230, 238
Barber, Red, 177
Barbour, Ralph Henry, 50
Barfield, Jesse, 271–72
Barnes, Ross, 11, 13, 14–15, 16
Barra, Allen, 299, 324
Barrow, Ed, 36, 55, 62, 77–78, 102, 104

Barry, Joe, 46
Bartholomay, Bill, 245
Baseball Encyclopedia, 98, 136
Baseball Magazine, 66
Baseball Writers Association, 75
Bats, 25, 28, 72–73, 189, 286–87, 317; Babe Ruth and, 71–72, 73; origin of, 8–9; pine tar and, 268–69
Batting averages, 23, 27
"Batting of 1894, The" (Chadwick), 28–29
Bauer, Hank, 164, 197, 198, 207
Baylor, Don, 255
Beadle's Dime Base Ball Player, 7
Beanballs, 27
Bearden, Gene, 155
Beatin, Ed, 19
Beck, Erve, 34
Beckwith, John, 136
Bell, George, 275
Bell, Gus, 193
Belle, Albert, 284, 291–92, 293, 310–11
Bench, Johnny Lee, 219, 234, 235, 236–37, 245
Bendix, William, 106
Bengough, Benny, 93
Bere, Jason, 312
Berger, Wally, 99, 193, 232, 275
Berkow, Ira, 304
Berra, Yogi, 150, 164, 194, 195, 198, 208, 209, 210, 217, 222, 242
Bevens, Bill, 151
Bichette, Dante, 284, 288
Billingham, Jack, 245
Birmingham Black Barons, 169
Blanchard, Johnny, 210, 217
Blomberg, Ron, 240
Blount, Roy, Jr., 120
Blue, Vida, 234
Boggs, Wade, 281
Bonds, Barry, 290–91, 295, 316–24; stats, 70, 71, 140, 287; swing, 73, 316–17; 1992, 283–84; 1997, 291; 1998, 300; 2001, xii–xiii, 317–23, 327–28, 330–31; 2002, 331–32
Bonds, Bobby, 238–39, 241, 278, 291, 320, 321, 322
Boone, Bret, xi, 323
Boras, Scott, 327
Boston Beaneaters, 30
Boston Braves, 190–91
Boston Red Caps, 17
Boston Red Sox, 38; Ruth and, 53–58, 61–64
Boston Red Stockings, 11–12, 14
Boswell, Thomas, 316
Boudreau, Lou, 148, 150, 155
Boundary Field, 31
Bouton, Jim, 222
Boxscores, 5, 7
Boyer, Clete, 220
Boyer, Ken, 222
Branca, Ralph, 157, 171, 174–79, 210, 283
Breadon, Sam, 88
Brenley, Bob, 325–26
Bresnahan, Roger, 33
Brett, George, 253, 266–69, 275
Brett, Ken, 243
Bridges, Tommy, 137
Brock, Lou, 221, 227
Broeg, Bob, 86–87
Brosius, Scott, 325
Broun, Heywood, 80
Brouthers, Dan, 24
Brown, Marc, 128
Browning, Pete, 24–25, 86, 100
Brush, John T., 33, 41
Buck, Jack, 273
Buckner, Bill, 247, 266, 273
Buhner, Jay, 284
Bulger, Bozeman, 42
Burdette, Lew, 198
Burgess, Smoky, 209
Burkett, Jesse, 27
Burks, Ellis, 288
Burns, Britt, 272
Busch, Noel F., 124
Bush, George W., 300, 324
Bush, Guy, 104, 112

Callahan, Pat, 19
Callison, Johnny, 228
Cameron, Mike, xi, xii, 314, 328
Camilli, Dolph, 117
Campanella, Roy, 131, 157, 158, 169, 173, 186, 201, 285
Campaneris, Bert, 242

Candlestick Park, 224–25
Cannon, Jimmy, 120, 177, 193, 211, 218
Canseco, Jose, 250, 276–78, 279–80, 284–85, 287, 329
Carbo, Bernie, 251
Carew, Rod, 240
Carlton, Steve, 265
Carrigan, Bill "Rough," 54, 55
Carter, Gary, 266
Carter, Joe, 281–83
Cartwright, Alexander Joy, 3–4, 8, 10–11
Cartwright's Rules of Baseball, 4
Cash, Norm, 217, 228
Caster, George, 139
Castilla, Vinny, 288–89
Cavarretta, Phil, 144
Cedeno, Cesar, 239
Cepeda, Orlando, 218, 220–21, 240
Cerv, Bob, 212
Cey, Ron, 256
Chadwick, Abraham, 179
Chadwick, Henry, 5–8, 15, 28–30, 42, 116, 129
Chadwick, Lester, 50
Chalmers Award, 79
Chambliss, Chris, 253–54, 257
Chandler, Albert "Happy," 160–61
Chapman, Ray, 76
Charleston, Oscar, 136
Chase, Hal, 51, 57
Chass, Murray, 259, 275
Chesbro, Jack, 37
Chicago American Giants, 131
Chicago Call, 132
Chicago White Stockings, 13–16, 18–22
Choking-up position, 9
Church, Bubba, 170
Cicotte, Eddie, 68, 69
Cimoli, Gino, 209
Cincinnati Red Stockings, 5, 10, 17
Civil War, 9–10
Clark, Jack, 272, 275
Clark, Will, 293
Clarkson, John, 27
Clearing the Bases (Starr), 99, 117, 278
Clemens, Roger, 300
Clemente, Roberto, 169, 208, 209, 230–31, 234, 237–38
Clendenon, Donn, 229
Coates, Jim, 209
Cobb, Ty, 25, 41–43, 46, 50, 58, 75, 77, 84, 89, 95, 118
Cochrane, Mickey, 94, 118, 141, 165
Colavito, Rocco Domenico, 200
Colbert, Nate, 240
Coleman, Vince, 250
Coliseum, 200–201
Collins, Eddie, 46, 50, 102, 125
Collins, Joe, 182, 186
Combs, Earl, 90
Comiskey, Charlie, 32, 35, 68
Conigliaro, Tony, 227
Connor, Roger, 19, 24, 77
Controlled Substances Act (1990), 277
Control pitchers, 162
Cool, Perry L., 183
Cooper, Mort, 141–42
Cooper, Walker, 151
Coors Field, 288–89
Cork balls, 44–45, 98–99
Corkins, Mike, 231
Covington, Wes, 197
Cowens, Al, 253–54
Cowhide balls, 250
Cox, Billy, 171, 175, 176
Cox, Bobby, 291
Crandall, Del, 192
Crane, Sam, 28
Cravath, Gavvy "Cactus," 49–50, 57, 77, 86
Crawford, Sam, 31, 34–35, 41, 42–43, 48
Creamer, Robert, 104
Creasey, Dewey, 136
Creatine, 303
Creighton, Jim, 9–10, 16, 76
Cronin, Joe, 110
Crosetti, Frank, 123
Crystal, Billy, xiii
Current Opinion, 65
Curtis, Chad, 313
Curveballs, 6, 63
Cuyler, Kiki, 48, 97

Daisy cutters, 7
Daley, Arthur, 211, 218

Daley, Bud, 214
Dalrymple, Abner, 21, 23
Daly, Tom, 28
Dandridge, Ray, 170
Daniel, Dan, 120, 213
Darcy, Pat, 251–52
Dark, Alvin, 175, 180
Dauer, Rich, 262
Dave Winfield Foundation, 271
Davis, Chili, 313
Davis, Eric, 271
Davis, Harry, 35–36, 46, 83
Dawson, Andre, 271, 274, 291
Dead balls, 30–31, 100, 116–17
Dean, Chubby, 139
Dean, Dizzy, 128, 129, 133
Deer, Rob, 71
Delahanty, Ed, 27, 29, 36
Dempsey, Jack, 75
Dent, Bucky, 259–60
DeWitt, Bill, 226
DHs (designated hitters), 239–40
Diamond Appraised, The (House and Wright), 38–39
Dickey, Bill, 143
DiMaggio, Joe, 87, 120–25; Jackson and, 232; retirement, 181; stats, 70, 71, 122, 127–28; swing, 120–21; Williams and, 127–28; 1940, 136; 1941, 138–40; 1946, 148–49; 1947, 150–51; 1949, 155–56, 157; 1950, 164; 1951, 163–64, 167, 180–81
Dinneen, Bill, 38, 40
Dixon, Rap, 134
Doby, Larry, 155, 163, 169, 186–87, 187, 240
Doerr, Bobby, 125, 156
Donohue, Pete, 99
Doubleday, Abner, 3
Dougherty, Patrick Henry, 40
Douglas, Phil, 77
Downing, Al, 222, 246–47
Doyle, Brian, 260
Doyle, Denny, 251
Drebinger, John, 105
Dressen, Chuck, 171, 173–74, 175
Dreyfus, Barney, 41, 84
Drug testing, 303–4, 329–30
Drysdale, Don, 220, 225–26
Duffy, Hugh, 23
Dugan, Joe, 77
Dugglesby, William, 239
Dunlap, Fred, 19
Dunn, Adam, 193
Dunn, Jack, 52, 53, 95
Dunston, Shawon, 331
Durocher, Leo, 110, 170, 174, 176, 177, 187
Dykstra, Lenny, 272

Eastwick, Rawly, 251
Ebbets Field, 172
Eckersley, Dennis, 273
Eclipse Park, 24
Edmonds, Jim, 315
Ed Sullivan Show (TV show), 178
Eephus pitch, 147–48
Egan, Ben, 53
Ehmke, Howard, 79
Elliott, Bob, 155, 191
Ellis, Dock, 234
Elysian Fields, 4
Emery balls, 49
Erskine, Carl, 175, 182
Erstad, Darin, 331
Essick, Bill, 120
Essigian, Chuck, 202
Evans, Darrell, 240
Evans, Dwight, 251
Evens, Darrell, 247
Ewing, Buck, 22
Exposition Park, 36

Faber, Red, 63
Face, Elroy, 208
Falkner, David, 183
Falls, Joe, 119
Federal League, 50–51
Feller, Bob, 121, 161
Fenway Park, 63–64, 126
Fielder, Cecil, 283
Figure-8 balls, 15
Fimrite, Ron, 258
Finley, Charles, 231, 242, 254–55
Fischer, Bill, 221
Fisher, Jack, 206, 216
Fisher, William, 14–15
Fisk, Carlton, 251–52

Flick, Elmer, 228
Flood, Curt, 229
Forbes Field, 84, 149
Ford, Gerald, 245
Ford, Russ, 49, 51
Ford, Whitey, 56, 197, 219
Forneris, Jim, 306
Fosse, Ray, 234
Foster, Andrew "Rube," 131
Foster, George, 251, 263
Foster, John B., 63, 64
Foul balls, 34
Four-seam fastballs, 326
Fox, Nellie, 199
Foxx, Jimmy, 84, 93–96, 117–18, 216, 223, 231, 300; stats, 109, 140; 1932, 101–2; 1938, 115–16; 1939, 126; 1945, 117–18, 142–43
Frazee, Harry, 61–62, 77, 148, 226
Free agency, 254–55
Freedman, Andrew, 33
Freehan, Bill, 228
Freeman, John Frank "Buck," 31, 56
Frey, Lonnie, 172
Frick, Ford, 76, 107, 161, 213–14, 217, 219
Frisch, Frankie, 80, 88, 99
Froelich, Ed, 107
Fullerton, Hugh, 42, 68
Fungo hitting, 28–29
Furillo, Carl, 162, 171

Gaetti, Gary, 306
Galarraga, Andres, 285, 288
Galehouse, Denny, 139, 155
Gallagher, Joe, 138
Gallico, Paul, 42, 105
Gambling, 16, 68, 81
Game schedules, 35
Gammons, Peter, 252
Garcia, Mike, 186
Garcia, Rich, 289
Garciaparra, Nomar, 295
Garman, Mike, 265
Garvey, Steve, 238, 247, 256, 257, 273
Gehrig, Lou, 82, 102, 200; stats, 70, 71, 109, 140; 1926, 87–88; 1927, 90–93; 1928, 93; 1930, 95; 1931, 102–3; 1932, 104–5, 107; 1934, 111; 1937, 119–20; 1939, 122–23
Gehringer, Charlie, 111, 118, 141
Gentile, Jim, 217
Giambi, Jason, 310, 329
Gibson, Bob, 222–23, 227, 228
Gibson, Josh, 133–35, 136, 183
Gibson, Kirk, 272, 273
Gilliam, Junior, 201
Gionfriddo, Al, 151
Giusti, Dave, 237
Glaus, Troy, 331, 332
Goldsmith, Fred, 19
Gomez, Lefty, 117, 124
Gonzalez, Juan, 70, 283, 287, 292, 293–94, 300, 310, 311
Gonzalez, Luis, 290, 323, 326, 329
Gooden, Dwight, 273
Gordon, Joe, 141, 155
Gossage, Goose, 259, 260, 267, 268, 272
Grace, Mark, 306, 325
Graham, Frank, 42, 82
Grange, Red, 75
Grant, Mudcat, 226
Gray, Pete, 142
Green, Shawn, xi–xii, 192, 287, 323, 328–29
Greenberg, Hank, 118–20, 141, 186, 278; stats, 70, 109, 145; 1938, 116; 1939, 126; 1940, 136–38; 1945, 143–44; 1946, 149; 1947, 151–52
Greenwade, Tom, 165
Griffey, Ken, Jr., 70, 284, 287, 288, 294–95, 296–97, 300, 310, 313–15, 324
Griffey, Ken, Sr., 295, 314
Griffin, Wilmot E., 54
Griffith, Clark, 32, 33, 50
Griffith Stadium, 149
Grim, Bob, 198
Grimes, Burleigh, 63, 96
Grimsley, Ross, 236
Groat, Dick, 208
Groh, Heinie, 72
Gromek, Steve, 155
Grove, Lefty, 91, 95, 218
Guerrero, Pedro, 271
Guerrero, Vladimir, 317, 328–29

Guidry, Ron, 259–60
Gullett, Don, 242
Gumpert, Randy, 166
Gwynn, Tony, 322

Haas, Mule, 95
Haddix, Harvey, 201, 208
Haines, Jess, 93
Hall, Dick, 215
Hall, George, 11, 15–16, 16
Hallahan, Bill, 111
Hall of Fame, founding of, 3–4
Hamaker, Atlee, 272
Hamilton, Milo, 247
Hand signals, 30
Harder, Mel, 121
Harding, Warren G., 65, 79
Harper, Tommy, 238
Harris, Bob, 139
Harris, Bucky, 150
Harrison, Robert L., 184
Hart, John, 291
Hartnett, Gabby, 99, 104, 128
Hartung, Clint, 175
Harwell, Ernie, 177
Hawkins, Wynn, 205
Heading Home (movie), 66
Hearn, Jim, 153
Heilmann, Harry, 77, 79
Helton, Todd, 323
Henderson, Dave, 272–73
Henderson, Rickey, 239, 250
Henrich, Tommy, 151, 157
Herman, Babe, 96, 99, 142
Herman, Billy, 87, 141
Hernandez, José, 301, 329
Hernandez, Keith, 261
Herrmann, Garry, 35, 62
Heydler, John, 62, 88
Higgins, Mike, 205
Hiller, Chuck, 220
Hillerich, John, 25
Hillerich & Bradsby Company, 25, 72
Hines, Greg, 317
Hines, Paul, 23
Hit-and-run, 30
Hodges, Gil, 162, 172–73, 182, 186, 195, 196, 201, 229, 243
Hodges, Russ, 176–77
Holder, John Henry, 7
Holman, Sam, 317
Home Run Baker's Double (movie), 50
Home Run Encyclopedia, xvi, 183–84
Home Run Heard 'Round the World (Branca), 178–79
Home runs: origin of term, 4, 6–7; science of, 69–74; top 100 hitters, 333–36
Hooper, Harry, 54, 55, 62, 142
Hooton, Burt, 257
Hornsby, Roger, 77, 84, 85–89, 96, 99–100, 109, 219
Horton, Willie, 228
Hough, Charlie, 257
Houk, Ralph, 212
House, Tom, 38–39, 247
Howard, Elston, 198, 221
Howard, Frank, 221, 232, 263
Howser, Dick, 268
Hoyt, Waite, 77
Hubbell, Carl, 107, 110, 111, 112
Huggins, Miller, 81, 90
Hulbert, William, 13–14, 16, 22, 23
Hunter, Catfish, 236, 253
Hyland, Frank, 248

I Had a Hammer (Aaron), 243
Incaviglia, Pete, 71
IPHs (inside-the-park home runs), 149–50
Irvin, Monte, 170, 187, 246

Jackson, Joe, 42, 45, 48, 68–69
Jackson, Reggie, 219, 231–36, 240; stats, 70, 109, 140, 194; strikeouts, 70, 232; 1971, 234–35; 1973, 242; 1975, 255; 1976, 254–55; 1977, 255–58; 1978, 258–59; 1980, 267; 1981, 269–70; 1982, 271
Jackson, Vincent Edward "Bo," 280–81
Jacoby, Stan, 179
James, Bill, 112, 161–62, 188, 197, 224, 274, 287
Jansen, Larry, 173, 175, 181
Jarvis, Pat, 238
Jenkins, Fergie, 234
Jenkinson, William J., 183–84
Jeter, Derek, 289, 295, 325, 326

Joe, Marse, 97, 104, 120
Johnson, Ban, 33, 35, 41, 42, 44–45, 61, 78, 115
Johnson, Byron Bancroft, 32
Johnson, Davey, xiii, 240
Johnson, Deron, 240
Johnson, Ernie, 198
Johnson, Howard, 271
Johnson, Judy, 131
Johnson, Lou, 225
Johnson, Walter, 38, 50, 55, 81, 134
Jones, Bobby, 75
Jones, Charley, 15, 17, 22
Jones, Nip, 198
Joyner, Wally, 280
Justice, David, 290

Kaline, Al, 194
Kandle, Matt, 104
Kansas City A's, 232
Kansas City Monarchs, 189
Keefe, Tim, 27
Keeler, Willie, 30, 154
Kell, George, 158
Keller, Charlie, 124
Kellner, Alex, 166
Kelly, George, 77, 84
Keltmann, Steve, 307
Keltner, Ken, 155
Kennedy, Adam, 329
Kent, Jeff, 328, 330
Kerr, Dickie, 64
Kieran, John, 92
Killebrew, Harmon, 70, 199–200, 225, 227, 230, 232, 234, 244, 263
Kim, Byung-Hyun, 324–26
Kinder, Ellis, 155
Kindred, Dave, 322
Kiner, Ralph, 70, 109, 146, 151–53, 156–57, 163, 185–86
King, Eric, 294
King, Martin Luther, Jr., 246
Kingman, Dave, 263–64
Klein, Chuck, 96, 101, 107–8, 109, 323
Klusman, Billy, 19
Kluszewski, Ted, 188–89, 193, 194, 199, 201–2, 221, 263
Knoblauch, Chuck, 313
Koenig, Mark, 90, 104, 105, 108
Kolp, Ray, 99
Konstanty, Jim, 162–63
Korean War, 145, 160
Koufax, Sandy, 80, 220, 221, 224, 225–26
Kruk, John, 282
Kubek, Tony, 198, 209, 214
Kucks, Johnny, 196
Kuechle, Oliver, 216
Kuenn, Harvey, 200
Kuhel, Joe, 110, 149
Kuhn, Bowie, 242, 244, 245–46
Kurowski, George "Whitey," 141–42, 143

Labine, Clem, 175
Lackey, John, 331–32
Lajoie, Napoleon, 32–33, 36–37, 42, 49
Lake Front Park, 20–21
Landes, Stan, 210
Landis, Kenesaw Mountain, 51, 68–69, 78
Landrum, Tito, 272
Lane, F.C., 66, 69, 81–82
Lane, Frank, 200
Lannin, Joe, 53
Lardner, John, 129
Lardner, Ring, 36–37, 42, 50, 66–67, 68
Larkin, Barry, 190
Larsen, Don, 196, 207
Larussa, Tony, 304
Lasorda, Tom, 272
Last Hero, The (Falkner), 183
Lau, Charlie, 266–67, 275
Lavagetto, Cookie, 151
Law, Vern, 208
Lazzeri, Tony, 87, 88, 123, 153
Lee, Don, 205
Lee, Thornton, 139
Leever, Sam, 40
Lemon, Bob, 186, 187–88, 259–60
Leonard, Jeffrey, 273
Leonard, Walter "Buck," 133, 136
Lewis, Duffy, 54
Leyritz, Jim, 290
Liddle, Don, 187
Lieb, Fred, 42, 46, 54, 68, 215
Life, 123–24

Linz, Phil, 222
Lira, Felipe, 299
Literary Digest, The, 65
Littell, Mark, 253
Live balls, 66–67, 278–79
Lloyd, Pop, 131
Lockman, Whitey, 174–75, 180
Lofton, Kenny, 332
Logan, Johnny, 198
Lolich, Mickey, 228, 234
Lollar, Sherm, 199
Lonborg, Jim, 227
Lopes, Dave, 247
Louis, Joe, 124
Louisville Sluggers, 25, 73, 317
Lowe, Bobby, 29, 200, 265
Luce, Henry, 123–24, 150
Ludurus, Fred, 49
Luque, Dolf, 110
Luzinski, Greg, 264–65
Lyle, Sparky, 259
Lynn, Fred, 250–51, 264, 272
Lyons, Jimmy, 136
Lyons, Ted, 218

Maas, Kevin, 323
McCarthy, Joe, 97, 104, 120, 122, 137
McCarthy, Tommy, 30
McCarver, Tim, 223, 331
McClelland, Tim, 268–69
McConnell, Bob, xvi, 98
McCormick, Frank, 128
McCovey, Willie "Stretch," 70, 218, 220–21, 299
McDougald, Gil, 181, 198, 209
McDowell, Roger, 273
McGinnity, Joe, 33, 37
McGraw, John "Muggsy," 32, 33, 37, 41, 46–47, 50, 77, 78, 84, 89, 97, 108, 109, 110, 111, 115, 118
McGregor, Scott, 262
McGriff, Fred, 283, 329
McGwire, Mark, xiv, 274–78, 296–97, 312; stats, 70; swing, 73; 1990, 280; 1995, 284, 285; 1998, 299–309, 319, 322–23; 1999, 316; 2000, 315
McInnis, Stuffy, 46
Mack, Connie, 30, 32–33, 50, 53, 83–84, 93–96, 102, 111, 115, 331
Mackey, Biz, 131
McKinley, William, 23
McLain, Denny, 223
McNally, Dave, 252
McNamee, Graham, 80–81
MacPhail, Larry, 156, 268–69
McRae, Hal, 253
McVey, Carl, 13
Maddux, Greg, 295
Magee, Lee, 57
Maglie, Sal "The Barber," 173, 174, 175
Maier, Jeffrey, 289
Malamud, Bernard, 172
Malarcher, David, 136
Malone, Pat, 100
Manning, Tom, 106
Mantilla, Felix, 201
Mantle, Mickey, 164–65, 168, 188, 193–99; Jackson and, 232–33; retirement, 223; stats, 70, 109, 194; swing, 168; 1951, 164–68, 180–81; 1952, 181–83; 1953, 183–84, 186; 1955, 195, 206; 1956, 195–96; 1957, 196–97, 198; 1958, 197, 198–99; 1960, 207–11; 1961, 212, 213–15, 217, 218, 302; 1962, 219–20; 1963, 221; 1964, 222–23; 1965, 224
Mantle, Mutt, 165, 167–68, 181
Manuel, Jerry, 310
Maple Rideau Crusher, 317
Marcum, John, 102
Marion, Marty, 143
Maris, Roger, 207–8, 306; 1960, 207–11; 1961, xiii, 212, 213–19, 302; 1962, 219–20; 1963, 221; 1964, 223; 1966, 223; 1967, 223
Marquard, Rube, 46, 47, 55
Marshall, John, 151
Martin, Billy, 182, 197, 255–56, 258–59
Martin, Pepper, 99, 129, 142
Martinez, Edgar, 316
Martinez, Ramon, 299
Martinez, Tino, 313, 324–25, 326
Mathews, Eddie, 70, 191–92, 193–95, 197, 198, 246, 265, 289
Mathews, Eddie, Sr., 191
Mathewson, Christy, 37, 42, 46–47, 50, 51, 325

Mattingly, Don, 270, 290
May, Dave, 248
May, Lee, 237
Mays, Carl, 61, 76
Mays, Willie, 168–70, 175, 181, 320; retirement, 242–43; stats, 70, 109, 194; swing, 73–74, 169, 224; 1951, 181; 1954, 187–88; 1956, 238; 1957, 238; 1961, 217–18; 1962, 220; 1966, 231; 1970, 230; 1971, 231; 1973, 241–42
Mazeroski, Bill, 208, 209–11, 282
Medwick, Joe, 129, 141
Meekin, Jouett, 27
Melton, Bill, 236
Messersmith, Andy, 252
Meusel, Bob, 77, 78, 80, 82, 87, 88
Meusel, Emil, 84
Mexican League, 154
Meyerle, Levi, 9, 14
Mick, The (Mantle), 168
Mickelson, Pete, 223
Milwaukee Braves, 191
Minner, Paul, 192–93
Minnesota Twins, 212–13
Mitchell, Kevin, 283
Mitchell, Paul, 255
Mize, Johnny, 116–17, 128–29, 140, 146, 151, 153, 156–57, 158, 182, 194, 299
Molitor, Paul, 138, 282
Monday, Rick, 272
Moon, Wally, 201
Moore, Donnie, 272–73, 283
Moreno, Omar, 261
Morgan, Joe, 109, 237, 251, 252
Morgan, Mike, 305–6
Mueller, Don, 175, 260
Munson, Thurman, 251, 255, 257
Murcer, Bobby, 236, 240, 241
Murphy, Dale, 250, 271, 275
Murray, Eddie, 262, 264, 287, 298–99
Murtaugh, Danny, 208
Musial, Stan, 70, 129, 141, 143, 153–55, 156–57, 206–7, 221–22, 243
Myers, Hy, 54

Narchildon, Phil, 139
National League Story (Allen), 14
Natural, The (Malamud), 172
Neal, Charlie, 202
Negro League, 131–36, 157, 169, 170
Nehf, Art, 80
Nelson, Rocky, 208, 209
Nettle, Graig, 253
Newcombe, Don, 157, 162, 173, 175
Newhouser, Hal, 139
Newsome, Dick, 139
New York Giants, 18, 35
New York Highlanders, 37
New York Mutuals, 5
New York Times, 65, 67, 132, 180, 275, 302
New York Yankees, 252–53; Ruth and, 61–82
Nicholson, Bill "Swish," 143, 144
Niedenfuer, Tom, 272
Nighttime baseball, introduction of, 115
"1953 Young Mantle Hits One" (Harrison), 184
9–11 terrorist attacks (2001), 318, 324
Nixon, Richard, 259
No, No, Nanette (musical), 62
Noble, Rafael, 170
Nolan, Gary, 235, 251
North, Bill, 255
Northrup, Jim, 228
Nuxhall, Joe, 109, 142

Oakland A's, 232
O'Farrell, Bob, 88
Official Spalding Guide, 15
Ogea, Chad, 285
Ojala, Kirt, 300
Okrent, Daniel, 309
Olive, Tony, 240
Olmo, Luis, 158
O'Loughlin, Silk, 41
O'Malley, Walter, 197
O'Neil, John "Buck," 133
O'Neill, James Edward "Tip," 24
Opposite-field homers, 286–87
O'Rourke, James Henry "Orator," 11–12, 14, 17–18, 29
O'Rourke Fan Club, 18
Ott, Mel, 70, 84, 96, 101, 107–10, 116, 140, 142, 187, 231

Pac Bell Park, 288, 317
Pafko, Andy, 174–75, 176
Paige, Satchel, 131, 132
Palmeiro, Rafael, 70, 287, 293, 311–12
Palmer, Jim, 232
Pappas, Milt, 215, 226
Park, Chan Ho, x–xi, 320, 321, 322
Parker, Dan, 182
Parker, Dave, 263
Parnell, Mel, 157
Parrish, Lance, 277
Pascual, Camilo, 195–96
Passeau, Claude, 140
Past Time: Baseball as History (Tygiel), 74–75
Patek, Fred, 190
Patterson, Red, 183
Pavano, Carl, 308
Pegler, Westbrook, 75
Pendleton, Jim, 191
Pennock, Herb, 80
Pepitone, Joe, 221
Perez, Tony, 228, 237, 251
Perry, Gaylord, 241, 243
Perry, Jim, 241
Pesky, Johnny, 149
Petrocelli, Rico, 227
Pfeffer, Fred, 21
Pfirman, Cy, 110
Phelps, Ken, 275
Philadelphia Athletics, 14, 32–33, 35
Piazza, Mike, 70, 313, 316
Pierce, Billy, 196
Pike, Lipman Emanuel, 17
Pillette, Duane, 166
Pine tar, bats and, 268–69
Piniella, Lou, 253
Pipp, Wally, 78, 82
Pippen, Roger, 52–53
Pirini, Lou, 191
Pitcher's mound, 27, 228; 60-foot 6-inch rule, 26–27, 28, 39
Pitching in the Pinch (Mathewson), 50, 51
Plank, Eddie, 37–38, 46
Platoon system, 156
Player pension fund, 160
Players' Fraternity, 51
Players League, 29
Players' Protective Association, 32
Podres, Johnny, 195, 202
Polo Grounds, 63–64, 65, 67, 78, 109, 151
Pope, Dave, 187–88
Post, Wally, 193
Postdated stats, 97–98
Potter, Nelson, 144
Powell, Boog, 226
Prager, Joshua Harris, 178–79
Pratt, Todd, 313
Puckett, Kirby, 290
Pujols, Albert, 126, 317, 323
Pulliam, Harry, 32, 35
Purdin, John, 238–39

Quinn, Jack, 19

Rabbit balls, 44–45, 48
Radbourne, Hoss, 27
Rains, Claude, 179
Ramirez, Manny, 70, 323
Randolph, Willie, 257, 260
Raschi, Vic, 182, 192
RBIs (runs batted in), 194
Reach, Al, 44
Reach Guide, 42
Rebound speed, 73
Redus, Frog, 136
Reese, Pee Wee, 158, 172, 195
Reserve clause, 14, 29, 32, 35, 160, 229
Resuchel, Rick, 280–81
Reuschel, Paul, 265
Reuschel, Rick, 265
Reuss, Jerry, 245
Reyes, Dennis, 304
Reynolds, Allie, 157
Rhodes, Gordon, 102
Rhodes, James Lamar, 187–88
Rice, Grantland, 42, 75
Rice, Jim, 236, 250–51, 255, 262, 264
Richardson, Bobby, 208, 211, 221
Richter, Fracis, 42
Rickert, Marv, 155
Rickey, Branch, 85, 129, 130, 154, 169, 171, 185
Riggleman, Jim, 301
Ripken, Cal, Jr., 287, 295, 316
Rivera, Mariano, 290, 326

Rivers, Mickey, 253, 257
Rizzuto, Phil, 141–42, 163
Roberts, Ric, 134
Roberts, Robin, 162–63, 164, 206, 224
Robertson, Bob, 273
Robinson, Brooks, 219, 226
Robinson, Eddie, 248
Robinson, Frank, 70, 109, 192–93, 218, 225–26, 230, 232, 240–41, 241, 275
Robinson, Jackie, 134–35, 157, 161, 169, 173–74, 175, 192
Rodriguez, Alex, 70, 287, 292, 295–96, 313–15, 327, 332
Rodriguez, Francisco, 331
Rodriguez, Henry, 301
Rodriguez, Ivan "Pudge," 311, 315
Roenicke, Gary, 262
Rogan, Bullet, 131
Rogers, Steve, 272
Root, Charlie, 104–5, 107
Rose, Pete, 89, 122, 234, 235, 236, 237, 261
Rosen, Al, 163, 186–87, 275
Rothstein, Arnold, 69
Rowell, Bama, 172
Rozek, Dick, 166
Rudi, Joe, 236, 237, 255
Ruffing, Red, 124, 126, 142
Rules of baseball, 3–4, 6, 26–27, 34
Runyon, Damon, 42, 54
Ruppert, Jacob, 62, 63, 66, 78, 81
Rusie, Amos, 27
Russell, Bill, 247
Russell, Jack, 110
Ruth, Claire, 217, 244
Ruth, George Herman "Babe," 31, 52–58, 61–82, 93; Aaron and, 243–44; bats and, 71–72, 73, 287; home run-to-strikeout ratio, 70–71; lifestyle, 74–75, 81–82; Maris and, 246; science of home run and, 69–74; stats, 70, 97–98, 109, 140; Walsh and, 75–76; 1914, 52–53; 1915, 53–54, 55; 1916, 54, 55; 1917, 55–56; 1919, 56–58; 1920, 64–65, 67–68; 1921, 77; 1922, 77–78; 1923, 79–80; 1924, 81; 1925, 81, 82; 1926, 87–88; 1927, 90–93; 1928, 93; 1931, 102–3; 1932, xiv, 93, 103–7; 1933, 111; 1934, 111; 1935, 112; 1961 home run race and, 211–12, 213–14, 217, 218–19
Ruthville, 79
Ryan, Nolan, 281

SABR (Society for American Baseball Research), xvii
Sacrifice bunts, 28, 30
Sacrifice flies, 26
Sain, Johnny, 153, 155
Salaries, 10, 50–51
Salmon, Tim, 330
Sandberg, Ryne, 283, 316
Santiago, Benito, 330–31
Santiago, Jose, 227
Santo, Ron, 244
Santos, Valerio De Los, 307
Sauer, Hank, 185–86
Savino, George, 102
Schang, Wally, 77
Schenz, Hank, 179
Schilling, Curt, 324, 326
Schmidt, Mike, 70, 219, 264–66, 268, 269, 274, 287, 289, 318
Schoendienst, Red, 163
Schulte, Frank, 46
Schulte, Fritz, 110
Schultz, Barney, 222
Scott, Everett, 77
Scott, Frank, 165
Seaver, Tom, 242
Sebring, Jimmy, 40
Seerey, Pat, 150, 161–62
Segregation, 130–36, 160–61
Seitz, Peter, 252
Selig, Bud, 241, 303, 304, 306, 322
Sewell, Truett Banks "Rip," 147–48, 222
Sex, hitting compared with, 232
Sexson, Richie, 323
Seybold, Ralph Orlando, 34
Shannon, Mike, 227
Shantz, Bobby, 209
Sherry, Larry, 202
Shibe, Ben, 44–45, 57, 61
Shibe, Tom, 57, 63, 67
Shocker, Urban, 87
Shore, Ernie, 53

Shumacher, Garry, 116
Sierra, Ruben, 295
Sign stealing, 137–38, 178–79
Simmons, Al, 84, 94–96, 102, 108
Simmons, Curt, 185
Simon, Paul, 124
Singleton, Ken, 262
Sisler, Dick, 162–63
Sisler, George, 67, 74, 79, 122, 162, 171–72
Sixty-One (Kubek), 214
60-foot 6-inch rule, 26–27, 28, 39
Skopec, John, 34
Skowron, Moose, 196, 208
Slaughter, Country, 129, 141–42, 149
Smith, Al, 199
Smith, Charlie, 223
Smith, Chino, 134
Smith, Eddie, 139
Smith, Elmer, 142
Smith, Hal, 209
Smith, Hilton, 131
Smith, Ozzie, 272
Smith, Red, 123, 157–58, 165–66, 170, 177, 245–46, 257
Smith, Reggie, 227, 256
Smith, Wendell, 135
Snider, Duke, 70, 162, 171–72, 176, 181–83, 186, 194, 195, 201
Snodgrass, Fred, 47
Soden, Arthur, 17
Somewhere in Georgia (movie), 50
Soriano, Alfonso, 325, 326, 329
Sosa, Elias, 257
Sosa, Sammy, xiv, 300–301, 327; stats, 70, 287; 1996, 296; 1998, 300–309, 312; 2000, 315; 2001, 323
Southworth, Billy, 87
Spahn, Warren, 155, 170–71, 198
Spalding, Albert Goodwill, 11, 13, 15, 21, 22, 44, 45
Speaker, Tris, 49, 50, 54, 58, 95
Spiezio, Scott, 331
Spitballs, 27, 63, 67
Sporting News, 7, 147–48
Sports agents, 76, 165
Sportsman's Park, 85, 86
Springer, Dennis, 322
Staley, Gerry, 189
Stallard, Tracy, 216–17
Stanky, Eddie, 177
Stargell, Willie, 70, 236, 237–38, 261–63
Starr, Bill, 99, 117, 137, 152, 278
Starr, Mark, 323
Staub, Rusty, 242
Stearnes, Norman, 131–32, 136
Steinbrenner, George, 239–40, 253, 255, 256, 259, 269, 270
Stengel, Charles Dillon "Casey," 80, 156–57, 164, 166–67, 182, 198, 209, 229
Stephens, Vern, 156
Steroids, 276–78, 303, 304, 329–30
Stobbs, Chuck, 183–84, 234
Stolen bases, 250
Stoneham, Horace, 175, 197
Stottlemyre, Mel, 222–23
Stovey, Harry Duffield, 22–23
Strawberry, Darryl, 271
Strike zone, 26, 161–62, 274
Stuart, Dick, 207–8
Sukeforth, Clyde, 175
Sullivan, Frank, 206
Sutter, Bruce, 266
Suttles, Mule, 132, 136
Sutton, Don, 256, 275
Suzuki, Ichiro, 323
Sweeney, Jim, 19
Swing, angle of, 73–74

Tarasco, Tony, 289
Tatis, Fernando, x–xi
Tattersall, John C., 194
Taylor, Jack, 38
Tenace, Gene, 235–36, 237
Terry, Bill, 96, 109–10
Terry, Ralph, 210, 220–21
Thomas, Bud, 126
Thomas, Frank, 284, 287, 292–93, 310–11
Thomas, Gorman, 71
Thomas, James Gorman, III, 264
Thome, Jim, 323, 329
Thompson, Hank, 149, 169, 170, 174
Thomson, Bobby, 151, 192; 1951, xiv, 173–79
Thurman, Mike, 308

Tiant, Luis, 226, 228
Tilden, Bill, 75
Time, 309
Tinker, Johnny, 51
Tobin, Jim, 143
Torrez, Mike, 255, 259, 260
Touch of Nature (movie), 50
Trachsel, Steve, 306–7
Tresh, Tom, 220, 222–23
Trimble, Joe, 193–94, 212, 214–15, 216
Triple Crown Winner, first, 22–24
Trout, Dizzy, 139
Turley, Bob, 198, 208
Turner Field, 289
Two-seam fastballs, 326
Tygiel, Jules, 74–75

Ultimate Baseball Book, 82
Updike, John, 126–27, 206

Valentine, Bobby, 304
Vaughn, Arky, 140, 142
Vaughn, Greg, 310
Vaughn, Mo, 287, 292
Veeck, Bill, 89, 188, 191
Veil, Bucky, 40
Ventura, Robin, 313
Verducci, Tom, 320, 322, 328
Vietnam War, 223, 228–29
Vincent, David, xvi
Vincent, Fay, 219, 270
Virdon, Bill, 208, 209
Voodoo balls, 49

Waddell, Rube, 37–38
Wagner, Honus, 36
Waitkus, Eddie, 162
Walker, Dixie, 151
Walker, Larry, 288, 318
Walker, Rube, 174
Walker, Tilly, 56, 77, 83–84
Walsh, Christy, 75–76
Walsh, Ed, 39, 48
Walters, Bucky, 137
Waner, Lloyd, 122, 142
Waner, Paul, 142
Ward, Aaron, 80
Ward, John Montgomery, 9, 18
Ward, Monte, 29, 30
Ward, Robert, 255
Warhop, Jack, 54
Washburn, Jarrod, 330
Washington Post, 178
Watkins, George, 99
W.B. Jarvis Company, 25
Weaver, Earl, 234, 262, 326
Webb, Mel, 150–51
Weight training, 277
Weis, Al, 229
Wells, Kip, 327
Wells, Willie, 131, 136
Wertz, Vic, 187
Westrum, Wes, 171
White, Deacon, 11, 13
Whitman, Walt, 3
Wilhelm, Hoyt, xii, 215
Williams, Bernie, 289, 313
Williams, Billy, 238
Williams, Charlie, 231
Williams, Cy, 67, 84–85
Williams, Edward Bennett, 298
Williams, Joe, 131
Williams, Ken, 77, 84–85, 148, 238
Williams, Lefty, 56–57
Williams, Matt, 284
Williams, Mitch, 282–83
Williams, Ted, 117, 124–28, 163, 195; DiMaggio and, 127–28; Musial and, 154–55; retirement, 205–6; stats, 70, 71, 127–28, 145; swing, 125, 148; 1940, 136; 1941, 138–40; 1942, 140–41; 1946, 145, 147–49, 150; 1947, 150; 1949, 155–56, 157, 158; 1956, 196; 1957, 196–97; 1958, 197; 1959, 205; 1960, 205–6
Williamson, Ned, 21, 56, 86
Wills, Maury, 220
Wilson, Artie, 170
Wilson, Don, 245
Wilson, Lewis Robert "Hack," 85, 95, 96–100, 216, 300, 304
Wilson, Mookie, 273
Wilson, Owen, 47–48
Winfield, Dave, 239, 269–71, 287
Wohlers, Mark, 290
Wood, George, 21

World Series, 40–41; 1903, 40; 1910, 46–47; 1915, 142; 1916, 54; 1917, 56; 1919, 57–58, 68–69; 1921, 77; 1922, 78; 1923, 79–81; 1926, 87–88; 1927, 90–93; 1928, 93; 1929, 95; 1930, 95–96; 1932, 103–7; 1933, 110; 1934, 118–19; 1935, 119; 1937, 124; 1942, 141–42; 1943, 143; 1945, 144; 1946, 148–49; 1947, 151, 155; 1948, 155; 1949, 157–58; 1950, 163, 164; 1951, 180–81; 1952, 182–83; 1953, 186; 1954, 187–88; 1955, 195; 1956, 196; 1957, 197–98; 1958, 198–99; 1959, 201–2; 1960, 207–11, 330; 1961, 219; 1962, 220–21; 1963, 221; 1964, 222–23; 1965, 225–26; 1966, 226; 1967, 223, 226–27, 227–28; 1968, 228; 1969, 228, 229; 1970, 230; 1971, 230, 231; 1972, 235–36, 237, 271; 1973, 242; 1974, 255; 1975, 251–52; 1976, 253–54; 1977, 256–58; 1978, 258, 261–63; 1980, 266, 267–68; 1981, 270; 1983, 282; 1984, 272; 1986, 273; 1988, 273, 276; 1991, 290; 1992, 282–83; 1995, 290; 1996, 290, 292; 1997, 290; 1998, 313; 2001, 324–26, 330–31; 2002, 331–32
World Trade Center terrorist attacks (2001), 318, 324
World War II, 138, 141, 142–45
Wray, John E., 116
Wright, Bill, 165
Wright, Craig R., 38–39
Wright, George, 9, 10, 11
Wright, Harry, 5, 10, 11
Wrigley Field, 84, 97
Wynn, Early, 186, 188, 218

Yankee Stadium, 78–79, 121, 122, 133–34, 289
Yastrzemski, Carl, 70, 206, 226–27, 251, 259–60
Yawkey, Tom, 102, 156, 197, 205
York, Rudy, 143, 148–49
Young, Cy, 27, 38
Young, Dick, 212, 214, 215
Yvars, Sal, 178–79

Zachary, Tom, 91
Zernial, Gus, 163
Zimmer, Don, 264
Zimmerman, Heinie, 47, 57

About the Author

Mark Ribowsky's previous books include *A Complete History of the Negro Leagues, Don't Look Back: Satchel Paige in the Shadows of Baseball, The Power and the Darkness: Josh Gibson in the Shadows of the Game; Slick: The Silver and Black Life of Al Davis,* and *He's A Rebel: Phil Spector, Rock's Legendary Producer.* A regular contributor to Playboy, Ribowsky lives in New York City.